James Glass Bertram

Sporting Anecdotes

Being anecdotal annals, descriptions, tales and incidents of horse-racing, betting, card-playing, pugilism, gambling, cock-fighting, pedestrianism, fox-hunting, angling, shooting, and other sports

James Glass Bertram

Sporting Anecdotes

Being anecdotal annals, descriptions, tales and incidents of horse-racing, betting, card-playing, pugilism, gambling, cock-fighting, pedestrianism, fox-hunting, angling, shooting, and other sports

ISBN/EAN: 9783337148881

Printed in Europe, USA, Canada, Australia, Japan

Cover: Foto ©ninafisch / pixelio.de

More available books at **www.hansebooks.com**

SPORTING ANECDOTES

BEING

Anecdotal Annals, Descriptions, Tales and Incidents

OF

*HORSE-RACING, BETTING, CARD-PLAYING,
PUGILISM, GAMBLING, COCK-FIGHTING,
PEDESTRIANISM, FOX-HUNTING,
ANGLING, SHOOTING,
AND OTHER SPORTS*

H. M. LLOYD.

NOW FIRST COLLECTED AND EDITED
By "ELLANGOWAN"

LONDON: HAMILTON, ADAMS & CO
GLASGOW: THOMAS D. MORISON
1889

PREFACE.

EVERY phase of social life presents aspects of interest not only to its immediate votaries, but to many who feel interested in the tastes of their countrymen, and in that sense it is hoped the present volume will be found instructive and amusing, not to sportsmen only but to others who do not pretend to such a designation.

Many readers will, probably, recognize in these pages incidents with which they are already familiar, but not a few of the stories will undoubtedly be new to them. Other readers will find the volume largely descriptive of what is, or has been, going on around them. Whether viewed historically, socially, or as matters of taste and habit, such circumstances and incidents bulk largely in the life of the people and necessarily attract attention.

Although much interested in the sporting habits and customs of past and present generations, the Editor may be permitted to state that he does not identify himself with the practices described or the opinions given by the writers drawn upon. And readers of the following pages, whatever their tastes may be, will doubtless be able to form their own conclusions of the moral, social, and historical bearing of what is narrated. All that has been essayed in forming this compilation is the bringing together of such anuals, incidents, and opinions of sport and gambling as most vividly bring into notice their salient features.

As will be seen on perusal, greater space has been accorded to "the turf" and its surroundings than to other sports and pastimes, horse-racing being regarded by the people of the present day as containing elements of greater interest than any other phase of sporting life.

CONTENTS.

An Earl's Stratagem	17
The Bookmaker's Plan	18
Tom King, the Comedian, in Luck	19
Christopher North's Breeches	20
In the Days of the Lotteries	21
Remarkable Derby " Sweeps,"	22
Unlimited Poker—A Terrible Trial	24
Playing a Desperate Game	25
The Fruits of Boxing Fame	26
Origin of Steeple Chasing	27
King of the Tipsters	28
Cock-Fighting in Olden Times	30
A Sabbath Keeping Trainer	31
Turf Tipsters and their Ways	32
Blind Anglers	33
Betting Ventures of " Public Form,"	34
" Old Thatchem's " Good Fortune	36
Remarkable Derby Dreams	37
Captain Barclay's Earlier Pedestrian Feats	39
Lucky Sir Joseph	40
Gamblers and Gamblers	42
An Astute Turf Diplomatist	44
Description of the Catching of a Big Salmon by a Little Boy	47
Slices of Good Luck	48
The Derby in the Year of George Third's Jubilee	49

CONTENTS.

His Ruling Passion Strong to the Last	50
Presents to Popular Jockeys	51
He Should Have let Well Alone—A Monte Carlo Story	52
Squire Osbaldeston's Gallantry	52
Playing Golf by Candle Light	53
Stories about the St. Leger	54
Captain Barclay walks a Thousand Miles in a Thousand Hours	55
Blair Athol's Race for the Derby	56
Grouse Shooting Match between Horatio Ross and Colonel Anson	58
Gambling on the Turf	59
"Music hath Charms"	61
Card-Playing in Great Cities	62
Turf Slang	63
Tom Parr the Trainer's Doings	64
More about Typical Tipsters	66
Lord Brougham's Clever Wager	67
About Webb the Wave Breaster	68
Blenkiron the Breeder	68
Pedestrian Feats of Long Ago	69
Money Earned by Popular Jockeys	70
Cheap Race-Horses and Steeds of Value	72
The Cock o' the Golf Green	73
Johnny Broome the "Pug of Fame"	73
Mrs. Thornton beats Buckle, the Great Jockey	74
The Tricycle as a Cure	75
State Lotteries	76
Davis the Leviathan Book-Maker	78

CONTENTS.

Treatment of High Mettled Racers in Infancy	79
How to Educate " Yearlings"	80
Accidents which lead to Fortune	81
Lord George Bentinck's Plan for Starting Horses in a Race	82
Jockey Worship	83
Pheasant Poaching	84
Hawking, Can it be Revived?	86
How to " Work" a Horse to Advantage	87
Singular Wagers	88
Told by the Proprietor of a Music Hall	89
How Jem Burn the Pugilist took an Insult from a Customer	91
Strutt's Notices of Cock-Fighting	92
A City Merchant's Wife dreams the Winner of the Derby	93
Natural History of the Salmon	94
First Appearance of the " Champion of England"	94
Card Playing: The Case of Lord de Ros	96
Cost of Angling	97
A Golfer's Elegy	98
What is Baccarat?	99
Baccarat Explained	101
Misers on the Turf	102
Going to the Derby	102
Athletic Feats performed by Captain Barclay	104
How to turn an Honest Penny on the Turf	105
A House of Bondage	106
From the Grenville Memoirs	107
About Bookmakers	108

CONTENTS.

About Cock-Fighting	109
Popularity of Cock-Fighting	110
Lotteries	111
London Gambling House described by Mr. Edmund Yates	113
Remarkable Feats of Pedestrians	114
The Duke of Wellington's Horsemanship	115
Poaching as a Fine Art	116
Investing the Stable Money	117
Gregson the Poet of the Pugilists	119
Growth of Gambling	120
Extent of Play in London Hells	122
Derby Story of £25,000	122
Glove Fights	123
Poetic Prophets of the Derby	124
A Sportsman's Epitaph	126
Crockford the Hell Keeper	128
Kingsley's Description of a Fox Hunt	129
Grouse Shooting and Business Combined	130
An Attempted Racing Fraud	134
About the Derby	135
Gambling in the Reigns of George III. and George IV.	135
Training the Arab Steed	136
Captain Barclay as a Runner	138
Value of Information in Racing Tactics	139
Leith Links and Golfing in 1766	139
How the Colonel was "Done"	140
What is a Main at Cock-Fighting?	141
A Reverend Bettor!	142

Paying for the Ducal Whistle	143
Visions and Omens of Bluegown's Derby	144
Gentleman Jackson	145
Character in Anglers	146
Russel of the Scotsman	147
Betting should be for Ready Money Only	148
About the Great German Lotteries	149
Judge Kenyon and a Prince of Wales	151
Mr. Max O'Rell's First Derby	152
"Billy's" Epitaph	154
The Rise of Lawn Tennis	155
Titled Gambling Ladies	156
Cock-Fighting Reminiscences	156
Bookmaking and Betting	158
In the Days of Dick Christian	160
The Clinker and Clasher Match	161
How Sir Tatton Sykes punished a Pugilist	162
Tricks of the Poachers	163
How George Payne lost his Fortune	164
About Derby Tipsters	165
One of Lord Oxford's Adventures	167
Feats of Captain Barclay's Father	167
The Bookmaker of the Outer Ring	169
The Royal Game of Golf	173
From Stable Boy to a Peerage	174
Mr. Mytton's Dare-Devil Feats	175
Jem Ward and the Editor's Lady	176
Distinguished Patrons of Cock-Fighting	177
Cost of keeping Race-Horses	178
A Fox that did not neglect Business	179

CONTENTS.

Curious and Eccentric Ways of finding out Winning Horses	180
Indigestion and Glenlivat	180
Arab Horses	182
Betting for and against : Canon Kingsley's Opinion	183
Hermit's Sensational Derby	186
Philosophy of Salmon Poaching	187
In the Days of the Regency	188
Value of Race Horses	189
What Scotsmen Achieve	191
Charles James Fox	192
About Young Eclipse and the Derby	193
Bobby Mumford gets a Character	194
Fortune's Favours	195
Cocking a Royal Game	197
Greyhound Stories	198
Golfing—The Duke and the Shoemaker	199
A Hundred Guineas to a Walking Stick	200
Ways and Work of an Old Time Jockey	202
The Bold Bendigo and Jem Burn	207
One way of Winning a Wager	208
How Bookmakers name Horses	209
Lord Palmerston and John Day	210
The Royal Cock Pit	214
Ready Money Betting	216
Grouse Driving Sport	217
Tipsters' Tricks and Temptations	218
Difficulties attending Horse-Race Trials	220
Of the Odds obtained in Betting	222

CONTENTS.

Novel Fox Chase	223
"The Blue Riband of the Turf:"—Origin of the Phrase	224
One of Lord Kennedy's Feats	225
Are Bookmakers as Black as they are painted?	226
How the Marquis of Waterford floored the Cock of the North	227
A Statesman at Play	227
Prize Fighting on the Derby Day	228
Fe-fi-fo-fum	230
Phantom Fortunes	231
The Making of a Sportsman	233
Cock-Pit Swells and Roughs	234
Macaulay's Picture of Newmarket	235
Newmarket in the time of Queen Anne	236
Messrs. Glitter and Flash Outwitted	236
Sportsmen's Fish	237
Who are the "Touts?"	238
Crockford's Clubs in London and Newmarket	240
Lord George Bentinck's Duel	242
What will Win?	245
One of Fortune's Frolics	246
Something like a Walk	247
Trading in Racing Tips	247
Ups and Downs of Turf Life	249
Colonel Mordaunt and other Cockers	250
The Biter Bit	252
Lord George Bentinck's Work on the Turf	253
Some Remarkable Wagers	254

CONTENTS.

Mr. Short Odds and Jimmy Hirst - - -	255
Falling among Thieves - - - - -	257
Charles James Fox and other Gamblers - -	258
Lord Glasgow on the Turf - - - - -	259
Sportsmen's Appetites - - - - -	261
How Lord George Bentinck sold his Stud - -	262
Squire Dimsdale's Death Ride - - - -	263
Charles Dickens on Battue Shooting - - -	265
Luck in Gambling - - - - - -	266
Old Coaching Days - - - - - -	268
Absurd Stories about Mr. Merry - - -	268
Wagers about Words - - - - -	269
In a London Gambling Club - - - -	270
About "Hedging" - - - - - -	273
No. 2,224 : Miss Mitford's Choice ! - - -	274
Good Advice to Anglers about killing Trout in August - - - - - - - -	275
Myttoniana - - - - - - -	277
Games of Chance and Gambling - - - -	278
Billiards in Paris - - - - - -	279
Stock Exchange Gambling - - - - -	281
"His Royal Highness" on the Turf - - -	283
True Story of a Lottery Ticket - - - -	284
How the Pugilist of the Period is trained - -	286
Charles Dickens and his Betting Cashier - -	288
Value of Racehorses : " Doncaster," - - -	289
How to bring up your Boys - - - -	291
Our Sports and Pastimes—The Professional Element - - - - - - - - -	292
Multiplication of Gambling Clubs in London -	293

Fondness of the Clergy for Cocking	294
No Friendship in Horse Dealing	295
The Derby in the House of Commons	296
King of the Gamblers	297
Singular Gambling Circumstance	298
A Clever Backer of Race Horses	298
Nimrod's Literary Work	299
How Fred Swindell began Business	301
Lord Petersham's Strange Visitor	301
Taking a Tip for the Cesarewitch	302
The Lord of the Valley	303
How Dickey Rayner was "Done,"	304
Delights of Trout Fishing	305
Gambling Chat	305
How the Jockeys rose to Power	307
L. S. D. of a Great Pugilistic Event	308
Beau Brummel's Luck at Cards	309
Billiards	309
Art of Placing Horses in Races	310
One of Mytton's Practical Jokes	311
Racing Conspiracies	312
A Waif's Tips	313
Dan Dawson's Crime	314
Model Yacht sailing on the Serpentine forty years ago	315
Mr. Cheerful's Betting-Shop	316
Mr. Snewing's dream	319
Dreams about Caractacus	320
How to perpetrate a Lottery Fraud	321
The Fate of Mr. Merry's Horse, Dundee	322

CONTENTS.

Pugilists after the Fight	323
Pleasures of Moorland Shooting	324
Miscellaneous Moorland Sport	326
Tattersall's	327
Gamekeepers' Tips	328
Gambler and Duellist	330
An Odd Catch	331
General Hutchinson on the Education of Sporting Dogs	333
Turf Slang	336
Cost of Scottish Out-of-doors Sports	337
Game Preserving, Pro and Con	338
Differences in Jockeys	341
Winning by the Skin of his Teeth	341
A Legend of the " Shires,"	341
How Anglers should cast Their Flies	343
Shakespeare as a Fox-Hunter	344
Golden Rule in Betting	347
Waiting for a Badger	347
How Jockeys used to Dress in the Days of Old	348
Captain Barclay's Rival	348
Epsom and the Derby	349
When Professional Riding began	349
Chifney in the Hunting Field	350
What a Jockey should be	350
Men with more Money than Brains	350
A Morning with the " Wizard of the North,"	351

SPORTING ANECDOTES.

AN EARL'S STRATAGEM.

THE late Earl of Grosvenor had a horse heavily engaged at the Craven Meeting [Newmarket], and a few days before he was to run a report was circulated that he coughed. But whence the report? Why, a man has been hired by a party (so "Nimrod" tells the story) to lie all night on the roof of his box to ascertain the fact which he proclaimed. His authority, however, being doubted, another worthy was employed to perform the same office on the following night; which, coming to the ears of the trainer, was immediately reported to his noble employer.

"Have we no horse that coughs?" inquired his lordship.

"We have one," was the reply.

"Then," said his lordship, "let him be put into the box on which the fellow is to pass the night, and if he does not catch his death from this cold north-east wind and sleet we shall do very well."

Of course the odds became heavy against the horse, from the report of this second herald, and his lordship pocketed a large sum by his horse, who won the race with ease. Still later, indeed, a very fair advantage was taken of a report circulated by the means of one of these watchers, vulgarly called "touters." Mr. Wilson was about to try a two-year-old colt, and had entered his trial for the morrow.

"We must not try to-morrow, sir," said his trainer.

"Why not?" inquired Mr. Wilson.

"We shall be watched, sir," replied the trainer, "and the old horse's (*i.e.*, the trial horse) white fore-leg will be sure to let out the cat."

"Leave that to me," said Mr. Wilson, "I shall be at the stable before you get out with the horses."

And coming prepared with the materials for the purpose, he painted the white fore-leg of the old horse black, and the fellow-

B

one of the colt white, and so they went to the ground. The old one, as may be supposed, ran the fastest and longest; but being mistaken by the touter for the young one, his fame soon spread abroad, and he was sold the next day to the noble viscount who had employed the watcher, for fifteen hundred guineas, being somewhere about eleven hundred more than he was worth.

THE BOOKMAKER'S PLAN.

SOME extraordinary stories have from time to time been told regarding the doings of owners of race horses. The following is one of them. A certain gentleman who was the happy possessor of a Derby favourite which he had caused to be backed to win him a very large sum of money, over a hundred and twenty thousand pounds, it was stated at the time, became somewhat uneasy, a fortnight before the day fixed for the race, about his prospects of receiving his money in the event of his horse winning the blue ribband of the turf. Sending for the commissioner he had employed to back the horse, he asked him to state with whom the bets had been made, and finding that over eighty thousand pounds would fall to be paid by one person, should Paddington (that was the name of the horse, which at the time was first favourite) win, he became very anxious indeed, so anxious that he determined to have a personal interview with the bookmaker, a man in a very large way of business, then known as "the leviathan." Sending for this person, Lord Buncombe asked him all sorts of questions about the forthcoming race which the man answered straightforwardly enough, and to the following effect:

"Your horse is favourite, my lord—first favourite—and we all lay as much as we can against the favourites; your commissioner has backed your horse with me to win eighty-eight thousand pounds. Can I pay you if your horse wins? Well, I have never yet broken faith with a customer, and hope to pay all I owe whatever the name of the winner may be. Not a satisfactory answer, my lord, how so? It is all I can say; you know I have to get paid by the losers who back the wrong horse, and of course if many of them should fail to come to the scratch with what they owe me, I might experience a difficulty, in such case money might be a little scarcer than usual, but I hope for the best—it is not a certainty you know, my lord, that Paddington will win."

His lordship did not relish this supposition, and knowing how highly the horse had been tried, and believing thoroughly in the honesty of his trainer and jockey, and of all his stable people, he at once told the bookmaker:

"Defeat is impossible, and you must back the horse yourself so as to ensure some of your money."

"That cannot be done, the horse is at too short a price; it would cost a very large sum to cover even half the money I stand to lose over Paddington: other men, you see, have backed the horse, and if it wins, my lord, I shall have to pay over a hundred and twenty-seven thousand pounds."

"Just so," said his lordship, "I am aware that the horse is a great favourite, and so, I fancy, is my filly for the Oaks."

"Yes, and if Paddington wins the Derby, my lord, your filly will come to even money for the race of Friday (the Oaks)."

"So I fancy, well now, suppose—"

"Yes, my lord, suppose what?"

TOM KING, THE COMEDIAN, IN LUCK.

THE following anecdote refers to a "slice of luck" that befell Tom King, the famous comedian. Having one night, in a tavern near Covent-garden, lost heavily at hazard, the actor with much resignation called for a bottle of wine to drink "good health" to his lucky opponent, who in return pressed Tom to "try again." Having no money, King refused to do so; but on his adversary saying that made no odds, as his word was good for a hundred times the amount of the stakes, play was resumed, and in a few hours Tom won two thousand five hundred and twenty pounds. When he got home he found his wife sitting up to receive him, and naturally enough a little inquisitive as to where he had been and what he had been doing; but to her inquiries he made no reply beyond saying in a peremptory manner:

"Bring me a Bible!"

"A Bible, Tom!" she exclaimed, followed by, "Have you been taking poison?"

"Bring me a Bible, can't you?"

"I suppose you have lost a lot of money, Tom? But never mind that; we can work for more."

As he refused to be comforted on any other terms, and as Mrs. King remembered there was not such a book perhaps in the house, she went to a neighbour's, borrowed theirs, and gave it to her husband, who then fell upon his knees, and made a fervent vow never to touch dice or cards again, his wife—a very good one—all the time trying to soothe his grief for some great loss. When he rose up he flung fifteen hundred and twenty pounds upon the table saying:

"There, my dear, I've won all that, and I shall receive another thousand pounds by noon to-morrow; but I hope to be hanged if ever I risk a guinea of it again at cards or dice."

Nor did he, but invested the money in property ere he was forty-eight hours older. Tom seems to have understood the whole art of gambling—"knowing when to leave off."

CHRISTOPHER NORTH'S BREECHES.

AMONG the "tid bits" of the Noctes Ambrosianæ occurs the following delightful little story of one of Christopher North's Sporting Adventures as told by "Tickler."

"Twenty-seven brace of birds, nine hares, three roes, and a red deer stained the heather on the twelfth beneath my single-barrelled Joe, not to mention a pair of patriarchal ravens and the Loch Erie eagle. It bore down on my dog Sancho, and would have broken his back with a stroke of its wing had I not sent a bullet right through its heart. It went up with a yell a hundred fathoms into the clear blue air, and then, striking a green knoll in the midst of the heather, went shivering along the black surface of the tarn till it lay motionless in a huge heap among the water lilies. I stripped instanter, and shot in twenty seconds a furlong across the Fresh. Grasping the bird of Jove in my right, I rowed towards the spot where I had left my breeches. Espying a trimmer, I seized it in my mouth, and on relanding, as I hope to be shaved, lo! a pike of twenty pound standing with a jaw like an alligator, and reaching from my hip to my instep, smote the heather like a flail. Braced by the liquid plunge, I circled the tarn at ten miles an hour. Unconsciously, I had taken my Manton in my hand and re-loaded it; suddenly up sprang a red deer. We were both going at the top of our speed when I fired. The ball pierced his spine, and the magnificent creature sank down and died without a convulsion. I sat down upon the forehead and rested a hand on each antler and sent Sancho off to the tarn side for my pocket-pistol, charged with Glenlivet. In a few minutes he returned and crouched down at my feet with an air of mortification. I understood him and hurried back to the spot where I had left my garments. Not an article to be seen save and except my shoes. Jacket, waistcoat, flannel, shirt, all melted away with the mountain dew. There was I like Adam in Paradise. A figure moved along the horizon—a female figure—and, as I am a Christian, I beheld my buckskin breeches dangling over her shoulders. I gave chase, six feet four in bare skin. As I neared her I saw she was making for a morass. Whiz went a ball within a stride of her petticoat. She dropped the breeches. I literally leaped into them, and like Apollo in pursuit of Daphne, pursued my impetuous career. Down went one after the other, jacket, waistcoat, flannel, shirt—would you believe it, her own blue linsey wolsey petticoat! Thus lightened, she bounded over the little knolls like a bark over the Sicilian seas; in two minutes she had fairly run away from me, hull down, and her long yellow hair streaming like a pendant, disappeared into the forest."

IN THE DAYS OF THE LOTTERIES.

AMONG the vast army of blackguards and men who lived by their wits a hundred years ago, there was a notorious sporting character, who went by the nickname of "Old Nick," his name being Nicholas Ward. Shakespeare says, "One man in his lifetime plays many parts," and certainly Old Nick carried out the poet's words by the variety of his pursuits. In bushy wig, with grave and Puritanical air, this scoundrel often mounted a tub in Moorfields, and in Whitefield vein held forth upon the iniquities of the flesh, and while he dealt out fire and brimstone with the most lavish profusion, an emissary went round with the hat. At the same time, in different parts of the town, he kept a billiard-table, a bowling-alley, a skittle-ground, and a hazard-table. On Newmarket-heath no man was better known or more avoided by the knowing ones; he was in league with every roguish jockey, every brother blackleg, and even with the highwaymen, who in those times infested the country, and if any person did chance to win off him, which was very seldom, he would be eased of his money before he had gone many miles on his homeward journey by some minion of the moon who had been put upon the lay by Old Nick, on condition that he shared the robbery with him.

One of Ward's most ingenious devices was founded upon the lottery mania, which at that time was at its height. Just before the day for drawing the tickets he would have handbills distributed, announcing that a learned conjuror at Westminster would foretell the numbers to be drawn each day during the lottery at half-a-crown a consultation. Disguised in a white wig, long beard, and gown covered with cabalistic characters, he would receive his numerous dupes, tell them to go into a certain street, take the number of the first hackney-coach that passed, multiply it by three, and then add three to the total number and then insure it in the first lottery-office they came to, which, of course, would be one of his own. "It will be a prize for certain," said the supposed conjuror. Sometimes a greenhorn would come back in a state of wrath to "the wise man" and complain that, although he had followed his instructions to the letter, he had drawn a blank; upon which he would prove to him that he had not taken quite the nearest office—he having opened a new one in the meantime—and would get another half-crown out of him. Having stripped a young fellow of every farthing at cards—including a sum that had been intrusted to him to pay a bill, for which he was liable to be prosecuted—a lady of respectability, who felt great interest in the young gamester, called upon "Old Nick" to ask him to refund a little of the booty.

"Sit down, my dear," answered the old villain, "and play with me at cards for all you have about you, and I'll win the clothes off your back and send you back to your young gentleman bare."

REMARKABLE DERBY "SWEEPS."

HUNDREDS of lotteries are every year organized over the great race for the Derby under the title of "Derby Sweeps," and many curious stories have been told regarding dreams and coincidences which have attended some of these speculations. Many of the stories have of course a family likeness, but the following is somewhat singular:

A man named Dugdale, a bookseller, carrying on business in Wych Street, London, who had taken some shares in the crown sweep organized in a neighbouring public-house for the Derby of 1840, drew for one of his tickets a horse called Launcelot, the other tickets representing horses of no moment, animals, in fact, not likely to run. The sweep was drawn on the Saturday previous to the race, and as there were over 340 subscribers, the first prize had been fixed at the value of £35, the second and third horses being set down to receive respectively £15 and £10, whilst the others which started were to receive half a sovereign each, any balance left over to be expended in a supper to the prize-takers. Dugdale used to relate that, on the Sunday afternoon, having dined, he was sitting in the little parlour behind his shop enjoying a smoke and a glass of stout, "and I fancy I had fallen asleep, but I have never been clear on that point," said the old man, as he used to tell the story; "at any rate, a young fellow came in, and as I was rising from my chair to ask what he wanted, he said, 'Sit still, Dugdale; I have only come to tell you that the horse you have drawn in the sweep won't win, although it is first favourite; take my advice, old fellow, and I know what I am speaking about: sell your ticket to Joe Evans —he fancies Launcelot, he'll give you a fair price—and then put all the money he gives you on Little Wonder—that's the horse as will win the Derby.' I was struck all of a heap," continued Dugdale, as he went on with his story, "at what I had just heard; I suppose it was a dream, for if the man was in my shop he had got out of it again wonderfully quick; anyhow, I had a visit on Monday morning from Joe Evans, who asked me if I would sell my chance; I said, 'Yes, I will, but it must be for money,' and to cut a long story short, I there and then parted with Launcelot for a fiver." "And did you back Little Wonder?" "Back it;—to be sure I did; I took 40 to 1 to fifty shillings, and drew the money the day after the race at an office in Long Acre, where there was a big betting list. But, look you, gents, what was still better, I bought the ticket for Little Wonder as well from a potman who had drawn it, and so you see I bagged the first prize."

One more story. The wife of a club steward in London, in which club a Derby sweep of considerable amount was annually drawn, dreamt that one of the members had sold his chance, which was Doncaster, to her husband, and that the horse won the race. Of course, like a dutiful better half as she was, the lady told her husband what she had dreamt; but he, good man, was a very matter-of-fact person, and pooh-poohed the matter, telling her there were better horses in the race than Doncaster, "and I've backed one of 'em, my lass, which its name it is Kaiser, and if that wins you shall have a new bonnet; there, old woman!"

Curiously enough, however, that actually took place which had been foreshadowed in her sleep. On the Friday preceding the Derby Day, the holder of the ticket in question said to the steward of the club, "Look here, Peters! I sail on Monday from Southampton for the East, and I want to be quit of this confounded ticket. I am told the horse has no chance of winning. If any gentleman will give you a guinea for the ticket, let him have it." Peters at once thought of his wife's dream, and replied promptly, "All right, sir; there's the money, and if no one takes the bit of pasteboard I shan't be broke. I backed Kaiser long ago, and that's the horse which, as I think, will win this year's Derby." As a mere matter of form, Peters offered the ticket to several gentlemen of the club, knowing pretty well they would refuse it, and in the end he had the pleasurable satisfaction of paying himself the sum of £150, due over the winning horse, the money being in his own hands as treasurer to the sweep.

UNLIMITED POKER—A TERRIBLE TRIAL.

The following sensational gambling story was recently published in an American paper:—

A young clerk in a New Orleans banking-house had been dispatched by boat with a parcel containing one hundred thousand dollars, to be delivered to the branch bank of the firm in Natchez. On the third evening the young man was induced to take a friendly hand at cards; and as all seemed fair and square, and the stakes were trifling, he did not refuse to renew the game on the following night. It was the old story; after a good supply of brandy-smashes, unlimited poker was proposed and agreed to; the game admits of enormous stakes and of two or three dozen people joining in, and the man who has the most nerve in "bluffing"—increasing his bet beyond his opponent—often succeeds in winning with a very inferior hand, as whoever outbids his adversaries can take the pool without showing his cards.

At midnight the clerk had lost all his own money except two hundred dollars, and his opponent, "an old sport," had determined upon cleaning him out at once and finishing the contest

It had been his deal, and he had managed to give the young man a very good hand, three queens and a pair of aces; but he had taken care to give himself a better, four kings. Still, the game did not depend so much upon the cards as the largest purse to "outbluff." Seeing he had a good hand, the clerk put down fifty dollars upon it, the gambler put down an equal sum and another fifty for "bluff." This necessitated the clerk to put down an equal amount and another fifty for "bluff" which exhausted his funds. Thereupon the old sport emptied his pockets and note-book, exclaiming:—

"That's eight thousand three hundred and fifty dollars — that's my pile. I give you ten minutes to cover it or I'll sweep up the lot."

The young fellow was in despair—all he possessed in the world was in that pool, and that gone he would find himself in a strange place utterly penniless. How could he account for this save by confessing the truth to his employers, and that would entail his instant dismissal? Suddenly a desperate thought suggested itself, and after a moment's hesitation, telling the lookers-on to see that neither money nor cards were touched, he rushed off to his cabin and returned with the hundred-thousand-dollar parcel entrusted to him. With a white face and trembling fingers he placed the precious packet upon the pool, stated the contents, and, in his turn, gave the gambler ten minutes to cover it, on penalty of forfeiting the stakes. It was neck or nothing. He knew not how many accomplices the fellow might have, or what means he might resort to to raise the sum, therefore the agony of those minutes as "the sportsman" went round to his pals and took counsel, may be imagined; in the meantime the packet was opened, his assertion as to its value verified, and thereupon Blackleg had to cry a go. As he swept up the pool it was with difficulty the young fellow saved himself from falling into a dead faint, so strong was the revulsion of feeling; but he made a vow that he would never again play a card for money, and the man kept his word.

PLAYING A DESPERATE GAME.

COULD the truth of a story which has been often told be relied upon, that must have been a gruesome sight which was presented to the sportsmen of the period when they had returned to London after witnessing the race for the Oaks of 1844. The "garter of the turf" in that year, as all who are versed in racing lore are aware, was won by a filly called Princess—a horse which the notorious William Crockford, and a few of his friends, had backed to win a large sum of money; but as on the previous evening the grim king had laid violent hands on the old gambler, and as death cancels all bets, there was consternation in the clique. "What can we do to get our money?" became a momentous question. The total amount due over the victory was far too much to be sacrificed without a struggle being made to obtain it, and accordingly, after much scheming, a novel plan was hit upon to secure payment of the bets. Only one or two persons knew of the paralytic seizure which had resulted in the sudden death of Crockford, and it was, of course, the interest of these persons to keep the matter secret. The idea hit upon by the plotters, should the horse Crockford had backed win the race, was to exhibit the dead man, in his habit as he lived, at one of the windows of his club, so that he might be seen by the passers-by after the race had taken place.

Persons were sent to Epsom to watch the result and to send off a pigeon with the news so soon as the struggle was over; they were also told to talk to all and sundry of Crockford's interest in the event just as if he were alive. In due time the bird came home to its loft containing under one of its wings the briefest possible chronicle of the event, simply the word "Princess." So far the conspirators had succeeded—the horse backed by the dead hell-keeper had, as he had anticipated when he backed it, won the Oaks. The second scene of the ghastly tragedy had then to be enacted. The corpse of Crockford was dressed in the clothes usually worn by the deceased, and the body being then placed prominently in the window was made by a little management to look as if it were alive. Many of the gentlemen returning from Epsom as they drove past to their clubs, saw the old man, "looking," as they said, "rather lively." By this means all the bets, which in consequence of his death had lapsed, were duly obtained, each of the confederates getting the amount for which he had respectively "stood in."

THE FRUITS OF BOXING FAME.

THE fame of the great battle between Heenan and Sayers was by no means confined to Great Britain and America; it extended to those continental countries where "the noble art" was as unknown as the stiletto was in London. Just after the Farnborough fight, Dymock, the Champion, who, according to ancient custom at the coronation of the Queen, rode up Westminster Hall and challenged any one who disputed Her Majesty's right of succession, was in Florence. One night when he was at a ball at the Pitti Palace, the whisper went round that the Champion of England was there, and as the word, even in Italy, was associated only with the renowned Tom Sayers, every one was anxious to get a glimpse of him. Sitting in a nook by himself, was a very little, shrivelled-looking old gentleman attired as a clergyman. This was Mr. Dymock. Group after group passed, staring and pointing at him and whispering, evidently much to his annoyance; indeed, that this quiet, retiring, and very *unmuscular* elderly gentleman should have been the hero of that tremendous fight was naturally a subject of the most profound astonishment. At last a loud-voiced and very pronounced Yankee woman stopped in front of him, and with that charming disregard for other people's feelings that characterises her nation, exclaimed:

"You don't mean to tell me that that's the fellow that licked Heenan? Well, I never should have thought it!"

Imagine Mr. Dymock's horror at being taken for a prize-fighter, even though it were the gallant Tom himself! An explanation ensued.

"Well," said the lady, "I didn't think you up to that sort of thing; but you look a plucky little chap!"

ORIGIN OF STEEPLE CHASING.

The following brief narrative has been given of the origin of Steeple Chasing, but the story cannot be authenticated. On a certain evening in the month of December, 1803, in the mess-room of the cavalry officers, then in winter quarters at Ipswich, a young captain named Hansum challenged anyone in the regiment to run against a certain favourite grey horse of his four miles across country for a pony. As the place was very dull at the time, a chorus of voices cried,

"Done, done!"

"Four miles and a-half under the saddle, from here to Nacton church, now. It's a moonlight night, the weather open, the country clear; we shall not find a better opportunity."

Ready for anything, the chorus assented and rushed of to prepare.

"I think we should all look interesting if we wore clean night-shirts over our uniforms and cotton night-caps on our heads," suggested one.

The proposition was hailed with acclaim. A complement of eight was soon ready to start, and a body of troopers was in the background to witness the fun. Whoop! away they went, in night-shirts and caps, making strong running for the lead, and lying well together. At the first fence one of the racers turned a somersault and horse and rider were landed in a muddy ditch, while a Major Medly, with his shirt-tail flying in the wind, vainly tugged at his old "trooper" to carry him over the same. The remaining six got safely across, and with some ups and downs reached Nacton Heath. But the last fence and field presented a most varied picture of reverses: one jumped smash through the middle of a five-barred gate; Hansum's grey, which had occasioned the challenge, took a strong hurdle, fence and bank in beautiful style; two were thrown. Yah! yah! yah! screaming and whooping like maniacs, the remainder clattered through the quiet village, startling the country folks out of their beds, and making them believe the French had landed and were upon them; but the sight of the white, shrouded figures in the cold moonlight, shrieking and urging on their horses, as if a troop of demons were in pursuit, filled them with terror.

> "The steam of their steeds,
> Like a mist of the meads,
> Veiled the moon in a curtain of cloud;
> And the stars so bright
> Shuddered in light
> As the unhallowed troop, in their shadowy shroud,
> Galloping, whooping, and yelling aloud,
> Fast and unfailing, and furious in flight,
> Rattled on like hailstorm and vanished in night."

KING OF THE TIPSTERS.

THERE is no end apparently to the devices adopted by those smart, but very unscrupulous persons who pretend day by day to foretell the winners of races—one plan of taking in the unwary, is to advertise from a well-known training centre, and have an arrangement made for the letters to be forwarded to

London or Manchester, or whatever town or city may have been selected as headquarters. When received, these letters are at once answered, the dupes believing that they are in communication with a person on the spot, who sees the horses at their training-work. Every now and again there is held in the sporting prints a washing of dirty linen; some tipster having a quarrel with his brethren, denounces him as a Turf rapscallion of the period, who ought to be tarred and feathered for his sins.

The unblushing effrontery of hundreds of the tribe would be simply laughable were it not for the money lost over their tips. Taking up one of these letters at random, on it are the names of four horses, not one of which proved successful in the event for which it was given. That, however, is a common enough occurrence, the annoying part of the business being that the scamp in his next advertisement coolly asserts that he sent his clients three winners and a non-starter! Three years ago a person came to the front in the way of tipstering whose mendacity was far beyond anything of the kind formerly experienced. He posed as "king of the tipsters," to gain which title he expended a little fortune in buying up a paper which asked its readers to fill up a coupon saying who in their opinion was the best Turf prophet of the times. The price of the journal in question was twopence, and as the man gave himself a good few thousand votes, the amount of money he expended must have been considerable; but the plan paid: the "mugs" flocked to obtain the advice of the "king of the tipsters," finding, as in all other cases, that it was useless: two winners to-day, three losers to-morrow, the winners being "odds on" chances. The infamous pests who batten on the rawest votaries of the Turf earn every year in the aggregate an enormous sum of money; even those of them who proceed on the no-win no-pay system earn hundreds per annum, as by sending different horses to different clients they make certain of selecting a few winners per diem.

"I have," said, lately, one of these tipsters, "over one hundred persons that I can wire to every day if I like. Each wire, as you know, only costs sixpence, for which I can give a list of four horses. Well, then, I risk a pound every day, and that enables me to select some forty persons from my list, and, as I claim to stand in to the odds obtainable for half-a-crown on two, at least, of my selections, the job pays me well, as men to whom you send a couple of winners to-day live in the hope of your doing still better to-morrow; but I never send two consecutive days to the same persons. I wait, generally, till I get my remittances; and every day brings me a score or two of letters with enclosures of dollars, half-sovereigns, and sovereigns. I am fond of the business; but I cannot say that any person following my advice would be the better of it at the end of the week. It has given me and my wife a good living for the last five years."

COCK-FIGHTING IN OLDEN TIMES.

COCK-FIGHTING is now a banished sport, and one that is illegal. "Cocking" was at one period a pastime of the most popular kind, and Cock-pits were to be found at all places where the sport of racing was carried on, although, as a matter of course, the fights could only be seen by comparatively few persons. Plenty of betting took place in connection with the work of Cock-fighting, and large sums changed hands on the results of mains and matches being declared—tens of thousands of pounds sterling. People came from long distances to see these mains fought out, ladies sometimes forming a portion of the company. In judging of Cock-fighting it must be remembered that about the end of the last century the public had few resources of an instructive or amusing kind to fall back upon after their day's labour had been achieved, and a main of cocks in such circumstances was warmly welcomed, and well patronised. Cock-fighting, as may be supposed, was well organised in the days when it was a British sport. There were persons who made it a business to train—or, as it was called, "feed"—the birds, and get them ready for battle. In this line of business, Gulliver and Potter were men who knew their work, and performed it well; it lay with them to feed and train the birds, and deliver them for battle properly prepared. Among the retainers of the noblemen and gentlemen of England there were always one or two persons who took naturally to cocking: connoisseurs in the various breeds of game-cocks, and able to prepare them for action. Such men were valued by their masters, and were able to show some sport in the stable-yard or in the harness-room when asked to do so. It was the above-named Joe Gulliver who "fed" the great match which took place at Lincoln for £5000. Some counties were more celebrated than others for their mains and matches. In looking over old works which treat of the subject of cocking we find notices of the sport which took place in the Preston pit, much patronised in his time by the Earl of Derby, a great patron of the sport. Most of the gentlemen who indulged in Cock-fighting had choice breeds of birds, which they perpetuated with careful attention.

A SABBATH KEEPING TRAINER.

MANY will perhaps be surprised at the title given to this anecdote, but the fact remains that old John Day was a strict observer of the Sabbath, never exercising his horses on that day, and he used to tell a story in support of his principle. One Sunday morning Mr. Padwick came down with a party to see his Derby favourite, Belgrade, at exercise. It would make thousands of pounds difference to him, he said, if his friends saw his horse out and his beautiful action when extended, instead of seeing him merely in the stable.

"Belgrade is your horse," replied John, "and so are the rest, and you can do what you like with them; and if you take them out Goater may go with them, if he likes; but you must excuse me."

Padwick accepted the compromise, and Belgrade and a few more were taken to the Downs. Galloping with an old horse, Belgrade suddenly became frightened at nothing, or, at least, at nothing that could be seen. Though generally of a most docile disposition, he now grew unmanageable; he dashed off at a furious pace down a steep hill that was almost a precipice; the boy who was riding threw himself off in a fright, and the animal pursued his headlong course. In vain did Goater on a hack and Padwick in his carriage give chase, Belgrade soon out-distanced them, after divesting himself of saddle, bridle, and every particle of clothing. Nothing more was seen or heard of him that night; but the next morning, just as John was about to set out to scour the country, a man called at Danebury to ask if a horse was missing, as one was caught in his yard late last night, and was now at the end of the barn tied up with a halter. A lad was despatched at once; it proved to be the missing horse, and the truant was brought back in a most terrible plight, and though, as we have stated, he had been the Derby favourite, strange to say, after that identical Sunday ride, he was never good for anything.

TURF TIPSTERS AND THEIR WAYS.

As all who have even a rudimentary knowledge of horse racing and its surroundings are aware, there is forever hanging about "the turf" a regiment of vampires calling themselves tipsters and racing mentors, who, if not exactly swindlers, are not far removed from being so. Many scathing exposures of their doings have been made from time to time, but in spite of all that has been written against them, they continue to fatten on the patronage of the fools whom they induce to deal with them.

A gentleman who has had numerous dealings with these persons, in order that he might expose their doings, says, "I made the acquaintance of one of these scamps in the year of Blue Gown's Derby. He was called Daniel—an admirable name for a professional prophet—and letters addressed to him at Beaufort Buildings in the Strand were punctually replied to. Where he lived I never knew; but on one occasion I obtained an interview with him, and was much astonished at the pitiful spectacle he presented. Thinking him to be, judging by his well written letters, a 'somebody' of the Turf world—I was not prepared to see the broken-down waif who met me by appointment. That he was a bit of a scholar I knew at once from his conversation as he spoke English grammatically. Our interview ended by my advancing him a sovereign, for which I received a tip or two which proved of no value. My next London tipster was a man who wrote from 'The Bell,' a public-house in Fleet Street. I never paid this man anything; but I received from him on five consecutive days five tips, all of which came off, and then never heard from him again, and who he was or what became of him I know not. The tipstering ranks have become greatly augmented since the days I am alluding to, or rather, the style of tipping has undergone striking changes—the telegraphic wires being now a wonderful factor in the account."

A gentleman connected with a chief provincial post-office tells me that turf telegraphic business has been about quadrupled during the last ten years, increased indeed to an extent that, were the figures made public, would seem incredible. Some of the most active of the working tipsters will send away from a prominent meeting, such as those held at Manchester or Liverpool, over a hundred wires in the course of the racing; and there are always several such men at work, for "paddock wires" and "final telegrams" have become the order of the day. In most cases the wires are not sent direct from course to customer;

one wire being sent to the tipster's head-quarters, from whence information is sent all over the country. One of the dodges now successfully worked, is for a man to operate as a tipster from more than one place and under more than one name. There is a scamp of the sort now busy swindling the lieges under seven aliases, and he is making money at the business. Persons who have an agent at various race-meetings frequently hit off a winner or two—a fact which they are not slow to proclaim. The following is a copy of one of the many shouts of victory which are set up on such occasions : "Done it again! Dick Richards' sixty-seventh grand *coup* has come off! Will give a cool hundred to anyone showing any of his wires which did not contain Imagination for the Summer Stakes. Dick Richards never sends 'even money' or 'odds on' chances, but always winners at good prices. Remember Bridewell (6 to 1), Oakum Picker (11 to 2), Gaolbird (10 to 1), and a host of others."

BLIND ANGLERS.

THE late Professor Fawcett was not the only trout fisher, who, although blind, was able to wield his rod with precision and success. A few years ago there was to be seen on Tweedside, actively engaged in piscatorial pursuits, Mr. William Rankin, who was known in the country round as the blind angler of St. Boswells, and who became by practice a proficient master of the art, able to cast a fly or land a trout as well as any of his contemporaries. Rankin lost his sight whilst working in London as a journeyman shoemaker, where he was attacked by small pox. It was hoped that by returning to St. Boswells, of which place he was a native, that his sight might in time be restored, but that hope was never realized, for as time passed it became only too certain that "his days were always to be nights," and that the seal set on his eyes would never be broken. When this fact became apparent, he went to Edinburgh, and blind as he was, learned the rather complicated business of a maker of fishing tackle. It proved to be the best thing he could have done, as it enabled him to obtain a living, and to keep himself and family in comfort and respectability. He had, since his boyhood, been a keen angler, and continued during his lifetime to enjoy his favourite recreation, knowing each cast of the Tweed as well as any of his contemporaries, and being blind he was not particular as to the hours during which he fished; his baskets of trout were envied by many a brother of the rod.

A brother fisherman who encountered Rankin on Tweedside and at once discovered by his style of throwing his fly that he was a complete master of the gentle art, thus speaks of the scene :—The picture was a strange and weird one :—that solitary fisherman, shut out for ever from the light of Heaven, pursuing his path steadily far in the deep flowing Tweed, with no earthly help at hand in case of need except his faithful dog; and, as all sound of him died away in the distance, I could not but reflect on the mercies of Him who, while shutting off from His servant the glories of light, had granted him an intensity of perfection in the senses of hearing and feeling, which went far towards supplying the lost blessing. Henceforth, I have associated the blind fisherman of St. Boswells with the blind naturalist whom Wordsworth commemorates in "The Excursion," each affording proof

> . . . . " That faculties which seem
> Extinguished do not therefore cease to be,
> But to the mind among her powers of sense
> This transfer is permitted,— not alone
> That the bereft their recompense may win,
> But for remoter purposes of love
> And charity."

The blind man's many exploits as an angler, and his proficiency in the busking of flies and the making of tackle, soon procured him patronage and business in the line of work he had taken up, but he was also an expert gardener, and could weed a bed of onions or a row of carrots with great success. His life was throughout a notable instance of the triumph of the man over an affliction, which, to many, would have proved insurmountable. Rankin was of a quiet and unassuming disposition, and was never once heard to bemoan his fate. He suffered during the last few years of his life from a painful disease which he bore with great fortitude: on 18th January, 1887, his remains were consigned to the grave in Lessendden kirkyard, where a concourse of mourning friends had assembled to evince their respect.

BETTING VENTURES OF "PUBLIC FORM."

MANY of those who are regular attendants of the various race meetings will recognize, under the name of " Public Form," one who has made his mark on the turf, as a persistent backer of horses, doing business on a large scale—no matter how small the odds may be which at the time are offered against the horses which he wishes to back.

As an example, it may be stated that "Public Form" took £2000 to £1000 that "Bend Or" would win the Derby, and of course won his money. The same person, incited by his success, backed "Versigny" for another race to win him £2000, and in doing so, required to risk about £1,200, so that, as the horse lost, he had only £800 of his gains left, a portion of which was lost over "Master Kildare" in the Gold Cup. The person here alluded to, well-known in betting circles by his "nick name" of "Public Form," is a heavy speculator, risking a stake of from £50 to £200, on even small races. In some seasons this betting man has been very successful, although from the rate of the odds against the horses which he backs (almost always favourites), he seldom secures a very big win, but if on occasion he thinks the chance presented a good one, he will not scruple to lay £700 to win £400, or he will take *even* money (pound for pound) against a chance if he thinks it a good one. "Public Form" backed "Iroquois" for the St. Leger, to win him a large sum of money, and waited with great patience during the time the horse was tossed up and down in the market as if it had no chance to win; being at length rewarded by seeing it first on the eventful day. When not present at a race-meeting, he backs his fancies with resident bookmakers on the system of "starting price," which means, that, if the horse does not start for the race specified, the transaction is null and void. This is a plan of backing horses very generally adopted by persons who do not go to the meetings. Bookmakers in town limit the price they lay on the ordinary and daily races to 10 to 1, and on larger events to 12, 14, 16 or 20 to 1, as the case may be, but generally speaking, the great majority of the horses start at short odds.

Curious dealings occur now and then at the "starting price game," as some call it. When horses start at a short price it is, of course, because of their previous good character, or that they are heavily backed by betters on the course. In order to invest a big sum a *coup* is necessary to success. A clique of persons will save a horse for some nice little race which they feel sure it can win. It is taken to the meeting, but the owner and his friends know very well that, if they were to offer to back it in the paddock, the price offered would not be worth taking. They contrive, in consequence, to let it be thought that it is not good enough to win, or that it has not been sufficiently trained. No one on the course backs it, and in consequence it is quoted in the papers next day as having started at 10 to 1 ; but, so far from the horse not having been backed, money galore has been sent to every town in the kingdom to be invested upon the horse at "starting price," and thus a comfortable little sum of probably £3000 will be won by the confederacy interested.

With reference to the "punting" indulged in by "Public Form," and other men like him, it will be obvious enough that a person betting such large sums runs heavy risks, more especially as he so seldom goes for big odds ; risks, however, are comparative, and it should be easier, therefore, to realise a 7 to 4 chance, than to obtain a win when the odds are 66 to 1, but in the latter case the bettor only requires to risk £15 to win a £1000. Some bold spirits, when they think the opportunity favourable, bet in the most fearless manner, going for "big money," often enough at the risk of those who will give them credit—backers of the kind indicated being not unfrequently careless of results. Occasionally a lucky *coup* will be made that, wisely handled, may prove the forerunner of a fortune. A man may bring off a double event which will yield him a couple of thousand pounds, or may win a thousand over a handicap, and so be able to inaugurate a career. On the other hand, a person may bet away every day for a season with all his might, and while possessing a fair knowledge and experience of what is needed to ensure success, may lose more than another man may win.

"OLD THATCHEM'S" GOOD FORTUNE.

Favours of fortune in betting are, generally speaking, ill-divided ; it sometimes appears as if the whole good-luck of the Turf was showered at some particular meeting on a drunken cab-driver, a worthless billiard-sharp, or an illiterate tailor. There are few men now on the Turf who are known to be "worth money," and who have earned all they possess in the betting-ring. The persons here alluded to have gone on the lines that "small fish are sweet," and have, at first at any rate, been contented with modest profits, taking care to keep carefully the sums gained. "Old Thatchem," who is the happy possessor of nearly a whole town in a well-known racing county, made the money with which he bought or built his houses at the race-meetings held in his own shire. His first slice of luck —he was then a day-labourer—was in realizing a bet of £10 to 10s. on Prince·s, for the Two-year-old Stakes at Doncaster, -1843. A sum of £10, forty-five years ago, was considered by a labouring man to be "money," and such was the opinion of "Old Thatchem." Not a penny of the £10 was parted with till the following year, when a sovereign invested on a horse called Kedge, for the Champagne Stakes, doubled the sum, whilst £2 invested on Beeswing for the Gold Cup added £16 to his hoard. In three years Thatchem was worth £100, which he invested in the purchase of a house. His ambition being stirred, he continued his painstaking and successful career, and soon became an adept at the business. Not that he was always successful in his selections. Many a time he felt the frosts of speculation, but on such occasions, like a prudent general, he was wise enough to desist from business for a brief period, so that his *luck* might have time, as he was wont to say, to come round again.

REMARKABLE DERBY DREAMS.

It may be affirmed without much fear of contradiction that the race for the Derby Stakes has proved a gold mine for dreamers. "The Derby" has now been run every year for more than a century, since 1780 in fact, and it is not a little remarkable that some fortunate person —more than one indeed— always dreams the winner of that race. It is sufficiently curious that it should be so, but it is true nevertheless ; and if the records of dreamland could be ransacked—that is, if any records are kept in such a fairy domain—it would certainly be discovered that from the day of the first Derby till now, that is, from the year when Diomed credited Sir Charles Bunbury with the blue ribbon of the Turf till the day when Ormonde brought the same honour to the Duke of Westminster, some one or other of the favoured children of the gods has been specially blessed with a revelation of the first of the Derby three—and in some instances all three made famous by the fiat of the judge.

Some Derby horses have been the hero of more than one dream. Spaniel is a case in point. That horse, which was the Epsom hero of 1831, was purchased from Lord Egremont, at a dinner-party in his own house in the spring of 1828, for the sum of one hundred and fifty pounds. When his new owner went to look at his purchase next morning, he said to the groom :

"He looks deuced like a weed ; I fear I've made a bad bargain."

"That you haven't, sir ; my wife, the night the colt was foaled, dreamed that he would win the Derby ; " and the dream came true.

"You can make a mint of money over Spaniel, if you like to try," were the words heard by Mr. Joseph Brown, a Yorkshire commercial gentleman of sporting proclivities, living for a little time at an hotel—the Buck's Head—in Glasgow, as he awoke one morning towards the end of April, 1831.

Mr. Brown was never very certain about the words ; that is to say, whether he had overheard them being spoken by some one, or whether, as he sometimes thought, they were a kind of supernatural revelation, and came from his own lips. No matter ; being bound, in the course of two days, direct for London, he lost no time on his arrival in making pointed inquiries about the horses engaged in the Derby, the betting, etc., and in the end had the courage to back the curious revelation which had been made to him, much, however, against the advice of his friends, who insisted that the horse had no chance whatever of winning the blue ribbon. He obtained a good price—40 to 1, to over £20—ten or twelve days before the race, and on the course at Epsom he was again induced to back the horse, by the circumstance of hearing a little boy saying, as the horses came on the course,

"That's it, pa ; that's the one I dreamed had won," when Spaniel appeared.

Having taken 50 to 1 to £5, he then stood to win more than a "cool thousand" by Spaniel's victory. On turning round to see whom the boy was addressing, he had disappeared in the crowd. Mr. Brown watched all the preliminaries of the race with very great attention, and more especially the race itself, which was won by his dream-horse, Spaniel.

By means of his thousand pounds Mr. Joseph Brown was enabled to become a partner in the firm for which he had hitherto been travelling as a bagman, and, curiously enough, never in all his life made another bet, although he annually attended Doncaster races for a period of sixteen years after Spaniel's Derby.

CAPTAIN BARCLAY'S EARLIER PEDESTRIAN FEATS.

The Captain's first match (for 100 guineas) was decided when he was of the boyish age of 17, by his walking six miles within an hour, fair "toe and heel," which he accomplished on the Croydon Road in 1796. Two years afterwards, he contested with a celebrated London pedestrian, a match over a distance of 70 miles, which he walked in fourteen hours, beating his opponent by several miles. In the following year he accomplished 150 miles in two days, having walked from London to Birmingham, round by Cambridge; and a few days afterwards returned in the same time by Oxford. His next important match was in 1801, when, for a bet of 2000 guineas, he undertook to walk 90 miles in 21½ successive hours, the ground selected being the line of road from Brechin to Forfar. After having accomplished 67 miles in thirteen hours, having incautiously partaken of some brandy he became sick, and was unable to proceed. He then renounced the bet, and the umpire retired; but after two hours he completely recovered, and could easily have finished the remainder of the distance within the time. He subsequently performed the distance between York and Hull in 1 hour 7 minutes and 56 seconds, within the specified time, thus retrieving his former loss, and gaining a bet of 5000 guineas.

In November 1800, he walked 64 miles in twelve hours, including stoppages for refreshments. Starting from Ury at midnight he went to Ellon, in Aberdeenshire, where he breakfasted, and returned to Ury by mid-day. Two years later he walked from Ury to the house of Dr. Grant at Kirkmichael, a distance of 80 miles. He remained at Kirkmichael a day and a night, without going to bed, and walked back to Ury by dinner-time of the third day, returning by way of Crathynaird, a detour which lengthened his journey by 20 miles. The distance altogether was 180 miles, over extremely ragged roads through a mountainous part of Aberdeenshire.

In December 1806, Captain Barclay accomplished a still more arduous task, having walked 100 miles in 19 hours over what was then one of the worst roads in the kingdom, and just at the break of a severe storm. From Ury he went to Charlton of Aboyne (28 miles) in four hours, stopped there ten minutes, and then proceeded to Crathynaird, an additional 22 miles. He remained at the latter place 50 minutes and returned to Charlton, where he refreshed for half-an-hour, and then walked back to Ury, completing the distance in 19 hours. Exclusive of stoppages, the time taken was only 17½ hours, or at the rate of 5¾ miles an hour on an average. In this walk the Captain was attended by his servant, William Cross, who also performed the distance in the same time. That Cross was no mean pedestrian is proved by the fact that in December 1808 he walked 100 miles in 19 hours 17 minutes on the Aberdeen Road, near Stonehaven. The Captain's staying powers were well exemplified in the following instances:—In May 1807 he covered 78 miles in fourteen hours over the hilly roads of Aberdeenshire. Leaving Ury at two o'clock in the morning, he attended a cattle sale at a place four miles beyond the Boat of Forbes, on the Don, where he remained five hours, walking several miles in the fields, and returned home to Ury by nine at night.

On another occasion in the following year, merely for amusement, he performed a most laborious undertaking. Having gone to Colonel Murray Farquharson's house of Allenmore, Aberdeenshire, the Captain went out grouse shooting at five o'clock in the morning, and tramped, at least, 30 miles on the mountains. He dined at Colonel Farquharson's house in the afternoon, and in the evening set off for Ury, a distance of sixty miles. He walked this in eleven hours, without once stopping. At Ury he attended to his ordinary business, walked to Laurencekirk (16 miles) in the afternoon, where he danced at a ball during the night, and returned to Ury by seven in the morning. Even then he did not go to bed, but spent the day partridge shooting in the fields. He had thus travelled not less than 130 miles, supposing him only to have walked eight miles while shooting at home, and also danced at Laurencekirk, without sleeping or having been in bed for two nights and nearly three days.

LUCKY SIR JOSEPH.

ONE of the most fortunate racing men of his own, or any other period of turf history, was undoubtedly Sir Joseph Hawley, the owner of Blue Gown and several other race horses of equal celebrity. This gentleman is reputed to have won more money by racing, than any of his contemporaries on the turf, and so well pleased was the noble baronet with his continuous good fortune, that on the occasion of winning the Derby with the above named horse, he presented the rider of the animal with the stakes won on the occasion, nearly six thousand pounds; a sum more than equal to the salary of a Chancellor of the Exchequer for one year! Sir Joseph Hawley's good fortune on the turf may be said to have originated with the purchase of a horse called Mendicant, bought from Mr. John Gully, at one time a prize fighter, afterwards a professional betting man, who in the course of years became a member of Parliament, and died, leaving, as has been said, a large fortune to his family. The horse in question (Mendicant) cost the baronet a sum of three thousand guineas, which, in the opinion of his friends, was a ridiculous price to pay for it; but as it proved, the bargain was a good one for Sir Joseph. Mendicant became in due time the sire of Beadsman, the winner of the blue ribband of the turf in 1858, a victory which in bets alone placed a sum of over £80,000 to the credit of Sir Joseph, who, in conjunction with a partner, had previously won a Derby, namely the race of 1851 with Teddington. The confederates won a large sum of money on the result of this race—not less, probably, than a hundred thousand pounds, and that the Derby of that year was remarkable for the large amount of betting which took place is now matter of history; one bookmaker is known to have paid his fortunate clients at least a hundred and ten thousand pounds. The jockey who rode Teddington received the honorarium of two thousand guineas. That horse, it is interesting to know, was purchased as a foal from a blacksmith for £250, and a thousand pounds additional should it win the Derby, a race which fell to Sir Joseph on four different occasions, Musjid being the Epsom hero of 1859, and Blue Gown crediting him with a similar honour in 1868.

With another son of Beadsman this fortunate sportsman won the great race of Doncaster, in 1869, the name of the horse being Pero Gomez, an animal which ran second for the Derby of the same year, and only lost it by a head; many indeed asserted that Pero Gomez in reality was the winner, and not Pretender. Sir Joseph in his time won many other races, some of them only less important than the Derby, such as the Oaks and the One Thousand and Two Thousand Guinea stakes, as also many of the larger handicaps of his day. In stakes and bets the owner of Blue Gown is reputed, in the course of his career on the turf, to have won close upon half a million sterling. It is a curious fact in connection with the turf career of the "lucky baronet," as he came to be called, that, when Blue Gown won the Derby of '68, the horse ran entirely

for the benefit of the betting public, not being fancied by his
owner, whose liking was centred on other two of his horses engaged in the same race, and which he supported to win him a
very large amount of money. Blue Gown long before the day
of the race had become a great public fancy, and been very
heavily backed to win; it took one betting man, it was reported
at the time, aided by a dozen of clerks, several days to write
out and send off the cheques for the different sums large and
small, which fell due to his clients over the victory of this
public favourite for the Derby. The reason of the horse being
so much liked by the betting fraternity, arose out of the following circumstance:—Blue Gown's Derby was sensational, but
the most exciting episode in the turf career of that horse took
place at Doncaster, when as a two-year-old he carried off the
Champagne Stakes. There were twelve starters, and Sir
Joseph Hawley's colt won the race, but did not get the stakes
because his jockey could not ride the weight. Other jockeys
knew this, and when he returned to be weighed he was
watched. Watson seized the beam, and appealed to Mr.
Chaplin, one of the Stewards. That gentleman ordered Wells
to sit in the scale till Admiral Rous could be summoned. Then
followed a bad quarter of an hour as the Admiral pronounced
against the winner for overweight. Mr. Chaplin inquired what
impost Blue Gown had carried. "No, no," replied the Dictator,
"this is bad enough—the public need not know how much
Hawley's horse really carried." As a matter of fact Blue Gown
had won carrying as nearly as possible 9 st., and this marvellous
performance, the public who stuck to him through evil and
good report, never forgot.

GAMBLERS AND GAMBLERS.

THE veracity of the following story is beyond question, its
truth having been more than once vouched for. In the days
when George the Fourth was regent, Mr. Scrope Davis was one
of the men of the period, *that* period, he was known as a
dandy, but it is proper to state that he was a cut above the
common run of that class of persons, being also a good scholar,
a wit, and a man of high intellectual powers, as also one of the
most inveterate gamblers of his time. One night at Crockford's Scrope was introduced to a young fellow named Hastings,

who had inherited a splendid fortune, which he had already impaired in such haunts as those.

"I shall cut this sort of thing soon," he said; "I am going to be married in a month, and, having had my fling, shall settle down to be a respectable *paterfamilias*."

After conversing for a while, the two went to the hazard-table and began to play. Davis was in luck that night, and won main after main. Several times he wished to throw up the game, but his opponent, who kept drinking champagne like water, was wild with excitement, and swore he would play on until fortune changed. The persistency of the fickle goddess on Davis's side now became so marked, that other gamesters left off playing and gathered round the two champions, watching their play with breathless interest. With white, parched lips that he was moistening every moment with wine, and feverish eyes, Hastings went on rattling the dice and throwing crabs, while Davis, whose face was scarcely less pale than his opponent's, almost as invariably threw the nick. Play continued all night and well into the morning, when Hastings, dead beat, hurled box and dice across the room, shivering a handsome mirror against which they struck, and throwing himself upon a sofa, covered his face with his hands, and sobbed out.

"I can play no more. I've lost all I have in the world: I'm a beggar!"

Hardened as they all were to such scenes, the most callous of the spectators could not repress a feeling of pity for the ruined man, who a few hours before had entered that room, rich, happy, with a bright future before him, and who now had not wherewithal to buy himself a dinner, for he had not only gambled away his money, but his carriages, horses, jewellery, household goods, everything. As Davis stood looking at him all this was running through his mind, and he thought of the young girl who was to have been his wife in a month, who, perhaps, loved him devotedly; her prospects were ruined with his. He touched him upon the shoulder.

"Mr. Hastings," he said, "listen to me: I will forego everything I have won to-night on one condition, and that is, that you will take a solemn oath never to touch cards or dice again."

The young fellow looked up at him, mute with astonishment. He could not believe his senses.

"I mean what I say," continued the other. "Do as I ask, and I will give you back absolutely all."

Down went the ruined gamester on his knees to take the oath, and blessed the man who had saved him from destruction, pouring forth, at the same time, protestations of eternal gratitude, while his generous conqueror gave him back money, assignments, IOU's—everything he had won.

"I will only keep one thing," he said; "that *dormeuse* of yours [a fashionable carriage of the day]. It will be useful to me when I travel."

Hastings rigidly kept his vow, married the girl he loved, and waxed richer and richer. The reverse of this was the fate of Scrope Davis; the fickle goddess deserted him, and in the course of a few years his fine fortune was gone. Over head and ears in debt, nothing seemed left to him but to spend the rest of his days in the King's Bench or leave the country. In this strait he bethought him of Hastings and the protestations of friendship he had made him. Without putting too great a stress upon these, he wrote him a letter, explaining his situation.

"On a certain occasion, which neither of us is likely to forget, you begged me, should I ever want a friend, to come to you, as you considered that all you possessed belonged as much to me as yourself. Without taking any such exaggerated view of your obligations, I now ask you for some assistance to enable me to weather the storm."

The reply came by return, cold and formal, scarcely polite—"Mr. Hastings regretted that he was unable to offer Mr. Scrope Davis *any* assistance."

Davis retired to France, where he spent the remainder of his days, gave up gambling, devoted himself to intellectual pursuits, and found greater contentment in poverty than ever he had in wealth.

AN ASTUTE TURF DIPLOMATIST.

ONE of the most astute diplomatists connected with the financial arrangements of the turf was Mr. Frederick Swindell, who, as the saying goes, "rose from nothing," and died leaving a fortune to his heirs, but the money he left, it is proper to state, was not all derived from his speculations on the turf, his excellent business capacity being exercised in connection with several commercial concerns of considerable magnitude. Along with several other sporting men he invested a large sum in the Burton Brewery Company, but the thing at one time looked so like a failure that his friends sold out at a great sacrifice. Not so Swindell, who, believing in its ultimate prosperity, put £20,000 more into the sinking concern in order to keep it afloat. Then he hired a number of men in town and country to go round to public-houses and hotels and inquire for this particular beer. Of course it was not kept; but they declared they could get it just above or just below, and saying they did not care for any other, walked out again. This being done persistently, orders from licensed victuallers began to pour in, and the article supplied being good, the management of the concern, thanks to the shrewdness of Swindell, was excellent, and in course of time the Burton Brewery became a real "good business."

With regard to the turf, an instance of this person's capacity for making the most out of a bad job was afforded in one of his transactions with Sir Joseph Hawley. They had made a match, but just before the time it was to come off Hawley's horse was taken ill and could do no work. The fact was kept as secret as possible, but Swindell always kept an army of touts, one of whom very soon discovered what had happened, and hastened to communicate the news to his employer. Now it so happened that the horse Swindell had engaged to run against the baronet's was in even worse plight, not being able to leave the stable at all. With most men there would have been an end of the business; not so Swindell. As soon as he heard the news his quick brain saw how to turn it to advantage. Summoning his trainer, he ordered him to bring up another horse, very much of the same colour as the sick one, and to hold his tongue as to what its name was, its age, or what it was intended to run for. This had the desired effect. The touts on the other side immediately jumped to the conclusion that this was the real Simon Pure engaged for the match; Swindell's spies made a point of confirming this supposition, and Sir Joseph was soon informed that the enemy was prepared to take the field. The match was for £200 a-side, half forfeit. Swindell went to Messrs. Weatherby's office on the evening of the horse's arrival and paid in two hundred pound notes to make stakes for the race that was to come off on the following morning. Just afterwards Sir Joseph came in and asked Weatherby if he had heard anything of Swindell's horse. The reply was that he had not, but that Mr. Swindell had just been in and paid his stake, so, of course, he intended to run.

"Then there is nothing left for me but to pay forfeit," said the baronet.

And the little transaction put £100 into Frederick's pocket.

Many attempts were made to "do" the great Frederick, but they never succeeded. One case of the kind may be cited by way of example. A certain owner had received from his trainer a most flattering account of a horse he had entered for the Chester Cup; he was in first-class condition, lightly handicapped, and was a really good thing, ran the report. Thereupon Mr. Swindell was commissioned to back him to win a large stake. To the surprise of our agent, however, this affected the market scarcely at all, the horse still standing at a long price. His suspicions were at once aroused, and although he had a great antipathy to visiting trainers or viewing horses anywhere except on the course, he for once overcame his aversion, and telegraphed to the stables to say he was coming. Upon arriving at the trainer's, that person met him, all smiles, and his inquiry as to the horse's condition was answered with, "Couldn't possibly be better."

Upon being taken to the stall there seemed to be no doubt as to the truth of the assertion, the gallant steed looking splendid. The visitor said he would like to see him gallop, but was told that he had just come in from exercise, and that it would not do to take him out again, and this of course looked feasible enough. Swindell had another look at him. According to the custom of many stables, the animal stood in a set of woollen bandages and these he asked to have removed. The trainer assured him it was quite unnecessary, and was quite contrary to his rules to unswathe a horse after he had been done up for the night. On this point, however, the visitor was not so compliant. He had *carte blanche* from the owner, he said, and he would not quit the place until his request was complied with. The trainer changed colour. He knew his man, and knew it was useless to beat about the bush any more. At first he said the horse had met with a slight accident; but the slight soon changed to severe—severe indeed! While exercising, the animal had come in contact with some sharp instrument that had nearly severed the main tendons of one leg. How such an instrument came upon the exercise ground was not very clearly explained, though doubtless there were people about who could have thrown some light upon it. In the meantime the trainer had been laying heavily against the horse, and, had it not been for the suspicion of Frederick Swindell, the accident would not have been known until the morning of the race, and Mr. Trainer would have netted a pretty considerable sum by his reticence—or roguery.

DESCRIPTION OF THE CATCHING OF A BIG SALMON BY A LITTLE BOY.

The following graphic description of the capture of a salmon in Loch Tay, is from the pen of a very young school boy, who had been permitted to accompany his father and uncle on an angling expedition; it is given just as it was written:—

"Dear mama,—Uncle David and Papa have caught a great big Salmon fish; it took the bait just as we were at lunch, and it was more than an hour before we could get it up into the boat. The salmon got away to the other side, and when the men turned the boat it did the same. Uncle David swore at the men two or three times, and Papa said 'd—n the brute, it's a perfect devil!' Papa was running all over with perspiration, and Uncle David had off his coat. One of the men fell over the side of the boat when he tried to catch the fish with a cleek. Uncle David swore again quite awful, and Papa was so excited that he cried out, 'Never mind, Duncan, let's get the fish.' It was a terrible sight, dear mama; but we got the man safe into the boat, and Papa then made him drink two capfuls of whisky. By this time the big salmon was lost, and Uncle David was awful ill-natured; but the fish, after all, was still on the line, and danced about here and there on the top of the water quite lively, and once jumpit nearly into the boat, and that excited Uncle David more than ever. He said to the men, 'Now, lads, you must get that fish; I'll give you a pound between you if you gaff it.' But we were a long long time in getting it, and Papa was afraid the line would break; it rushed about as if it was mad, then it sank far down to the bottom and remained quite quiet for a long while, then up it would come again, and dash about round and round the boat. At the long and the last, it came rushing on one of the oars and stunned itself, and before it could come out of its fit, Duncan had pulled it on board, at which Uncle David was very proud, and there and then pulled out his purse and gave the men a pound note to divide between them. Papa was greatly pleased, and shook both Duncan and Roderick by the hand. Roderick felled the big salmon by giving it a blow on the head, and then Uncle David gave the men some more whisky. Papa thinks the fish will weigh more than thirty pounds."

SLICES OF GOOD LUCK.

Many incidents have from time to time occurred—indeed are always taking place on the turf—which if recorded in a truthful way would certainly prove interesting to the reading public. Recently, for instance, by a mistake on the part of a telegraphic operator, a Manchester gentleman received from a London bookmaker an unexpected cheque for twelve hundred pounds. The circumstances of this case were as follows :—the telegraph message was, " Have sent you cheque for hundred to back Dreamer for Haymarket Stakes run at 3.30." The clerk operating had several other messages on his hand of a similar kind, all of them referring to different horses, and in operating he put in the message instead of Dreamer, the name of an animal he had himself backed, called Creamcheese, and which proved to be the winner ! The gentleman, a frequent customer of the bookmaker, posted his cheque in a registered letter without remark, and on reading the result of the race in an evening paper thought, as a matter of course, that he had lost his money ; his surprise therefore may be imagined when on the Monday following he received a cheque for thirteen hundred pounds. He thought at first some error had occurred but said nothing (as is the custom in such cases among betting men), and found out afterwards that he was indebted for his stroke of good fortune to the blunder of the telegraph clerk.

A wonderful slice of luck befell a gentleman who, accompanied by a lady friend, had gone racing to Kempton Park. Before leaving for the race-course the gentleman in question had been so fortunate as to receive payment of an old debt of a thousand pounds which had been sent to him in a single bank note for that amount, folding it up, he, unthinkingly, placed it in his pocket-book among five ten-pound notes, which for the time being was all the ready money at his command. Being in good credit with the bookmakers, Mr. Blank did not require to do more than, as it is called, bet " on the nod," which means pay or receive on the following Monday, the usual day of settling for betting men. Having backed, as it proved, the winning horse—Amphion, and also Screech Owl for a place, he came back to join his lady friend (they were engaged to be married); she at once asked him what he had done.

" Backed Amphion," was the reply. " That will be lucky, she said. " I dreamt last night it had won : have you paid your bet ? "

" No, I have not, there is no occasion, my credit is good."

"Well, I have no doubt of that, Alfred, but do oblige me by putting on other ten pounds in ready money."

Under such circumstances to hear was to obey, and Alfred going up to the man he had made his previous bets with, said: "Look here, Fry, I want you to lay me the odds against Amphion to this note in ready money."

And taking from his pocket-book, as he thought, one of his tenners, he handed the bookmaker the note for a thousand pounds which he had that morning received. Nor did he discover what he had done till on going to receive, the bookmaker asked if he would take a cheque for the amount, as he had not such a sum of ready money at hand. Mr. Blank on seeing the figure saw in a moment what had happened, but keeping his own counsel pocketed the cheque for twelve thousand pounds.

THE DERBY IN THE YEAR OF GEORGE THIRD'S JUBILEE.

THE race for the Derby had, by the year of George III.'s jubilee, began to attract a considerable degree of public attention, although, as we can all read for ourselves, it was not till another twenty years had elapsed that the struggle began to be really popular with the people. The conditions of the race then were very much like what they are to-day. This can be shown by quoting the rubric, which ran as follows:—Thursday, May 18th. The Derby Stakes of fifty guineas each, half forfeit, for three-year-old colts, 8st. 7lb., and fillies 8st. 2lb. The owner of the second horse received a hundred guineas out of the stakes—one mile and a half." As at present, the sums raced for were provided by the owners of the animals running, the proprietors of the grand stand (as at present) not contributing one penny to the fund. That is, at least, one point in which the Derby remains unchanged since the days when "good King George reigned o'er us."* In 1809 the Derby was won by Pope, by Waxy, out of Prunella, by Highflyer. There were forty-five horses entered for the race, ten of which came to the starting point, and the total value of the stakes amounted to 1,375*l*. The value of the Derby Stakes in the Jubilee Year of Queen Victoria was a little over 5000*l*; and it may be guessed

* A considerable sum is now, however, provisionally added to the Derby stakes.

that probably more than twenty times the number of people looked on at the race than saw the struggle between Pope and Wizard, which resulted in Goodison, the jockey of Pope, winning the race by a neck just as they were upon the winning post. The rider of Pope, as told in one of the chronicles of the race, rode his horse with much skill and judgment.

It is eighty years since that Derby was run; and it is curious to speculate as to how many persons may now be living who saw it run, at an age, that is, when they would be able to comprehend the meaning of the struggle. Mr. Gladstone, the ex-Premier, is, we believe, now at the age of eighty. He could not see Pope win the Derby; and any five-year old child who might be present on Epsom Downs on that occasion, will have attained his eighty-fifth year—a brave old age indeed. The writer once conversed with an old Yorkshire man at Doncaster, who had seen forty-six St. Legers run, his visits to that famous race course having extended over a period, so he told us, of sixty-two years, his first appearance at the St. Leger having taken place when he was seven years of age along with his grandfather, who officiated as ostler in a livery stable at Newcastle-on-Tyne. He rode all the way on a led horse, taking a good few days to accomplish the distance, and resting all Sunday at a hospitable farm-house.

HIS RULING PASSION STRONG TO THE LAST.

THE following is a true story of a Squire of small means who lived in the county of Cornwall, whose eccentricities of conduct are still kindly remembered by many who knew him. During his career, this gentleman dearly loved fox-hunting, and, possessing a clever "whit-faced horse," which carried him brilliantly over Roughtor and Brownwilly, he valued him more than gold. Being attacked by serious illness, which brought him face to face with an enemy he could no longer escape, and having lived a free-and-easy kind of life, with more thought for the present than a future world, the clergyman of his parish deemed it his duty to pay him a visit, and impress him with the momentous approach, and, if he could, with some serious view of his coming end.

"You are going on a long journey, sir," said the good parson, "and surely you should make some preparation for it, before it be too late."

"I've no wish to travel," replied the sick man; "this place suits me well enough."

"But, sir, 'tis to a better country I would direct your thoughts, where—"

"A better country, did you say?" interrupted the other, impatiently—"give me only a thousand a year and my old whit-faced horse, and I'd never wish to see a better country than our Cornish moors."

Finding him utterly impracticable, the parson then took his leave with manifest but unavailing "signs of sorrow."

In a very short time afterwards, being dressed in his top-boots and scarlet hunting-coat, he was carried down to a settle near the kitchen fire, where, as volumes of smoke curled up from his lighted pipe, the spirit of this hardy Cornishman passed away, and, let us hope, in spite of himself, took its flight to a better land.

PRESENTS TO POPULAR JOCKEYS.

A JOCKEY given to a little rhyming thus made up a list of the presents made to him in the course of a couple of seasons by persons who had betted on the success of the horses which he rode to victory—

"A nice little dog-cart—two very smart hunters,
A hobby-horse for Bob and a match-box of gold;
Ten 'fivers,' two Christmas hampers from Gunters,
And of golden yellow boys—seventy-two all told:
Some cases of mumm, five dozen old port—
A ring with an emerald and a pair of nice slippers
Just right for the wife, other things of that sort:
While along with the fizz came a sharp pair of nippers,
A donkey for Jackey, an Alderney cow,
A box of cigars, a full dozen of hats,
Two prime Stilton cheeses, a fat heavy sow,
A portrait of Bessie and two drawing-room mats,
Ten gallons Scotch whisky, a barrel of bitter—
A silk gown for the wife, a cloak for her girl,
A pin for my scarf with a bright golden glitter
And in a glass case a nice little squirrel."

HE SHOULD HAVE LET WELL ALONE:—A MONTE CARLO STORY.

SOME years ago a young man arrived at Monte Carlo with 300,000 francs in his pocket—those who knew said so. With a sum like that, one can struggle; but that is not enough, one must have some head, which the passions cannot run away with. This young man plays—loses—gains—loses again—and gains again. The struggle had continued far into the afternoon.

In the evening the bank had required to replenish. Again the gain of the player continued. Mons. Blanc goes early to bed. About half-past ten (they close at eleven) there remained nothing in the bank, and the players, chiefly the gaining ones, insisted on the bank being again replenished. Notwithstanding the lateness of the hour they went to call up Mons. Blanc, and returned with 60,000 francs, which were again won by this insatiable, happy child of fortune.

The following morning at the rendering of accounts all the employés gathered round M. Blanc and lamented to him his loss, the individual having gained 300,000 francs and more. M. Blanc, on the strength of his millions, only smiled, and rubbed his hands.

He turned to his valet de chambre, "Baptiste," said he, "where lives this monsieur?"

"At the Hotel de Paris."

"Go and see if he has *left*."

Baptiste goes there. They tell him that monsieur is still there.

"Oh then," says M. Blanc not another word.

In fine, the player plays again, and not only loses the 300,000 francs which he had gained but his own 300,000 besides, and 50,000 more, which he had borrowed. He leaves completely drained out.

SQUIRE OSBALDESTON'S GALLANTRY.

"LIKE all true fox-hunters, 'the Squire' was not insensible to the charms of females, when beautiful, as is pleasantly illustrated in the following anecdote. On one occasion while on a visit to Lincoln, he met at a dinner-party, previous to a county ball, the beautiful Miss Burton, afterwards Lady Sutton. It happened that Miss Cracroft, a rival beauty, had a nosegay in which was a hot-house flower of exceeding rarity. It attracted general admiration, and Miss Burton especially admired it, whereupon her rival, for some private reason or another, twitted her after the manner of dear friends. This was not lost upon Osbaldeston. Pleading an excuse after dinner for leaving the wine-party, he got upon one of his horses, and rode to the house of the person from whose conservatory the flower had been obtained, twenty-five miles distant, and brought back another and more brilliant specimen, which Miss Burton displayed in triumph at the ball-supper. The distance was accomplished at night in about four hours."

PLAYING GOLF BY CANDLE LIGHT!

Of the many anecdotes told by the gallant Captain (Horatio Ross) to his friends, there is none which will interest Scottish ears, in particular, so much as the following description of a game at golf by night. At the race ordinary at Montrose, Lord Kennedy and the late Mr. Cruickshank of Langley Park, both good players, "got up a match of three holes, for five hundred pounds each hole, and agreed to play it then and there. It was about ten or half-past ten P.M., and quite dark. No light was allowed, except one lantern placed on the hole, and another carried by the attendant of the player, in order that they might ascertain to whom the ball struck belonged. We all moved down to the golf-course to see this curious match. Boys were placed along the course, who were quite accustomed to the game, to listen to the flight of the balls, and to run to the spot where a ball struck and rested on the ground. I do not remember which of the players won the odd hole; it was won I know by only one hole. But the most remarkable part of the match was, that they made out their holes with much the same number of strokes as they usually did when playing in daylight. I think, on an average, that they took about five or six strokes in daylight, and in the dark six or seven. They were, however, in the constant habit of playing over the Montrose course." Perhaps golf is, upon the whole, the surest athletic game that can be played, notwithstanding all its chances and "hazards;" a man may be in play or out of play, but scarcely ever makes a total fiasco, as happens occasionally to the best of sportsmen with his gun.

STORIES ABOUT THE ST. LEGER.

Yorkshire teems with St. Leger stories of all kinds, and Yorkshiremen of all grades have recollections, pleasant or otherwise, of the great race for the blue ribband of the North, and of the curious characters who came to Doncaster to assist at its celebration, such as the eccentric James Hirst, who came to the paddock dressed from head to foot in sheepskin garments and drawn in a carriage of his own make by his tame dogs or occasionally by an ass, and surrounded by half a dozen of tame foxes.

On one occasion ten false starts had to be endured by the spectators before the genuine race was run; this was in Altissidora's year, when there were seventeen runners under the charge of the starter. A speculative occupant of the grand stand when the eighth false start had taken place laid 100 to 20 against the next attempt being successful, and also 100 to 30 against the tenth, and of course won his money. In the year 1819 the St. Leger was run twice! Two years afterwards Gustavus, which had won the Derby, was expected to win the St. Leger also, but he was defeated by Jack Spigot, a Northern horse.

On this occasion was fought the first great struggle between the Southern and Northern trainers, and the latter, who entertained a profound contempt for the Newmarket men and their plans and training, prophesied that they could never win a St. Leger on the Town Moor of Doncaster—a prophecy which was speedily shown to be erroneous, and the race is seldom won now by a horse that is trained in the Northern stables, the latest Yorkshire trained winner being Apology.

The writer, during various visits to Doncaster, has held converse with men who had seen thirty, and even more, St. Legers run for right off the reel, and has heard stories of the good or ill fortune which befell them in their financial speculation. In the year Hannah won he met an ent' usiastic old tyke who had witnessed the victory in question, and had attended nearly fifty anniversaries of the race, walking, on some occasions, a distance of sixty-seven miles to witness the St. Leger. One of this old man's reminiscences struck the writer as being somewhat remarkable. On asking him if he was fond of having a bet on the horse he fancied, he said he was, and proceeded to narrate that, in the year 1830, he was working in the neighbourhood of Birmingham, having just been married to a young woman of that town, who had been a domestic servant in the house of a manufacturer. True to his colours, a day or two after his marriage he set off for Doncaster, and was present on the Town Moor when Priam, the hero of that year's Derby, succumbed to Mr. Beardworth's colt Birmingham.

"Yes, I backed the winner, sir, and took home a bit of money with me, which pleased the wife; you see, sir, although everybody said Chifney's horse was bound to win, I was bent on having my money on Birmingham, not because I had come from that town, but because he was out of Filho de Puta, which was the first St. Leger winner I ever saw. There was a big field, and as I had fifty shillings on, I was in the shakers till the brass was again in my pocket; I got wet with the rain, and I was all of a sweat as well, thinking that Priam would do me out of my money—it was a near thing; but I landed, and I was so excited over the matter that I never heard the thunder."

CAPTAIN BARCLAY WALKS A THOUSAND MILES IN A THOUSAND HOURS.

THE following is a brief account of the great feat accomplished by Captain Barclay in walking a thousand miles in a thousand successive hours on which he started on the 1st of June 1809. The conditions of the match set forth that the great pedestrian for a bet of a 1000 guineas was to go on foot at the rate of one mile in every hour. The Captain, when he commenced this great feat, was in fine condition, in the best of health and spirits, his weight being 13 stones and 4 pounds, but when weighed after finishing he scaled only 11 stones, thus losing in the course of his walk no less than 2 stones 4 lbs. He walked in a sort of lounging gait, without any apparent extra effort, scarcely raising his feet more than two inches from the ground. His dress was adapted to the weather, sometimes a flannel jacket, and sometimes a loose, dark grey coat, but he always used strong shoes and lamb's-wool stockings. Towards the close of his task the spasmodic affections in his legs were particularly distressing, but it was an astonishing fact that his appetite continued to the end as good as ever, and to this fortunate circumstance his success must be largely ascribed.

We give a statement of the Captain's meals during the match, which, we fear, are antagonistic to the rules laid down by more modern trainers. He breakfasted at 5 A.M., when he ate a roasted fowl, drank a pint of strong ale, and then two cups of tea, with bread and butter. Lunch at twelve—the one day beef-steaks and the other mutton-chops, of which he ate a considerable quantity. He dined at six either on roast-beef or mutton-chops, and his drink was porter and two or three glasses of wine. He supped at eleven on cold fowl. In addition to the foregoing, he ate such vegetables as were in season, and the total quantity of animal food he took daily was from five to six pounds. Extraordinary excitement prevailed during the last days of the walk, and the Captain had ultimately to be roped in to prevent his being impeded by the crowd.

The multitude that resorted to the scene of action was unprecedented. Not a bed could be procured at Newmarket, Cambridge, Bury, or any of the towns and villages in the neighbourhood, and every house and vehicle was engaged. The betting all through was in Captain Barclay's favour, and so strong was the confidence in his success that, although excessive odds were offered against him towards the close, no bets could be obtained. The aggregate sum that changed hands is supposed to have amounted to £100,000. When the last mile was finished the Captain was put into a hot bath for a few minutes, after which he went to bed, and by next morning he was in perfect health and entirely free from pain. So great were the recuperative powers of Captain Barclay that five days from the conclusion of this extraordinary walk he joined the expedition to Walcheren at Ramsgate, and embarked with it as aide-de-camp to Lieutenant-General the Marquis of Huntly.

BLAIR ATHOL'S RACE FOR THE DERBY.

THE following narrative, abridged from Baily's popular magazine of sports and pastimes, may be relied upon as giving the true tale of Blair Athol's Derby victory:—"It was not until the morning before the race that I felt certain Blair Athol would start. On the Derby day I saw John Day of Danebury, and in talking over the Derby he remarked that 'Harry Hill had said that Blair Athol would run well, and nearly win.' When such an unfailing oracle as Harry Hill spoke, one could not go far wrong in following his judgment.

"For that year's Derby thirty horses went to the post. There was a long delay owing to the fractiousness of an obstinate brute named Tambour Major, an animal that, judged by his actions, would have been more at home in Sanger's Circus than on a race-course. What with dancing on his hind legs, pirouetting like a harlequin, and fiercely kicking out at intervals, he became a nuisance and a terror to the jockeys on the other horses. He caused many false starts, which took a good deal of 'go' out of some of the competitors. While this brute's antics proved so annoying, and made most of the other horses restless, Blair Athol stood his ground in a quiet and unconcerned manner, merely swaying his head to and fro, taking no notice of the tumult around.

Snowden, Blair Athol's jockey—Yorkshire like his horse—a strong and resolute rider, sat quietly in his saddle, keeping a wary eye on Tambour Major. In several of the false starts Blair Athol took no part whatever. The flag was lowered once more. Snowden thought it was another false start, but the starter had become disgusted with Tambour Major and the flag was raised no more for that Derby. When Snowden realised this he set his horse going, but the others were before him, and he had to be content with a stern chase. He was in the rear until Tattenham Corner was reached, but Blair Athol was going well within his own speed, and Snowden became aware that he had the pace of the best of the field. And once round that dreaded corner, Snowden saw that the horses in his front were so close together that he could not get through. Amidst the din of the horses' feet, as they thundered over the turf, could be heard Snowden's voice shouting to the jockeys (who had unwittingly blocked him) to make way. At this time, Tom Aldcroft on General Peel held a good position, and, to all who closely watched the race, it seemed as if General Peel would win; but when the way was once clear, Snowden called upon the white-faced chestnut in the most resolute manner, not forgetting to dig the spurs into his sides. In spite of the enormous stride of General Peel, Blair Athol gained upon him, inch by inch. Now the white-face reached his antagonist's quarters; now his girths; now his head; and then, as deafening and ringing cheers rent the air, the son of Blink Bonny rushed like a whirlwind past the big son of Young Melbourne, and won the Derby of 1864 by two good lengths.

"On the day of the race Mrs. Jackson, wife of the owner of the horse, was staying at James Bland's house at Isleworth. Mrs. Jackson and Mrs. Bland were at an open window, watching for the return of their husbands, and wondering which horse had won. Mrs. Bland first espied the gentlemen as they drove up to the house and exclaimed:—'I wonder what can have won? Mr. Jackson has some laburnum round his hat.' 'Laburnum!' cried Mrs. Jackson, 'that means green and gold—I'Anson's colours! Then BLAIR ATHOL has won!'"

GROUSE SHOOTING MATCH BETWEEN HORATIO ROSS AND COLONEL ANSON.

THIS great match, which was much spoken of at the time, and has been frequently referred to since, was made on a boat on the Thames whilst the gentlemen were returning from a pigeon shooting display at the Red House, Battersea. Captain Ross has himself told the story of this contest, and we relate all that took place in the sportsman's own words.

"The terms were," says Mr. Ross, "that I should make my appearance at Milden Hall prepared to shoot against any gentleman that Lord de Roos should name; that we were to start at sunrise by the watch, and shoot until sunset, without any halt; that no dogs should be used, but that we were to walk about forty or fifty yards apart, with two or three men between, or on one side of us; that it was not necessary any birds should be picked up, the umpire's seeing them drop was to be considered sufficient. The bet was two hundred pounds a side, but to that I added considerably before the event came off.

"We all breakfasted at Milden Hall by candle-light, and were in line ready to start at the correct moment when (by the watch) the sun had risen, for we could see no sun, as the country was enveloped in mist. Colonel Anson was a particularly fast and strong walker, and seemed to fancy he was able to outwalk me. So off he went at 'score' pace (I merely guess it), probably from four and a half to five miles an hour. I was not sorry to see him go off at 'score,' as I knew I was in the highest possible state of training, and that I was able to keep up that pace for fifteen or sixteen hours without a halt. Everything was conducted with the greatest possible fairness. We changed order every hour, and as Colonel Anson was quite able to hold on the great pace, we were fighting against each other as fairly as two men could do.

"The Colonel had luck on his side, for though in the arrangement of the match, as made by Lord de Roos, everything was fair, still by mere chance birds rose more favourably for him than for me, and in the course of the match he got eleven more shots than I did; the consequence was that he at one time was seven birds ahead of me. About two o'clock, I saw evident signs of the Colonel having near about 'pumped' himself. 'The Old Squire' rode up to me, and said: 'Ross, go along! he'll lie down directly and die'—he fancied he was viewing a beaten fox. I was thus able to go right away from the Colonel; and, as the birds were so wild (in consequence of the crowd and noise) that few shots were got nearer than fifty or sixty yards, I gradually made up my 'lee-way.'

"A quarter of an hour before the expiration of the time, Mr. Charles Greville and Colonel Francis Russell rode up to me, and said Colonel Anson was unable to walk any more, but that he was one bird ahead of me, and that Lord de Roos had authorised them to propose to me to make it a drawn match. I had a great deal of money depending on the result (about one thousand pounds), and had not had a shot for the last ten minutes, so, after a moment's consideration, I came to the conclusion that, at that late hour, when the birds were all out of the turnips and feeding in the stubble, it was too great a sum to risk on the chance of getting a brace of birds in a quarter of an hour, I therefore agreed to make it a drawn match. I was as fresh as when I started, and in the excitement of the moment, and perhaps a little anxious to show that I was not beaten, I said to the assembled multitude (about five to six hundred people) that I was ready then and there to start against any one present to go to London on foot against him for five hundred pounds, or to shoot the same match next day against any one for five hundred pounds."

GAMBLING ON THE TURF.

Those who are unacquainted with the magnitude of the "racing speculation" of the present day will find matter for reflection in the following figures which are worthy of all credence and illustrate vividly the part played by the horse as an instrument of gambling.

All that can be won on the racing arena in one season in stakes is a little over £400,000, and that sum divided among the horses in training (say from two to six-year-olds), would only represent a nominal amount to each, and no man who pursues the pastime of racing from pure love of the sport can, in the face of the enormous expenditure which is necessary, possibly reimburse his outlays from any stakes he may win. A well-informed sporting writer said lately that one owner had in recent seasons paid for " entries" alone, over £40,000. With such outlays, what signifies the winning of a few paltry handicaps, or even a Derby or Oaks, or both of these classic events with a St. Leger added? In one year (1865) of his career on the turf, a French racing magnate won close upon £60,000, in England and France. That was, undoubtedly, a large sum for one year, but when it was incorporated in the accounts of seasons which proved less productive or resulted in loss, it was as pence to pounds. Other prominent supporters of the turf have in their day experienced similar vicissitudes of fortune. In the year 1863, a gentleman (the owner of Macaroni) came to the front who carried all before him, and in winning the Derby, took out of the ring, in absolute money, the largest sum ever won over that celebrated annual struggle.

Calculation, as brought to bear on the turf, is best exemplified, however, in the war continually being waged between bookmakers and backers. In this battle the chance and luck of the racing arena come into prominent view. The £400,000 annually fought for by owners, is as a drop of rain added to the ocean, when compared with the enormous sums which are annually gambled for on the race-courses of the kingdom, and in the clubs where betting is now carried on all day long, and during the night time as well. One has but to visit the inclosure of any well known seat of racing sport to know how vast are the accumulated sums which change hands over each race. Ready-money bookmakers have been known to draw £700 over a small handicap, and to lay the odds to over £2000 on a good betting race in one day ; the total sum involved at meetings where over a couple of hundred layers of the odds are to be found loudly shouting for business must indeed be large. Only the other day the fact was recorded of a bookmaker's clerk, who beginning with a sovereign (he was speculating on his own account), was so fortunate as to end his endeavours by pocketing a sum of £1,300. Such tales have often been told ; when Fortune bestows her favours the grateful recipients are prone to boast of the fact ; on the other hand, when Fortune frowns, nothing is said, the loser has then to bear his "bad turn" as well as he can. It is needless to say that for one winner of the kind alluded to there are ninety-nine losers.

"MUSIC HATH CHARMS."

The following little sketch appeared recently in *Rod and Gun*, a weekly newspaper devoted to sporting matters:—

Scotsmen, as every Englishman is aware, cannot see a joke; but it is sometimes a disastrous mistake to suppose that they cannot make one.

It was a fine morning at the beginning of the season. Sport had been fair the day before; but those who had done well were thinking it not impossible to do better. They had all got up before the sun, and the landlord of the inn could not understand why they were late for breakfast. He consulted Boots.

"Where have the gentlemen gone, Boots?"

"Don't know, sir,—leastways can't tell where they've landed. One by one they began to come downstairs about six o'clock, all askin' me, confidential like, the same question—where could they find a piper?"

"Aye! and what did you say?"

"O, I told them all the pipers I knew in Killin or round about, and they all set off hard as their legs could carry them."

By-and-bye, a good half-hour after breakfast had been ready, the gentlemen, one by one, re-appeared. Each was looking more solemn than the other; and the kitchen was full of natives skirling their pipes into tune.

The explanation of the extraordinary assemblage came out as the porridge plates were being carried away.

"What's amusing you, Laird?" asked one of the English gentlemen, the editor of a well-known Liberal newspaper in Manchester, addressing a kilted young man struggling to repress an embarrassing mirthfulness.

The Laird was not loth to answer; but as his tale began to unfold the gentlemen were loth to hear. They blushed like school-girls. The day before, the English editor had turned away, and gone to another part of the loch, in a rage at the Laird, with whose boat his had been keeping company a hundred yards apart, for having caused his piper to enliven matters with a tune. At the pier that night, however, the piper was able to report that, immediately after "Macrimmon's Lament" had begun to sound upon the waters, his master had hooked and landed a 43-pounder. Three other fish had followed rapidly. "In fac'," Donald said, as he was showing off the Laird's basket to the gentlemen, "the fush stopt takin' only when I could plaw no more—wi' fair exhaustion. A' the time I played, they wis' ruggin' and tuggin' at the meenow like mad, and thoosands and thoosands were poppin' up their noses at the stern o' the boat, tae see ta pipes in operaashun. Pipes always maks 'em tak' in Loch Tay."

CARD-PLAYING IN GREAT CITIES.

As is known there is a great deal of card-playing as well as other kinds of gambling, constantly going on in London, but it is said by persons who have been inquiring into the incidence of play that very little gambling takes place in that metropolis compared with other capitals. This is an undoubted fact, more money is lost and won in a night in the Oriental Club at Constantinople than changes hands in half a week in any club in London; while at the Jockey Club in the city of Mexico heavier play may be witnessed any evening than can be seen anywhere in London; that there are fifty places in New York where gambling goes on for every ten in London, and that at the Club in Shanghai, or at Singapore, the stakes are heavier than in most coteries in this capital of ours.

The following statements have been made as to the card-playing in London :—

In London we do not play for high stakes. Stop ! At a few places we do, fitfully, but not often. I was present one night, when a well known "society man" lost £3,200 at baccarat, but I have seen £7000 lost in half the time in the Turkish capital by a Bey, who was a relation of the ex-Khedive of Egypt, Ismail.

Strange as it may appear, an Englishman is not naturally a gamester. He does not like to risk his money foolishly and recklessly. He will play for a few pounds; but if he be badly hit, he will go away. Look at what we see at Monte Carlo. Who are the gamblers there? The Russians, the Americans, the French, and, in a very small way indeed, the English.

Look at the clubs, and you will find that in all the respectable ones whist is the game chiefly in vogue, with sixpenny, shilling, half-crown, and crown points.

You have all heard the tale of the Prince of Wales's visit to Lord Beaconsfield, and the whist party at which Mr. Bernal Osborne assisted.

"What points shall we play, sir ?" asked the then Premier.

"Pound points, I think," said the Heir Apparent.

Upon which Mr. Bernal Osborne, seeing the countenance of

his chief fall, remarked, "I think, Sir, the Prime Minister would prefer Crown points!"

"But poker is played very extensively in London, now," you will say.

I grant you that General Schenck did introduce and popularise that game; but I do not find unlimited poker played much.

I did hear once of a game in the chambers of a well-known barrister, at which a wealthy Jew paper-owner, a learned counsel, a young lordling or two, and a literary man assisted, at which a great sum was lost, so large as to be the talk of the town. And I heard once of a gambling game of poker, at which a cheque of two thousand pounds or so changed hands, a cheque that was never honoured. But these games are rare; very rare now that several inveterate gamblers have died.

TURF SLANG.

THE language of the turf abounds in slang phrases, some of which are expressive. In accounting, five shillings are known in betting circles as a *dollar*; a pound is called a *quid*; *fivers* and *tenners* are respectively five and ten pound notes. A *pony* is turf slang for twenty-five pounds; a *century* means, of course, a hundred; while a *monkey* represents a sum of five hundred pounds. The *odds* is represented by the figures for or against the chances of the horse, and the principal turf market is in London, and is open daily at a large building in Wellington Street and at Tattersall's. It is the big bookmakers who "set the market," *i.e.*, fix the rate of the odds which are seldom if ever commensurate to the chance of the horse. A *stiff one* is a *dead 'un*, or a horse which is in *the cart*; in other words, an animal which will not compete, but will probably be *scratched* (that is, struck out of the race) or made safe before the day appointed for its decision.

Skinning the lamb denotes that the bookmakers have a clear book as regards the winner; in other words, have not betted against it, and have, therefore, nothing to pay. The origin of the phrase is not given in the *Slang Dictionary*, and the writer has not been able to trace it.

Milking is a word which in the slang of the turf implies that the owner of the horse is obtaining money on the certainty of its not ultimately being allowed to run in the race, or, if it runs, on the certainty of its not winning. Winning a race cannot be made an absolute certainty, but losing a race can. "We shall do with our own horses as we please ; enter them or not, as seem fit to us ; and we do not ask the public to back them, nor yet to pay the expenses of their training :" that is the general reply of the owners to the accusations embodied above. There are, of course, owners of horses who enter more than one animal in a race and act quite an honest part in doing so ; the merits of the animals may be so nicely balanced that even on the eve of the struggle they will be unable to settle which is the best one. The owners who do this, it is safe to assume, do not make their living on the turf.

TOM PARR THE TRAINER'S DOINGS.

In the opinion of that best of all retailers of racing gossip, Thomas Coleman, there has been no cleverer man on the Turf than Tom Parr of Letcombe, near Wantage, in Berkshire. No man picked up horses at such small prices and won big handicaps with them afterwards as he did ; he generally sold them well, too, into the bargain after he had skimmed the cream off. You remember Malacca winning the Cambridgeshire in 1856 ? Parr had bought him for eight sovereigns. They said, after he won, he had been in a cab ; but that was nonsense. The trainer rode him as a hack, and galloped him with his horses at exercise, thus found out he could go, and prepared him for the Cambridgeshire. The next year he won with Odd Trick, another horse he had picked up for a little money.

But the best of all was Weathergage, a horse cast off from the Duke of Bedford's stables by Admiral Rous and Bill Butler. They actually sold him to Armstrong for £40 ; and this was how Parr came to get hold of him : he was sitting with me in Mr. Linton's hotel during the Northampton race-meeting, when Robert Sly the jockey came in and said, "That's a nice useful horse, and one that will win some plates, that Admiral Rous has sold to Armstrong for £40, out of the Duke of Bedford's stable." Parr, hearing this, slipped out, went to Armstrong, and offered him £60. Armstrong said he had bought him for Frank Clark, but he would ask him if he would take the £60. Mr. Parr did buy the horse at the price he offered, and won a race or two with him ; then he put him in the Goodwood Stakes, which he won, beating a large field of good horses. Before he started for this the Duke of Bedford offered Mr. Parr 1000 guineas for him back—a pretty compliment to the judgment of Butler as trainer, and Admiral Rous as manager of the stud. A joke went round the ring at the time, they said *the Duke of Bedford was below Parr.*

The same trainer also won the Cesarewitch Stakes with him the same year, and many other races, and then sold this £40 cast-off for 2500 guineas. He bought another colt called Contentment, by Archy, for £100, entered him in the Metropolitan Stakes, and sold him for 2200 guineas before the race, in which he ran third. How he bought little Saucebox for a small sum, and won the Leger with him, besides other stakes, you know, beating Rifleman, who ran second, and for whom 8000 guineas was refused before he started; also Oulston, for whom £3000 was refused I know, as I had a commission myself to offer that for him, for a clergyman, before the race; yet Parr beat them both with a £200 plater. But, you see, he never overdid them. The silly creatures think the more they gallop them the faster they go; but a lot of the best horses are used up at home, and if not, they lose their force of going.

Poor old Mr. Thelluson was very near selling Rataplan for 800 guineas, as they had blistered his hocks for curbs. There was nothing the matter with them; and it was only done to get the horse out of him. I told Parr about it, and he went to see him, and, as Mr. Thelluson was short of money, he lent him £1100 on the horse, and afterwards wrote him out another cheque for £50, which was very liberal. He agreed to take the horse to train and run, and to divide the profit, and he won upwards of twenty races with him—King's Plates and some good handicaps. I had a horse called John Bull in the Goodwood Stakes with him, and the day before I asked Parr to lead my horse a gallop round the Stakes course. He got on Rataplan himself and led mine. In the gallop he threw a fore-shoe. I never saw a shoe fly so far before; it went into the bank of the plantation. Parr rode Rataplan himself in the race, and I believe the Bribery mare won. He was never over-galloped in private, or he would not have won a third of the races, and would have been broken down into the bargain.

MORE ABOUT TYPICAL TIPSTERS.

It would not prove at all difficult to paint the portraits in type of a score of the men who, knowing that some people have more brains than money, are always endeavouring to obtain a share of the latter commodity. The hard cash expended by gamblers on the turf for racing counsel is undoubtedly enormous, but if those in search of such phantom gold could only know the men they deal with they would very speedily button up their pockets. There is Sam Sneak, for instance, who pretends to know stable secrets, and to send "paddock snips," as he calls his precious finals, well, he is a person who had been some years clerk to a small ready-money bookmaker, and who, after pretending to conduct the business of his late employer (who died suddenly) for the benefit of his widow and fatherless children, had to be ignominiously discharged for embezzlement.

Setting up as a tipster, he advertised himself as being an owner of race-horses and always in "the know" of good things. He issues daily, at least a hundred lies from his brazen-faced mint, and has a hundred companions who every day do just as he does. Then there is "Billy Button" who has twice "done time," as the saying goes when a man has been in prison for theft. "Billy" has found a congenial hiding-place on the race-courses and daily sends out his *tips* with more airs than any honest man would think of adopting. "Tom Tiddler," who solicits business on the "unsurpassed system of mutual benefit to backer and tipster," was two years ago a potman in a Manchester public-house; now, as he boasts, he can pay a clerk five-and-twenty bob a week to do his correspondence with the mugs, and have a tenner clear for his pocket after paying office rent and all expenses. "It's a rare paying game," says Tom.

Several of the shrewdest turf adventurers of the period have of late put on an air of much respectability, and advertise after the following manner:—

"Mr. Henry Howard St. Clare, late of Buxton, begs to intimate that he can impart some occasional information of great importance to turf men who will favour him with their club or private address. Professional betting men need not apply to Mr. St. Clare."

That is a style which is sure to bring a dozen replies to "the Gracechurch-street Chambers," and by-and-bye business results. St. Clare is an old gentleman's servant, with a considerable knowledge of the world, and intimate with a few valets who are in the service of "swell" racing men, from whom he gains some knowledge of what is doing at Newmarket and in other training stables, in consequence he is often able to season his tips with an occasional really "good thing." These he makes the very most of:

"Kindly put me on a sovereign when you make your own investment," is the plan he adopts.

"I have been put to much expense to obtain such important information, and I know it to be so good that I take the liberty of asking you to name it to your brother-in-law, Sir—."

This man (he still goes on) is so clever that if he makes only three or four hits in a year he can live like a "fighting cock." Unbounded cheek is the characteristic of this person; and Mr. St. Clare, it may be remarked, has many brethren equally as clever and quite as unprincipled as himself.

LORD BROUGHAM'S CLEVER WAGER.

LORD BROUGHAM was not exactly the kind of man you would expect to hear a good betting story about; but there is one told of him that makes Scotch canniness hold its own beside Yankee shrewdness. Once, when a youngster, he was at Dumfries, attending the Caledonian Hunt, and dining at the table with a number of choice spirits. Everybody was betting; and Brougham offered to wager £50 that not one of the company would be able to write down the kind of conveyance in which he would go to the races next day. The bet was accepted, everybody scribbled a guess, and no one proved to be right; for Brougham had made up his mind to be carried thither in a sedan chair, which no one had ever thought of. When the time came for return he offered to bet the same amount as before, that no one would be able to write down the name of the vehicle he had chosen to return in. Everybody taxed his ingenuity to the utmost to think of the most *outre* modes of conveyance, and for that very reason everybody was again baffled, for Brougham had cunningly taken a chaise and pair, which was so simple that no one dreamed of mentioning it.

ABOUT WEBB THE WAVE BREASTER.

"You have only to do something uncommon to become famous or at any rate notorious," said the late Mr. Dickens to an acrobat who called upon him asking counsel. This is a truism which many know by experience and have benefited from or suffered by; Captain Webb was an example of what we mean.

Until taken up by the sporting correspondent of a London newspaper he was nobody, but no sooner had the pressman taken him in hand than he became a celebrity. After the channel feat had been accomplished all and sundry wanted to know and shake hands with the hero of the exploit. The man who formerly often had to want a drink could not move now a dozen yards without festive admirers wishing him to partake; and many a man gave Webb gold to walk with him in some conspicuous thoroughfare, in order that he might say he was on familiar terms with the great swimmer. Webb was seen going the pace during the Agricultural Hall mixes, and the late hours and debauchery were so different from his original rough, sea-faring life that the pace soon began to tell. When once a man begins to taste the adulation of the mob it is as the very breath to his nostrils, and soon poor Webb could not live without it. Finding he had survived the notoriety created by his Channel feat, he inaugurated another to revive his waning fame; and that, as everybody knows, was to swim the Cataracts of Niagara. Had he been in the same form as when he crossed the Channel, he would have accomplished this feat; but he depended on his original strength and staying power, and found too late he had lost them, that in this fight with the cataracts the victory, as all the world is aware, remained with them.

BLENKIRON THE BREEDER.

Mr. BLENKIRON, the famous breeder of blood stock at Middle Park and the founder of the great race run annually at Newmarket for two-year-old horses—the "Middle Park Plate," made a fortune in the business referred to. He began life in the Great Metropolis in a commercial way, but having a penchant for the turf used to enter with zest into several of the sweepstakes for the Derby which are so popular in all parts of

London. Being so fortunate as to gain the first prize in one of those—not less than a thousand pounds—he began to turn his attention to the breeding of horses, and commencing in a humble way attained in the end a very large degree of success, and bred in his day some of the grandest horses on the turf. His first sale of blood stock took place in 1856 when he sold thirteen lots at an average of £111 per head. Twenty-three sales in all were held at Middle Park, and the average of these showed the figure of 250 guineas. The greatest prices were obtained for blood stock in what are known as the plunging years of 1864-5-6-7 and 8, when an average of £446 was attained ['67]. In the days referred to the price paid for a yearling was of no moment—men were then betting to win or loose in thousands over a fifty pound plate. Mr. Blenkiron paid the greatest attention to his work and bought the grandest breeding horses that money could purchase. Some of the prices he obtained for his yearlings were remarkable, but curiously enough, it is rarely the case that juvenile blood stock sold at a high figure blossom into racers of repute.

PEDESTRIAN FEATS OF LONG AGO.

The following feats may be commended to the attention of the pedestrians of the period.

Spence, a chairman in Paisley, walked from the cross of Glasgow to Edinburgh, a distance of 42 miles, in seven hours and twenty minutes without much apparent fatigue.

On 15th April, 1812, Lieut. Groats undertook, for a wager of two hundred guineas, to go 72 miles in 12 hours. He went from Blackfriars Road to Canterbury and thence back to Stroud. He performed the first fourteen miles in two hours. When he had gone 60 miles he was much fatigued, but by the aid of refreshment and rubbing, he was enabled to proceed and accomplished the distance within a minute of the time allowed.

In August, 1809, Captain Walsham of the Worcestershire regiment of Militia, walked the distance of 60 miles in 12 hours, with ease; and afterwards rode 30 miles on two curricle horses in two successive hours, for a wager of 120 guineas.

On the 18th Sep., 1811, Mr. Mealing, a gentleman of fortune in Somersetshire, started to go 540 miles at the rate of 30 miles a day for 18 successive days, and to perform the distance in 18 different counties, which he accomplished, and won 500 guineas. He was reduced from 14 st. 8 lbs., to 12 st. 4 lbs.

Mr. Canning, a gentleman in Hampshire, walked 300 miles in less than 5 days. He started at the turnpike road, four miles from Basingstoke, at four in the morning, and went sixty miles in 14 hours. He finished his task two miles from Yeovil in Somersetshire by eleven at night on the fifth day. He was apparently so little fatigued, that probably he could have continued for several days, but in the course of the journey he lost twenty pounds weight.

Lieutenant Halifax of the Lancashire Militia, walked two miles an hour for one hundred successive hours, near Tiverton in Devon, in March, 1808. This was a great performance, as he could not have more than fifty minutes' rest at one time, during four days and nights. He was much distressed: his legs were swollen, and his whole frame was exhausted. His courage, however, never failed him, and he completed the task amidst the shouts of the multitude that this extraordinary experiment had attracted.

Captain Thomson of the 74th regiment, while stationed at Aberdeen in the year 1808, undertook to *walk* twenty-one miles in three hours. He started on the 5th of May at the seventh milestone on the Ellon Road, returning to the 4th until he should perform the distance, which he accomplished in four minutes and a half less than the time allowed.

Among other feats performed by Captain Barclay of Ury it may be mentioned that he walked 64 miles in twelve hours including the time requisite for taking refreshment. He started from Ury at midnight, and went to Ellon in Aberdeenshire, where he breakfasted and returned by 12 mid-day. This walk was performed as a trial preparatory to a match he had undertaken to accomplish in December following. He had engaged to go 90 miles in 21 hours and a half for a bet of 500 guineas, but having unfortunately caught cold, was unable to attempt the feat.

MONEY EARNED BY POPULAR JOCKEYS.

In ordinary cases a jockey receives £5 for a winning mount, and two pounds less for a losing one, but, in these days of hot competition and turf money-making, an owner will think nothing of giving a boy a cheque for £500 if he wins an important handicap. "It is well," some will say, "to be a clever jockey. Where is the professor in any of our universities that will receive such a sum for even a whole course of his best lectures? What minister that ever mounted a pulpit will be paid £500 for the best sermon he ever preached?" It is, of course, the boy's honesty that is bought, not his skill; a bookmaker could square a bad boy by giving him double the sum. One or two jockeys earn as much (including the presents they receive) as £6,000 in the season. Two or three of the best of them hold retainers from crack sportsmen entitling them to so many hundreds a-year, and earn besides large allowances for their winning and losing mounts. A popular jockey is sometimes "retained" by several noblemen and gentlemen, one having the first call on his services, another the second, and so on in rotation. He is, of course, paid by them all, and has thus the chance of riding all the best horses of the period. A jockey, too, gets more presents, and those of far more value, than a popular clergyman. We have heard of the latter getting an occasional pipe of port wine, but it is not at all an uncommon occurrence for a jockey to get ten or twelve cheques, each for a hundred pounds, in the course of a year from men who follow his mounts.

At one period jockeys were sadly spoiled. Some years ago, when a few men went crazed about racing matters, and lost their patrimony on the turf, thereby beggaring their families, it was the fashion to pet the jockey lads of the day; they were made much of, and were often seen in the dining-rooms and drawing-rooms of their patrons, and were occasionally taken to the opera by duchesses! No wonder, then, that some of them lost their heads, and, to use an expressive phrase, "went to the bad." But there are jockeys *and* jockeys. There are certain riders who would not "pull" a horse for any sum of money that might be offered to them, whilst there are not a few who would do any piece of dirty work for a sovereign.

Some trainers who "work the oracle" either for themselves or their patrons would not directly corrupt their boys by giving them orders to pull a horse; they take other means to ensure their ends being arrived at; but it is known that an unscrupulous bookmaker has bribed a jockey before now. All jockeys are bound to ride to order; they are very seldom invested with any discretionary power. A trainer or employer will so instruct his jockey as to ensure what he wants coming to pass, and yet use such language as will keep him clear of consequences should any inquiry follow the running of a beaten horse.

CHEAP RACE-HORSES AND STEEDS OF VALUE.

"YEARLINGS," said the late Mr. Merry when he purchased All Heart and No Peel, afterwards known as Doncaster, "are a fearful lottery." He was right in saying so, although at the time he was drawing a prize and didn't know it—he was, in fact, for a sum of 950 guineas, purchasing the Derby-winner of 1873.

Horses, which, comparatively speaking, have been bought for an old song, have proved of great value, winning no end of rich stakes, and ending their career probably at the stud, where their value has been immense. Thormanby, a Derby-winner of 1860, which belonged to Mr. Merry, cost only £350. Voltigeur and Caractacus were purchased for less than 300 guineas each; Kettledrum was obtained for 350 guineas; so was Chattanooga, which won the Criterion Stakes. Early Bird's price was only 70 guineas. The following anecdote related in Parliament by Mr. Gerrard Sturt is *apropos* :—"In 1835, there was a little mare which belonged to a country apothecary at Newcastle, and her vocation was to go up one street and down another, leaving pills and what-not; well, this little mare of nominal value produced in as many consecutive years three of the best animals of their respective periods, namely, Rubens, Selim, and Castrel." The Deformed was purchased as a filly for £15, with her engagements in four large stakes, all of which she won! She was afterwards sold to a Captain Salt for 1,500 guineas, and was re-purchased for a brood mare at 300 guineas, sold again for 600 guineas to the Marquis of Waterford, at whose sale she was purchased for her Majesty's breeding stud.

The blood stock from which yearlings descend is of commensurate value. As an example of the fact, it may be stated that Formosa, a brood mare, changed hands for 4,000 guineas, Scottish Chief was bought for 8,000 guineas at Dewhurst sale, and a few years ago Blair Athol, described by Mr. Tattersall when he was brought into the sale ring, as "the best horse in the world," was purchased by the Cobham Stud Company for £12,000. Breadalbane, another fine horse, realized £6,000, but Doncaster, winner of the Derby of 1873, and second in the St. Leger stakes of the same year, changed hands for £14,500; whilst the owner of Springfield refused an offer of £10,000 for that horse, to be paid at the end of his racing career! Marie Stuart, the heroine of the Oaks and St. Leger, was last sold for £8,000.

THE COCK O' THE GOLF GREEN.

ALEXANDER M'KELLAR, ironically called *The Cock o' the Green*, and rendered famous by Kay including him among his *Edinburgh Portraits*, spent his life pretty much on Bruntsfield Links, playing by himself when unable to procure an opponent, and was even not unfrequently found practising at the "short holes" by lamp light. His golf-hating wife, annoyed by his all-absorbing passion, on one occasion carried his supper and his night-cap to the Links. But M'Kellar, blind to satire, good humouredly observed to his better half that she "cou'd wait if she likit till the game was dune, but at present he had no time for refreshment."

JOHNNY BROOME THE "PUG OF FAME."

OF the many stories that are still in circulation about the doings of that well-known pugilist Johnny Broome, the following is not generally known. Enjoying one day a ride out on a cavalry charger, he jumped over a navvy who was eating a bit of dinner under a hedge. "Where are you coming to?" growled the man; "do you want to kill a fellow?" "No; only to frighten you a bit," answered Broome, coolly, flying over his head and the hedge back again. Having stopped to talk with a farmer a minute or two, up came the navvy—a tall, well-built fellow, at least six feet in his boots. "Get off that horse," he said. "What for?" asked Johnny. "You get off that horse," repeated the navvy, beginning to strip; "and I'll give 'ee the biggest hiding you ever had in your life." "Then I won't get down," said Johnny, "as I shouldn't like that." "You'll have it whether you like it or not, 'cause I'm going to pull you off." "Then, I suppose, I shall have to do as you tell me," said Broome, jumping down, simply buttoning up his cutaway coat across the breast.

A looker-on, who knew nothing about the men, would have considered it a terribly unequal match—five feet seven to six feet, ten stone to thirteen. They squared for a moment, the navvy made a rush, but Johnny quickly landed him a smack on the nose that floored him like a shot. The fellow, much amazed, jumped up and snorted through his crimson conk. "I know what you are; you wait a bit," and, running down to a stream, he began to bathe the damaged organ.

"Time!" shouted Johnny. "I'm coming," was the answer; "you won't serve me like that again, Mr. Swell; I'm up to you now." Coming to the scratch, the son of toil instantly closed with his adversary, and seized him by the shoulders. Johnny wriggled and worked until, getting him fairly on the hip, he threw him over, his big boots describing a circle in the air, while Broome adroitly planted his knee on his stomach as he fell with a tremendous "Ugh—h—h—h!"

"Get up!" said Johnny. And very slowly the discomfited man rose to his feet. "Will you have any more?" inquired the conqueror. The navvy made no response. Then gathering himself up with an air of theatrical dignity, Broome thus addressed him: "Man, it is necessary I should teach a lesson to you and your class. You thought, because I am a gentleman, I could not defend myself. You have discovered your mistake. Know in future how unsafe it is to take such liberties, and when you meet a gentleman, touch your hat."

MRS. THORNTON BEATS BUCKLE, THE GREAT JOCKEY.

A LADY made her appearance on the turf in 1805, in a match in which she was opposed by Buckle the most famous jockey of the period; the race was run over a distance of two miles, and victory fell to the lady. As may be supposed the event excited quite a sensation, Mrs. Thornton being beautifully dressed for the occasion, in a purple cap and waistcoat; and her skirts were nankeen coloured, and being short, enabled those assembled to see her embroidered stockings and purple shoes, which looked very nice. The lady has herself commemorated the event in the following verses:—

> To the post we advanc'd, at the signal to start,
>   Brisk I flourish'd my whip over Louisa's ears;
> When springing a-main, by a resolute dart,
>   I gain'd a whole length of the jockey of peers;
> That advantage to keep as I rode fleet along
>   Behind me full many a glance did I throw—
> I soon found I'd the foot, but Allegro was strong,
>   And the jockey of peers carried weight, as you know.

I tried then to cut the third post pretty close,
  At the same time the length I had gained to preserve,
Gave whip to my mare but she kicked at the dose,
  And—a vile little devil—attempted to swerve ;
I chang'd, and a left handed cut brought her to,
  But Buckle 'tween me and the post made a push,
And lay neck and neck with me all I could do,
  Not seeming to value my efforts a rush.

I led him, however, at length to a slough,
  Where he sunk to the fetlock at every stroke,
The Buck had the bone—he press'd hard at me now,
  And seemed to enjoy much the best of the joke ;
But I cross'd at the next post, and stretching my hand—
  As I hoped to be saved without malice or heat—
I put all his trials of skill to the stand,
  For the jockey Buck I nearly threw from his seat.

He recovered his saddle, by seizing the mane,
  My mare darted forward as swift as the wind,
Nor heard I of the horse or Buckle again,
  Till I turn'd and beheld them come panting behind ;
My pleasure alone that sensation defines,
  Which the Laplander courts from the breeze of the south,
When I saw my Buck distance'd, and dashed up the lines
  With my mare hard in hand, and my whip in my mouth.

Mrs. Thornton, it may be mentioned, had on a previous occasion been matched to ride against a Mr. Flint, by whom she was beaten, greatly to her chagrin.

THE TRICYCLE AS A CURE.

Dr. Oscar Jennings has been giving his views upon the tricycle as a means of health. He says :—" When I began cycling I had been taking short exercise for three months. I had endeavoured to make a beginning in fencing, and had gone so far as to purchase the necessary implements, and pay for a month's lessons in advance. I had also tried walking. Horse-riding had not done what I wanted ; to commence fencing at my age was a *corvée*, and according to the initiated, was likely to continue one for many months. Walking alone was far from cheerful, and I soon said that nothing short of the direct necessity would induce me to continue this mode of taking a constitutional. As a forlorn hope—one never-to-be-forgotten day I mounted a tricycle. At the end of the first ride I foresaw its possibilities. What it has done for me may be judged from two facts—first, I have lost 14 kilos. of superfluous fat; secondly, I am always ready to rise at 6 a.m., and this, to borrow a cycling expression, used by no means to be 'my record.' Rational cycling, more than any other athletic exercise, tends to promote the *mens sana in corpore sano.* There is every reason to believe that in a near future the medical profession will take up cycling as they have rubbing. Naturally, it will receive a high-sounding name, and doctors will then recognise it as a method of 'cure.'"

STATE LOTTERIES.

"YESTERDAY afternoon, at about half-past six o'clock, that old servant of the state, the lottery, breathed its last, having for a long period of years, ever since the days of Queen Anne, contributed largely towards the public revenue of the country. This event took place at Cooper's Hall, Basinghall Street; and such was the anxiety on the part of the public to witness the last drawing of the lottery, that great numbers of persons were attracted to the spot, independently of those who had an interest in the proceedings. The gallery of Cooper's Hall was crowded to excess, long before the period fixed for the drawing (five o'clock), and the utmost anxiety was felt by those who had shares in the lottery for the arrival of the appointed hour. The annihilation of lotteries, it will be recollected, was determined on in the session of parliament before last; and thus a source of revenue bringing into the treasury the sums of £250,000 and £300,000 per annum will be dried up. This determination on the part of the legislature is hailed by far the greatest portion of the public with joy, as it will put an end to a system which many believe to have fostered and encouraged the late speculations, the effects of which have been and are still severely felt. A deficiency in the public revenue to the extent of £250,000 annually, will, however, be the consequence of the annihilation of lotteries, and it must remain for those who have strenuously supported the putting a stop to lotteries to provide for the deficiency." See Hone's Every-day Book, vol. 2, p. 1502.

This is certainly one way of looking at the matter; but Charles Lamb puts the abolition of lotteries in another and very ingenious point of view, which, as like all that he has ever written is most clever and amusing, I lay before my readers. Writing in "The New Monthly Magazine" under his well-known *nom de plume* of Elia, he says :—" The true mental epicure always purchased his ticket early, and postponed inquiry into its fate to the last possible moment, during the whole of which intervening period he had an imaginary twenty thousand locked up in his desk. And was not this well worth all the money? Who would scruple to give twenty pounds interest for even the ideal enjoyment of as many thousands during two or three months ? ' *Crede quod habes et habes*,' and the usufruct of such a capital is surely not dear at such a price. Some years ago a gentleman, in passing along Cheapside, saw the figures 1,069, of which number he was the sole proprietor, flaming on the window of a lottery office as a capital prize. Somewhat flurried by this discovery, not less welcome than unexpected, he resolved to walk round St. Paul's that he might consider in what way to communicate the happy tidings to his wife and family; but upon repassing the shop he observed that the number was altered to 10,069 ; and, upon inquiry, had the mortification to learn that his ticket was blank, and had only been stuck up in the window by a mistake of the clerk. This effectually calmed his agitation ; but he always speaks of himself as having once possessed twenty thousand pounds, and maintains that his ten minutes' walk round St. Paul's was worth ten times the purchase-money of the ticket. A prize thus obtained has, moreover, this special advantage ; it is beyond the reach of fate, it cannot be squandered, bankruptcy cannot lay siege to it, friends cannot pull it down, nor enemies blow it up ; it bears a charmed life, and none of woman-born can break its integrity even by the dissipation of a single fraction. Show me the property in these perilous times that is equally compact and impregnable. We can no longer become enriched for a quarter of an hour ; we can no longer succeed in such splendid failures ; all our chances of making such a miss have vanished with the last of the lotteries.

" Life will now become a flat, prosaic routine matter-of fact ; and sleep itself, erst so prolific of numerical configuration and mysterious stimulants to lottery adventure, will be disfurnished of its figures and figments. People will cease to harp upon the one lucky number suggested in a dream, and which forms the exception, while they are scrupulously silent upon the ten thousand falsified dreams which constitute the rule. Morpheus will stifle Cocker with a handful of poppies, and our pillows will be no longer haunted by the book of numbers.

"And who, too, shall maintain the art and mystery of puffing in all its pristine glory when the lottery professors shall have abandoned its cultivation? They were the first, as they will assuredly be the last, who fully developed the resources of that ingenious art; who cajoled and decoyed the most suspicious and wary reader into a perusal of their advertisements, by devices of endless variety and cunning; who baited their lurking schemes with midnight murders, ghost stories, crimcons, bon-mots, balloons, dreadful catastrophes, and every diversity of joy and sorrow to catch newspaper gudgeons. Ought not such talents to be encouraged? Verily the Abolitionists have much to answer for!"

DAVIS THE LEVIATHAN BOOK-MAKER.

This personage of the racing world, who died a few years ago, leaving a very considerable fortune, was one of the heaviest betting men of his day, and at one time made a book to lose £100,000 on the Derby, and began his career in life as a journeyman carpenter in the establishment of Messrs. Cubitt the great London builders. He commenced betting in half-crowns, and having a sort of genius for figures, speedily found out the right side to take on the turf—namely, that it was always better to lay the odds against all the horses in a given race, than to back one of them to win. He soon discovered that, to offer backers a slight advantage over the prices laid by his competitors in booking, was an aid to business. By-and-bye, when he came to get information of a valuable kind from men in "the know," that is, from persons who knew which horses were intended to run in different races, as also those that had won a good trial, he would back such animals to win him a good stake and often proved successful. He betted to large sums, and was known to pay away large sums of money over horses which had been heavily backed with him, but his accounts were always ready. The morning after Teddington had won the Derby, he sent a cheque for £15,000 to one of his customers who had backed the horse to win that amount. Curiously enough, "the Derby" was of no use to Davis as a money making centre, he indeed lost large sums from time to time on that race, but he made up for these amounts by what he won on large handicaps. It was Davis who invented the "betting lists," which, a few years since, were seen in all large cities. These lists were hung up in various public houses, a figure of the odds being placed against each horse's name, the figures being altered from time to time, as the odds against the horse increased or lessened. Davis called at the houses where his lists were shown, in the course of the evening, and lifted the money drawn, and was ready to pay all who had won as soon as the name of the winning horse was known. Lists have been abolished for some years and ready money betting rendered illegal by act of Parliament.

TREATMENT OF HIGH METTLED RACERS IN INFANCY.

THE following details of the infantile life of a race horse are from the pen of an expert in such matters, and are of more than usual interest, and at all events will be new to all but those who are familiar with the routine of a training stable.

When the foal is born what becomes of him? By what process is he converted into a high mettled racer? The finest trainer of two-year-olds the Turf ever knew (the late Joseph Dawson) was of opinion that when a foal was born, nothing was too good for him. No matter what natural nourishment his mother gave him he always fed his foals on the richest Alderney milk. Stimulating foods of all kinds of light digestion were given him, so that by Christmas he was well grown and able to withstand the variations of our climate, and was full of natural courage, with strength to display it, as he gambolled round his dam in the paddock that was allotted him. In a few months after his birthday he would stretch himself out, and by exercise increase his strength and appetite. Then the finest Scotch oats were crushed and given him, with old hay, mixed with carrots or vetches. This stimulating food expanded his powers, aided his growth, and his natural instinct soon developed his galloping powers.

Yearlings, as a rule, are fed thrice a day, an occasional dose of linseed oil being given. In cold weather they get beans and peas in addition to their other food—oats, carrots, and hay. They have homes to lie in and shelter from the wet. These are always open to the paddock, so that the yearlings may go out and enter at will. If fed regularly, they will always "eat up" before going out again, whilst they will pick what scour they can find out of their pasture. Dutch clover is indispensable in breeding paddocks, and is easily propagated. Some yearlings require four feeds a day. That fact will always make itself manifest to their attendant. Just as children vary in their appetites, so do yearlings. It is best to tie them up during feeding time, and to handle and accustom them to treatment they will have to undergo when in a training stable. In May, cavessons and lunging reins are put on. The yearling is then led along the high roads to accustom him to noise and traps of various descriptions. This is done to prevent shyness; it gives the yearling confidence, and enables him to be taken through villages and towns with safety. Those who breed for sale never give a yearling too much work. They make them plump and fat with artificial foods, which require months to sweat off.

HOW TO EDUCATE "YEARLINGS."

It is always considered to be good odds on a private breeder's yearlings racing sooner than a public breeder's. To this fact Lord Falmouth's and the Duke of Westminster's successes are to be attributed. Their yearlings were fed with the idea of racing, not for sale. It is from this cause—over feeding—that so many high priced yearlings turn out useless as racehorses. The first thing a trainer does when he gets a yearling is to understand him. He may be a sulky or a generous animal, a good feeder or a bad one. He treats him accordingly. The trainer's life at this time is full of anxiety.

The first thing in the education of the yearling is to bit him. This requires great care, because the bit must be made to press equally in all its parts, or the yearling's mouth will be spoiled, and he will become nervous and difficult to ride. When his mouth has got used to the bit, the best plan (after he is backed) is to exercise him in it in the shape of a figure of 8 along with other yearlings. The bit will then use his mouth to an equal pressure, and make it as nearly equal in all its feeling as it is possible to get it. After being exercised for several days in this manner, the pupil will turn to the merest touch.

Lesson second is to put on the roller and crupper, with side reins attached to the bit, and crossed over his withers; and thus attired the yearling is lunged, i.e., trotted to the right and left alternately, so as not to put too much pressure on either leg. A month's practice will suffice for the bitting and lunging. Then the saddle is added, and the yearling is driven with a pair of long reins, and twisted and turned and pulled back in all fashions, so as to use him to any emergency he may afterwards meet, and be asked to overcome by his rider.

Mounting is the next step; and this must be done gradually. The rider first leans gently on the saddle, then more heavily, and when the pupil has got used to this, and does not resent it, the rider sits down in the saddle fairly and squarely. The yearling is then considered "backed." Great care is required in this process, for the heels of a yearling are as quick as lightning, and no man ought to approach him in his box even unless he has been educated to the manners and ways of yearlings, for until you gain their confidence in and out of the box you can do nothing with them. After a yearling has been once "backed" he can be led and jogged along in all sorts of paces until he rides nicely, and can be trusted to go with the head and the heel either in a trot or a canter. When he arrives at this stage the real work of preparing him for the race course begins.

ACCIDENTS WHICH LEAD TO FORTUNE.

THESE are many, and could they all be set down with truthfulness in honest print, would form an interesting and curious record: take the following as an example. It refers to an episode in the life of a man who at one time was of some account in the racing world—Harry Hill, who, as the saying goes, had "risen from nothing," to be a man of mark on the turf, a man, in short, who made a ten thousand pound book regularly on every big event during the year. Having heard of the success some had met with who went—figuratively—a bit beyond their own doorsteps to lay out their money, he went one year to Doncaster to see the Cup run for, and without much trouble got rid of the money he had in his pocket, except about five shillings, which, though not enough to pay his fare

F

by coach back to Manchester, was still enough to take him there by the more humble conveyance of Shank's pony, missing his road just after he had crossed the Dearn River, and he, stopping at a small cottage to enquire his way, noticed a window in which a pane had been stopped with the manuscript of an old ballad to keep out the draughts, while the pane next to it had been strengthened by pasting on it a £20 Bank of England note. The persons who lived in the cottage did not know the value of the piece of paper they had used for so common a purpose, not being able either to read or write, and so Hill had little difficulty in buying "the picture," found months before on the high road, for the small sum of one shilling! Again in funds, like Whittington, he "turned" his footsteps, invested part of his windfall on next day's racing events, was fortunate in his venture, and on those of the other days as well, clearing altogether over eighty pounds. To his credit, be it said, he repaid the old folks the twenty pounds, to, as may be easily imagined, their great joy when they found themselves the possessors of a sum so much beyond even their wildest dreams of opulence.

LORD GEORGE BENTINCK'S PLAN FOR STARTING HORSES IN A RACE.

LORD GEORGE BENTINCK, among his other turf reforms, reformed and simplified "the start." It was his lordship who engineered the mode now practised, and the following brief particulars of which may prove interesting to persons unacquainted with turf practices:—"Lord George's way of starting horses in a race was as simple as effectual, and was carried out in the following manner. In the first place, it needed a starter whom the jocks, instead of daring to disobey, had, as in their feelings towards Lord George, an enthusiastic desire to please: hence he undertook to illustrate his own mode of securing the horses and the public from the ever-occurring disappointment of a false start, and, flag in hand, marched in the van of the quivering phalanx quite unattended to the starting place on the noble course of Doncaster, in full view of the tens of thousands regarding him with admiration from the Grand Stand and the rising part of the ground. Hitherto, the functionary who had performed the office of starter, after doing his best, or rather his worst, to put the horses in line, simply ordered the jockeys to 'go!' as frequently having to recall them by a distant signal after they had galloped a great part of the distance, by reason of some obstinate brute—man or horse—refusing to obey the order and remaining fresh for the next essay.

"Lord George rectified this very inefficient plan by an equestrian trigger of his own invention, viz., the posting a man with a flag directly in view of all the jocks—on whom they were to fix their undivided attention and to 'go!' without fail, on pain of a pecuniary fine, on seeing the colour dropped in front. The main duty rested with the noble chief in getting the horses in line, a manœuvre he accomplished by great patience and occasionally walking them backwards and forwards, till assured on his own part that they were so, when he, standing on their flank—unseen by horse or rider—suddenly lowered his flag, in signal to the man ahead to do the same; when, if the jockeys were disposed to act at all fairly, or a horse was not especially restive, a false start was next to impossible. On this occasion the immense field bounded off at the first signal, notwithstanding it was Lord George's maiden essay, like a charge of veteran Mamelukes. The countless throng cheered the gallant starter with deafening shouts of delight and admiration; and cheered again, as, taking off his hat and bowing in acknowledgment, he mounted his hack and cantered down the course."

JOCKEY WORSHIP.

THE large sums earned by jockeys during the last thirty years have of late attracted much attention. The vagaries of Fortune are never so obvious as when that much courted lady bestows on some "unlettered lad," the income of a first-rate lawyer or great merchant. "Why did my parents not place me in a training stable, instead of sending me to Oxford?" said, three years ago, a country rector, passing rich on four hundred pounds a year; "had they done so, I might now have been earning annual thousands." Just so. Still there are those who defend the extravagant sums paid to the riders of our race-horses; but all men who love the sport of horse-racing for itself, have set their faces against the sort of idol-worship which of late years has been set up in our training stables. It is curious, that of three boys, all natives of the same parish, all about the same age, and all of them launched on the world at the same time, one a few years ago was a popular jockey, earning, about the time of his death, some two thousand a year; another had become a hardworking City clergyman, holding a living valued at three hundred and twenty-seven pounds per annum; the third of the little band working ceaselessly at the bar, and at "literature" as well, could only fill in his income in the tax-paper as being (and it was precarious) four hundred pounds. The jockey-boy's father had been groom and gardener to the father of the barrister, and he had married a young woman who had served in the house of the clergyman's parents.

PHEASANT POACHING.

PHEASANT poaching, although profitable, is difficult to carry on with success, and the art of "removing" these beautiful birds—which are annually bred on the chief estates of the kingdom in tens of thousands at considerable cost to the landlords—in a quiet way requires to be very carefully studied.

Among southern woods and coverts the pheasant poacher is usually a desperate character; but not so in the North. North country poachers are more skilled in woodcraft, and are rarely surprised. If the worst comes to the worst, it is a fair stand-up fight with fisticuffs, and is usually bloodless, but liberty by flight is the first thing resorted to.

It is a good thing for the poacher, and his methods of work, that the pheasant is rather a stupid bird. There is no gainsaying his beauty, however, and a brace of birds, with some excitement thrown in, are worth winning even at considerable risk. While engaged in poaching I have noticed that the pheasant has one great characteristic. It is fond of wandering, and this cannot be prevented. Watch the birds; even when fed daily, and with the daintiest food, they wander off, singly or in pairs, far from the home preserves. This fact we knew well, and were not slow to use our knowledge. When October came round, they were the very first birds to which we directed our attention. Every poacher knows year by year that it by no means follows that the man who rears the pheasants will have the privilege of shooting them.

There is a time in the life of the pheasant when it disdains the scattered corn of the keeper, and begins to anticipate the fall of beach and oak mast. The pheasants make daily journeys in search of this, and consume it in great quantities. They feed principally in the morning, dust themselves in the roads or turnip-fields at noon, taking a ramble through the woods in the afternoon, and one thing is certain, that when wandered birds find themselves in outlying copses in the evening, they will probably roost there. These are the birds to which the poachers pay their best attention. When wholesale pheasant poaching is prosecuted by gangs, it is of course in winter, when the trees are bare. Guns, with the barrels filed down to shorten them, are taken in sacks, and the pheasants are shot where they roost. Their forms stand sharply outlined against the sky, and they are invariably on the lower branches. If the firing does not immediately bring up the keepers, the game is quickly deposited in bags, and the gang makes off. And it is generally arranged that a light cart is waiting at some remote lane end, so that possible pursuers may be quickly outpaced. The great risk incurred by this method will be seen when it is stated that pheasants are generally reared close by the keeper's cottage, and their coverts surround it. It is mostly armed mouchers who enter these, and not the country poacher. There are, of course, reasons for this. Opposition must always be anticipated, for, speaking for the nonce from the gamekeeper's standpoint, the covert never should be, and rarely is, unwatched.

Then there are the certain results of possible capture to be taken into account. This effected, and with birds in one's possession, the poacher is liable to be indicted upon many concurrent charges, each and all bearing heavy penalties. Than this we obtained our game in a different and quieter way. Our custom was to carefully eschew the preserves, and look up all outlying birds. We never went abroad without a pocketful of corn, and day by day enticed the wandered birds further and further away. This accomplished, the birds may be snared with hair nooses, or taken in spring traps. One of our commonest and most successful methods with wandered birds was to light brimstone beneath the trees in which they roosted. The powerful fumes soon overpowered the birds, and they came flopping down the trees one by one. This method has the advantage of silence, and if the night be dead and still, it is rarely detected. Away from the preserves, time was never taken into account with our plans, and we could work systematically. We were content with a brace of birds at a time; we usually got most in the end, and with least chance of capture. The cost of rearing pheasants in the home coverts runs to about two shillings each.

HAWKING, CAN IT BE REVIVED?

A MOST interesting account of this enjoyable sport might easily be compiled. The origin of "falconry" is lost in the annals of hoar antiquity; its history, however, can be traced back to the middle of the fourth century, but even before then hawking had been practised abroad. At one period the sport was greatly followed in England, and no young man of rank was thought accomplished who had not devoted a portion of his time to the training and flying of these birds. Edward the Third was exceedingly fond of hawking, and took with him in his invasion of France thirty falconers mounted on horseback, so that the passion he entertained for this sport might not be interrupted.

In England only persons of the highest rank were permitted to keep hawks, and stringent laws were laid down for the government of the sport, but in time the pursuit of birds in this way was opened up, so that the sport could be indulged in with more freedom. Hawks were valuable birds at one time in England: at the beginning of the seventeenth century a hundred marks is set down as having been paid for a gos-hawk and a tassel-hawk, and in those days a hundred marks was a considerable sum of money. The training of the birds to do their work well was a matter involving constant work and watchfulness, and in consequence really well-bred hawks were deemed worthy of being presented to kings. Different kinds of birds had different values; the tercel was meet for a poor man, the sparrow-hawk for a priest, the gos-hawk for a yeoman, the marlyon for a lady, the sacre and the secret for a knight, the peregrine for an earl, the falcon of the rock for a duke, the falcon gentle and the tercel gentle for a prince, the ger-falcon and the tercel of ger-falcon for a king.

In old sporting literature numerous references are made to the art of hawking, and we have been told that in the olden times no person of rank moved about without his dogs and hawks. These birds are considered to be emblematic of the high position of their owners, "no action was more dishonourable than for a man of rank to give up his birds." We sincerely hope to see hawking again take root and flourish in merry England.

HOW TO "WORK" A HORSE TO ADVANTAGE.

ONCE upon a time, a certain racehorse of rising fame was purchased by a small syndicate of bookmakers in order that he might be prepared to win the Derby. The nominal owner was a gentleman of position in society, but that the animal was a bookmaker's horse to all intents and purposes came to be received as a fact in turf circles. As to the horse itself, it was of good breeding, and that it was a superior animal had been demonstrated by its winning an important two-year-old race. A large sum of money was given for it, £8,000 being named as the price. It was generally understood among the initiated that The Pelican (so we will call the horse) was being "worked" with a view to winning the blue riband of the turf, and as a consequence it was quoted at a long price for another important race in which it was engaged, and which fell to be run previous to the Derby. For *that* race an ostentatiously public trial of the horse was made, when it finished a long way behind another animal trained in the same stable.

But in spite of all that was said to have been done to prevent success, the horse won the race it was not intended to win, much doubtless to the chagrin of those interested, who had been quietly backing it very largely at the best odds obtainable for the Derby; and if it had not won the other race, long odds would have been got about it for the Derby. That classic race it did *not* win, but it won another stake, of nearly equal importance, at a later period of the year. In the meantime, at one of the most fashionable meetings of the season, it displayed what may be called in *italics* some awfully "out and in" running. First of all, it won a stake of the value of nearly three thousand pounds, starting with odds of two to one *against* it; then it lost a stake worth about seven hundred pounds when it started with odds of six to one *on* it; then it lost another stake at the same meeting, being easily beaten on both occasions by far worse horses than it had previously vanquished! In the newspapers of the day the racing of The Pelican was much commented upon, as was also the appearance of the animal. When it ran on the second occasion it was asserted that it was in great pain, and that it had suddenly been taken ill. As a matter of course, ill-natured people insinuated foul play, but no proof was given, while curiously enough some very heavy bets were gained by one or two bookmakers on the second and third occasions of its running, a large coal and iron-master, it is said, having backed The Pelican to win to the extent of ten thousand pounds, which went into the hands of the bookmakers. That gentleman, we believe, never makes a bet now, till he sees the horse which he intends to back at the starting-post! We give these details for what they are worth. That they occurred "once upon a time" is certain.

SINGULAR WAGERS.

ONE of the most singular of the many curious bets which have been from time to time recorded, was decided at York early in the present century. The money risked in the wager was only five shillings, and the bet was to be won by the person who appeared in that which should be adjudged the most extraordinary costume. One of the gentlemen came to the place agreed upon, the Castle Yard at York, his dress being trimmed all over with bank notes, ten guinea notes and five guinea notes being liberally used, his hat also was trimmed with notes, whilst a purse of gold was placed on its brim by way of ornament. A label pinned to the back of his coat announced his name to be "John Bull."

The other gentleman was got up in peculiar fashion, on one side he appeared to be a negro, on the other a woman; as a negro he was booted and spurred, on the woman's side he displayed a fine petticoat, a silk stocking and slipper, his cheek coloured and patched as was then the fashion. The judges gave their verdict in favour of "John Bull," who was declared the winner. "It is the money that has done the trick," said one of the onlookers, and so the five shillings were handed to the man covered with bank notes.

For the relation of another curious wager, Horace Walpole is responsible. "It happened on a very hot day, that a member of White's Club was seized on entering the hall with sudden illness, and fell to the floor apparently dead. Several who were present, at once began to wager on the occurrence, and heavy bets were made as to whether death had taken place or the man had only fainted. A doctor being sent for, came and prepared to bleed the man, but was at once stopped in his humane intention, by those who betted he was dead: they said it was not fair to them, as they had staked their money on death!"

TOLD BY THE PROPRIETOR OF A MUSIC HALL.

I.

"Well, gents, it's no use mincing the matter, as you know I'm a big man now, and this fine place is all my own—it's free hold and I built and furnished it, and it's one of the best music halls out of London. This is how it happened, I'll tell you the truth. I was at York Races, down on my luck, broke, in fact, stone broke, and was looking about to see how I could best get a chance to earn a dinner, when who should I see but old Bill Dawkins, who used to pal with me years before, when we went backing horses at the meetings round about the big village.

"'Look here, old man,' says Bill, 'I'm making a little book, taking dollars and half dollars only, but see here, Bob, my clerk is off on the beer, confound him, and I am stuck if I don't get a penciller; what do you say, I'll make your day's work worth a sov. at least to you?'

"'I don't mind,' says I, 'if it's fair and square, but I'm not for any welshing game.'

"'All serene, my boy, my work's all above board; I can pay if I lose; I'm only making a small book, not going more than a tenner on any one race, and I'll not get easy broke.'

"Well, we went to work, and for the first three races we had almost nothing to pay, a non-favourite having won each time that had not been much backed. In the fourth race we took a deal of money, and as there was a long delay at the start, Bill went off, as he said, to Collins' tent to get a bite, saying I could go next time. By-and-bye the race was over, and a horse won against which we had laid a lot of money; but Dawkins never came back. I told the people who were waiting to be paid where he had gone, and some of them went to get him—but as very speedily appeared, he had bolted, and left me to face the angry crowd.

"What happened then, you ask? well, I will tell you, there was a shout of 'drown the Welsher.' It was in vain that I attempted to explain, I was seized upon and knocked about at an awful rate; I was knocked down and kicked till I was utterly helpless, my clothes were torn off my back, and I was left bruised, bleeding and naked at the back of one of the tents. I shall never forget how I was treated; it was something awful what I suffered."

II.

"No, I couldn't move for pain, and dared not get up if I

had been able, do you see, for want of clothes to cover my nakedness. What I should have done I don't know, the police would not help me; but at last, after I had told my story to a few persons who came from the drinking-booth, a woman came to me; she said, 'Here, put on them trousers, and take this old cow skin waistcoat, they belonged to my husband, dear man, who was killed three weeks ago.' It seems she had brought them to the course to try and sell them.

"It would take too long to tell you all how I got about again. Some of the fellows who were drinking in the booth, believing my story, subscribed twenty-seven shillings to set me going. Well, to cut it short, I went out one day, after about a week, to try and get the cowskin vest changed for a cloth one, but was unsuccessful, and taking it off at night I began looking it over, and at the neck found what I thought would be some pieces of paper put in for lining. It did not occur to me that it was anything else, but as part of the sewing had given way, it was easy enough to pull out the paper lining as I fancied it was. Well, judge of what my feelings were when I did so, and saw that my hand was full of bank notes!

"I must have fainted, I think, at any rate, when consciousness came back, it seemed to me that I had been dreaming, but all the same the notes were there on the floor. I had got lodgings partly out of charity from the man who managed the booth at the back of which I had been so terribly ill-used. At first I thought I should tell my landlord, then it seemed but proper I should go to Mrs. Wainright who gave me the vest, and give her the money.

"'Steady, old man, keep steady,' I said to myself, 'think it over first,' so I did nothing, but sat down trying to think it over.

"'How much was there?' you ask, well, believe me, I speak the truth, when I say there was five five-pound notes and three tenners, they were on a York bank.

"What did I do? I'll tell you. I waited till next day and then I took the vest to a dealer, and telling him it was a valuable theatrical property, I said I wanted to sell it, and to buy a new suit of clothes, right away."

III.

"And now, although it seems more like a romance than sober truth, here's what took place next, as sure as I'm a living man.

"The dealer said, 'Well, I can fit you out, and can get you a customer for your cowskin vest, leastways, I'll try,' and with that he sent a boy to tell Tom Darley to come and speak to him. Now then, this is what happened.

"'That's a thing I can be doing with,' said the man—he was a comic singer—'you shall have a ten pound note for it, if you like, so help me bob.' You may easily guess that I couldn't believe my ears, in fact, I thought the man was mad.

"'Listen,' says he, 'it's this way, there's a dollar for the cowskin, put it on Doncaster for the Derby, that's the horse that'll win, and it's blessed price, so help me bob, is 40 to 1, you'll get that now, from the Ham seller in this very city of York.'

"Well, you'll think me a big mug, but that man so convinced me, he was so earnest about the matter, that I backed the horse. I put five pounds on with the Ham seller, as he was called, who laid me two hundred pounds to the money, and when I got to London I backed it again and again, till I stood to win a thousand pounds and—thank God—it came off. I saw it win.

"Not likely, I paid to Mrs. Wainright all the money that was in the vest, and a ten pound note besides. She looks after my music hall, lights the fires and keeps it clean, and there is a man sitting beside us who can tell you that the story I have been telling is a true one; that man's name is Tom Darley; he is now my stage manager."

HOW JEM BURN THE PUGILIST TOOK AN INSULT FROM A CUSTOMER.

The following is an incident which really occurred in Jem Burn's own "pub." One of his most regular customers was a master tailor who carried on business in Bond-street. Now Jem had a desperate liking to see the hearths in his parlours and elsewhere kept clean, and if no one whose duty it was to do so was at hand he would rush in with a hand-brush and sweep back any dust or ashes which had come too far to the front.

The Bond-street tradesman happened on one occasion to be near the fire, and said, after one or two invasions of the kind, "If that buffer comes here any more with his brush I'll kick him." "My nevy," who had probably been within earshot of the argument, heard some one present say to the man ready to provoke a breach of the peace, "Ah! you try that on, and you will be soon sorry for it." "I'll bet you a bottle of wine I do if he comes in here again with his brush," was the rejoinder. "Done," was the reply; "will you make it half-a-dozen?" "Yes," said the man from Bond-street, and he won his wager easily, as in the course of a few minutes in came the host, brush in hand, and, as he stooped down to perform the duty of sweeping back, he was saluted with a gentle kick. Jem simply said, when the tailor's boot came in contact with his body, "Oh; am I in your way? I am so sorry," and quietly walked out. But then it must be remembered that the tailor was an old and valuable customer, while he who had to pay for the half-dozen of wine was a stranger, one who, according to Scripture and the manners and customs of those days, should be "took in."

Burn made a great deal of money in his business but somehow failed to keep it; if he had been more miserly, and remained more at home, he would have become a wealthy man. So far as lending went, Burn could not well help himself, for when a man had spent two or three pounds in his house and wanted a half-sovereign, he could not easily refuse it. Champagne then was fifteen shillings a bottle, and port and sherry proportionally dear to what they are now, so that if swells did borrow occasionally, it was not altogether a loss. Jem himself could chaff well, and, what was better by half, take a joke even when practised on himself as has just been shown.

STRUTT'S NOTICES OF COCK-FIGHTING.

In Hone's edition of Strutt's well-known book on English sports and pastimes, some desultory notices of cock-fighting may be consulted; but we were disappointed in our search for a consecutive history of the art and practice. "This barbarous practice," he says, "which claims the sanction of high antiquity, was practised at an early age by the Grecians, and probably still more anciently in Asia. It is common in China, and was practised by the Romans." It can be traced back in England to the period of the twelfth century; and probably originated as a childish sport among schoolboys. It was for centuries a custom of the scholars of all schools to present game-cocks to their masters, and it was the universal practice to "fight them" in the forenoon. In Scotland, too, the same custom was observed, and it is within the knowledge of many now living that game-cocks were given to the schoolmasters on Shrove Tuesday. We are in possession of a heavy denunciation of one branch of the sport of cock-fighting, which was known as the Welch main, and was arranged on the following scheme : Sixteen pairs of cocks, being arranged for battle, fight with each other till half of the number are placed *hors de combat*, then the sixteen which have proved victorious are fitted again ; then the remaining eight are made to fight out the battle ; and so on, till one only of the original number is left victorious. " It is a scandalous shame that such work is tolerated, thirty-one cocks in all being killed."

A CITY MERCHANT'S WIFE DREAMS THE WINNER OF THE DERBY.

THE following dream was vouched for at the time of its occurrence as having actually taken place. One winter's night, Mrs. Clifton, the wife of a merchant in the city of London, dreamed she saw the Derby won by a bay horse, ridden by a jockey wearing a green cap, and a brown jacket with crimson sleeves ; and having faith in the vision, she urged her husband to risk a few pounds on its truth ; but he, finding no such jockey-belongings in the official list of colours worn by the riders, naturally laughed at the idea. However, the lady, with feminine persistence, dreamed her dream the orthodox three times, and at last persuaded her sceptical spouse to promise to take her to Epsom, and back her colours for twenty pounds, if they put in an appearance. Shortly before the Derby Day, Mr. Gratwicke, the owner of the then Derby favourite, changed his colours to chocolate body, crimson sleeves and white cap ; and when *Doleful* appeared on the course with his rider thus attired, Mr. Clifton asked his wife if that was near enough for her. She, however, would have a green cap ; and presently, to her husband's astonishment, Mr. Gratwicke's despised second horse, *Merry Monarch*, cantered by, carrying a jockey with a cap of the desired hue. Encouraged by this unexpected sight, the wine-merchant hurried into the ring, invested his twenty sovereigns on his wife's champion, and in a few minutes found himself the richer by a couple of thousand pounds !

NATURAL HISTORY OF THE SALMON.

THERE is much that to the angler is curious and romantic in the natural history of the salmon. At every stage of its career it has been invested with something like magic. Till recently, but little was known of its habits or history. It was supposed to appear in our rivers first of all as a smolt. Where the smolt came from no one knew. Like Topsy, it was supposed to have "grow'd," but from what? was the question. The smolt was almost universally held to be the young or fry of the salmon in the first year of its age. Had it not been found that naturalists have all along been in error on this point, we must have come to the conclusion that nature had lavished her choicest powers on the development of this king of the waters.

For a long series of years no naturalist took the trouble to watch the spawning beds or to ascertain how long it was till the young fish burst from the egg. No person seemed to know how it looked on its first appearance in the river, or what size it was on being hatched, or whether the supposed time of its birth was right—the month of February or March. But suddenly, indeed with something like dramatic effect, it appears in our salmon rivers as a smolt, several ounces in weight, on its way to the sea. Making its way down to the great deep, and escaping all the dangers incidental to its infantile career, it returns to the place of its birth, in August or September, a beautiful grilse of many pounds' weight! And, if still so fortunate as to escape capture—for we very stupidly kill even our grilses before we permit them to propagate their species—it once again migrates to the sea, and then returns, converted by the magic wand of some briny harlequin into the majestic salmon, that is eagerly hailed by the anxious fisherman, and politely requested to render up its valuable life, much to the future delight of expectant epicures.

FIRST APPEARANCE OF THE "CHAMPION OF ENGLAND."

THE late Jem Ward, the well-known "Pugilist and Painter," wrote, or had written for him, an account of his own life, but it was not quite a veracious chronicle : at all events there are some colourable statements in it, and these have tempted us to compile the following "memorandum" as to his *début* as a "pug," which took place in the year 1822 :—"The principal novelty was the introduction of a new Black Diamond, and although a bit rough, yet now and again his shining qualities so far peeped out that curiosity asked 'Who is he?' 'Where does he come from?' 'Is he a novice?' The replies were: His name is Ward; he is an East-ender; he has put the quiet on all who have tried him; he is a sharp one in a turn-up, but what he may do in the ring is another matter. However, he can be backed against anything of his weight (twelve stone), barring 'the Gas' (Tom Hickman). Ward was matched with Spencer. Like most new-comers, he displayed too much eagerness, and more milling than generalship. He received good encouragement from the amateurs present, and his nob was pronounced to be a fighting one."

So promising a youth could not long want the opportunity of distinguishing himself upon a sterner stage than the Fives Court. He soon found friends, and in less than six months— on June 12, 1822—fought his first battle in the ropes, at Moulsey Hurst, with Dick Acton, a shoemaker, whom he beat in six rounds, and won high approval from the *cognoscenti* by his quick hitting. It was now the universal opinion that a new light had appeared in the pugilistic world, and when a match was arranged between Ward and Bill Abbot, the conqueror of Oliver, for £50 a-side, the event was looked forward to with the greatest eagerness. The battle took place on October 22, in the above year, and never, perhaps, within the annals of the Prize Ring were high-raised hopes so wofully disappointed. It was evident very early in the fight that the new man had the victory in his own hands; but it was equally evident that he did not intend to avail himself of his superiority, and when Abbot was so distressed that he could hardly have knocked a fly off a leaf Jem went down before his touch, and at last, to bring the farce to an end, pretended to swoon, so as not to answer to the call of time. "It is impossible to describe the consternation, as well as indignation, expressed by the amateurs. So barefaced a robbery was never before witnessed in the annals of pugilism."

The case was referred to the Pugilistic Club, before whom James Ward was summoned to answer for his conduct. Very pale and crestfallen, the young man for a time stammered out excuses; but at last, bursting into tears, confessed that it was a cross. "But I knew nothing about it till I was in the ring," he said; "then my backers told me I must *not* win. If I did

I should be ruined and they'd be ruined; but if I lost they'd give me a hundred pounds, but they haven't kept their word."

Although there was no doubt that Ward was more sinned against than sinning, the Club could not condone such conduct, and he was there and then expelled the Ring. As soon as sentence was pronounced, up jumped big-hearted Tom Cribb. "I've never done anything wrong myself," he said, "but I believe he's a poor, deluded, ignorant young chap, and that he's been led away; and I, for one, will give him a quid." This good-natured example was followed by many others present; and, with a heavy heart, Ward went forth, if not a penniless, a disgraced man.

CARD PLAYING: THE CASE OF LORD DE ROS.

It would not be difficult to fill a large volume with an interesting series of card-playing anecdotes. The following is one in which Mr. George Payne took part: it was given in one of the biographical sketches that appeared in the newspapers at the period of his death, prefaced by the statement that for upwards of fifty years of his life he had spent more hours at the card table than any two of his contemporaries.

The fashionable, private game of cards about forty years since was *Écarté*, and many were the merry bouts thereat which Mr. Payne fought out with several distinguished adversaries. It is a tradition of Limmer's Hotel that he and Lord Albert Denison, afterwards the first Lord Londesborough, sat up all night at that famous but now extinguished hostelry, and that when they separated, Lord Albert, having lost about £30,000, proceeded to the adjoining temple of Hymen at St. George's, Hanover Square, to be married to his first wife, Miss Henrietta Forester, sister of Lady Chesterfield, and Lady Bradford.

With the same companion and playing the same game, Payne set out from London in a post-chaise to pay a visit to a country house in the New Forest. As the story is told they played all day, and when night fell a lamp in the roof of the chaise was lighted, and they proceeded to deal and propose without intermission. Payne was in a run of luck, with £100 staked on each game, when both became aware of the chaise having stopped, and that the post-boy, who had lost his way, was tapping lustily with the butt end of his whip at the window of the post-chaise. "What do you want?" said Mr.

Payne, testily. "Please, sir, I have lost my way." "Well let us know when you have found it," was the rejoinder.

The case of Lord de Ros which excited at the time a "great sensation," and has been narrated over and over again in various fashions, came on in the year 1837 and was quite a *cause celebre.* His lordship had for a long period been a player chiefly at Ecarté and Whist in West End London clubs, and was so steady a winner, that in the winter of 1836, rumours began to circulate that his play was not fair, but he declined to take the hints which were given him. Being closely watched on several occasions, he was detected in the act of marking the cards, and performing also the sleight-of-hand feat known as *sauter la coupe.* The chief among many accusers were Mr. Payne, Mr. Brooke Greville, Lord Henry Bentinck and Mr. Cumming. Lord de Ros returned to England as soon as he heard of the scandal, and having traced the accusations to their source, was ill-advised enough to bring an action for libel against Mr. Cumming, which was tried before Lord Denman and a special jury, on the 10th of February, 1837. The sensation produced by the trial was profound; the court was crowded with ladies and gentlemen, and the excitement in all circles was very great, so much so that the *Times* of that date gave a verbatim report. Mr. Payne was spoken of most disrespectfully by Sir John (afterwards Lord) Campbell as one of those who, he said, had conspired to trump up the charge against Lord De Ros, who lost his case which had taken the shape of an action for libel against a Mr. Cumming.

COST OF ANGLING.

ANGLING has during late years become a rather expensive pastime. On Loch Tay, for instance, two persons can have a boat for three days at a charge of £4 10s., which with the men's wages and luncheons will come to £6 for the period indicated or £3 each person. Boats and men can also be hired for one day or for a week as may happen to be convenient. The following is the authorised tariff at Killin as per (the printed regulations issued from the Breadalbane Estates office): Cost of a boat per week £5, men's wages per day, two to each boat, 3s. 8d. each; for a single day a boat costs 25s., or, if occupied by two persons, 30s., the two boatmen having, of course, also to be paid. According to the regulations, "anglers are not obliged to provide lunch for the boatmen, and those who are kind enough to do so are most earnestly requested not to give more than a soda-water bottleful of whisky between the two boatmen." Some good-natured fishers introduced the custom of giving the boatmen their lunch, and now it costs each hirer of a boat about 4s. to provide sandwiches and whisky for his two men.

Salmon fishing whether from a boat on a loch or from the river's brink is the finest of all sports although costly. As a Manchester man once said, "I have had some capital fishing on Loch Tay, but looking at the pastime from a business point of view, it does not pay—my fish have cost me at the rate of exactly 11s. 3d. per pound weight." The amount of money annually expended in the upholstery of angling, in travelling expenses and in the rental of water, if it could be accurately computed, would undoubtedly show a large total. A recent writer on the economy of sport, in order to arrive at some figure more or less accurately representing the cost of angling, says, "There are probably in all parts of the United Kingdom over half a million persons who fish, and who will over head spend every year an averge of fifty shillings each, on tackle, travelling, and living expenses." That brings against the cost of sport a sum of one and a quarter million sterling. Another gentleman has calculated that the total cost of angling to the disciples of old Isaac, is not less than one million sterling per annum! The fish caught are in most instances of no commercial value.

A GOLFER'S ELEGY.

THE following verses on the occasion of the early death of Tom Morris (professional golfer) appeared in *Chamber's Journal*, and as many may not have seen them, and those who have, forgotten them, we reproduce them here.

> Beneath the sod poor Tommy's laid,
>   Now bunkered fast for good and all;
> A better golfer never played
>   A further or a surer ball.
>
> Among the monarchs of the green
>   For long he held imperial sway;

And none, the start and end between,
  Could match with Tommy in his day!

A triple laurel round his brow,
  The light of triumph in his eye,
He stands before us even now
  As in the hour of victory.

Thrice belted knight of peerless skill;
  Again we see him head the fray;
And memory loves to reckon still
  The feats of Tommy in his day.

In vain, to trap his flying sphere,
  The greedy sands yawned deep and wide,
Far overhead it circled clear,
  Nor dropped but on the safer side.

In vain along the narrow course
  Entangling whins in ambush lay,
But never hazard was the source
  Of grief to Tommy in his day.

Who can like him with Fortune deal,
  And from the fire undaunted snatch,
With steadfast heart and nerve of steel,
  The desperate hole that won the match?

To him alike were tee and rut,
  From both he found his certain way,
And who could predicate a put
  Too long for Tommy in his day?

" For all in all our Tommy take,"
  The verdict of the links will say,
" We n'er shall look on one who'd make
  A match for Tommy in his day."

WHAT IS BACCARAT?

BRIEFLY answered it is a game of cards of the most " gambling kind," which to some extent has usurped the place of " Napoleon," and is now being played by thousands of people in the Clubs of

London and other large cities and towns, to the hurt of hundreds, more especially in houses where it is suspected the cards are tampered with, or in which clever modes of cheating pre-arranged by groups of confederates take place ; it has been affirmed indeed by a clever Frenchman that over sixty modes of cheating at Baccarat have been detected.

One informed writer on the game says, that with a reliable confederate, the dishonest banker's chance of sweeping the board is an easy one. A code of signals is arranged, usually one which merely involves matter-of-fact actions and movements, which an ordinary bystander watching the play would spontaneously go through. . The confederate stands, cigar in mouth, at the back of the punters with other on-lookers. He takes care never to look at the banker, which might arouse suspicion, but signals the state of the punter's cards by simply removing the cigar from his lips when the punter's cards count five, or emitting the smoke with great deliberation when the punters have very good hands and so forth.

The following very clever feat was successfully accomplished in the course of play some three years since. One of a party of players who generally took the bank, experienced an extraordinary and inexplicable run of luck, having, after four nights' play, won £23,000. After careful scrutiny, it was at length noticed that when he took the bank he was in the habit of casually laying down his silver cigarette-case on the table, and deftly dealing the cards so that their faces were reflected on the burnished silver. The trick conceived by a well-known player at the Palais Royal Club at Paris not very long ago was equally clever. As banker he invariably won large sums. This continued some time, and though the packs of cards and his mode of play were scrupulously watched by large numbers of interested self-constituted detectives, everything seemed fair and above board, till one evening, after the banker had won the large sum of 300,000 francs, the committee determined to have the pack of cards which had been used submitted to microscopic examination by an expert. The most minute specks of phosphorus were then discovered on the back of each card, arranged on a definite plan, by which the value of each card was denoted. These spots could not possibly be seen by the naked eye, and the reason why the banker invariably wore dark-coloured *spectacles* was then apparent. He could see the phosphorus marks while the punters could distinguish nothing.

BACCARAT EXPLAINED.

THE game is somewhat difficult to explain in writing—as to teach it requires the practical manipulation of the cards. To play Baccarat is an offence against the law, the game being illegal, but the punishment for playing it is so light that the risk is run by thousands of gamblers. That the element of chance altogether swamps the modicum of skill and judgment which the game affords to players is evidently the opinion of the legislature, who declare baccarat "an unlawful game," while whist, écarté, and picquet are considered "games of skill," and therefore legal.

The following explanation of the mode of play is the best we have seen; it appeared in a weekly magazine some months ago. The leading principles, says the writer, are the same as in *vingt-et-un*, the aim of the players at Baccarat being to get as near the number of nine pips as possible. Half-a-dozen whist packs are used, and are well shuffled. The banker (who invariably has to pay a stiff sum for the post) sits in the middle of a long table, having the players—"punters" is the technical term—to his right and his left. He deals two cards, face downwards, to the players seated on his right-hand table, and two to those on his left hand—the players having first planked down their stakes—and then deals two to himself. The punters have the option of taking another card, and the banker enjoys the same privilege, but his third card is dealt face upwards. The deal having been completed, the banker has to reckon with each of the two divisions separately with regard to winnings and losses. To take an example. Suppose the sum of the banker's cards is 6, of the right hand punter's (A) 7, and of the left hand punter's (B) 4, and that there is £740 on A's table, and £500 on B's table, the banker would take B's £500, he having a number nearer the nine than they, and would have to pay £740 to the lucky punters on his right hand, thus losing £240 on the *coup*. If again, say, the banker had three, and the cards of the punters remained the same, he would of course lose £1240 on the round. There is plenty of excitement about the game, as the time occupied in each round rarely exceeds a minute. Tens and court cards do not count in baccarat, which simplifies matters considerably. In some of the clubs where this game is played the person who offers to put down the largest sum to be played for is made the banker.

MISERS ON THE TURF.

In all histories of the turf, mention is made of John Elwes, who in his day obtained notoriety as a miser, but another miserly turf celebrity has not been so much noticed, viz: "Lade the Lawyer," who abandoned the courts of law for the racing paddocks, breeding and training a number of horses at his seat at Cannon Park, in Hampshire. His attention was principally directed to endeavouring to win country plates, as he never sent a horse to Newmarket until two years before his death, when he won both classes of the Oatland Stakes with a horse he christened Oatland in honour of the event. His saving propensities extended to his stables as well as to his kitchen and pantry; and so wretched was the condition of his numerous stud when, after his death, his horses were sent to be sold at Tattersall's, that they excited universal pity in the towns and villages through which they passed between Hampshire and London. The man was systematically parsimonious; he would drive his curricles and greys the fifty-seven miles between London and Cannon Park without taking them out of the harness, or giving them more than a handful of hay and a drink or two of water, nor did he ever think of eating or drinking by the way, but made the journey unattended, as he considered servants on the road were more expensive than their master, who required nothing.

GOING TO THE DERBY.

You may go to the Derby anyhow, for the saint is far from particular. You may go with four horses and a private drag, or upon a skeleton frame, with a barrel of small beer upon it, to sell by retail on the course, and drawn by a skeleton donkey. Or you may go in a furniture van, if the "Glass with care," which is so prominently painted upon it, affords you greater assurance of safety. Or you may go in an advertisement-van, of which there are hundreds, whose inmates perhaps carry the combination of business and pleasure to the highest attainable degree. Or you may go in a pleasure van, pure and simple, with evergreens and babies and a brass-band. Or you may go in a hansom cab, bearing your luncheon-hamper on the top of it as a maiden bears her pitcher, with the less desirable liquor in it, from the well. Nay, you may even go in a life-boat, for we saw one wending its inland way upon wheels to the saint's abode, as though it had been the shrine of Neptune; nor were the nautical inmates so much out of their element as might have been expected, for we noticed that most of them were already half-seas-over. For what we know to the contrary, a good many people may go in balloons—but we set down here nothing but things certain, and which have occurred under our own eye.

About a quarter of a million of the more zealous devotees, who do not mind the risk of being squeezed to death, and the certainty of having their pockets picked, patronise the Rail; but we confine ourselves to describing the Road—which, after all, is the Derby. If, as in the *Arabian Nights' Entertainments*, folks could be taken to Epsom on enchanted carpets, and set down there in a twinkling, not the best and brightest piece of Brussels that was ever made should transport me thither. The race itself only lasts two minutes and a half, and is but as the flash of a rainbow. To go and return is what, I know, most makes men happy, and most keeps them so; and I think I may say the same of the women and children. At every wayside dwelling, whether consequential villa, "standing in its own grounds," and looking quite aware of the fact; or farmhouse, whose pastoral air increases the Pandemoniacal character of the passing scene by contrast, there are mothers at the windows holding up their babes, girls with their younger sisters, and beautiful servant-maidens demonstratively happy in the attics.

The luckier portion of the fair sex, who actually form part of the procession, are also in the highest spirits, but it must be confessed that the majority of them are not young. What is the correct explanation of this misfortune, we do not know; but the popular belief, as expressed without hesitation or reserve, is that these are the ladies who will not let their husbands stir anywhere without them. "*Couldn't* she trust you, old gentleman?" was an interrogation put to more than one respectable Paterfamilias in our hearing, whose voluminous better-half had banished him to the edge of the driving-seat of his pony carriage; and these cruel satirists, and the occasional grazing of the wheel, no doubt did somewhat dull the glories of the day for him. The lady, on the other hand, always seemed to take the remark in excellent part, as a pleasing tribute to her matrimonial supremacy; and, at all events, it never spoiled her appetite. The extent to which these middle-aged females ate and drank was the subject of our incessant wonder and apprehension. After consuming the rations they had brought with them in their vehicles, it was they who, under pretence of "giving the horse something," retarded the mighty pilgrimage at every place of refreshment, and divided the delay with the accidents.

ATHLETIC FEATS PERFORMED BY CAPTAIN BARCLAY.

It is probably not generally known to pedestrians and other athletes, that Captain Barclay's feats were detailed at great length in a volume devoted to "Pedestrianism," published at Aberdeen in the year 1813. This volume, in addition to giving a very full account of the great feat he accomplished of walking a thousand miles in a thousand successive hours, contained numerous other particulars of Barclay's powers of endurance and feats of strength, some of which were remarkable. It is well known that by the extraordinary development of the muscles of his arms, Captain Barclay was able to perform feats of strength which few men could equal. While with his regiment in Suffolk in 1806, he offered a bet of a 1000 guineas that he would lift a weight of half a ton from the ground. The bet was not accepted, as it was universally believed that what he undertook he could accomplish, no matter how difficult. To prove that his offer was no vain boast the Captain procured a number of weights, fastened them together by a rope through the rings, and lifted the whole clear off the ground. The weight was ascertained to be 21 half hundredweights, or half a hundredweight over half a ton. Afterwards, with a straight arm, he threw a half hundredweight a distance of eight yards, and put the same weight over his head a distance of five yards. But perhaps the most extraordinary performance of this extraordinary man was done in the mess-room of the 23rd Regiment. Captain Keith, Paymaster of the regiment, a man who weighed eighteen stones, stood upon Captain Barclay's right hand, and, steadied by his left, he was thus lifted up and set on the table.

Pugilism being a fashionable vice of the Captain's day, the "manly art" naturally found in him an ardent patron, and several of the most celebrated members of the "Fancy" underwent a course of training at Ury previous to engaging in decisive contests. Among these was Tom Crib, who was prepared at Ury for his great battle with the Black Molyneaux, which took place in September 29th, 1811, and resulted in victory for Crib. During his training Tom took long tramps into the Highlands, and derived great advantage from the severe exercise of following Captain Barclay. Crib was altogether nine weeks at Ury, during which time he occasionally gave lessons in sparring in Stonehaven. Although professor of a brutalizing sport, Crib was of a humane and charitable disposition. He made frequent visits to Aberdeen while in training, and while walking in Union Street of that city one day, he was accosted by a poor woman who poured her sad tale into his ear. Tom's heart was touched, and he emptied his pockets into the woman's lap, who remarked, as the pugilist walked away,

"Surely that is nae a common man."

Captain Barclay also trained Alexander Mackay, a Badenoch man, to fight Simon Byrne for the championship. Mackay was a man of large stature and enormous strength, but notwithstanding these advantages he was no match for Simon Byrne's science, and the fight terminated fatally, Mackay being knocked down by a blow from the effects of which he died soon afterwards. Byrne, it is said, left the ring without a scratch on his body. It was related at the time that Captain Barclay was so chagrined at the result that he challenged Byrne, thrashed him, and won the belt. This, however, is supposed to be without foundation.

HOW TO TURN AN HONEST PENNY ON THE TURF.

In cases of turf-gambling, the proverbial "honour among thieves" is nearly always duly observed. There are certain gentlemen on the turf just now who are owners, or nominal owners, of race-horses who chum together, or at least never oppose each other, in the betting-ring.

There is, for instance, let us say, that little clique, or syndicate, composed of Lord Brown, Viscount Jones, and Sir Robinson Robinson, who keep between them some twenty-eight horses, a selection from which they enter in the more important races of the season; and it is a noticeable fact, that the animals which are reputed to belong to this clique are more "worked" in the turf market than the horses of any other individuals. It has been said, indeed, by some morose critics, that more money is annually carried off by the horses of this clique which do not win races than by those which do win! It is not an uncommon circumstance for Viscount Jones to say to Pike, the leviathan bookmaker, " I think my horse, The Shark, can win the Rotten Row Handicap : you can, I suppose, lay me for self and friends twenty-five monkeys (£12,500), and in that case work the horse as you please." "All right, my Lord," replies Mr. Pike ; " I'll lay you what you want, upon condition you don't interfere with the market, but leave all to me ; and, by-the-by, my Lord, what about Flatcatcher ? " " Oh, Flatcatcher was beaten in the trial and has no chance."

All being left to Mr. Pike as arranged, what is the result ? The result is, that Flatcatcher speedily becomes first favourite for the Rotten Row Handicap, at three to one, while Sir Robinson Robinson's Dummy also becomes a hot favourite ; but The Shark wins, and a cheque for the requisite number of monkeys is duly handed over to the representative of the clique, whilst it is not at all improbable that Lord Brown and Sir Robinson Robinson may have derived some little additional advantage of a monetary kind by the " working " of their horses. If these two gentlemen had struck the animals entered in their names out of the forthcoming contest the moment it was known that The Shark was the best of the lot, they would have acted the part of honest men, but so long as horses are only kept to be gambled with, it is in vain to expect such persons to play a straightforward part on the turf.

A HOUSE OF BONDAGE.

ANOTHER great gambling club which at one time flourished in London—it was only second to Crockford's in the splendour of its appointments—was directed by the Bonds and was known as the Junior St. James'. Its proprietors made a fortune. The late Lord Beaconsfield gave a sketch of it in one of his novels. Bond, it has been told, began life as an obscure prize-fighter, and hearing that money was to be made at racing he went upon the turf. He lost £600 to some officers in the Guards, and greatly surprised them by paying up. A few nights afterwards the loser and winners met in the crush-room of Drury-lane theatre ; when Bond told the officers he was about to open a club—i.e., a gaming house—in Duke-street, and respectfully solicited their patronage, which they promised and kept their word. A week after the opening of his house he was worth £5,000, and in twelve months he removed to magnificent premises next to Crockford's, where the bank was the same as at that establishment, £10,000.

"From the back parlour of an oyster-shop my hazard table has been removed to this palace," says Mr. Bond Sharpe in the romance of *Henrietta Temple;* "had the play been foul, this metamorphosis would never have occurred."

Disraeli gives a full description of the splendour of the place, the dining-room with its gold plate, goblets of carved ivory set in precious stones, cups of ruby glass mounted on pedestals glittering with gems. In the drawing-room were chairs that had been rifled from a Venetian palace, and couches that were the spoils of the French Revolution, glass screens in golden frames, a table of mosaic mounted on a gold pedestal. An agent had been employed to ransack Europe for these treasures, while his cook had been *chef* to Charles X. The author, however, evidently had the House of Crockford in his mind's eye as well as the establishment of the Bonds. One writer in describing the place and detailing the enormous amount of gambling which took place wound up by saying that to many the club had proved a house of *Bondage.*

FROM THE GREVILLE MEMOIRS.

In connection with the Derby of 1833, the following story is related by Charles Greville, in the famous "Greville Memoirs:"—"Just before the race Payne told me in strict confidence that a friend of his—who could not appear, on account of his debts, and who had been much connected with turf notorieties—came to him and entreated him to take the odds for him to £1,000 about a horse for the Derby, and deposited in his hand a note for that purpose. He told him that half the horses were made safe, and that it was arranged that this one was to win. After much delay, and having got his promise to lay out the money, he told him it was my horse. He did back the horse for £700; but the same person told him if my horse *could* not win, Dangerous *would,* and he backed the latter likewise for £100, by which his friend was saved, and won £800 (Greville's horse lost). He did not tell me his name, nor anything except that his object was to pay his creditors; and he had authorised Payne, if he won, to retain the money for that purpose."

ABOUT BOOKMAKERS.

Bookmakers, as a rule, make large sums of money through the gullibility of the public, who back no end of horses. All the chances of the unholy war of betting are in favour of the bookmaker; he is well posted up by his touts as to what is occurring on the training-ground; the money sent to him to back different horses affords him a constant clue to what is going forward. He gets to know where it comes from, who sends it, and their position as to knowing which horses are meant for a particular race; and so he is able to judge, if he is not in "the know," which horses are stiff ones, and which are likely to compete. In fact, all the fools who throw away money in backing horses play into his hands; he sifts the information they give him, and has their cash into the bargain. Some bookmakers have been stigmatised by Dr. Shorthouse as being "swine." As a general rule, the men on a race-course in the betting line are coarse in their language and illiterate to a degree, many of them being scarcely able to pronounce the names of the horses they lay the odds against, and nearly all of them garnish their conversation with oaths.

Many of the bookmakers who attend a race-meeting are thorough swindlers, the typical name for them being "welchers;" they are men, many of them, who would rob their mother if she came and made a bet with them. Some who are daily seen in the ring have "convict" legibly stamped on their foreheads; and we once heard a gentleman say of a well-known bookmaker that if he were to appear for trial in a criminal court, the jury would not ask for any evidence of his crime to be produced, but would say "Guilty," whenever they looked upon the man. It is pitiful to think that by the gullibility of the public a lot of these ignorant roughs should make fortunes, be able to keep carriages, and live in their elegant mansions. Many a poor fellow has been ruined, and his family reduced to beggary, by the machinations of these men and their congeners. They "lay" against a *stiff* horse with avidity. With the utmost glee, they will laugh over their feats of this kind, and speak with sad contempt of the men that bring the grist to their mill.

Of course, there are many very good men even among bookmakers—men of taste and cultivation—jewels in a pig's snout, so to speak—men who can not only read, but men who can write as well—ay, and write elegantly, too. And the gentleman bookmaker, who receives his visitor politely, and does not garnish his conversation with a volley of strange oaths, is just as acute at his trade as the others; he can fight a rogue with a rogue's weapons, but would not on any account become an accomplice of mere swindlers. He makes a legitimate book, and holds his own in the race for wealth, and is not averse to tell a friend about a "good thing" when he knows it.

ABOUT COCK FIGHTING.

COCK-FIGHTING was at one time a national sport as a public exhibition, and there are persons still alive who can remember that when at school cock-fights were encouraged, the school-master being presented with the beaten birds. Public matches were held as a matter of course, and these were always well attended by the sporting men of the period. Harking back for some sixty years we find in the racing calendars of that date, long lists of cock-fights, as also a summary of the cock-fighting laws. Brettle, the pugilist who, although he could not read or write much, was never tired of showing a book written by Gulliver, a famous handler of cocks. The feeders and trainers of those birds were many, and there are doubtless men still living who can remember the time when Colonel Mellish and Sir Francis Boyton fought main after main against each other at Bootham Bar. The feeders and trainers in those days were thought as highly of as the popular jockeys of the present time, and, as the Druid tells us, "It was often the custom to fight cocks by candle-light amid a perfect babel of bets." No race meeting was at one time considered perfect unless a match with a main of cocks was included in the programme. The nobleman who gave his name to the great race run at Epsom, the Earl of Derby, was a breeder of game cocks, and took great delight in his choice breed of birds, and his example was followed by many other gentlemen, who thought it as good sport to fight their cocks as to hunt their foxes. Some of the old Lancashire families were as proud of their breeds of fighting fowls, as other men were of their high mettled racers.

Among the most prominent cock-fighters of the past were Lord Sefton, Captain Whyte, Mr. Price of Brynypys, Lord Derby, Mr. Leigh of Lyme, and Sir Watkin Wynn—the three latter being especially formidable in mains fought at Preston,

Newton, and Liverpool. And within our own times General
Peel and Admiral Rous have been often heard to declare their
partiality for a sport now fallen so greatly into disfavour, and
not long before his death the Admiral, in a letter to the *Times*,
advocated the continuance of the sport.

The cocks were carefully tended and "groomed," and also
daintily fed, their condition being ascertained by their weight.
Before a fight they used to be weighed as carefully as jockeys,
or even more so, and it is not long since Kent and Surrey
fought a main "in a walled in orchard," attached to a country-
house belonging to a local gentleman, who entertained a large
company at breakfast prior to this encounter. The battle was
between fifteen birds on each side, ten pounds a battle, and two
hundred pounds on the main. Surrey depended upon its
black-reds, and Kent upon its duckwings—the latter, according
to the account, being "completely outcocked and outset," the
victory remaining with Surrey, who won nine battles to its
opponent's three.

POPULARITY OF COCK FIGHTING.

How, it may be asked, did cock-fighting die out in these
islands? Oliver Cromwell is said to have, with the greatest
reluctance, suppressed the Royal Cock-pit in 1654. Yet the
game lived until half of the present century had passed.
There was a time when some of our most famous admirals
never went to sea without carrying cocks enough to fight a
main with, and we have it on the authority of George
Cruikshank that the Duke of Wellington was a frequent attendant in Tufton-street, Westminster, which used to be the
headquarters for cocking matches in the metropolis. Themistocles, we are told, once halted his army in order that his
soldiers might witness a cock-fight, addressing them in words
which, according to O. Meara, won the highest approval from
Napoleon I. "My gallant friends," Themistocles says, "these
two cocks are not fighting for their country, nor for their
paternal gods. They do not endure danger and pain for the
sake of their offspring, or in the sacred cause of liberty. Their
sole motive is that one is heroically resolved not to yield to the
other."

In a work published by Colonel W. H. Scott, entitled
"British Field Sports," cock-fighting was placed alongside of

hunting, racing, coursing, and fishing. The author touches the objections to the game when he says, "Is not this indolent kind of humanity nearly allied to a cowardly fear of death?" Cock-fighting in a booth is pronounced horrible. Weighed, however, in the balance of reason and fact, it is attended with less cruelty than the others. He argues that the game cock, being kept in a state of comfort and happiness until the day of battle, it is a pleasure for him to fight, and that to deny him that pleasure would be a sin. "Let those," Colonel Scott concludes, "who entertain such enmity to cock-fighters rather transfer their hatred to dog-fighters and bull-baiters." On the other hand, it was only a few years before, when the then Secretary of State for War, the Right Honourable Charles Wyndham, made an excellent defence in the House of Commons of bull-baiting which he wound up with the assertion that, "the bull is his Majesty's best recruiting sergeant."

In writing about Mr. Merry, Mr. William Day says, " I am told by one likely to know, and therefore am ready to believe that at one time he (Mr Merry) possessed more game fowls than any other person in the world, keeping thousands of game cocks at a time entirely for the purpose of matching them, and seldom had a less number. It was his singular fancy to breed all the birds of the same colour—black breasted reds—In his business, which he carried on with Mr. Cunningham as his partner, he accumulated an immense fortune, but big as it was, it was increased, I believe, in no despicable manner by his luck or good management at cocking. Many of the battles he fought were for fifty guineas a side, and five hundred guineas the main, and not a few were fought for much heavier stakes. On this sport in those days, as on racing to-day, large sums were lost and won, and from all I hear Mr. Merry's balance was usually on the right side." The site of one of the Glasgow Cock-pits is now occupied by the printing and publishing offices of the *Glasgow Evening News*.

LOTTERIES.

AN interesting book, says an eminent English barrister, Mr. F. Brandt, might be compiled from the anecdotes and stories with which the newspapers and other publications overflowed in the palmy days of lotteries, showing how one man was lucky, another unlucky, how beggars became rich, and how ragged boys from the street, on the turn of the wheel, were raised high above their previous state of poverty. The advertisements in prose and doggrel verse became a literature by itself, and the squibs and epigrams of the day were tinged with a lottery colour, and flavoured with a lottery taste almost unintelligible in these virtuous times. An account of the different modes in which lotteries were drawn, the instruments used, the precautions against unfairness, &c., would be interesting.

The tickets were drawn from the wheel by Bluecoat boys, and it is a fact, that an order was issued from the Lords of his Majesty's Treasury, that the managers on duty should see that "the bosoms and sleeves of his coat be closely buttoned and his pockets sewed up, that he shall keep his left hand in his girdle behind him and his right hand open with his fingers extended," together with other precautions calculated to render cheating by the concealment of tickets or otherwise impossible. When it is stated as a fact that poor medical practitioners used constantly to attend in Guildhall when a lottery was drawn to be ready to let blood in cases where the sudden proclaiming of the fate of tickets in the hearing of the holders was found to have an overpowering effect, I think it will be admitted that it was high time to put an end to these exciting but deleterious games.

Incredible efforts were made to postpone the evil day, but in vain, and on Wednesday the 18th of October, 1826, the last state lottery was drawn. During the summer of that year the lottery office keepers almost incessantly plied men, women, and children throughout the United Kingdom with petitions that they would "make a fortune in the last lottery that can be drawn." Men paraded the streets with large placards on poles or pasted on their backs announcing the imminent death of all lotteries. Bills containing the same information covered the walls, were thrown down areas and thrust into the hands of passengers along the street. Prices of tickets were said to be rising, and in a word the inhabitants of the great metropolis were in a state of chronic ferment.

One of the most important of the "contractors" in this last lottery was a man whose name was or purported to be Bish. He organised processions of fantastically attired men, bands of music, vehicles outrageous in size and gorgeous in colour. He had ballads (of some of which I am credibly informed the late Sam. Lover was the author) headed by rough woodcuts printed and circulated, and advertisements of every sort and kind disseminated, all having the object of informing the public that the last lottery was about to be drawn, and that BISH of 4 Cornhill and 9 Charing Cross, was the only man with whom they could safely deal. This was the system pursued by all lottery contractors, but BISH we find out-Heroded Herod in this the last state lottery. Although it was said that shares in the last lottery went up to a premium, there seems considerable doubt whether in fact they were not arbitrarily raised, and whether in truth many tickets did not remain in the hands of speculators unsold to the last. Not infrequently these "remainder tickets" took a big prize.

LONDON GAMBLING HOUSE DESCRIBED BY MR. EDMUND YATES.

IN his exceedingly interesting book of memories recently published by Mr. Edmund Yates, that gentleman tells his readers something about the London gambling houses of fifty years ago. "You pull a bright nobbed bell which responded with a single-muffled clang, and the door was opened silently by a speechless man, who closed it quickly behind you. Confronting you was another door, generally sheeted with iron, covered with green baize; in its centre a small glazed aperture, through which the visitor, in his temporary quarantine, was closely scrutinised. If the survey was unsatisfactory—if, that is to say, he looked like a spy, or a stranger merely prompted by curiosity—he was bidden to be off, or in case of need thrust out by the strong and silent porter. If he were known, or looked 'all right,' the door was opened, and the visitor passed up richly-carpeted stairs to the first floor. The front room was set apart for play; a long table, covered with green cloth, divided by tightly stretched pieces of string into the spaces for the 'in' and 'out'—the game being hazard—and a few chairs for the players. The croupiers, each armed with a hooked stick, instead of the usual rake, for the collection of the money, faced each other in the middle of the table; the shutters were closed and thick curtains drawn. The back room was given up to the substantial supper of cold chicken, joints, salads, which, with sherry and brandy, was provided gratis. In the places I have named the play was perfectly fair, so there was no occasion for the presence of sham players, 'bonnets,' as they were called, who acted as decoys. The company was composed mostly of men about town, the majority of them middle-aged, with occasionally a lawyer, a West-end tradesman, and almost invariably a well-known usurer, who came there not to play, but to ply his trade.

"Money was lost and won without display of excitement. I never saw anything approaching 'a scene' in a London gaming-house. The greatest excitement was when once, about 2 a.m., in the middle of the play, after a sharp whistle outside, which caused the croupiers at once to cut and clear away the strings dividing the table, and to cover it with a white cloth, swallowing, as some said, the dice—at all events, hiding them, we heard a tremendous crash below, and found the police were breaking down the iron doors with sledge-hammers. The scene was very like that so cleverly portrayed in *Artful Cards* (a piece produced at the Gaiety with Toole); when the inspector and his men entered, they found a few gentlemen peacefully supping, smoking, and chatting. We had to give our names and addresses, but never heard any more of it."

REMARKABLE FEATS OF PEDESTRIANS.

FOSTER POWELL, the most celebrated walker of his day, was seldom equalled in long journeys. One of his achievements was walking from London to York and back again in six days, in the year 1773, a feat which he afterwards excelled upon several occasions.

A Mr. Joseph Edge, of Macclesfield in Cheshire, 62 years of age, walked one hundred and seventy-two miles in forty-nine hours and twenty minutes.

John Batty, 55 years of age, walked seven hundred miles in fourteen days, on Richmond race course. His table of distances achieved was as follows: first day, 59 miles; second, $53\frac{3}{4}$; third day, $52\frac{3}{4}$; fourth, 51; fifth, 51; on the other days he walked respectively 51, 43, $42\frac{3}{4}$, $44\frac{3}{4}$, 51, 51, 51, $54\frac{1}{2}$, 51, $36\frac{1}{4}$, and at the close of his task, had five hours at his credit.

In the course of the year 1792, a Mr. Eustace walked from Liverpool to London in four days, being then in his seventy seventh year; the distance between the two cities is over two hundred miles. One journey from Chester to London, when eleven years younger, he covered ninety miles on his first day out.

In the month of February, 1808, a Mr. Downer walked four hundred miles in ten days, for a bet of one hundred guineas; he was much fatigued, and lost two stones in weight. On another occasion Downer walked twenty miles in two hours and forty minutes. At another time when he matched himself to go thirty miles in three hours and a quarter, for a wager of one hundred guineas, he failed, the task being evidently too much for him.

THE DUKE OF WELLINGTON'S HORSEMANSHIP.

IF the following little bit about the great Duke's horsemanship at the coronation be kept in mind, it will prevent the loss of a good number of sovereigns and half sovereigns, many of which coins used to change hands in wagers on the subject of his grace's performance on the circus horse.

In the work on "The Duke of Wellington" by Sir William Fraser, will be found an account of an amusing incident which occurred at the coronation of "the first gentleman in Europe," George IV. The Duke of Wellington, who at no time of his life had been an expert rider, having to act as Lord High Constable of England for the day, and in that capacity to ride beside the hereditary Champion of England, took the wise precaution of hiring a horse from Ducrow's Amphitheatre. The duties of the Lord High Constable and Lord High Steward were to ride up on either side of the Champion, and after the latter had received the gold goblet from the hands of the King, to back their horses the whole length of Westminster Hall to the door. This being an unusual movement for a horse, the Duke took care that his steed should be disciplined day by day to retrograde with proper dignity. The intelligent animal learned his lesson only too well, as the sequel will show. The great day arrived. The King was in his seat. The peers, and peeresses, and everything that was great in the kingdom had found their proper locality in Westminster Hall. The great doors were thrown open; and a sight which eclipsed all other sights enchanted the spectators. The Champion of England, in brilliant armour, entered between his supporters. Nothing could be more imposing.

The hero of Waterloo, wearing his coronation robes, his ducal coronet placed rather forward on his brow, and bearing in his right hand the bâton of a field-marshal, bestrode with great dignity his noble steed, duly caparisoned for the occasion. The sight was irresistible. The peers, peeresses, and commoners rose to their feet: a wild burst of cheering echoed through that vast and picturesque roof. What was the horror of the spectators; what was the dismay of the Sovereign; and what must have been the feelings even of that iron soul, that had confronted death in every shape unmoved, when the intelligent animal which he rode, assuming that the noise was the preliminary to his turning round, as he had been trained to do, instantly did this: and advanced backwards towards the Sovereign with his head pointing to the door by which he had entered Westminster Hall! As children say at the end of a good story, "What did they do then?" Some of those in attendance with great difficulty succeeded, to use a sailor's expression, in "slewing" the animal round; and possibly by dint of holding the bridle, and caresses, enabled the great Duke to approach George the Magnificent in a decorous and dignified manner.

POACHING AS A FINE ART.

THE following clever ruse adopted by a poacher is worth printing.

I had conceived the idea of openly shooting certain well-stocked coverts during the temporary absence of the owner. These were so well-watched that all the ordinary measures at night seemed likely to be baffled. To openly shoot during broad day and under the very eye of the keeper was the essential part of the programme. And to this end I must explain as follows. The keeper on the estate was a new one lately come to the district; and upon two occasions when I had been placed in the dock I had been described as a "poacher of gentlemanly appearance," and the "gentleman poacher," again." (My forefathers had been statesmen for generations, and I suppose that some last lingering air of gentility still attached to me.) Well, I arranged with a confederate to act as bag-carrier, to be very servile, and not to forget to touch his cap at pretty frequent intervals.

After "making up" as a country squire, and providing a luncheon in keeping with my assumed squiredom, we started for the woods. It was a fine morning in the last week of

October, and game—hares, pheasants, and woodcocks—was exceedingly plentiful. The first firing brought up the keeper, who touched his hat in the most respectful fashion. He behaved, in short, precisely as I would have had him behave. I lost no time in quietly congratulating him on the number and quality of his birds; told him that his master would return from London to-morrow (which I had learned incidentally), and ended by handing him my cartridge bag to carry. A splendid bag had been got by luncheon time, and the viands which constituted this meal were very much in keeping with our assumed position. Dusk came at the close of the short afternoon, and with it the end of our day's sport.

The "bag" was then spread out in one of the rides of the wood, and in imagination I can see it now—37 pheasants, 9 hares, 5 woodcocks, a few rabbits, cushats, and miscellaneous. The man of gaiters was despatched three miles for a cart to carry the spoil, and a substantial "tip" gave speed to his not unwilling legs. The game, however, was not to occupy the cart. A donkey with panniers was waiting by the covert side, and as soon as the latter was packed, its head was turned homewards, over a wild bit of moorland. With the start obtained, chase would have been fruitless had it ever been contemplated—but it never was. I need not detail the sequel to the incident here, and I may say that it was somewhat painful to myself as well as to my bag-carrier. And I am somewhat sorry to say that the keeper was dismissed by the enraged squire as a reward for his innocence. As to the coverts, they were so well stocked that after a few days' rest there appeared as much game as ever, and the contents of our little bag was hardly missed.

INVESTING THE STABLE MONEY.

"FOLLOWING the stable money" is considered by some bettors a safe mode of betting; for, as a rule, the stable money is not invested till a horse has been so well tried that it is thought it cannot lose the race. When the owner of a horse trained in some good stable is known to be backing it, and that all the patrons and hangers-on of the stable are following suit, then the betting men are pretty sure the horse in question will see a shorter price, and yield good "hedging" before the day on which the race is run.

Whilst the betting on important handicaps, and some other

races as well, is in progress, large backing commissions are frequently thrown into the market by owners of horses. These are executed by persons in the confidence of the owner or trainer, or perhaps by some important adherent of the stable; but the person usually appointed to execute a commission is generally a bookmaker in a large way of business. The secret of the trial, the weights carried by the competing horses, and the lengths by which the race was won, may or may not be communicated to the agent employed; he may be told no more than Asterisk has won a great trial for the Chester Cup, and that the owner, for himself and friends, wishes at once to back that horse to win him twenty thousand pounds. Then Asterisk will come in that day's market; and, as the commissioner and his friends will also back the horse on their own account, the price against him soon begins to lessen. Telegrams are despatched at once to those towns where there are betting agents, not only to Manchester, Nottingham, Liverpool, Glasgow, Edinburgh, and Dublin; all the "little" men or petty bookmakers in London will be "sharped" on behalf of Asterisk as well, and by four o'clock of the day on which the commission was commenced the owner will probably be apprised that he stands to win his thirty thousand pounds at the average odds of 18 to 1.

Large commissions are frequently executed with considerable cleverness, especially when the horse to be backed has already become a favourite in the market, in consequence of being fancied and backed by the general public. An effort will at once be made to "knock him out" if possible, or drive him back a few points in the betting, so that the stable money may be invested to greater advantage than would otherwise be the case. Rumours will be put in circulation of the horse having become lame, or being "off" his feed," or that he has been beaten in his trial; these manœuvres, if they are successful, will induce the required panic. All who have backed the horse, or who, in turf parlance, have helped themselves before the owner could do so, will now be anxious to bet against him, and the desired retrogression in the price list will be obtained; the stable money will then be quietly invested, and the betting public will be electrified next morning at seeing the horse quoted at a shorter price than before!

GREGSON THE POET OF THE PUGILISTS.

THE man who was best known as the songster of "the pugs" was—Bob Gregson, who could both sing the praises of Boxers and box.

In early days he had been able on occasion to display his powers. There was, as the story goes—and a sketch of Gregson's life has been published—a touch of romance about his early career. A Lancashire lad, his first set-to was in defence of the lady of his love, whom some other swain at a fair endeavoured to wrest from him by force. Bob fought valiantly in her defence, and after a struggle which lasted a full hour, came off victor. After that his fame rose rapidly, and a gigantic collier, who had hitherto been hailed as champion of the neighbourhood, resigned the title to him; soon afterwards he was engaged in another contest, in which a woman figured very prominently. A farmer's widow of Ormskirk having been importuned by one of her men, Bill Halsall, to doff her cap of woe for a second bridal wreath, she determined that her hand should be won only by daring deeds. Not being quite as exacting as the damsel who threw her glove into the lion's den for her lover to fetch, the Ormskirk widow declared that she would be Mrs. Halsall on only one condition—that he challenged and beat Bob Gregson. Love gave the rustic courage, and he forthwith dared the champion to fistic combat.

Bill fought very desperately, but the Fates were against him, and at the end of an hour he was picked up senseless and carried out of the ring. In little over a week, however, "the god of soft desire" had roused him to another trial; once more he stood up before his conqueror, but only again to fall before Bob's prowess. So impressed, however, was the hero by Bill's pluck and gallantry that he undertook to intercede with the hard-hearted fair one, and his advocacy proving successful, Halsall was rewarded in the desired way.

When death, in 1808, claimed poor Bob, his universally acknowledged successor to the crown of bays was Jack Fogo—who, from the bluish tint of his complexion, the redness of his nose, and a generally pinched expression of features—had obtained the nickname of Frosty-faced Fogo. This new poet of the ring was a shoemaker by trade, but with a soul above leather. Nature had not fitted him for a gladiator, and his passionate admiration for the sport of the arena had to vent itself in poetry instead of pugilism; the old files of *Bell's Life* abound in the effusions of Jack's muse, some of his efforts being far from bad in their way. Though not a fighting man, Jack was a personage of very considerable importance in milling circles, and one to be considered and conciliated; for, though most of the heroes could not read the verses composed in their honour, Jack could sing and recite them, and to see the unknown characters which held them up to the admiration of contemporaries and posterity was a very pleasing spectacle to the subject. Again, Fogo was a walking cyclopædia of the ring, and had every battle from the days of Broughton and Slack to Jack Randall's last at his finger ends, and his decision was taken as law. His effusions were always signed, "Poet Laureate of the Ring," and he faithfully fulfilled the duties of his office in singing the famous deeds of the heroes of the day.

GROWTH OF GAMBLING.

WHEN an occasional "revelation" of a highly sensational sort is made by means of a police raid on some one or other of the gambling houses of London, there are people who turn to each other in their astonishment at what has happened and ask, "Can this be so?" Those, however, who have been behind the scenes of the "Modern Babylon," express no surprise when such events take place, knowing well that there are thousands of men in that vast city to whom gambling is as the salt of life; and so it has been for a long period,—games of chance being entered into with relish by all classes. When upon a recent occasion the police apprehended a large number of card players, much newspaper comment was, of course, evoked, one journal embracing the opportunity of giving a brief sketch of gambling history which is worth preserving in book form. As the paper in question asks, admitting that at the present time gambling is widely prevalent, *when was it not so?*

So far as this country is concerned, it is certain that the Normans brought with them the love of gaming. They were conquerors; they came by their possessions easily, and they as easily exchanged them among each other at the gaming table. Old statutes, moreover, show that punishment was provided for artificers and persons of humble condition for frequenting houses where dicing and carding went on, instead of spending their time in a more innocent and profitable manner. The laws against gaming were, however, not by any means rigidly enforced until the Reformation.

To Henry VIII. belongs the honour of causing the conviction and castigation of keepers of gaming-rooms, and of inflicting to boot a fine of 6s. 8d., on each player. That gambling hells were absolutely suppressed during the Reformation period and the years that followed, is, nevertheless, more than doubtful. However this may be, they flourished once more in the reign of the "Merry Monarch." That was a golden time for the gambler. Readers of Harrison Ainsworth's "Old St. Paul's" may remember the terrible incident of the gamester who stakes his wife on the cast of the dice, and loses. They will also recall how the winner proceeded to secure his prize only to find that she was stricken down by the plague. The event is said to be no fable but actually founded on fact. Gambling in Charles the Second's day was furthermore not limited to noble men and squires. It was common to every class, and young apprentices by the score were to be seen swaggering in the gaming house and challenging its frequenters to "throw a main." Duels, brawls, and broken heads were of course amenities usual to such places. For a neat little picture of the time—though, to be sure, the date was a good deal earlier than the Restoration—attention may be directed to Scott's "Fortunes of Nigel," and to the scene in which the young apprentice goes to a tavern kept by a Frenchman, loses his money, and lunges with terrific fury at the bully Culpepper. Shadwell's plays on the subject are also very instructive reading.

In Queen Anne's day, cards became more attractive than dice. The papers of Addison and Steele teem with reproaches levelled at the vice. The two best-noted hells of that time were Shaver's Hall, on the site where now stands the Princess's Theatre; and Piccaddili House, at the corner of Windmill Street, described as a "fair house for entertainment and gaming." But bad as things were then, they were not nearly so scandalous as in the middle of the eighteenth century. No shame attached itself at all to wagering and gaming during that epoch. Nearly everybody betted and gambled; and the ladies of the highest rank were not only passionately fond of cards, but they were notorious for cheating at play as well, and with the utmost effrontery. The clergy, moreover, whatever they might have said in the pulpit, sat down with the rest. The Countess of Bernstein at Bath, and the Chevalier Balibari at Berlin and other German towns, are fair types of a century in which the passion for gambling was prevalent all over Europe. Dr. Johnson was heard to wish that he had learned to play cards when at Oxford; and on more than one occasion defended gaming when the practice was attacked in his presence. It is noteworthy that club gambling also attained great notoriety about the middle of the eighteenth century. There was White's Club, originally established as a chocolate house in 1698, where the game of hazard was played daily for enormous stakes. Everything, moreover, served as a pretext for a wager among the members; even the accident of a man being carried insensible into a neighbouring house, bets being freely made as to whether he was dead or not.

EXTENT OF PLAY IN LONDON HELLS.

At Brookes's, a club in London where gaming was extensively carried on, Fox lost and won prodigious sums at faro and macao. It was at Brookes's that Beau Brummel won £20,000 at a sitting from Mr. Drummond, the banker. Dice playing was in favour at the Cocoa Tree, and the records of that club tell of a famous throw which meant the winning or the losing of £180,000. George IV., when Prince Regent, was practically the founder of Watier's hell, as the said Watier had been the Prince's servant, and was started in business under Royal patronage. All these resorts were, however, eclipsed by Crockford's in St. James's Street, the proprietor of which was commonly reported to have won two millions in less than thirty years, and who actually died in 1844, worth half a million. Though hundreds were ruined, there were, nevertheless, instances of great fortunes made at the gaming table. General Scott, for example, gave it out as no secret that he had netted over £200,000, by playing chiefly with the Duke of Portland and George Canning. Instances might be multiplied. Those quoted, however, are sufficient to show that there is nothing very new in the present state of things.

DERBY STORY OF £25,000.

Apropos to the struggle of Ellington for the classic honours of Epsom Heath, I must repeat the following little story of £25,000 which was won by his trainer. Mr. Thomas Dawson, of Middleham, had backed that horse to win a very large stake, the sum mentioned above, in fact, and in consequence of the

Derby candidate being defeated a few days before the great event, it was found impossible to hedge the large sum for which owner and trainer had backed their horse, and thus, much against their will, they were both of them compelled to win their money! On the Monday following the race, Mr. Dawson was duly paid his winnings at Tattersall's in good notes of the Bank of England. Settling being well over, the happy trainer "dined," entertaining a friend or two to all the delicacies of the season on the occasion, in honour of Ellington's success.

Dinner well over, the lucky trainer prepared for his return, part of his preparation being to pack away his winnings—the £25,000—in an old leather hat-case, which being without a lock, required to be fastened with a piece of string. Mr. Dawson was sound asleep when his train arrived at Northallerton, where, having to change to another carriage, he was duly awakened by the guard, but in the hurry to transfer himself to the waiting train he forgot his treasure, and left the old hat-case tied with the bit of string to proceed on its travels. It was carried to Newcastle, Edinburgh, and ultimately as far north as Aberdeen, before it was claimed, because, in the days of Ellington, telegraphic activity was not quite so much developed as at present. In the meantime the astute trainer evinced no particular anxiety, and made no fuss—he did not in any way announce his loss; he knew how to wait, and in due time his patience was well rewarded by the return of the treasure laden hat-box, with its valuable contents intact—the bit of string never having been untied by any Peeping Tom of the railway.

GLOVE FIGHTS.

What constitutes prize-fighting? It may be roughly defined as a contest in which two men endeavour to reduce each other to insensibility by blows for the sake of winning a sum of money. But there must be some other meaning, or public announcement would not be made of coming battles which answer exactly to the above definition. Thus, in a Newcastle journal of good repute, there recently appeared an account of a boxing match arranged between two professionals. The stakes are £100 a-side, and the heroes will be allowed to punch one another for twenty rounds unless one succumbs previously. It is true, gloves are to be worn for the sake of appearances, but the articles which go by that name in these encounters are very different from the legitimate "mittens." Except in this particular, and in the limitation of the number of rounds, the brutal business will be carried out exactly on prize-fighting lines. Yet so convinced are the promoters of the exhibition that they have kept within the four corners of the law, that they propose to hire a large public hall at Newcastle for the purpose. Nor do we doubt that it would prove a very remunerative speculation. The question is whether the law should allow itself to be diddled in such a flagrant manner. If so, then it would be far better to legalise prize-fighting at once, and let game chickens work their sweet wills upon one another as in the good old times. There is something to be said for that course, but nothing for the present pretence of suppressing the "noble art," while winking at its continuance under the most flimsy disguises. Glove fights of long duration in light gloves for heavy stakes are, to all intents and purposes, prize fights, and the "fancy" recognise them and relish them in that character and in no other.

POETIC PROPHETS OF THE DERBY.

At one time, say forty years ago, there were a great number of persons who made it their business to offer prophecies for the Derby, some of those in the sporting journals being uttered in poetic phraseology of a kind which sometimes attracted attention, whether the prophecy came off or not. The practice of giving poetical prophecies began about the year 1837, when "Vates" gave the winner, making a fortunate commencement. His lines ended with the following couplet:

> " 'Tis over, the trick for the Thousand is done,
> George Edwards on Phosphorus the Derby has won."

Some other excellent hits of a like kind were made by other writers who were not only able to "spot the winner," as it is called, but were able as well to convey their prophecy in excellent lines. One of the most successful poetic tips ever given for the Derby appeared in *Bell's Life* on the Saturday before the race. It was from the pen of a well-known writer, and was signed "Orange Blossom." The following is an extract from the poem:

> " Caractacus, whose wondrous shape
> Sets every country mouth agape ;
> And if, of the outsiders there,
> One horse should pass the winning chair
> Enrolled in the successful three,
> Be sure Caractacus is he."

Caractacus won the Derby of 1862. Blair Athol was the hero of numerous poetic tips, one of which wound up with the following lines :

> " In short, if you'd summer in clover,
> And send to the Devil the Jews,
> Believe me the Derby is over,
> Blair Athol can't possibly lose."

The following Derby epigram gave first and third for the race, Lord Lyon and Rustic :

> " While members at Westminster hotly debate
> Whether gentry or workmen shall govern the State,
> The members of Tattersall's have the same shout,
> They know but two rivals, the Lord and the Lout."

Another of the doggrel Derby tips that was circulated in Bluegown's year proved prophetic ; it concluded as follows :

> " 'Tis the Lord of Kingsclere the Derby will win,
> All his three horses, we are told, are to spin ;
> Bluegown and the Green One are tips of the town,
> And as Rosie won't do, I plump for Bluegown."

These are not perhaps the best examples of Derby poetry that could be selected, some of the poems occasionally being really spirited and at the same time poetic. Poetic tips for the Derby are not so common now as they were twenty odd years ago. A recent confession of a tipster, telling us the mode of construction, honestly explains that the difficulties of tipping in language that is at all poetic, are sometimes so severe as to necessitate a departure from public form, and the prophesying of a horse the name of which shall be sufficiently easy to manipulate.

A SPORTSMAN'S EPITAPH.

The Editor gives this remarkable production, which ingeniously introduces the names of so many race horses, at full length: it is the longest epitaph that ever came under his notice:—

SACRED
TO THE
MEMORY OF JOHN PRATT, ESQ.,
OF ASKRIGG IN WENSLEYDALE,
WHO DIED AT NEWMARKET, MAY 8, 1785.

A character so extensive, so various, so valuable,
As to astonish the age he lived in.
Though small his patrimony,
Yet, assisted by that, and his own genius,
He, for upwards of thirty years,
Supported all the hospitality
Of an ancient Baron.

The excellent qualities of his heart
Were eminently evinced
By his bounty to his poor relations,
His sympathetic feelings for distress,
And his charity for all mankind.
Various and wonderful were the means
Which enabled him with unsullied reputation
To support his course of life;
In which he saw and experienced
Many trials and vicissitudes of FORTUNE;
And though often hard pressed, whipped, and spurred
By that Jockey Necessity,
He never swerved out of the course
Of Honour.

Once, when his finances were impaired,
He received a seasonable supply
By the performance of
A MIRACLE.
At different periods he exhibited
(Which were just emblems of his own life)
A CONUNDRUM, an ENIGMA, and a RIDDLE.
And, strange to tell, even these
Enriched his pocket.

A SPORTSMAN'S EPITAPH.

Without incurring censure,
He trained up an INFIDEL,
Which turned out to his advantage.
He had no singular partiality
For flowers, shrubs, fruits, or birds,
Yet for many years he maintained a FLORIST,
And his RED ROSE more than once
Obtained the premium.
He had an HONEYSUCKLE and a PUMPKIN,
Which had brought hundreds into his purse;
And a PHŒNIX, a NIGHTINGALE, a GOLDFINCH, and a CHAFFINCH,
Which produced him thousands.
In the last war,
He was owner of a PRIVATEER,
Which brought him several valuable prizes.
Though never famed for gallantry,
Yet he had in his keeping, at different periods,
A VIRGIN, a MAIDEN, an ORANGE GIRL, and a BALLAD SINGER,
Besides several MISSES,*
To all of whom
His attachment was notorious:
And what is still more a paradox,
Though he had no issue by his lawful wife,
Yet the numerous progeny and quick abilities of those females
Greatly contributed to augment his supplies.
With all his seeming peculiarities and foibles,
He retained his PURITY
'Till a few days before his death, when
The great CAMDEN† spread the fame thereof so extensively
As to attract the notice of his Prince,
Who thought it no diminution of royalty
To obtain so valuable an acquisition
By purchase;
And though he parted with his PURITY
At a great price,
Yet his honour and his good name remained untarnished
To the end of his life.
At his death, indeed,
Slander, in the semblance of pity,
Talked much of his insolvency,
And much of the ruin of individuals;

* *Miss Timms, Miss Lightfoot, &c.*
† *Afterwards named Rockingham.*

But the proof of his substance,
And of a surplus,
Equal, if not superior, to his original patrimony,
Soon answered, refuted, and wiped away
The calumny.
To sum up the abstract of his character,
It may be truly said of him
That his frailties were few,
His virtues many;
That he lived
Almost universally beloved,
That he died
Almost universally lamented.

CROCKFORD THE HELL KEEPER.

MR. JOHN TIMBS in his admirable "Curiosities of London," gives the following sketch of this Turf Baring of his day: Crockford started life as a fishmonger in the old bulk shop next door to Temple Bar without, which in time he quitted for play in St. James'. He began by taking Watier's Old Club House where he set up a hazard bank, and won a great deal of money; he then separated from his partner who had a bad year and failed. Crockford now removed to St. James's Street, had a good year, and built, in 1827, the magnificent club house which bore his name; the decorations alone are said to have cost him £94,000. The election of the club members was vested in a committee, the house appointments were superb, and Ude was engaged as *Maiter d'Hotel*. "Crockford's" now became the high fashion. Card tables were regularly placed, and whist was played occasionally; but the aim, end, and final cause of the whole was the hazard bank, at which the proprietor took his nightly stand, prepared for all comers; this speculation was enormously successful. During several years everything that any body had to lose or cared to risk was swallowed up; and Crockford became a millionaire. He retired in 1840, "much as an Indian chief retires from a hunting country when there is not game enough left for his tribe," and the club then tottered to its fall. After Crockford's death in 1844, the lease of the Club House thirty two years, rent £1400, was sold for £2900.

KINGSLEY'S DESCRIPTION OF A FOX HUNT.

PERHAPS one of the best descriptions of a fox hunt ever written is from the pen of Canon Kingsley, who, although a parson, was fond of all kinds of sport. On his way to visit an old parishioner, mounted on an old hunter, he finds himself by an accident, all at once in the van of a fox-chase. He listens, and hears a light foot-fall through the ferns. A hare appears, her great full eyes full of terror, her ears aloft to catch some sound behind, who, turning short, vanished into the gloom. She had been put up, but what put her up? A blackbird screams, and the old mare on which the Canon is mounted, gives a spring in the air as an old dog-fox, as red as the ferns between which he glides, and with legs as black as the ploughed land over which he had previously passed, emerges into the open. It is a hunted fox; the mare trembles under the Canon's legs. The fox is well in front, not seeing the clerical spectator of the scene; so he sits in the middle of a ride, turning his ears right and left, scratching one of them with his hind foot, seemingly to hear better. Reynard hears the cry of the hounds, and is up at once and off again. He knew the ground well, for beneath was a patch of sand-heaps mingling with great holes, amid the twining fir-roots, and feels he is safe. So off he quietly trots, lifting his toes delicately, and carrying his brush aloft as a signal of defiance. Suddenly he halts at his first entrance of shelter, examines it with his nose, goes on to a side entrance and examines that, and then another, and another, only to find them all stopped. Reynard cogitates for a moment, and, after scratching his ear as before when in a difficulty, and sitting down to do so, he is up and off at his best pace, for louder and louder come sounds which make the Canon's heart leap and causes his old mare to spring again into the air. Following the hounds can be seen the form of many a good fellow, not very clever or very learned men, or very anything, except plucky, gallant fellows, but he knows them all, and wishes naturally to join in the hunt, which, at the same time, would not be ecclesiastical. His heart is with his friends, with Jackson, with Molyneux, with Baker, with Saumarez, and a lot more of good fellows; but then it would be unclerical to follow, though he and his horse were quite in accord this should be done.

The thud of a hundred horses' hoofs comes over the springy vegetable soil, plunging, jingling, struggling through the heavy ground, bursting for a moment as it reaches a sound spot. The hounds feather a moment, and, still a spectator from afar off, Canon Kingsley, with his heart in the sport, watches. Reynard's footsteps have puzzled them. Then in a moment old Virginal's pace quickens; a whimper, and away she goes fullmouthed through the wood, and the pack after her, but not Canon Kingsley, who feared, though his heart was in it, to do anything of that kind. Then a race began, Reynard taking the Roman-road, keeping, however, to the narrow-fringed grass pathway, and by doing so brushes off his scent upon the twigs at every stride. The hounds over-run the scent, halt, and put down their heads for a moment, but with one swift cast, and almost when in full speed, they hit it off again. On they go fifty yards farther into the heather, when their head show first in a half-cleared valley, among turnips and a partial wilderness. A brook then intervenes, and through a growth of firs, when the hounds are again at fault and Monsieur Reynard escapes, which, from his pluck and powers of endurance, he thoroughly deserves to do.

GROUSE SHOOTING AND BUSINESS COMBINED.

I.

THE following burlesque account of the "wiles" of a company promoted to facilitate business by renting a moor and inviting persons likely to take shares, or otherwise aid the scheme on hand, was written some thirty years since, and will be quite new to the present generation of readers. Those who were in the secret assert that what is told is truth under a very thin disguise, and they nicknamed the shooting, "Man trap Lodge—"

"To be let, the desirable shooting of Glen Toddy, comprising 4000 acres (Scotch) or thereby of moorland, abounding with grouse, ptarmigan, black game, snipe, duck, and hares, and capable of being rendered a favourite resort of the red deer which teem in the neighbouring forest of Glen Heverill. Glen Toddy is the theatre of some of those scenes by field and flood which thrill the hearts of the readers of Waverley. It was considered by the immortal Scott one of the most romantic spots in his Caledonia stern and wild. Castle Toddy is a self contained house, replete with every modern comfort and convenience. For terms apply to the proprietor, The MacToddy, Castle Toddy, by Toddyburgh, Whiskeyshire. N.B. Or to the proprietor's agent, Andrew Blackmail, Esq., Writer, in the burgh aforesaid."

Such is the advertisement which greets the eye of W. Promoter, Esq., as one fine summer morning he is reading his *Times* over the family breakfast table at No. 500, Hyde Park Gardens, W. Mrs. Promoter has long dinned in his ears that it is due to that station in life to which it has pleased Providence to call him that he should rent a grouse moor. The present is a favourable moment for renewing her instances, seeing that Promoter has just made a very good thing out of his share in helping to float in the market that freshly launched scheme, "The Tooth-picking by Machinery Company (Limited)."

Moreover, he is beginning to experience the truth of what the doctor some time ago told him—viz., that he must for a time drop work and take to relaxation and exercise, if he hopes to get rid of that nasty numb sensation in the left arm and side which the doctor declares is the result of anxiety and brain work, and probably the direct consequence of the protracted and harassing law proceedings instituted against him a year ago by certain shareholders of "The Association for Manufacturing Gunpowder from Salt Water (Limited)," which was then wound up pursuant to an order in Chancery.

The advertisement of The MacToddy, whose touching allusions to Waverley stir the soul of Maggie Promoter, render this sprightly lass an ardent advocate with her father. The long and short of the matter is, that upon no better sort of information than that inserted in those prospectuses which he is himself so clever at drawing up, Promoter proceeds to open negotiations with The MacToddy, whom he addresses direct : firstly, because it seems the more dignified course ; secondly, because he imagines that this gentleman may be more easily dealt with—that is, haggled with—than his agent. Little does the city man know the business qualities of the shaggy eye-browed chief of Clan Toddy, or the pertinacity with which that veteran Gael will insist upon no abatement from the rent first demanded, as also upon the payment by the incoming tenant of the wages of all game-watchers employed on the moors throughout the spring and summer.

At length, after a due amount of coquetting on either side, an agreement is made whereby Promoter "binds himself, his heirs, and assignees, to rent all and whole the aforesaid land, self-contained house, &c. &c., for the present season—that is to say," &c.

II.

Any anxiety he might entertain regarding the collecting of dogs, keepers, and other appendages of a moor, is now appeased by the receipt of a printed card, which sets forth that Roderick MacRamrod, gunmaker, at Toddyburgh (to H.M. the Queen), undertakes to supply all such requisites on most moderate terms. Moreover, MacRamrod is warmly recommended by a friend whom at this stage Promoter calls into consultation; we allude to the Honourable Gerald Nèredowille, third surviving son of Baron Nèredowille in the peerage of Ireland, formerly page of honour to her Majesty the Queen; afterwards ensign and lieutenant in the Bombardier Guards; afterwards a Queen's messenger; afterwards of Boulogne; thus far we quote an old file of the *London Gazette*, but from motives of delicacy we here stop the quotation, and for the "at present" of that record substitute the statement that Gerald is now a director of sundry joint-stock companies lately introduced to the public by Promoter and his associates. The Hon. Gerald and Promoter are invaluable to each other. The one requires money, and gets it in the shape of director's fees; the other requires a "good name" to insert in lists of directors; and if it pleases him, or rather the share-holding public, to consider the name of this sprig of nobility as good, why, that is their business.

Mrs. Promoter, on her part, is nothing loth to have her house honoured by an honourable who goes out and in like a tame cat, and invites himself to dinner without ceremony—that is, when not better engaged elsewhere.

With woman's tact, Mrs. Promoter insists that this man of the world shall be invited to accompany the party to the north; where his experience of shooting matters and quarters, and his commanding manners, will prevent any awkward "gaucheries" that might happen were Promoter suddenly pitchforked, without a Mentor, into the unwonted character of sportsman.

Nay, more, a thought flashes across the brain of the mother; a romantic glen; the attractions of Miss Maggie attired *en chasseur*; the daily, hourly association of the young couple (according to Burke, the Hon. Gerald was born in the year 1818); the barony of Nèredowille in *posse* (his two elder brothers are as yet sonless)! Yes yes, Mr. Nèredowille *must* be of the party.

III

To the invitation which speedily follows, this gentleman, who despairs of being asked elsewhere, gives a gracious assent, and undertakes to arrange the necessary equipment for the glen even from the stores of good things from Morel's to the costume proper for Maggie—to wit, a straw hat with a gray ribbon, a jacket and skirt of hodden gray stuff, the skirt being cut short, so as to display a due extent of ribbed gray worsted stockings and hob-nailed boots laced in front; the costume being completed by thick yellow dog-skin gloves, and a small race-glass swung over the shoulder.

Promoter Père, the vain old rascal, is, after a proper show of resistance on his part, persuaded to go in for knickerbockers and a blouse-like jacket belted at the waist, and intersected by pockets without number. He dared not ask the sober tailor, who for years has decked him out in the orthodox style of City respectability, to concoct such outlandish garments; so one day, returning westward from work, he is conducted by Mr. Nèredowille into a Scotch warehouse, where he is measured for a shooting suit, to be built from a bale of what looks to him like a drugget for a staircase, but which is pronounced by his adviser to be admirable stuff; but this is indeed beyond a doubt, for, as the shopman tells him, the Marquis of Blueblood has just ordered a dozen suits of that identical pattern.

Any qualms that Promoter may have felt regarding the singularity of his intended costume, or the possibility of his making a guy of himself, are relieved by the pictures which, in this emporium, replace the placards of the fashion stuck up in an ordinary tailor's shop. It is clear from the graven images which Promoter there regards, that the Scotch are a universally kilted race, with countenances, moreover, which, in the police-sheets, would be described as "forbidding," very different from the smug-faced, pink-cheeked gentleman depicted in the periodical *Modes de Paris*.

But let us cut matters short by supposing that, marshalled by the Hon. Gerald, the Promoters have reached Glen Toddy a day or two before the twelfth, so as to give the gentlemen time to "walk their shooting boots easy," to ascertain the merits and defects of their newly acquired dogs; and to find out the best ground on the hill, and the best manner of working it.

AN ATTEMPTED RACING FRAUD.

THE great fraud which was attempted to be perpetrated in connection with the race for the Derby of 1844, excited, at one time, a vast amount of comment. What then occurred may be briefly related. Two of the most heavily-backed horses in the race of that year, Leander and Running Rein, started under protest. Both were suspected of being improperly described as three-year-old colts, while the last named was said not to be himself at all, but another animal altogether. Curiously enough, Running Rein contrived to settle his fellow-suspect's pretensions by smashing his leg so utterly as to necessitate his destruction, and after doing that mischief came in an easy winner. Winning the race was one thing, getting the stakes proved a more difficult matter. Colonel Peel, the owner of the second and third horses, the last man in the world to allow himself to be defeated unfairly, determined, with the aid of Lord George Bentinck, to unravel the so far successful conspiracy.

After much preliminary legal skirmishing, the case of Orlando versus Running Rein came before the Court of Exchequer for decision. Baron Alderson presided, and among the counsel engaged we find the names of Cockburn, Lush, James, Thesiger, Kelly, and Martin. The issue submitted to the jury was, "Whether a certain colt called Running Rein, which came in first at a certain race at Epsom, was or was not a colt foaled in the year 1841, whose sire was the Saddler and dam Mab?" Mr. Cockburn undertook to prove the affirmative, and trace the colt day by day, week by week, month by month, and year by year, from the moment he was foaled to the moment he won the Derby. Unfortunately for his client, the other side did all this, and proved pretty plainly that the so-called three-year-old Running Rein was really a four-year-old named Maccabeus, bought by a Mr. Abraham Levi Goodman in 1841, and kept in retirement at Northampton until 1842, when he was taken to London, and installed in the true *Saddler* colt's quarters—that animal thenceforth becoming invisible; while another horse was hired to do duty as Maccabeus, this second impostor requiring the exercise of the dyer's skill to make him pass muster. When the trial had proceeded far enough to render its result easily guessed, the judge ordered that the Derby winner should be produced in court, "to satisfy the conscience of the court and the curiosity of the jury," whereupon the innocent cheat became *non est*. His cause was virtually abandoned, and Orlando declared the actual winner of the Derby of 1844.

ABOUT THE DERBY.

STARTING on its career with thirty-six subscribers, the Derby was exactly half a century old before its subscription list boasted a hundred names; after that, its progress was rapid—the second hundred was reached in another seventeen years; and in 1866, it attained its maximum, with two hundred and eighty-three entries, the actual value of the prize amounting to seven thousand four hundred pounds. This great stake coming entirely out of the pockets of the owners of horses; for the Derby, while attracting a greater crowd of sightseers than any other race in England, and by consequence greater profits to the lessee of the course, unlike the principal races at other meetings, receives no subsidy from the purse it helps to fill. Although so lately as 1855, the rich reward in prospect drew but twelve competitors to the post, one can hardly realise a Derby being contested by half-a-dozen horses; but that was the number upon two occasions—in 1783 and 1803. Indeed, before 1824, the field never exceeded sixteen; assuming its largest proportions in the Exhibition year of 1862, when the boy-ridden Caractacus made an example of his thirty-three opponents. Even that respectable field seems small compared with the number of horses engaged; but it must be remembered that the horses are entered when yearlings, and two years make sad havoc with hopes of owners. It is calculated that each animal putting in an appearance for the Derby represents an expenditure of four hundred pounds—leaving his original cost out of consideration altogether—while but one first class racer is produced among every hundred foals; so the wonder is rather that so many should be ready to pay five-and-twenty sovereigns for sending their horses on a hopeless errand.

GAMBLING IN THE REIGNS OF GEORGE III. AND GEORGE IV.

"PLAY," as it was called in those days, was greatly indulged in; the public and private records of the period contain numerous details as to the large sums lost and won at cards and dice.

During the latter part of the reign of George III., during the Regency, and in the days when George IV. was king, gambling in private and in semi-private clubs, as well as in the public hells, was carried on nightly to an immense extent, hundreds, thousands, nay, tens of thousands, being staked on a card or a throw of the dice. Women, too, sometimes played as high as men; in the papers of the period we find such paragraphs as "The amount lately lost at play by a lady of high rank has been variously put down at sums ranging between £200,000 and £700,000," and "The Marquis of H——d is said to have been so successful at play this season, as to have cleared £60,000." "The Earl of B——e has won upwards of £50,000 clear of all deductions." "A Right Reverend is stated to be amongst those who are losers on this occasion."

Here is another paragraph, "The noble marquis, who has been so great a winner this season at hazard, never plays with any one, from a prince to a common, without having the stakes first laid on the table. His lordship was always considered as a sure card, but now his fame is established, from the circumstance of his having cleared £35,000, after deducting all his losses for the last six months." Another form of gambling of that period took the form of lotteries. Thousands of persons tried their luck in the lotteries, which were continued in England till October 1826, when the last of them was drawn. The State derived a large revenue from the lotteries of the time, and among thousands of people there was a feeling of regret at their being suppressed, which, as a writer said, was done "in the interest of public morality, many worse things being left standing which should also have been abolished."

TRAINING THE ARAB STEED.

The training of the colt is begun by his being shackled with clogs; and persons who have seen this mode of breaking think it a really admirable system. The clogs prevent the animal from entangling itself in the halter, or from getting into the manger, or from lying below it, and from a multitude of bad habits which are incidental to other modes of training. Not till it is over two years old is the colt ever saddled or bridled, and then the utmost care is taken not to fatigue the animal; as a preliminary to the mounting of a full-grown rider, they are frequently led up and down with a pack-saddle on their backs and a bit in their mouths which is covered with undressed wool. At length the man mounts the colt in order to complete its education. Before it has only been allowed to carry a child on its back, now it is made to feel the power of a master hand—the great object in view being to accustom the animal to ungrudging obedience.

At first, the colt gets only light work, and is ridden without spurs, and but little force is used. His owner canters him around among his belongings, using (as seldom as he possibly can) a light cane, just to remind his horse that he has a master; immense pains are taken not to "tout" or harass the animal, but to train him in the way he will have to go; he is always addressed in a gentle voice, and gently forced to do what is required, till in time no opposition is experienced. One bit of business it is deemed of the utmost importance he should be taught from the beginning of his training, and that is to stand stone-still while his rider is dismounting, and not to stir after he has dismounted. The value of such training was seen when an Arab rider was shot and fell from his horse—it stood still, till it was remounted.

The training of these animals is so complete, that any person might ride one of them to market—pass the bridle over the horse's neck, let it fall to the ground, then, placing a brick or stone upon it, go away on business, remain absent for an hour or two, and come back in the certainty of finding his colt where he left it. It is, of course, by the exercise of patience and painstaking that such results are insured; but then, what will an Arab not do for his steed? As one of their proverbs says, "The horseman makes the horse as the husband makes the wife." The best results are, as a rule, the fruits of the kind of training described; in a bivouac the rider sleeps beside his horse, his head pillowed on its shoulder. Horses, like men and women, differ in their tempers and dispositions, and some are met with of such a fiery disposition that they cannot be broken-in by gentle means. For such as these, provision of an austere kind is made, the rider in such a case chastising his horse by means of large and sharp spurs, with which he inflicts severe wounds upon its belly and flanks. In their earlier years the Arab horses are fed with much care and discrimination, their food being in accordance with their age, temperament, and work.

The Arab horse (see *Baily's Magazine*) is taught to drink the milk of the camel and the ewe. A milk diet is greatly approved of, because owners of horses think that it is good for the health of the animal, and strengthens without fattening it. Camels' milk is also said to be imbued with the power of impartin speed of limb to those who drink it, whether man or horse. Another point connected with the feed of a horse in the desert ought to be studied by trainers at home, that is, that the animal should be made to eat barley. "Had I not seen the mare produce the foal I should have said it was the barley," is an Arab saying. Another saying is, "When you purchase a horse feed him with barley till you know the measure of his stomach—a good horseman ought to know the measure of barley suited to his horse as exactly as the measure of powder suited to his gun."

CAPTAIN BARCLAY AS A RUNNER.

As a running man of superior swiftness and power of endurance Captain Barclay made a big mark, and much to the astonishment of persons who thought he would not succeed, succeeded to admiration. It was in 1803, that Captain Barclay first appeared before the sporting world as a swift runner, having undertaken to run a quarter of a mile against John Ward, one of the swiftest sprinters in England. The Captain accomplished the distance in fifty-six seconds, and beat his opponent by ten yards. While stationed at Eastbourne, in Suffolk, with his regiment (the 23d), he ran two miles within twelve minutes; and at the same place, in a one-mile contest with Captain Marston of the 48th Regiment, Barclay ran the distance in five minutes and seven seconds, and won the match, and with it a bet of 100 guineas. He did better than this shortly afterwards in a mile run for 500 guineas with a celebrated Manchester pedestrian, on which occasion he covered the mile in four minutes fifty seconds. Still more remarkable was his performance in December, 1808, when he was matched against a runner of the Duke of Gordon to go from Gordon Castle to Huntly Lodge, a distance of eighteen miles. Barclay ran the first nine miles in fifty minutes, although the road was very steep and rough, and accomplished the whole distance in two hours and eight minutes, beating the Duke's man by five miles. He had no previous preparation for this run, which was started on immediately after breakfast.

VALUE OF INFORMATION IN RACING TACTICS.

BOOKMAKERS and other betting men take much pains, and incur a great deal of expense, in order that they may be well informed as to the doings of the various racing stables. Information flows to them from many sources, because they have numerous hangers-on, whose duty it is to keep them posted up in the facts and occurrences of the training grounds. At Newmarket and elsewhere—near all training grounds, indeed—there are persons stationed, employed either by bookmakers or backers, whose duty it is to communicate with the utmost celerity every important item of intelligence connected with certain horses. Should these horses fail to appear on the exercise ground at the customary time, should they only walk instead of gallop, or should they pull up lame after their canter, then these *touts*—a ragged regiment, it must be confessed—hie at once to the post-office and *wire* to those who have employed them.

The intelligence thus conveyed is promptly made use of, and its effect, for or against a horse, speedily becomes obvious by means of the price current, and when it is seen that Asterisk has receded in the betting list from 16 to 1 to 25 to 1, it may be concluded that the horse only walked that morning, instead of galloping as usual; while if the odds have receded still further, then the backer of the horse may conclude that Asterisk has not been seen at exercise, and that, in consequence, there is something radically wrong with the animal. It is astonishing how soon the mishaps which occur to racehorses are made known to those interested in the betting; it is frequently the case, indeed, that a man who has backed a horse will know of its having broken down on the training ground long before the man who is its proprietor! Instant use is, of course, made of such information in the turf market.

LEITH LINKS AND GOLFING IN 1766.

SMOLLETT, writing in 1766, thus notices the game, and describes its votaries as he found them at that period :—I never saw such a concourse of genteel company at any races in England, as appeared on the course at Leith. Hard by, in the field called the Links, the citizens of Edinburgh divert themselves at a game called golf. Of this diversion the Scotch are so fond, that, when the weather will permit, you may see a multitude of all ranks mingled together in their shirts, and following the ball with the utmost eagerness. Among others, I was shown one particular set of golfers, the youngest of whom was turned of fourscore. They were all gentlemen of independent fortunes, who had amused themselves with this pastime for the best part of a century, without having ever felt the least alarm from sickness or disgust; and they never went to bed without having each the best part of a gallon of claret in his belly. Such uninterrupted exercise, co-operating with the keen air of the sea, must, without doubt, keep the appetite always on edge, and steel the constitution against all the common attacks of distemper.

HOW THE COLONEL WAS "DONE."

THE victims of the horse-coper are numerous, it is a case of one down another come on. No example stops the buyer, like the moth he flutters to his doom and the " confidence trick " is enacted over and over again. In the triumph of " coping " I think the Irish beat the English.

One of the former had bought, for £15, a lady's old pet mare. Having always been well-kept, it presented a rather taking, and even young, appearance, at the fair to which Paddy soon afterwards conveyed it. Near where the fair was held a regiment was stationed, and on the first morning the Colonel came down to have a look round. He spotted the mare at once. " Is this *your* mare ? " he inquired, addressing the dealer. " Troth, sur, she ought to be," answered the other, " as I got her in a nock, and gave £50, and a mare worth £60, besides losing half a score on the dhraw." " How old is she ? " " I'm towld she's six off, but you can look at her teeth." While the Colonel was attempting to perform this operation, the mare, as Paddy knew she would, made a savage bite at him, which cut short the investigation.

" Can she jump ? " was next asked. " Faith, I never tried, and am too old for that sort of thing; but if you'll come down a bit of the road, I daresay we shall find some gossoon that won't mind risking his neck." Proceeding a little way, they came upon a ragged urchin, the dealer's son, who had been planted on that particular spot. " I say, you boy," said Pat, pretending not to know him, " could you ride this horse over a fence ? "

"I'll give you a shilling," said the Colonel, "if you'll take that gate." It was a five barred, opening into a field exactly opposite the spot where they were standing. Up the gossoon scrambled on to the mare, and took the gate in splendid style, then galloped her round the meadow two or three times. Making for the gate to leap into the road again, the father shouted, "No, no; she might mark herself coming down upon the rough stones."

The Colonel satisfied that she could both jump and go, after some haggling, bought her at a hundred guineas. When he took her home, all his brother officers admired her, and considered he had got a bargain. Next day there was a fox hunt; full of spirit she went splendidly. The first leap was over a high hedge into a meadow; she took it as cleanly as she did it the day before, and away she went for a broad ditch that divided the field from a road. Arrived at the jump she stopped so suddenly that she nearly threw her rider, but neither spur nor whip would induce her to leap. He tried her at a gate lower down, but with no better success. And now to reveal the secret. She had been trained by her groom, as a sort of trick, to leap over a high fence into a paddock when she was turned out to grass, consequently, whenever her head was turned towards a green field she would take gate or fence, however high, but would not leap at all under any other circumstances. As a hunter she was useless, and enduring a round of chaff from his friends, the Colonel was glad to take twenty pounds for his bargain.

WHAT IS A MAIN AT COCK-FIGHTING?

The largest main of which any note can be found was fought at Lincoln about 1820. The stakes were £5,000 the main and £1,000 the battle. Seven battles were fought, and the winning cocks were victorious in five of them; thus landing for their owner the nice round sum of £8,000 in stakes, beside bets. Gilliver, a trainer (or more properly "feeder") of great note at that time, had the care of the successful cocks. Indeed at that period he seems to have been almost invincible.

Perhaps it will not be out of place here to define what is signified by the term *main*, which is not now familiar to many people. A "main," then, is the match or undertaking to fight cocks made between any two persons, and is generally arranged by proper articles being drawn up and signed by the contracting parties. Any number of cocks may be matched in a main, and of any weight; but perhaps the most usual form of contract would run somewhat as follows: "A B and C D undertake to 'show' or produce on the   day of   twenty-one cocks, between the weights of 3lbs. 8ozs. and 4lbs. 10ozs. All that weight within one ounce of one another to fight for £   per battle, and a further sum of £   to be staked, to become the property of the owner of the cocks winning the greatest number of battles."

Many other conditions were inserted as to the length of spurs, extra battles, &c.; but the above form the principal. It will be thus seen that should the cocks all be nearly of the same weight, a good many battles—possibly twenty-one—might ensue; but should the birds of one owner run from 3lbs. 8ozs. to 4lbs. 2ozs., and those of the other from 4lbs. 4ozs. to 4lbs. 10ozs., very few, if any, would come near enough to each other in weight to be matched, or, as it is called, "fall in." Hence many large mains have been decided by one or two battles; but the usual number is perhaps from seven to thirteen battles out of twenty-one cocks shown.

A REVEREND BETTOR!

Those who do know even a little about betting know very well that it has now become a trade or business, and that the kind of boys so often said to be ruined are neither wanted nor needed by the "professionals" who follow the business. The "backer," in fact, is usually a hard-headed fellow who knows quite well what he is doing, and for whom, when he loses his money, not much sympathy need be felt. The constant endeavour of the backer, his thought by day and his dream by night, is to obtain money from the bookmaker. To enable him to gain his ends he has at his command a host of touts and tipsters whose business it is to instruct ignorant backers, and tell them the names of the horses which they should back. And the backer does his best to ensure success; it is on record that some of them have succeeded in obtaining considerable sums of money. Let it not be supposed then, as a general rule, that bettors on horse racing results require to be protected from themselves by the sort of grandmotherly legislation that has of late come into vogue. Were it not that we are forbid to tell the secrets of the prison house, we might a tale unfold, that would somewhat surprise those who have never been behind the scenes. We might name not a few of the good folk of Glasgow and other cities who frequently have their "sov," or even as much as a "fiver," on the favourite. A somewhat curious circumstance occurred three years since in the kirk circles of a town not very far from Glasgow. A young preacher was filling a pulpit for a few weeks in the absence of "the minister," in whose house he lived during the period while he was on duty. In that house, the morning paper taken in was the *Glasgow News*, and the housekeeper, with an observant eye, observed that the part of that journal which was turned to first and most eagerly scanned, morning after morning by the preacher *pro-tem* was the page which contained the sporting intelligence and the notes of *Souter Johnny's* boon companion *Tam o' Shanter*. For that preacher of the gospel there was also required the six o'clock evening edition of the same paper, which was perused even more eagerly than the morning edition. The housekeeper of that house was still more astonished when the eloquent young minister gave her a memorandum of his washing written on the back of a Boulogne betting list.

PAYING FOR THE DUCAL WHISTLE.

AN interesting story is told regarding the racing career of a certain noble Duke whose success on the turf has been quite phenomenal. As a youth he had incurred some debts of honour which he desired to pay. He went to a moneylender, but the Jew at first was not inclined to let him have the money on easy terms.

"The Duke may live twenty years; you may die in the meantime," said the Hebrew. The borrower could not deny this, and was ready to give liberal interest.

"I will tell you what I will do," said the Jew. "You will give me your word that when you become the Duke you will pay me £10,000, and I will give you £1000 now."

The Duke closed with the offer, and a few weeks after the old Duke died the new Duke remembered his bargain and instructed his agent to pay £10,000 in spite of the remonstrances of his lawyer, who insisted that a promise so extravagant was not binding. This is probably a revival of a turf story often told, that ended the same way. The Jew gave a loan to a young gentleman, the son of an enormously wealthy father, of a sum of £2000, on condition of being paid four times the amount at the death of the old gentleman (at the time of the transaction he had passed his seventy-third birthday). No bill or bond was signed, the money lender being satisfied to consider the loan a personal debt of honour; remarkable to relate, the Jew died within twelve months after the transaction.

VISIONS AND OMENS OF BLUEGOWN'S DERBY.

It would appear from what transpired after the race, that the victory of Bluegown had been the cause of more dreams and omens than any other horse. One of the omens of that year "went the round" shortly after the race: A gentleman from Birmingham had taken his wife and daughter to London for a few days, *his* idea in doing so being to visit Epsom and see the Derby run for, the lady's idea being, to use a familiar phrase, to try and "do her husband out of a new dress." In walking past Regent Circus she exclaimed:

"Oh, look dear, at that dress, *This Beautiful Blue Gown of Lyons Silk, only £4 12s. 6d.* Oh, how nice it is, just my fit! I'm sure you'll buy it for me, Charley, won't you, dear?"

Curiously enough, "Charley" had at that very moment been cogitating over the Derby, wondering what would win, and fancying in his mind's eye that it was sure to be one of Sir Joseph Hawley's three—but which? Ay, which was the problem! The way in which his wife emphasised the words blue gown at once decided him—it was as if a load had been taken off his mind, and so he replied briskly:

"Look here, Charlotte, my lass; I'm going to back Bluegown for the Derby, and, if he wins, that dress shall be thine, and a bonnet to suit."

The sequel need not be told. Charlotte, anxious about her gown, insisted on being taken to see the race, and, sitting on Barnard's stand, had the gratification of hearing the shouts of the excited mob at Epsom as the victorious Bluegown passed the post, winner of the coveted Blue Ribbon of the Turf in 1868.

As an instance of the ruling passion strong in death, it may be mentioned that a man named Lowry, who acted at one time as a tout to the late Mr. Padwick, said to his wife whilst he lay dying: "Bluegown is a certainty for the Derby, my lass. Promise me that you will back it," and she gave the required promise, doing as she had been requested by her husband, and won her money.

The following is "another of the same." Returning from Epsom on the night of Bluegown's Derby, I got the coachman to set me down at a point near Cremorne Gardens, as I wanted very much to see "the fun" incidental to a Derby night. At the gate I met an acquaintance, well known in sporting circles, George Morton (Big George), a traveller in the hosiery line, and a good fellow to boot. "Glad to see you, old man. Come and have a drink. I have landed a thou. over Bluegown, and almost against my will, too. I stood Rosicrucian, but I had such a confounded funny dream, that I was obliged to back the 'Gown' at last." On hearing the word 'dream,' I cocked my ears, thinking I would obtain a story for my collection; and so I did. "Well," said George, in answer to my request for his dream, "this is it. You know the business I'm in. One night at Manchester there came to me a mysterious visitor—in my sleep I mean—a lady, who said, 'George, mind, I shall require a blue gown to match the blue stockings you have given me.' I remembered the dream at breakfast, but did not connect it in any way with Sir Joseph's horse, but, strange to say, I dreamt it again, and yet another time, and that is the way I have won so much. It dawned upon me at length that my dream was a tip for the Derby, and so I backed Bluegown to win me a few hundreds, and then stood in with a friend who had the horse in a double event."

GENTLEMAN JACKSON.

AMONG the many good stories told by Captain Ross was the following about Gentleman Jackson *apropos* to the prejudice entertained against pugilists. "A man, who only recently died, and who was deservedly one of the most popular and best fellows that ever lived, and who played a great *role* as a politician, was in his younger days a patron of the 'Ring.' His wife did not approve of this, and expressed surprise that a really great man, as her husband always was, should take pleasure in the society of such ruffians as prize-fighters. So he resolved to play the lady a little harmless trick. He invited Jackson to dinner, and when he arrived said, 'Remember, you are *Colonel* Jackson, who has fought in the Peninsula and Waterloo, &c.' Colonel Jackson was announced, and was very graciously received by the hostess; he talked well, had a fund of anecdote, and was evidently on a footing of familiarity with most of the great men of the day. When he had gone the lady was loud in her praises of the 'colonel,' whom she pronounced to be one of the most agreeable and delightful men she had ever met. 'You must ask him to dine with us again, my dear.' 'With the greatest pleasure,' answered the husband, with a merry twinkle in his eye; 'but when he next comes you must receive him as Mr. John Jackson, the pugilist, and not as Colonel Jackson, a Peninsular hero.'"

CHARACTER IN ANGLERS.

MORE "characters" are to be met with in the pursuit of sport than in almost any other phase of life. Among anglers there abound a large number of the fraternity displaying peculiar modes and manner both on their own account and while helping others. A capital hand in the way of aiding one how to do it, and how to land his fish, used to dwell on the banks of the Isla at one time, a fair trouting and salmon stream, although at particular dates the par and the smolt became a clamant nuisance. The person alluded to was very fond of a dram, and no sooner had he got a taste or two from the flask, than he began a never-ending chatter which no hint, or even command, could stop. A brother, whom he occasionally deputed to take his place, was quite a contrast in manner, and rarely indulged in more than three words when gaffing a fish—I am now speaking of salmon. Upon one occasion when a gentleman was struggling with a pretty fish in a place on the Isla, a very deep pool, where it was somewhat difficult to land it, Tam proved equal to the occasion, he doffed his nether garments, and at the proper moment dropped into the water, and with great difficulty, secured the fish; "got it in," was all he said. Had his talkative brother accomplished a similar feat, he would have gabbled over it for at least twenty minutes. A taciturn old gentleman of Tweedside, was always attended by "Dawvid," his man, who was as silent as himself, and for hours on some days they never exchanged a word. "Dawvid" knew his duties, and performed them in silence, gaffed his master's fish when the time came and handed him his lunch, speaking never a word.

One day the old angler entered on a keen fight with a big fish, and after having it on his hook for an hour and seventeen minutes, it was seized by "Dawvid," and safely grassed. All that was said on the part of the master was, "Is that it?" and the man replied "Imphim!" (meaning, yes). Most of the well-known Scottish anglers of rural districts display individuality of character—they have, many of them, a large store of quaint sayings that are worth listening to. A well-known Scottish editor used to say that he could always get a few striking political points for his articles from an old village shoemaker with whom he occasionally fished in some of the tributaries of Tweed. On Loch Leven the boatmen are obliging, and always ready to give a hint or two to fishermen who require a little coaching when they visit a particular locality. One of them, "Old John," was a perfect magician when he had the rod in hand; he could "conjure with it," as Mr. Francis of the *Field* once said to the editor of the *Scotsman*. "Ay," responded Mr. Russel, "especially after he has emptied your flask."

Among angling eccentrics may be named Jock Smail, at one time a fisherman of the Scottish border, whose powers of fish-catching used to be exercised on the Teviot, the Jed and the Kale. He was a fly-fisher of the first order, and was often able to fill his basket out of a pool from which no other angler could lure a single trout. But he had a higher claim to distinction among his fellows than his prowess as a fly-fisher—he discovered, and *for years* kept his discovery a secret, the killing powers of the minnow as a bait for salmon. Jock did not even take his father, "auld Rob Smail," into his confidence, but the old man watched him, and one day pounced upon him unexpectedly, just as he was engaged in landing a heavy example of a bull trout in the river Teviot.

RUSSEL OF THE SCOTSMAN.

No angler was better known on Tweedside and in the South of Scotland than Mr. Russel; he was a notable fisher and *bon vivant*. Entertaining strong opinions on men and things, he was never slow to express his sentiments, no matter what the subject might be, whether theatrical or theological. On one occasion he said of a minister of the gospel, " He calls himself an angler for men's souls. Poor fellow ! if he be as poor a hand in the pulpit as he is on the river side it will be precious few souls he'll catch." Another time he said of a well-known *paper angler,* " Him catch a salmon ! It's far more likely that the salmon will catch him." Although Mr. Russel's book, " The Salmon," was not a success, in a commercial sense, it well deserved to have been so, because it is full of the subject, and discusses the natural history, legislation and economy of the salmon fisheries, as well as the sport it affords to the angler, in a learned and loving spirit. Mr. Russel fought manfully in those battles of the salmon which were so common a quarter of a century since ; but to be the editor of the great Scottish organ of liberal opinion, he was wonderfully conservative in all he said on the subject of salmon fishing economy. His articles in the " Edinburgh," and " Quarterly " Reviews attracted attention, and it is these papers, as well as portions of his " Scotsman " articles, which compose his book, " The Salmon."

BETTING SHOULD BE FOR READY MONEY ONLY.

THERE ought to be no other kind of betting than betting for ready money. In the earlier years of the turf it used to be the case that all stakes were tabled down, and among the officials of the Jockey Club there is still, we believe, an " official stakeholder." As it is in vain for legislators or moralists to try to put an end either to betting on the results of races, or to gambling on the Stock Exchange, or to that which goes on at the whist and loo tables of " swell clubs " or in private houses, it would be as well that our ministers and members of parliament should endeavour to regulate it by bringing it within the pale of the law. As to the advantages to be derived from betting in ready money they are so obvious as not to require to be further referred to. If a man were required to plank down his five, ten, or twenty pounds every time he made a bet, he would think twice before he opened his mouth in the presence of a bookmaker. It is when a man becomes *involved* that he steals, or embezzles, or forges, to get out of his difficulty ;

few men we should think would rob in advance so as to enable them to make a bet. Therefore, if horse racing is to endure and betting is to continue—of which there can be little doubt —the bookmaker must become of more and more importance and his office will have to be magnified, his business will require to be regulated, and he personally, will have to take out a license. There are men we know who will hold up their hands in horror at such a proposition; but let it not be forgotten that we regulate "the accursed drink trade" as some people call it, nay more, we condescend to take millions out of its regulation, why then, to use a vulgar expression, should we "worry on the tail of the cow" after having swallowed the body of the animal?

ABOUT THE GREAT GERMAN LOTTERIES.

I.

No feature of modern civilisation is more remarkable than that the Germans, who claim to be more intelligent than the people of other nations, keep themselves in a perpetual whirl of excitement by means of the gigantic money lotteries which are periodically organised in several of the larger towns and cities of Germany, notably in the city of Hamburg.

As large supplies of tickets for these lotteries are invariably forwarded to this country "on approval," it may serve the good purpose of preventing many from keeping them, if the *modus operandi* of conducting these institutions be briefly described by one who has had practical experience of their working and results. Nothing can be said in their disfavour, so far as impugning the honesty of those who are responsible for them goes, because their management is "guaranteed by government," and the prizes announced are honestly given, whilst the business incidental to the drawing is conducted in a thoroughly straightforward way in presence of witnesses, official and otherwise, who, doubtless, would scorn to lend themselves to any questionable practices.

The prizes in the various lotteries range downwards in amount from 200,000 marks to 20 marks. They are of many different values, the smaller ones, of course, being predominant. "In the most fortunate events," says the prospectus, "the highest prize will amount to 500,000 marks," (£25,000). That sum would be obtained by any person who should prove so fortunate as to draw the last of the big prizes, provided it were the highest of them all, namely, 200,000 marks, a bonus of 300,000 marks being in that case added; this bonus, it may be observed, always attaches to the last of the big prizes which is drawn. The five highest prizes are usually 200,000, 100,000, 60,000, 40,000, and 30,000 marks, then follow five sums of 15,000, and 20 of 10,000 marks.

II.

In these lotteries the drawings are accomplished in seven series, the last being the greatest of all, yielding 28,500 prizes, and the sum referred to as bonus. The prices charged for tickets increase as the drawing proceeds—for a chance in the first drawing the cost is only six marks, and in the event of a prize being taken the matter is at an end, unless the "fortunate prize-taker" pleases to go on. In the event of his failing to obtain a prize, it is understood that the ticket must be renewed for the second drawing at a cost of 12 marks, and, if again unsuccessful, for the third drawing, the ticket for which is priced at 18 marks. A complete set of tickets, which all who begin may be forced to take, amounts to 126 marks, which is equivalent to £6 4s. sterling, and even after that sum has been disbursed the chances are that the infatuated gambler who proceeds so far in the venture may be rewarded by obtaining a prize of 115 marks, of which class of prize 26,850 are set down to be drawn; but, in all likelihood, the final drawing will be concluded and no prize will have been taken.

With a degree of cunning, however, that has gauged human nature pretty well, a gratis ticket for the first drawing in the next lottery is presented to all the losers, so that they may be lured into the net. Having waited for the result, no further action need be taken; the user of the ticket need not, unless he pleases, go on, but, as a rule, the agents with whom he has been dealing usually get him to go on once more, in the hope of being able to announce to him that his ticket has earned one of the capital prizes.

As has been indicated, the *bona fides* of these German money lotteries is above suspicion; the drawings are regulated by a set of seventeen rules, which provide for all the contingencies which are likely to arise. The operation of controlling, shuffling numbers to be drawn, casting them into the wheel, and the drawing itself, is attended to by a functionary of the Treasury Board, two public notaries, and a delegate from the general public. In regard to the process of drawing, the tickets simultaneously extracted from both wheels, namely, a number ticket and a prize ticket, are, in evidence of this correspondence folded together one into the other, then filed on a string, which remains in official custody. The result shown by the string alluded to shall conclusively and definitely settle any question as to the prize awarded to the respective number. A considerable discount is exacted on paying the prizes from the amounts mentioned on the tickets; the rate ranges from 10 per cent. on the smaller prizes to as much as 15 per cent. on those of 1000 marks and upwards. Sums of money won in these lotteries cannot be arrested by creditors.

III.

In looking over the lists of winning numbers, one cannot but be struck with the "runs of luck" which fall to consecutive numbers in the case of the smallest of all the prizes (145 marks). Runs of three and four figures are exceedingly common, and in cases five, six, seven and even eight consecutive numbers can be picked out from the list, as for instance:—201-2-3-4; 735-36-37-38-39; 931-32-33-34-35-36-37-38; 1717-18-19-20-21-22-23. With such runs (be it noted after six previous draws) and with one prize to every blank, one would suppose that to take two tickets would to a certainty secure a prize, but in "lotteries" there are no "certainties" and, even should one prize of the lowest amount be obtained, that would only re-imburse the cost of one ticket, leaving the gambler £6 out of pocket. The writer knows an instance of three tickets being purchased, and yet no prize was obtained. As has already been remarked, "no feature of modern civilisation is more remarkable than that the Germans should keep themselves in a perfect whirl of excitement by means of the gigantic money lotteries which are periodically organised in several of the larger towns and cities of Germany."

JUDGE KENYON AND A PRINCE OF WALES.

THE following note regarding the firmness of a judge in dealing with the Prince of Wales of a former period is worth reprinting. The matter refers to the licensing of a gambling house, a licence being then necessary for such places. The applicant was named Martindale, and on the name being mentioned in the course of another case Lord Kenyon said that "he remembered in a case tried before him, that Mr. Martindale's certificate as a bankrupt was proved of no legal effect because he had lost certain sums of money by gaming. It had been mentioned that spacious premises were preparing in which this person was to keep a gaming-house, under the patronage of an illustrious person. That could not be done without a licence. He trusted the magistrates would do their duty to the public—granting such a licence would be contrary to their duty ; there were gaming houses enough already."

When this became known, the Prince at once addressed a letter by the hand of the Attorney-General, demanding retractation and apology, which contained the following passage :—"It is true I have assented to my name being placed amongst others as a member of a new club, to be under the management of Mr. Martindale, merely for the purpose of social intercourse, of which I can never object to be a promoter ; especially as it was represented to me that the object of this institution was to enable his trustees to render justice to several fair claimants. Give me leave to tell you that you have totally mistaken my character and turn, for of all men universally known to have the least predilection to play, I am perhaps the very man in the world who stands the strongest and the most proverbially so upon that point." Lord Kenyon, however, stood to his guns like the man he was, and in his reply said : " I have for years laboured to put an end to gaming. Many inferior offenders have been brought to justice, but no effectual prosecutions have commenced against the houses in the neighbourhood of St. James's where examples are set to the lower orders which are a great scandal to the country." It was something at the time indicated to have such a judge on the bench.

MR. MAX O'RELL'S FIRST DERBY.

THIS clever writer, in a communication to a weekly journal, gives the following account of his first Derby. Though I have spent sixteen years in England I had never seen the Derby until to-day. Can there be in the whole world such a dirty, hooting, swearing, brazen-throated, foul-mouthed crowd to be seen ? And I am told that things are vastly improved, and the scenes to be witnessed to-day are no match for the Derbys of Auld Lang Syne! And what a road! From Westminster we drove over a route strewn thick with bills, paper débris, advertisements of fusees, advertisements of the gospel tent to be found on the course, with orange peelings, cocoanut shells, empty bottles.

The only redeeming feature in the whole thing seemed to me the treatment of horses, the care with which they were driven, and at intervals, along the road down, watered and refreshed. On the course I saw a man furiously driving and whipping a poor horse which had unfortunately got into his company, quite set upon by an indignant crowd that looked likely to make a very good amateur R.S.P.A. The working man is no doubt better aware than any one who talks to him of humanity to his horse, that it pays to treat the animal well. Looking at the way in which he is often found treating his wife, the extra-gentleness extended to Dobbin may arise from shrewdness. Or is it something else? "A fellow-feeling makes us wondrous kind." In the carts, cars, shandrydans that I passed on the road, there were three distinct types of face: the bulldog, the fish, and the sheep. What an unlovely company occupied each cart, with its layer or two of men in front, and all the women (the females, I should rather say) stowed away behind in true British fashion.

Where there was an apparent absence of any linen on the persons of the men, there was an extra display of ostrich feathers on the wonderful hats of the women. As the various vehicles discharged their cargoes, some truly amazing toilettes that had been blushing comparatively unseen, in the carts on the way down, now joined in the general jarring and swearing. One, noted carefully in detail, will give an idea of many, though I doubt if it could have been outshone on the whole course. Dress of sapphire blue silk, covered to the waist with beaded frills; a gigantic hat of crimson velvet surrounded by a wide band of gold lace, and further adorned with a long and broad encircling plume of a dazzling apple-green hue. The finishing touch was put to this attire by a train of black lace, which started from the waist and trailed a long yard behind its wearer.

Just after witnessing the check in the career of the Jehu whom the crowd took in hand for lashing his horse, I stumbled upon a female fight. Two enraged creatures, with fine feathers and foul tongues, were in the thick of a quarrel which they evidently intended to settle on the spot. No interference here. On the contrary, hearty encouraging cries from the male bystanders of "Go it, old gal, I'll 'old yer 'at," and other evidences of the absence of any intention to spoil sport.

The main business of the day on the Downs is evidently eating, drinking, and getting photographed. I will venture to doubt whether a half of the people who flock to Epsom on Derby day see a horse race. Horseplay there was of course in plenty. Is it not an invariable accompaniment of every British holiday-making in which the masses take part? On the whole, however, it must be admitted that it was a good-tempered crowd, rough and rowdy, but not riotous; ridiculous and dirty, but with here and there a diverting touch, such as the impromptu foot-bath of an individual who removed the dust from his boots by calmly swilling a pail of water over them. To fun pure and simple the nearest approach seemed to be the wearing of a big bonnet by a man.

How the cockney loves a holiday, and how he will toil at taking it! It would be hard to say wherein the pleasure of the Derby lay for the six fellows whom I noted going down with a hand cart. I say *with*, for only four of them were upon it, No. 5 was in the shafts, and No. 6 pushed behind. Where they had joined the stream I cannot of course say, but when we passed them they were on the Epsom side of Tooting, and with baskets on board were clearly enough bound for the course, if not for the grand stand. To one who goes to mingle in the crowd and not to look on from the grand stand, the impression left is not a pleasant or a cheerful one. I returned home feeling that if horse racing was instituted for the improvement of the equine race, it has certainly not conduced much to the improvement of the human one.

"BILLY'S" EPITAPH.

The following epitaph on a famous sporting dog called "Billy," is from the pen of that famous sporting journalist, Mr. Pierce Egan, and appeared originally in *Bell's Life*.

"The celebrated hero of the canine race, to the joy of the rats, lost his *wind* on Monday, February 23, 1829, in Panton Street, Haymarket. The body-snatchers and dog-priggers are outdone upon this suit, and the remains of Billy, instead of being obscured in clay, are preserved in an elegant glass case and gilt frame. The ex-champion, Tom Cribb, who liked Billy when alive, still likes him although told out. Billy was the property of Charley Aistrop when he last barked out an adieu, although Cribb was his tender nurse up to the time he gave up the ghost. The rats, it is said, are extremely glad to find that Billy has left no successor to give them the nip." Then follows a monody upon Billy's death, in imitation of "Not a drum was heard," from which we select the following verses as the best:

> "Not a *bark* was heard, but a mournful whine
> Broke in cadence slow from the race canine;
> And the pricked-up ear and the wagging tail
> Were drooping low 'mid the gen'ral wail.
>
> "'Not a bark was heard—e'en the snarling cur
> Had his ivories closed, and without demur
> The dustman and beggar and sweep let pass,
> So down in the mouth the whole race, alas!
>
> "Not a bell was toll'd, not a shop was shut,
> Not a searcher deigned his fives to put
> On the lifeless corse of the Prince of Dogs,
> Whose history every history flogs.
>
> "Not a bark was heard, but a lively squeak
> Was echoed from rat to rat (a whole week),
> From Whitechapel Church to Piccadilly,
> Of ' Long life to grim Death for boning Billy.'"

THE RISE OF LAWN TENNIS.

THERE is scarcely any modern game of skill which has "caught on" both in England and America during modern times more universally than lawn tennis, and unlike the game of croquet, which afforded such ample opportunities for flirtation, it has come to stay. The secret of its popularity is probably owing to the presence of the ladies, and the becoming dresses which may be worn by the sex, as much as to the opportunities it affords for physical exercise and the exhibition of grace and skill. Like cricket, it is pre-eminently a game for sunny skies and green swards, for quick eye and ready hand, for sound lungs and agile legs. But there the similarity ends, for while cricket—except on some very extraordinary occasions—is devoted to men, lawn tennis, by its including the fairer and weaker sex amongst its votaries, appeals to a larger and more extended constituency.

TITLED GAMBLING LADIES.

A RICH harvest of gambling anecdotes might be gathered from the numerous memoirs and biographies of important persons which have issued from the press during the last half century; indeed, acting on Mr. Lockhart's maxim that from any four books on a given subject you may easily compile a fifth, such a collection of really interesting information as to the personal habits of many notable people who lived and flourished at the end of the last or the beginning of the present century, might be brought together as could not fail to command the attention of the reading public and prove singularly attractive. In the days referred to, " play " ran high and thousands changed hands at the dice or card table at all hours of the day and night. The evil of course was declaimed against, and strenuous efforts made to abate or abolish it, and in 1799 Lord Chief Justice Kenyon, in one of his charges, recommended the prosecution of fashionable (unlicensed) gambling establishments, saying, "If any of the guilty parties are convicted, whatever may be their rank or station, though they may be the first ladies in the land, they shall certainly exhibit themselves in the pillory." The following week Gilray had a caricature of Lady Buckinghamshire and Lady Archer in the pillory. About that date and long before, ladies of quality gambled even more heavily than men, and, as is well known, ladies of title kept gambling houses in the first half of the eighteenth century. An entry in the journals of the House of Lords, dated 29th April, 1745, distinctly proves the fact, for according to it, Ladies Mornington and Cassilis claimed privilege of peerage in resisting certain peace officers while in the execution of their duty, " in suppressing the public gaming-houses kept by the said ladies," but the plea of the fair and noble claimants was not allowed. At that time, gambling-houses were licensed in the same way as public-houses and music-halls are now, and it was for not being so that the castles of the two ladies named above were invaded.

COCK-FIGHTING REMINISCENCES.

NEWMARKET, of which place James I. and his grandson, Charles II., were what would to-day be termed *habitués*, has always ranked very highly amongst the lovers of " feather," and within, comparatively speaking, modern times, the theatre, which stood near the Rutland Arms, served as a cock-pit during the winter months. Mr. Gurney, the Norwich banker, whose pens were on the Exning-road, was a staunch patron of this pit, and both here and on the Mill Hill (in the present Wesleyan Chapel) the Gurney "pies" and "black-reds" earned for themselves undying fame. To such an extent was the sport carried on at Newmarket, that, scarce half a century ago, the following were only some of the "grooms" who had their own feeding pens in or near the famous racing town, viz., Jem Robinson and Dick Prince, on the Mill Hill; Joe Rogers, in close proximity thereto; Harry Neale and Sam Chifney, in Shakebag; and the Boyces, in the High street. Closely following the above worthies, and at a critical period in the history of the sport, for they had to contend not only with an opponent whose name appeared in the articles, but also with the myrmidons of the law, came Frank and William Butler, Sam Rogers, and Jem Godding, *inter alia*, and bravely they fought for the heritage bequeathed to them by their forefathers.

During these go-ahead days there is nothing more refreshing, or more interesting, than a chat in the smoking room of a Newmarket hostelry (or on the Heath, if a smoking suit is not the taste), with the veterans whose memories carry them back to the days when Lord Derby and Mr. Gurney fought their great matches in the town.

One has an anecdote of some famous cock who killed his adversary before he left his setter's hands; another, of a stag who went scathless through seven battles; whilst, mayhap, a jockey expresses his willingness to bet £5 against any cock that has "run" in a trainer's yard, for, he adds, "you see, they physic their horses so!" Physic'd or not, they had some rare birds, and many a good one travelled by the Chesterford road, slung to the back of the "Magnet," the night coach from London to Newmarket, in the days when the white-legged cocks from Knowsley were thought as much of as *Priam*, or, as a worthy old trainer told me but yesterday, as the mighty *Plenipo* himself.

Second only in importance to the London and Newmarket mains were those fought at Chester and York. Of the former pit, the Egertons, Cottons, Warburtons, and Leighs, of Lyme, were the great supporters; whilst Sir Francis Boynton and Colonel Mellish (the patron of Jem Belcher, the prince of pugilists and the friend of George, the Prince Regent) were especially fond of the one near Bootham Bar, in the Minster City. Preston, in the North, and Stamford, in the South, were also celebrated for the great mains fought at these places, and on which sums were wagered that would put the modern plungers, be they punters at baccarat or backers of horses, quite in the shade. The Preston pit is now, I believe, a nonconformist chapel, and that at Stamford, on my last visit, was doing duty as a newspaper office. It is recorded that the famous Joe Gilliver once fed a match at Lincoln, in which the main money was 5,000 guineas, added to a stake of 1,000 guineas each battle, to say nothing of the bets that would most assuredly be made during the progress of the fighting. It is also satisfactory to know that Gilliver was the winner of this important engagement, five out of the seven battles falling to the veteran's share.

A story is still remembered of an elderly maiden lady, who complained of being unable to sleep when a passenger of the coach in question, on account of the crowing of these outside customers—the first time her rest had been broken in such a ruthless manner. Of a truth, she was of a different nature to the widow of the late Sir Henry Boynton, who used frequently to tell with delight how she had often ridden forty miles on a pillion behind her husband, to assist at cock matches in Yorkshire.

BOOK-MAKING AND BETTING.

MANY of the persons who, as the saying goes, "make their living on the turf," make no bones about "milking" the public by means of an animal that is not intended to run, or if it runs is meant to be last in the race instead of first. "Milking" is the slang term which is used to denote these "robberies" of the public. All such practices tend to promote the office of the *Bookmaker*. This person may either be in league with an owner of race horses and an executant of his wishes, or he may simply be a layer of "the odds," without taking any part in the working of what are called "stable commissions." It is his business to lay the market odds against all the horses in a race; and generally speaking, he is able on most of the great handicaps of the season to earn a good profit. Only one horse can win, and the bookmaker obtains for himself all the sums of money which have been deposited with him, or promised to him if he gives credit, on the nineteen or twenty horses which have been beaten in the contest.

It is by estimating what is done by the bookmaker that we obtain an insight into the losses of the turf. Only one horse, as we have said, can win a race, whilst many may lose it. For some popular handicaps as many as a hundred and fifty animals may be entered to compete, and half of the number may be betted upon to greater or lesser amounts.

At one time there were bookmakers who would stand to pay fifty thousand pounds over a popular handicap. But these days are gone. Betting men have become so numerous, that the books they engage for are much smaller than they used to be. There are hundreds of betting men now for the tens there were a quarter of a century since. Considering the magnitude of the business, it would be no exaggeration to say that there is far more money lost over horse-racing than goes into the pockets of the winning owners. The public not only make up the amounts which are won by the successful men, but they also pay the "piper" in a large measure when the horses lose. It is the public who yield the bookmakers their handsome profits, and who pay all the miscellaneous expenses of the turf. There are not twenty backers of horses who can keep themselves at the game, yet thousands rush upon the turf year after year, anxious to try the lottery, each thinking that he is the person who is destined to succeed. But they fight an unequal battle; the "bookmaker" is sure to win the game in the end.

A determined stand has been made of late years against what is called "ready-money betting," and an Act of Parliament has been passed to put it down. Originally, when a bet was made, the money was staked by both the parties to it, in the hands of a neutral person, who paid the sum to the winner when the event was determined. Now, among "gentlemen bettors," and those gentlemen who keep accounts with the larger bookmakers, no money changes hands till after a race has taken place. We do not approve of betting in any shape, thinking the world quite able to move on without it; there cannot be any doubt that betting has become a huge social nuisance, and if it could be altogether suppressed, both among rich and poor, a mighty good would be accomplished.

IN THE DAYS OF DICK CHRISTIAN.

THE Druid has many stories to tell of the doings of Dick, of which the following is one; it is given here as told by Dick himself. "The Marquis of Hastings was one of my pupils. I was two months at his place before he came of age. He sent for me to Donington and I broke all his horses; I'd never seen him before. The first meet I went out with him was Wartnaby Stoke Pits. I rode by his side, and I says, 'My lord, we'll save a bit distance if we take this fence.' So he looks at me a bit queer like, and he says laughing, 'Why, Christian, I was never over a fence in my life.' 'God bless me, my lord, you don't say so!' and I was quite took back at hearing him say so. 'It's quite true, Christian, I really mean it,' says he. 'Well, my lord,' says I, 'you're on a beautiful fencer; he'll walk up to it and jump it. Now I'll go over first.' 'Well, if I fall off you won't laugh at me,' he says, not looking very comfortable. 'That I won't, my lord,' I answers. 'You put your hands well down on his withers and let him come.' It was a bit of a low-staked hedge and a ditch; he got over as nice as possible, and he gave quite a hurrah like, and he says, 'There, I'm over my first fence, that's a blessing.' Then I got him over a great many little places, and he quite took to it, and went on uncommon well. Years afterwards, at Six Hills, the day before Clinker and Clasher ran their great match, when he had a lot of nobs about him, he calls out, 'Here is my old tutor; I was never over a fence till he showed me how'—and then he told the gentlemen all about it. Whenever I saw him he always joked me about it. He was a nice gentleman to teach; he'd just do anything you told him. That's the way to get on."

Here is another. "I'm a good 'un to waste; you wouldn't think it, though, to look at me; I'm so thick across, and there's not much to come off my legs. Well, I once got off twelve pounds in about as many hours. I was at it one way or another from half-past four one afternoon till six next morning. I was at Birmingham, and Captain Fendal he wanted me to ride 11st. at eight o'clock to enter him, and I turned the scale at 11st. 11lb. So he would have me go into a hot vapour bath. I went in on his grey horse at Alcester next day, and he had to be there usual time—twenty minutes—and a man comes, 'How do you feel?' 'I feel very well,' I says; 'I'll be in a bit longer.' Then he comes back with a tray, and begins: 'Gentlemen sometimes has coffee when they're in a bath.' So I puts my head out of the little hole; I was tied in, you see, and I says, 'D—n your coffee; I'm hot enough outside and in; take it away.' In five minutes he comes again, and I says : 'I'm doing uncommon nicely; just you wait.' It was pouring off me then. Well, when that five minutes was over he didn't ask me what I'd like to do, but he whips the curtains away, wraps me in a blanket, and has me off across the passage to another room, under a reg'lar pile of blankets for half-an-hour. My heart, how it did bump to be sure! I'd just been and overdone it. Then the Captain he'd been and got the physic, and a precious stiff dose they'd mixed for me. They dressed me, and the Captain and I went off in a chaise. When I was two miles off Alcester I got out and walked, and the Captain he went on to get me a bedroom ready. When I got to the inn Mason and Becher and Powell were all there in the coffee-room; they'd come down to ride. When I went in they says : 'How are you, old cock?' and then the Captain comes in with his, 'Well, Dick, how are you after your boiling?' At six next morning he knocks at my bedroom and up I gets. I went into a grocer's shop and asks them to weigh me. I said, 'Put in eleven stone.' The Captain he says, 'Nonsense, Dick; you'll be six pounds more than that.' I said, 'I know I'm right,' and it's as true as I sit here alive I could scarcely pull the eleven stone down—the weights had the best of me. The Captain wanted me to have some breakfast, but I said, 'No; a very little will fetch me up.' So I had a cup of coffee and a bit of boiled bacon, and a shaving of bread and butter, and just two glasses of sherry; that made 11st. 4lb.; it's a ticklish thing is weight—but I rode the race and won it."

THE CLINKER AND CLASHER MATCH.

THE following relates to the much-written-about Clinker and Clasher match. It was for £1,500 a-side, and Dick rode Clinker and Squire Osbaldeston Clasher. "We weighed at Dalby, the Squire and I—bless me! I was never in such condition, and away we trotted to Gartree Hill. 'Captain Ross,' he says to me, 'you must wait.' 'It's giving away a certainty,' I says, 'and if I get a fall then I'm all behind.' But it was no manner of use talking. Sir St. Vincent Cotton and Mr. Gilmour started us, and Mr. Malin was umpire. We rode 12st. a-piece; I was in tartan, and the Squire, of course he'd be in green. When we were at the post he says, 'Now, Christian, I know your orders, but one thing I do ask, if I fall don't jump on me.' I said, 'I give you my word, Squire, I won't.' The gentlemen, they could hardly keep with us, and some had two or three horses fixed. We was almost touching one another over Sharplands. 'Squire,' I says, 'you're beat for a hundred pounds;' but he made no answer. I got over the rails at Twyford Brook. Clasher hits 'em with all his four legs, and chucked the Squire right on to his neck. Clinker took 'em like a bird. The Squire he lands in a bog, and his horse makes a dead stop; it did take a deal out of him. Then I jumps right into a dung heap up to Clinker's knees. We'd no idea them things was there. Going up to John o' Gaunt's Field we was together, but I turns to get some rails in the course—he was such a good 'un at rails was Clinker. I thought we was winning, but down he comes at the last fence, dead beat, lies for some minutes, then gets up lively as ever, but in no manner of form, looking round as a hoop. They held Clasher up, and flung water in his face, and he won in the last hundred yards from superior training. The Squire did ride that match day, to be sure. I went up to call on him one afternoon at St. John's Wood, and he pointed to that picture of the finish hanging up opposite the fireplace, and he says to me, 'Dick, that Clinker and Clasher day beat me a deal more than the 200 miles match.'"

HOW SIR TATTON SYKES PUNISHED A PUGILIST.

THERE are, at least, a hundred good stories told of that fine old sportsman, Sir Tatton Sykes, and the following is one of them. When paying one of his annual visits to London, after he had ridden, as usual, every yard of the way from Sledmore, Sir Tatton called at Tom Spring's, in Holborn, and, speaking in his usual shrill tone, asked to be served with a tankard of the oldest and strongest ale. The only other person in the room besides himself, was a square-set, broad-shouldered man, evidently a member of the pugilistic profession. When the tankard was brought in by the barmaid, the fellow said, mimicking Sir Tatton's voice, "Here, Betsy, bring that ale to me, and take a jug of mild ale to that old woman." Sir Tatton looked at him steadily for a moment, then, without a word, buttoned up his coat and turned up his cuffs. The pugilist was up in an instant, never doubting that he would finish off such an antagonist with one blow of his fist, but Sir Tatton, quick as lightning, had planted a thunderer upon his jaw, and away they fought, hammer and tongs, for ten minutes. At the end of that time the professional found himself in the coal-scuttle, and so severely punished that he declined another round. "Now, my lad," said Sir Tatton, "you can drink up the ale and welcome, and after doing so, you can go home and tell your wife you have been well thrashed by an old woman."

TRICKS OF THE POACHERS.

A VERY clever dealer in game, carrying on business in Glasgow, and who, having been in the trade all the working part of his life, had the reputation of being a very shrewd person. But for all his experience and knowledge he was once upon a time very cleverly "done" by a band of poachers, in the matter of a "deal" in pheasant eggs. The men alluded to were in league with a country dealer and being very hard up for money took him into their confidence, and arranged to supply the Glasgow poulterer with a few dozens of very fine eggs, all of them from keepers who were giving up hand-rearing. Glad to do a stroke of business, a contract was at once entered into, and in due time the eggs arrived. The town buyer, in order to see that all was *en regle*, put the eggs to various tests, and although he made them out to be a first class lot, still there was a something about them he did not like, an undefined something, however, which he could not solve. The trade in the eggs grew and was carried on for three or four weeks, when at length a gentleman who, liking the look of the commodity, had bought largely at first, and ordered an additional lot, found out to his great astonishment that, instead of hatching pheasants, he was only breeding bantams! The undefined "something" felt by the purchaser was solved! The eggs had been dyed, and the dying was done so skilfully as to defy identification. The country dealer was imprisoned for the fraud in which his connivance was clearly enough proved, but unfortunately, the other scoundrels who had had a finger in the pie escaped the consequences of their guilt.

HOW GEORGE PAYNE LOST HIS FORTUNE.

MANY interesting stories and anecdotes have been published from time to time relating to the social and turf career of the late Mr. George Payne, who during his life time was a popular person on all the race courses of the kingdom, and who betted on nearly every race that he witnessed. Unlike Sir Joseph Hawley (of Blueskin renown) who made a fortune on the turf, Mr. Payne may be said to have lost one. This gentleman inherited from his father, who was killed in a duel, estates which, when he came of age, yielded an income of £17,000 per annum, likewise a sum of £300,000 in ready money, so that his yearly income could not have been less than thirty thousand pounds, all of which took unto itself wings and flew away, in other words, Mr. Payne's great fortune was lost on the turf and at the gambling tables; he was never lucky on the turf, and had a sum of £30,000 to pay for racing losses at the very beginning of his career. There was no position in life which Mr. Payne might not have aspired to; Parliament and such honours as it might ultimately lead to, was open to him, had he chosen to offer himself as a candidate. But as a writer recently said while commenting on his career: He squandered health, wealth, and happiness in gambling, and disdaining the temptations of Parliament, though often urged to stand for his native county, where he was so popular that he would have been placed at the head of the poll whenever and as often as he chose to offer himself as a candidate for election, he preferred the attractions of the turf, the chase, and the card-table. In addition to trying his luck at the card table and in the betting rings of the various race courses of the country, Mr. Payne was a keen speculator in all kinds of produce and in stocks and shares of various kinds, and of his adventures in that line, various stories have been told, some of them being of a rather amusing kind; the following is one of them which he used to tell himself, with much good humour; it relates to a transaction in the purchase of tallow into which he entered upon one occasion. It was during the Crimean war a friend advised him that tallow was sure to rise and recommended him strongly to buy a lot of P.Y.C., or "prime yellow candle." Acting upon this advice, he went to the City and betook himself to a broker in Mincing Lane with whose address he had been furnished. Having given instructions that ever so many tierces of tallow should be bought for him, he added the information that his address was at Steven's

Hotel, Bond Street, and was asked by the clerk whether it was "for delivery?" Not understanding the question, he answered in the affirmative, and forgot all about the matter until, a fortnight later, he was astonished at having a greasy document put into his hand, with an announcement that "the man had come with the tallow." Going to the door, he found a cart full of tallow casks standing before it, and, as far as the eye could reach, a similar string of carts behind it.

"Never trust me," he exclaimed to a knot of friends whom he found at the Turf Club, "if Bond Street was not choked with tallow carts up to Oxford Street. That," as he often said subsequently, "was my first and last transaction in tallow." Mr. Payne's personal expenditure was at all times very large. An old Newmarket trainer, who knew him well, calculated that in times anterior to the introduction of railroads, Mr. Payne had spent more money in chaises-and-four than would have sufficed, if capitalised, to yield a competency to a man of moderate desires. The amount expended in travelling during his long and active life must have been enormous.

Another story that Mr. Payne used to tell about himself may be given here. Whilst one day on his way to Goodwood races he was taking his ticket at the railway station, when through the crowd there was thrust a hand which tapped him on the shoulder. "Take me one, George," said a tall man well dressed in a costume rather horsey than elegant. Mr. Payne took the ticket and handed it over to the free-and-easy speaker, who said, "Thanks, George: settle at Goodwood," and disappeared in the crowd for ever and aye. Never from that moment did Mr. Payne set eyes upon that hardened welsher, and he was never tired of telling the story and of laughing over it.

"You see," he used to add, exegetically, "more people know Tom Fool than Tom Fool knows. I did not know him from the dead, but thought I must have met him abroad somewhere. Clever rascal! he is welcome, I am sure, to his fraud and the proceeds."

ABOUT DERBY TIPSTERS.

THE fact that people sometimes dream the Derby winner, and that their dreams have occasionally been realized, was at one time actively taken advantage of by the ever-industrious tipsters to put money in their purses. The style of advertisement which some years ago was usual may here be repeated : "A lady who is totally ignorant of horse-racing has just had the extraordinary good fortune to dream the result of the Derby. The horse—the name of which will be given by a friend of the lady—is not one of the leading favourites. Terms, half-a-crown in postage stamps. *N.B.*—The money received will be distributed in charity.—Apply to Mrs. B—M—L—," etc., etc. This clumsy imposture was speedily detected by various persons, as "the lady," with some ulterior motive in view, no doubt, sent a different horse to persons who applied from different towns, as was at once found on the meeting of a gentleman residing in Perth with an Edinburgh friend, each of whom had sent for the fortune-yielding dream.

The accomplished tipster, whether he has a dream to retail or not, usually resorts to tactics similar to the above in order to obtain the largest possible number of shillings. That he gives the winner and a horse for a place in the Derby to some of his customers is, by this way of doing things, assured. If he has, say, a thousand applications for his tip, he will prepare probably half-a-dozen circulars, each containing a different selection of horses. Taking tips on this year's [1884] Derby as an example of the way business is done, the series of tips may be arranged as follows : " Queen Adelaide or Harvester to win, Departure's dam colt, a place." That may be number one, whilst number two may read as follows : "I think Talisman or Harvester certain to win, and Richmond will be sure to get a place." Another circular may be worded as follows : " Osborne's people are cock-sure about Waterford; back it for win and 1, 2, 3 ; my own fancy is Richmond, although Harvester is bound to run well."

It will be seen from these specimens of the tipster's art that pains are taken to " grow " the business. In future circulars " Chanticleer's " great tip of " Harvester for the Derby " was advertised in all the sporting papers, and a rattling business resulted on the St. Leger and some of the great Autumn Handicaps, a similar mode of doing business being, of course, resorted to, with a similar or even greater degree of success—there are thousands of persons who are ever ready to give a shilling for the straight tip, whether from " Chanticleer," or some other tipster. The inventive tipster, as I may call him, has, however, been largely superseded by the professional tipsters who communicate their prophecies to the daily and other journals, most of which now devote a considerable portion of their space to the affairs of sport.

ONE OF LORD OXFORD'S ADVENTURES.

Few men ever sacrificed so much time or so much property on practical or speculative sporting as the "sporting" Earl of Oxford, whose eccentricities are too firmly indented upon "the tablet of the memory" ever to be obliterated from the diversified rays of retrospection.

Among his experiments of fancy was a determination to drive four red-deer stags in a phaeton, instead of horses, and these he had reduced to perfect discipline for his excursions and short journeys upon the road; but, unfortunately, as he was one day driving to Newmarket, their ears were saluted with the cry of a pack of hounds, which, soon after crossing the road in the rear, caught scent of the "four-in-hand," and commenced a new kind of chase with "breast high" alacrity.

The novelty of this scene was rich beyond description.

In vain did his lordship exert all his charioteering skill; in vain did his well-trained grooms energetically endeavour to ride before the deer; reins, trammels and the weight of the carriage were of no effect, for they went with the celerity of a whirlwind.

Luckily, however, his lordship had been accustomed to drive this set of "fiery-eyed steeds" to the Ram Inn, at Newmarket, which was most happily at hand, and to this his lordship's most fervent prayers and ejaculations had been ardently directed.

Into the yard they suddenly bounded, to the dismay of ostlers and stable-boys, who seemed to have lost every faculty upon the occasion.

Here they were luckily overpowered, and the stags, the phaeton, and his lordship were all instantaneously huddled together in a barn, just as the hounds appeared in full cry at the gate.

FEATS OF CAPTAIN BARCLAY'S FATHER.

Some good stories have been told of the feats of strength performed by the father of Captain Barclay (a Quaker), the hero in his day of the greatest pedestrian feat which had ever been accomplished, namely, the walking of a thousand miles in a thousand successive hours, as will be found recorded in another part of this volume. The following anecdote will show that the Captain's father was possessed of almost herculean strength of body.—While walking in Ury grounds one morning he found a tinker grazing his donkey in one of the grass enclosures near the roadside. Mr. Barclay at once ordered the animal to be removed. This the tinker refused to do, whereupon Mr. Barclay lifted the donkey in his arms and threw it clear over the hedge into the road. The tinker, who knew the character of the man he had to deal with, thereupon jumped over the hedge and tossed the animal back into the field, only to find it the next instant again thrown out. This game of shuttlecock went on until the life was tossed out of the poor "cuddy," whereupon Mr. Barclay, struck with the extraordinary strength of the tinker, took him to Ury House, where he was feasted for some time, and was sent away with the price of more than the donkey in his pocket.

Of the many stories of which Mr. Barclay was the hero, the following, which was related by Sir Thomas Dick Lauder, is interesting :—A stalwart Highland soldier named Ian More, or Big John, had been badgered by the officers of his regiment into fighting a famous English boxer. The Highlander, although he entered the ring, did not seem inclined to strike, but latterly got so stung by the insults of the Englishman that he lifted his hand, and with one fell swoop of his clenched fist he smashed the skull of his antagonist and laid him dead at his feet. Ian was soon after this discharged, and on his way home to Strathconnan he stayed one night at Stonehaven. Here the landlord of the inn informed Ian of a short cut through the parks of Ury that would considerably shorten his journey, but at the same time he was warned that if the Laird found him trespassing he would turn him back.

"Tak' care," said the landlord, "and no meet the Laird, for he's an awfu' chiel, though a Quaker."

Ian, confident that he could hold his own in an encounter even with so terrible a man, said he would run the risk, and soon after sunrise took the forbidden path. He had not got far on the road, however, when he met Mr. Barclay, who informed him that no one was allowed to go that way, and he would have to turn back.

"She be sorry tat she has angered her honour," said Ian, bowing submissively, "but, troth, it be ower far a gate to turn back noo."

"Far gate or short gate, friend, back thou must go," said Mr. Barclay.

"Hoot na ! she canna gang back," said Ian.

"But thou must go back, friend," said the Laird ; "and if

thou wilt not go back readily, I'll turn thee back, whether thou wilt or not."

"Hoot, toot, she be no fit to turn her back," said Ian, with one of his broad, good-humoured grins.

"I'll try," said the Laird, laying his hands on Ian's shoulders, to carry his threat into execution.

"An' she be for tat," said Ian, "let her lay doon her wallet, and she'll see whether she can gar her turn back or no."

"By all means, my good friend," said the Laird, who enjoyed a thing of the kind beyond all measure. The wallet being quietly deposited on the ground, to it they went; but ere they had well buckled together, Ian put down the Laird beside the wallet with the same case that he put down the wallet itself.

"Ha!" said the Laird, as much overcome at a defeat which he had never before experienced as he had been by the strength that produced it, "thou didst take me too much o' the sudden, friend; but give me fair play. Let me up and I will essay to wrestle with thee again."

"Weel, weel," said Ian coolly, "she may tak' her ain laizier to rise, for her nainsel' has plenty o' sun afore night."

"Come on, then," said Mr. Barclay, grappling again with his antagonist and putting forth all his strength, which Ian allowed him full time to exert against him, whilst in defiance of it all, he stood firm and unshaken as a rock.

"Noo, doon she goes again!" said Ian, deliberately prostrating the Laird a second time, "an' gin tat be nae enough she'll put her doon a third time, sae tat she'll need nae mair puttens toon."

"No, no, friend, enough for this bout; I own that thou art the better man. This is the first time that my back was ever laid on the grass. Come away with me, good fellow—thou shalt go home with me." Ian sojourned for a fortnight at Ury House, and then proceeded homewards to Strathconnan.

THE BOOKMAKER OF THE OUTER RING.

(From Blackwood's Magazine.)

THE bell rings. I wend my way to the paddock. "Five shillings entrance." "Not for Jack," say I to myself; but I catch sight of an old trainer whom I knew very well in years gone by. I buy a card, and hail him through the narrow openings of the paling fence. He looks astonished.

"What! you squire? what the—well, what are you up to? You always were a rum 'un;" and he looked at my clothes, "what ever," and he relapsed into good old Berkshire—"what ever beest thou arter?"

"Too dirty," said I, "for the grand stand or enclosure; but, look here,—for auld lang syne, mark the winners on my card; p'raps I'm hard up, anyhow I want to bet, so just—I've not deserted my wife and children, I've not mortgaged my lands, but I'm just on the spree."

"Always was as mad as a hatter from a boy,"

he audibly muttered; but he took the card, marked it very carefully, slowly, and deliberately, returned it. "There you are, squire; I've done more for you than I would for any blessed man on this course, but—" and then

Some parting injunction bestowed with great unction,

which afterwards

I strove to recall, but forgot like a dunce,

and off I went studying the card.

A man—his name I can recall, for it was on his hat, "Dicky Dawkins, Bookmaker"—was shouting the odds. "Six to one bar one for the first race!" he cried. His dress was strange; his hat was tall and white, bar his name and titles inscribed on it in large black letters; his coat was in stripes of red and white, eke so his nether garments.

"What do you bar?" I shouted.

"The Fotheringay Colt, captain, and three to one against 'im."

I looked at my card. Fotheringay Colt marked. "I'm on for five shillings." I dubbed down the dust, got my ticket, and ah! bless my honest old friend, the trainer! the colt won in a canter. And so on all through the day—almost always winning, thanks to my good old friend, until the last race, and then my modest adventures had resulted in a gain of ten guineas. My card was consulted again; Maid of Perth marked for the last—a selling race. "What against Maid of Perth, Mr. Dawkins?"

"Evens, my noble general;" how quickly I got promotion.

"Done," said I; money and ticket quickly followed.

She won, but only by a short head, and I rushed towards the stand of the man in motley. But what a crowd was there.

A specious, civil kind of rascal made for me, touching his hat. "A heavy settling, sir. It may be," confidentially, " the last comers may have to wh'stle for their money, for the bookmakers are hit devilish hard; but if you'll give me your ticket; I know Mr. Dawkins, sir, right well, sir; believe I have the honour, sir, to know you, sir; also from Loamshire, sir; mum's the word, sir; no offence, I hope. A small commission, sir, and you shall have your money, sir, before you can say Jack Robinson."

Oh, what a fool I was! I have a temptation to swear even now when I think of it; I gave him my ticket and half-a-crown, and before I could say Jack Robinson he was gone—never, oh, never to return.

He was gone!—" abiit, excessit, evasit, erupit!" Gone also was my ticket, lost my half-crown.

I waited till all the crowd round Dicky were paid, and then, feeling like a most awful fool, approached the great man.

"You will quite remember," said I, "our last bet; evens you laid against Maid of Perth. A friend of yours took my ticket, ten guineas, but he has not come back."

A volley of oaths was my answer; no longer was I a noble general or a gallant captain. I was—but " words are wanting to say what; what a man shouldn't be, I was that." Our voices rose; a crowd collected, and as I had no wish to get into a disreputable row I said—" Well, at least give me the name of the hotel where you put up at in Salisbury." A hotel card was flung to me with an oath, and I walked away and bided my time. As I tramped into Salisbury, Dicky and his friends passed me in an open waggonette, and placed their fingers in that objectionable way to their noses whereby the noble Briton signifies that he holds you in contempt.

"Tout vient a qui tait attendre," said I to myself; and at length I reached my hotel, got shaved, washed, opened my portmanteau, arrayed myself in my best clothes, got out my card case, and proceeded, strong in temper, strong in sense of injury done to me, to seek the redoubtable Dicky Dawkins. Arrived at his hotel, I sent up my card.

"Cannot see you, sir," said the grinning waiter; "Mr. Dawkins is dining—never does business after seven p.m., sir."

I brushed past him. I found Mr. Dawkins' room by the smell of dinner; there he was with some dozen of the gang dining so well, and I was so hungry.

"Ten guineas, sir, if you please, that I won off you on Maid of Perth, and before you swallow another morsel," I said.

He looked at me—some of the gang rose up with oaths and threatening aspect.

"Oh, sir, I don't like to be disturbed at my meals, but sit down, sir, take a bite and a drink with us, and we shall wash out the debt; you were the gentleman who gave up his ticket, so you said—old dodge that—but I'll give you a good dinner, and your whack of liquor; but if I pay you one farthing I'll be—"

"Mr. Dawkins," I interrupted, "I'll eat with you, drink with you, or fight with you; but first," and I came close up to him, "I'll have ten pounds ten shillings out of you. Now, look here! I saw that rascal who took my ticket—ah! by heavens, there he is now, trying to slink off! Sit down, sir, sit down, or it will be the worse for you. Well, I saw him on the course talking to you; but here is better proof, he is eating at your table—one of your respectable friends. Now, unless you fork out the ten guineas, I'll tell you what I'll do. I'll go and swear a conspiracy to defraud against you and your gang; and the rascal knows me if you don't, and knows that I am a man of my word, and also a magistrate for two counties. So, which is it to be? Ten guineas down on the nail, or a warrant applied for? Possibly you yourself or some of your friends know the inside of a cell already."

Well, sometimes brag is a good dog, but only if it is not brag, solely, purely, and simply, but has something stronger behind.

Telegraphic winks, nods, and signs passed between Dicky and his confederates, and he caved in.

"Pay the gentleman the money," he cried to a man with a leather bag on his shoulders; and forthwith I took, counted carefully, and pocketed my lawful dues.

"And now, Mr. Dawkins," I said, "as you have made me too late for my own dinner, I will accept your kind offer of hospitality," and I took a chair and seated myself; and though the company was rather silent at first, as the hock and champagne went round they gradually thawed.

I much enjoyed my dinner, which was most excellent, but when bowls of punch were brought in with the walnuts I beat a hasty retreat.

THE ROYAL GAME OF GOLF.

By Mr. W. Dougall, Captain of Royal Musselburgh Golf Club.

Our first King James was fond o' games,
 But golf he liked the best ;
And aye since then, our wisest men,
 Its virtues hae confessed.
For far and near, fresh greens appear,
 Increasing day by day ;
New clubs arise, and greatly prize
 Our royal game to play.

There's nocht I ken, sae guid for men,
 As exercise and air ;
And golf's the game that gi'es that same,
 A' sports beyond compare.
Then tee your ba' and drive awa'
 Whene'er a chance ye hae,
'Twill gi'e ye health, mair worth than wealth,
 Our royal game to play.

A foursome set, o' lads weel met,
 Has pleasures nane can feel,
Except the few, 'gainst foeman true,
 Quite worthy o' their steel ;
For nane e'er thinks, when on the links,
 O' cares that on us weigh,
We travel miles, wi' cheery smiles,
 Our royal game to play.

Each ither club should hae a rub,
 Against its neebor men,
And though aince beat, the match repeat,
 And fecht it ower again.
'Twill gie new zest to do our best,
 Bring friendships by the way ;
Sae let us mix, and matches fix,
 Our royal game to play.

FROM STABLE BOY TO A PEERAGE.

THOSE persons who are fond of reading a good biography, should procure and peruse the life of "one of the most remarkable men," the late Lord Palmerston said, he had ever conversed with, namely the memoirs of Thomas Ward who began his career as a stable boy in a sporting establishment in Yorkshire, and ended a career of usefulness as a person of title and a man of mark, having in the end attained to great honour in a foreign country.

Baron Ward's story has been told at great length by a competent writer, but a brief notice is all that can be given in these pages. When he had finished "his time" in the training stables, young Ward journeyed to London to make his fortune as many another lad has done who fancied the streets of that city to be paved with gold. It was by accident, however, that the stable boy got his first chance, finding in Hyde Park the tide in his affairs which led to fortune.

While wandering about one day, watching the riders in Rotten-row, he noticed a gentleman on a horse over which he had lost control; springing forward, at the risk of being trampled to death, he caught the bridle of the restless animal, and, though he could not save the rider from being thrown, he, at least, broke his fall and prevented the furious animal kicking him. The gentleman thus aided proved to be the Duke of Lucca, and, being impressed by the lad's courage and ingenuous manners, took him into his service, and, on his return to Italy, made him head groom. Ward acted as jockey, rode races successfully, for his master, and was able to reduce the expenses of his stable one half without diminishing the splendour of his stud, which the Duke thought the finest in Italy. His Highness soon began to entertain such a belief in his capacity that he gradually initiated Ward into State affairs, consulting him in all perplexing matters.

Ward soon became a person of great importance, and was constantly being entrusted with the political business of his master. He never thought of hiding his humble origin, on the contrary, the portraits of his parents in their home-spun clothes were hung in the splendid saloon of his palace at Parma, and he married a Viennese woman of humble birth.

One element of Ward's success may be referred to. Without any educational foundation, this extraordinary man contrived to write and speak German, French, and Italian; but, strange to say, the moment he expressed himself in English, it was with a broad Yorkshire dialect.

In the year 1848, his master, who had promoted him to be his confidential minister, despatched the ex-jockey to Florence on a confidential political mission of great importance, which was no less than to convey to the Grand Duke of Florence his master's abdication of his Principality. The Duke hesitated to receive in a diplomatic capacity one whom he had only heard of as a groom. In reply to his objections the envoy produced a commission, making him viceroy of the Duke, which was to be acted on if the Grand Duke raised any obstacle or refused to see him.

Soon afterwards his patron's rule was violently terminated by the revolution of 1848, and he and his trusty servant escaped with some difficulty and retired to an estate near Dresden. Thanks to the able management of Ward, the hereditary States of Parma and Placentia were recovered after a time: but the Duke abdicated in favour of his son, under whom Ward was even more than ever a favourite, being now admitted to be more than a match for the first Italian diplomatists. Upon one occasion being despatched to Vienna as an envoy from his little Court, he astonished the domineering Austrian minister, Schwartzenberg, by the extent of his capacity, being the only one who could make head against him.

The young Duke, or Charles III., as he was entitled, was assassinated in 1854 before his own palace; after that Ward retired from public life and took to agricultural pursuits in the neighbourhood of Vienna.

Without a sigh of regret for the splendid position, as a companion of princes, he had occupied during so many years, Ward passed the remainder of his days in retirement,.following the, to him, humble occupation of a farmer.

MR. MYTTON'S DARE-DEVIL FEATS.

He was driving me (Nimrod) from Shrewsbury to Chillington to dinner, and after one or two trifling occurrences, such as knocking down a bullock, and breaking a shaft of the gig on the road, we found ourselves in an awkward predicament. By having taken a wrong turn, on approaching the house, we found ourselves in a field with no means of getting out of it, except by a gate by which we had entered, and we were already behind time for dinner. "We'll manage it," said Mytton;

"*this horse is a capital fencer;* so do you get over the fence (a hedge and ditch) and catch him." He then merely unbuckled the bearing-rein, gave the horse a cut with his whip, and over he came, gig and all, without the slightest accident.

Having shown a friend over his stud at Halston, and also his hounds, he told him he had something still better worth his seeing in reserve for him; and on opening his coach-house doors, he thus addressed him : " You see that gig. Last night it was carried clean over my lodge gate, and it is not a bit the worse for it; nor, as you have seen, is the horse that carried it over."

Now this sounds rather marvellous; but the inhabitants of the town of Wrexham, in Denbighshire, can well remember a somewhat similar circumstance occurring at a villa close to that town, some twenty years back. A horse, the property of Mr. Watkin Hayman, ran away with his gig from the door, and carried it over a high palisade gate, without injury to either himself or the gig. I went the next day to see the gate, and the only impression left upon it was the fracture of one of the spikes, or points, of the top rail.

Mytton would wantonly seek accidents from gigs and phaetons; and, latterly, I never entered into one with him, but on condition of his having nothing to do with the reins. I remember seeing him get out of his phaeton at the hall door at Halston, and instead of letting a servant drive it round to the stables, start the horses off by themselves at a gallop; and, strange to say, they conducted the carriage safely into the yard, although they had two rather sharp turns to make, and one gate to go through.

JEM WARD AND THE EDITOR'S LADY.

THE Editor of a sporting journal who had a "lady" wife—a woman of sentiment—requiring some information that he thought the veteran pugilist, Jem Ward, could furnish, he invited him to call upon him one Sunday morning. When the wife was made acquainted with the coming visit she was annoyed : "You must take him into your own room then; don't let me see him," she said. Jem arrived in good time and was conducted to the Editor's study; while the lady of the house shut herself in the drawing-room.

After chatting pleasantly for a time, and nursing one of the younger boys—who was told to remember in after life that he had once sat upon "a champion's" knee—Ward said, "By-the-by,——, I have never had the pleasure of seeing your wife; pray, introduce me." The host probably enjoying the situation, went downstairs. "It can't be helped," he said; "you'll have to see him; I assure you, you won't find him half so bad as you suppose." Resigning herself to the infliction, the lady awaited the appearance of the man whom she had pictured with a bullet head, closely-cropped hair, a nose flat with his face, a spotted belcher twisted round a bull-like throat, dressed in velveteens, and expressing himself in a gin-and-fog voice. Now, Jem Ward was the very antipodes of all this, having a handsome, well-formed nose and being quite a dandy in his dress, in fact, looking more like a half-pay officer than anything else. "What!" she exclaimed, when the pugilist had taken his departure; "do you mean to tell me that that good-looking, gentlemanly old man has been a prize fighter; I was quite delighted with him!"

DISTINGUISHED PATRONS OF COCK-FIGHTING.

It has been more than once asserted that Oliver Cromwell, notwithstanding the fact of his being a Puritan and being desirous to suppress all vain pastimes, had some love for cock-fighting. Many men of mark might be named who liked the sport and took part in it; some of our fine old admirals always carried game-cocks to sea with them that they might, with their officers, enjoy a main on the briny. The Duke of Wellington was not infrequently to be seen at the famous headquarters of the sport in Tufton-street, Westminster. The northern gentry used to be great patrons of cock-fighting. Mr. Frederick Swindell was fond of telling how he once lost his last guinea to the late Earl of Derby in a main, fought somewhere between Aintree and Liverpool. And some famous mains were fought at York between the birds of Colonel Mellish and Sir Francis Boynton. Nor was the south behind in the sport. Beckford, author of "Vathek," whose library was sold some years ago, used to tell how, when on a visit to an old Cornish family, the game-cocks were brought into the dining-room after dinner, and two or three mains were fought during the evening. Dr. Bellyse's toast,

"The Turf and the Sod," will be familiar to many a sporting man. The sturdy old doctor was a rare hand at this sport, and fed his birds upon an extraordinary diet, among the ingredients of which were eggs, sugar candy, water, hot bread and milk, barley, rice, and rhubarb.

COST OF KEEPING RACE-HORSES.

The following document is an exact copy of a Newmarket trainer's bill so far as the figures are concerned, the names of the parties and the nomenclature of the horses are fictitious, however, the object being simply to illustrate the £. S. D. of training :—

1835.
   John Brown Jones, Esq.
      To Henry Robinson, Newmarket.

Blood Hound	From July 1st to Sept. 30th, ...	£32	10	0
	Clothes 7s. Tonics 21s.	1	8	0
Arethusa	Do. Do.	33	18	0
Benbow	Do. Do.	33	18	0
	Expenses to Liverpool	18	5	0
	Do. Paisley	21	0	0
	Do. Doncaster	12	12	0
Invincible	From July 24th to Octr. 9th, ...	24	12	0
	Expenses from Sandown Park ...	1	10	0
	Clothes	0	3	6
Terrible	From June 11th to Sept. 30th, ...	39	5	0
	Expenses from M. Park	3	10	0
Dusty Bob C.	From June 11th to Sept. 30th ...	42	15	0
Musician	From Sept. 16th to 30th ...	5	0	0
	Expenses from Doncaster	3	12	0
Clarinet	From July 1st to 16th	5	7	0
	Expenses to Liverpool	17	7	0
		£297	2	6

A FOX THAT DID NOT NEGLECT BUSINESS.

It is rather curious to find an instance of a fox seizing its prey whilst it is itself engaged in running from danger, but that mighty hunter, the Rev. John Russell, encountered such an experience on one occasion. He had found a fox one fine-scenting morning on the outskirts of the moor, and was bringing him at a trimming pace over the wide heathery waste of Hawkridge Common, and thence into the hanging woods that crown the Barle with such majestic scenery, when Russell's ear was attracted by the wild screams of a woman, apparently in the greatest distress. The hounds at that moment were running exactly in the direction of the hubbub; and as Russell rode up to the spot, he beheld a woman rushing frantically after them, and catching sight of him, she exclaimed in a voice of agony, "Oh! Mr. Russell! that there fox hath a tookt away our little specklety hen; I seed un snap un up, and away to go, I did!"

"Then," said Russell, "I'll kill him and give you another hen," and on he went with the hounds.

The woman was the wife of a poor charcoal-burner, living in a turf-cabin, and passing a lonely existence in the solitude of those wild woods. On that one hen and her lively cackle, announcing the good news of a fresh-laid egg, depended, perhaps for days together, her sole supply of animal food: it had been as a pet lamb to her; had shared the crumbs of her scanty meal, and had been her companion in many a lonesome hour, when no other living creature was near. No wonder "the rocks and hollow mountains rung" with the cry of her distress: Eurydice herself could scarcely have been more lamented, nor his hive of bees by the shepherd Aristæus.

But the avengers were on his track; and, with no refuge at hand, die he must for his heartless theft. And die he did directly afterwards, for, within two gunshots of the spot, just over the Barle, the hounds ran into him; while the dishevelled carcass of the "poor little specklety hen," still warm with life, was picked up by the disconsolate owner, bringing the deed home, without a shadow of doubt, to the rapacity of that hunted fox.

CURIOUS AND ECCENTRIC WAYS OF FINDING OUT WINNING HORSES.

MANY stories are to be found in the annals of the turf of curious or eccentric modes of divining the winners of important races, as the following collection of anecdotes will bear witness. "A turf writer who believes in luck was at Croydon, and being undecided what to back in a certain race, he took his pencil and, shutting his eyes, made a haphazard thrust at the entries on his card. The pencil fell on the word "Gubat," one of the runners, but no one knew much of the horse, and the speculator's friends ridiculed the idea of "that" winning. But the scribe was not to be put off, and was able to secure a long price about Gubat, whom he had the pleasure of seeing flash past the post at the head of a large field.

I have heard of other occasions when despairing punters, baffled in their attempts to back a winner, have resorted to the most curious modes of divining. Two gentlemen, for instance, tried the plan of holding a stick between them, and by that means found out first, second, and third, in one of the less important of the spring handicaps. One of the pair on a latter occasion beheld, as he slept, a vision not of Corrie Roy's victory in the Manchester Cup, but of a lad on horseback arriving at the stables flourishing a telegram containing the news of the horse's success in that race. Of this dream or vision there need be no question; the gentleman who saw the scene is at the present time lessee of one of the largest hotels in Glasgow, and on the morning of the race told several of his friends that Corrie Roy would win it.

INDIGESTION AND GLENLIVAT.

A PAGE or two of this book might be easily filled with quaint stories of racing tips and omens, many of which are curious because of their sheer absurdity, such as one that tells of a man who, finding a black beetle in the water with which he was about to wash himself, felt warranted in backing the Beadle for a race to be run on the same day, and which was won by a horse so named. A confirmed gambler passing a music-seller's shop on the morning on which the Goodwood Stakes were to be run for, saw a portrait in the window of that most wonderful fiddler, Paganini, an event which caused him to back that horse for the great Goodwood handicap. But the sequel of this story is the most curious part of it : strange to say, next day, having resolved to purchase the portrait of the eminent violinist with a portion of the cash he had won over the event, he called at the shop, but found that the likeness had been bought by a man who, like himself, had won a little money over the race.

Some commercial gentlemen who were sitting several years ago at breakfast in the Crown Hotel, Edinburgh, on the morning of the day the Lincoln Handicap was to be run for, were commiserating with a brother of the road on his poor appetite.

"Ah, gentlemen, I cannot help it. I dare not eat that kidney," he said; "if I did, I should be ill all day."

"And what then is your complaint?" was asked.

"Oh, indigestion, indigestion; nothing else, I can assure you."

At that moment the waiter, a well-known local sporting man, had entered the room with a dish of ham and eggs, and on hearing the word "Indigestion," at once jumped to the conclusion that the conversation had been about the forthcoming handicap, and that a horse so-named (appropriately by Plum Pudding) would win, made a point of backing it, and so gained a good few five pound notes.

Mr. Robert Smart, so well known at one time, as the lessee of Frater's Rooms in Edinburgh, and also as the owner of several fairish racehorses, had given to him a presentiment of the victory of Glenlivat. "Bob," as he was familiarly called, was a great connoisseur of whisky, his advice being often asked by friends who desired to make a purchase in that line; happily, Bob, a few nights before the Chester Cup of 1871 was run for, dreamed that a gentleman for whom he had *never* made a purchase of whisky said to him, "Mr. Smart, I am obliged by the trouble you took about my whisky; I'm told to get some more of it—it's the finest Glenlivat ever distilled, so I am told. Please buy me another twenty gallons." The incident dwelt in Smart's recollection, and on Sunday evening, whilst reading *Bell's Life*, it suddenly occurred to him that he had been favoured with a capital tip for the Chester Cup of the following Wednesday. On the Monday "Bob" lost no time in backing Glenlivat; he put twenty pounds on the horse, which duly won the race.

ARAB HORSES.

As is well known, the English race horse has been made what he is by an infusion of Arab blood, and of late years much has been made of the fact, and old stories relating to the circumstance are being revived and reprinted. It was an officer of high rank in the French army who first gave to the world genuine information about the Arab horses. General Daumas having applied to the Emir for information as to the origin of the Arab horse, Abd-el-Kader told him, in his letter of reply, that he was like unto a fissure in a land dried up by the sun which no amount of rain will satisfy; nevertheless, that to quench, if possible, his thirst for knowledge, he would go back to the head of the fountain, for the stream is there always the freshest and most pure.

"Know, then," he went on, "that when Allah willed to create the horse, he said to the south wind, 'I will that a creature should proceed from thee—condense thyself!' And the wind condensed itself. Then came the angel Gabriel, and he took a handful of this matter and presented it to Allah, who formed of it a dark bay horse, saying: 'I have called thee horse, I have created thee Arab, and I have bestowed upon thee the colour dark bay. I have attached good fortune to the hair that falls between thy eyes. Thou shalt be the lord of all other animals.' He signed him with the star on his forehead—sign of glory and good fortune. Adam being allowed to choose, wisely preferred him to that wonderful mule Borak, on which Mahomet journeyed through the heavens, and was told that he had done well to choose his glory and the eternal glory of his children."

The horse, says Abd-el-Kader, is in more sympathy with the warrior who rides him than the weaker mare. "Let a horse and a mare receive exactly the same sort of wound, and one that is sure to be fatal, the horse will bear up against it until he has carried his master far from the field of battle; the mare will sink on the spot, without any force of resistance."

The first man after Adam who mounted a horse was, teaches the Emir, Ishmael. Allah taught him to call the horses, and when he did so they all came galloping up to him. He chose the best, and broke them in. But afterwards the breed degenerated, and the only faultless stock was that possessed by Solomon, called Zad-el-Rakeb, to which every real Arab steed must trace its pedigree. Some Arabs of the Azed tribe went up to congratulate Solomon upon his marriage with the Queen of Sheba. When they were about to leave Jerusalem the Noble, they had neither money nor provisions, so they said to Solomon, "Thou art a great king; bestow upon us wherewithal to take us home." Solomon gave him one of his pure breed of horses, and said, "There is food. When you are hungry set your best rider with a lance upon this horse; gather fuel, light a fire, and by the time the fire burns he will bring you meat." And so he did. Abd-el-Kader declares from his own observation that the Arab horse varies in colour with the soil on which he lives. Where the ground is stony he is usually grey, and where the ground is chalky he is usually white. According to the Koran, the horse prays three times a day. In the morning he says, "O Allah, make me beloved of my master." At noon, "Do well by my master, that he may do well by me." In the evening, "Grant that he may enter Paradise upon my back."

BETTING FOR AND AGAINST: CANON KINGSLEY'S OPINION.

Various controversies have taken place in regard to betting, both as respects its morality and utility, and many different opinions have been elicited on the subject in all its phases. The following extracts have been made from a series of letters about betting which were printed a few months ago in an important provincial journal:—

For.

The ethical objection to betting—viz., that it is wrong to make money by the loss of another person—is easily answered. In the first place, no one in ordinary commercial life ever dreams of regarding it. If A. and B. make a contract about the sale of a commodity, and the result is disadvantageous for A., B. does not on that account hesitate to enforce the bargain. During the coal famine here many owners of mines were losing heavily by having to supply coal at prices contracted for before the spurt, but no one accused the buyer of wrong dealing in enforcing the agreements. In fact, were this fantastic objection regarded in commerce, it would soon destroy all enterprise and speculation. At least two highly honourable professions—

doctors and lawyers—make money by the pain and losses of their fellow-creatures, but no one outside Bedlam would say that their conduct was wrong. It is certainly true that an honourable man would not take an unfair advantage of another, and if bookmakers as a class were weak and innocent and inexperienced, it would not be right for backers to make money out of such weakness, innocence, and inexperience. But bookmakers are the sharpest, shrewdest set of men in existence, and hence the objection does not apply at all.

Betting has got a bad name, chiefly because we hear of cases where it has done harm, and we do not hear of the reverse cases, which are more numerous than is generally supposed. An insolvent debtor pleads betting as the cause of his ruin, but a man who has averted bankruptcy by speculation on the turf does not usually advertise the fact. Of course, there are a class of nervous excitable people to whom betting is absolute ruin, but that is not an argument against the practice in the abstract. There are people who must either be teetotal or make beasts of themselves, but that is no argument against a glass of beer for those differently constituted. To many persons turf speculation is a pleasant and profitable form of amusement, affording a pleasurable, but not undue, excitement, and a nice addition to income.

If you will allow me, sir, to give my own experience, I may say that, though for some time past I have indulged in the above amusement, I have never neglected my business, never lost a minute's sleep, and am financially very much benefited.—

AGAINST.

I have never betted myself, but I have worked beside men who could not take their food when they had money on a race. One chap said to me the other day. "I have a trifle on the 'Cup,' and I feel all in a funk." One has but to visit Newgate Street or the Big Market [Newcastle] to find all classes represented, from the errand boy to the merchant; men from the factory and others from behind the counter; even the street arabs have joined together to have "something on." Nor does it end here, for *women* are becoming fanciers of the turf. All have an eager look, and are keenly asking for the latest information from each other, and all have a "sure thing" from some source. The bookmakers watch the group with one eye and the policemen with the other, and so get their books well filled.

Where the money has come from or how it has been raised,

it will be as well, perhaps, not to ask, for "such a horse is sure to win," and all will be right. But, if our racing prophets are so sure of winners, why do they not become millionaires? They are *not* sure. It is in many cases only a guess, and a very vague one, and yet thousands will risk money that does not belong to themselves, and others that which should support their families, on this uncertainty! Men will neglect their work, women will neglect their homes day after day—everything else must be set aside for this betting.

What a variety of facial expressions are displayed! It is actually pitiable to see betting people after the race is over. It is then that the reaction sets in; remorse seizes the loser, and even those who have won are flung into wild excitement, while all must off to the public-house—some because they have lost, and others because they have won. There they are joined by a lot of sponges who hang about bars among betting men, and often he who has won is out of pocket.

Now, I say, in conclusion, that no one can defend such a practice, though many are content to be lured on by its influence to the bitter end. But, to imitate the "talent of the turf," my selections to win the public from its evils are:—

1. If the same amount of thought were devoted to ordinary business, many would be in good positions who are not.
2. It causes men to neglect their work, and makes them irritable both in their workshops and homes.
3. It leads to drinking, for most bets are either made or paid in public-houses.
4. It pollutes what would otherwise be pleasant sport.
5. It is degrading the youth of England, and has landed many of them in misery.
6. It is absorbing the mind of all classes in the land, and causing them to neglect other and more profitable study.

What Kingsley Said.

"Of all habits gambling is the one I hate most, and have avoided most. Of all habits it grows most on eager minds. Success and loss alike make it grow. Of all habits, however much civilized men may give way to it, it is one of the most intrinsically *savage*. Historically it has been the peace excitement of the lowest brutes in human form for ages past. Morally it is unchivalrous and unchristain. (1) It gains money by the lowest and most unjust means, for it takes money out of your neighbour's pocket without giving him any·

thing in return. (2) It tempts you to use what you fancy your superior knowledge of a horse's merits—or anything else—to your neighbour's harm. If you know better than your neighbour, you are bound to give him your advice. Instead, you conceal your knowledge to win from his ignorance; hence come all sorts of concealments, dodges, deceits. I say the devil is the only father of it. . . . I found myself forced to turn my back upon racecourses, not because I did not love to see the horses run—in that old English pleasure taken simply and alone, I can fully sympathise—but because I found that they tempted me to betting, and that betting tempted me to company and to passions, unworthy not merely of a scholar and a gentleman, but of an honest and rational bargeman or collier."

HERMIT'S SENSATIONAL DERBY.

WITH odds of 1000 to 10 laid against him, Hermit won what was in many respects a most sensational race. The nett value of the stakes reached the handsome amount of £7000, and the owner of the winning horse, Mr. Chaplin, was set down as having pouched the large sum of £100,000, he was reputed indeed, to have lifted from bookmakers and others, bets to the extent of £141,000 in all; the odd money, however, was "bespoken" by those friends who "stood in," and some other friends who were not forgotten in the hour of victory. On no previous Derby had such a large stake been landed by the owner of the first horse.

The amount of money which changed hands over " Hermit's Derby" must have been very large; indeed, a well-known racing nobleman, who "died on the turf," stood to lose upwards of a hundred thousand pounds. So it was reported at the time, but Lord Hastings, the nobleman in question, had a setoff to his losses in the form of "contra"—cross and place bets, &c.; at any rate, however hard he may have been hit, his account was duly settled on the Monday after the race. One of the sensational bets about Hermit's chance of winning the Derby, of which there were many, was that of £180,000 to £6000, taken by Captain Macell from the Duke of Hamilton in the previous summer. Happily for his Grace, the bet had long before the eventful day been declared " off, by consent." There were several big winners over the event, in addition to Mr. Chaplin, two of whom, as it went the rounds of the newspapers of the period, took £50,000 each out of the ring; such statements must, however, be taken with the proverbial pinch of salt. The victory of Hermit was most unexpected as the state of the odds tend to show. The horse was bought as a yearling for a sum of one thousand guineas. It is a remarkable fact that the Derby of 1867 was run in a snow storm. Since the date of the memorable race, the horse has been at the stud, and has proved like a gold mine to his owner; it has been jocularly said, indeed, that Hermit produces a larger income to Mr. Chaplin than three of his best farms.

PHILOSOPHY OF SALMON POACHING.

It has never been very easy to determine with any degree of certainty whether it is the pleasure or the profit of the pursuit that impels men to take to salmon at a time when their capture is not only illegal, but uneconomic and cruel as well. Judging from the readiness with which even very large fines are paid, we might set down the impulse of salmon poaching to the fact of its forming a profitable occupation during the winter time for weavers and shoemakers who have a fancy for a little adventure. One man of the name of Herries, a labourer, was fined some time ago (his third offence) in the sum of £85 15s "in all," for fishing in the Nith, near Dumfries, with a net calculated to let nothing escape larger than a minnow! No one need have any hesitation in denouncing such piratical fishing. It deserves to be severely punished. There are some kinds of poaching which even the severest naturalist or economist might "wink" at, seeing how much can be said on both sides of the game laws; but no person should give sanction to the "harrying" of the waters by wholesale netting at the very time when the fish require to be protected. It is no excuse that the animals caught by Herries and his companion, were only sea trout—hirlings and greylings—the men were very likely on the prowl for salmon, and would certainly not have refused to capture any number of these fine fish, if they had been able to obtain them. A poacher that by chance takes a salmon during the open season, is in some degree excusable, seeing how he has been tempted, but the man who deliberately sweeps the salmon beds with a fine net during the spawning season deserves to be imprisoned without the option of a fine. If the fish cannot at that period of their lives be allowed to perform in peace the grandest function of their natures, only one result can follow, and that result has often been fore-shadowed—it is the ultimate extinction of the salmon.

IN THE DAYS OF THE REGENCY.

In the days of the Regency, sport knew no pause, but went on at rapid pace from one year's end to another. These were the days of Tom and Jerry, racing, cock-fighting, boxing, and pigeon shooting, gave constant work to all who cared for such pastimes. Great men thought nothing of engaging in a boxing match.

Lord Mexborough and Fletcher Norton were at one time Jackson's favourite pupils, and so nearly matched that a challenge was given and accepted between the two to try which was the better man. Such a sensation was created by this event that on the afternoon on which it was to come off, Rotten Row was literally deserted by the male sex. Jackson's rooms were crammed, the passages, and even the stairs being crowded with perspiring swells unable to get admission, for it was regarded as a match of the House of Lords against the House of Commons. Both combatants were light-weights, and splendid boxers, and for a long time victory hung in the balance, for while Mexborough was quicker at the out fighting, Norton was the stronger in the rally; but strength prevailed at last, and my lord was knocked clean over the benches, and the tremendous cheers of the Commons proclaimed Norton the victor.

Grantly Berkeley tells us, that after a dinner at Crockford's, the tables would sometimes be put aside and the room converted into an arena, wherein Tom Spring and Owen Swift, and other famous boxers of the day, would amuse the company with a display of their science. At other times the room would be temporarily turned into a cock-pit, and a main would be fought by candle-light. Lord Byron was particularly fond of boxing, and was one of John Jackson's pet pupils. In one of his notes to "Don Juan" he speaks of the famous fighter affectionately as his "old friend and corporeal master and pastor," and letters to him, written in a familiar strain, beginning "Dear Jack," and ending with "Believe me, dear Jack, &c.," are still extant. " At

Harrow," he says—and it will be remembered that the poet had a club foot, which of course in sparring was greatly against him —" I fought my way very fairly; I think I lost but one battle out of seven, and that only from the unfair treatment of my opponent's boarding-house where we boxed. I had not even a second." Again, speaking of a school friend, he writes : " He was pacific, I savage ; so I fought for him, or thrashed others for him, or thrashed himself to make him thrash others whom it was necessary, as a point of honour, he should so chastise."

VALUE OF RACE HORSES.

I.

The race horse of the period is undoubtedly the most valuable animal in the kingdom. It would not be difficult to compile a list of a hundred horses which, during a few years, have changed hands as yearlings, for a quarter of a million sterling. Four years ago, over twenty thousand pounds were obtained for a dozen of the yearlings, bred by Mr. Chaplin at Blankney, four of which changed hands, each at a sum of 3000 guineas, or upwards. In the course of 1887, a sum of 3000 guineas was obtained for one yearling, and for animals of that age sold in any one year, total amounts ranging from 100,000 to 160,000 guineas, have been drawn by the auctioneers. Some time ago, still larger sums used to be paid for yearlings, and for mature horses amounts ranging from two to ten thousand guineas have not been thought unreasonable when the buyer coveted what he fancied was a " really fine bit of stuff."

The value of a race horse cannot be assessed by any kind of intelligent rule—its value, indeed, is just what it will fetch when it is offered for sale, and although its veins may be filled with the bluest of blue blood, it may not, as a race horse, if bought as a yearling, be worth a twenty pound note when it comes to be tested. Only one animal can win the Derby in each year— true, the same horse may also prove victorious in two or three other races of like value, but of the two thousand race horses, which are annually saddled for the work of the turf, not half a dozen, perhaps, of those which have cost a thousand guineas and upwards, will earn the price paid for them. The buying of horse flesh is in the nature of a lottery. It has happened before now, and will happen again, it is always happening in fact, that an animal bought for less than a hundred guineas has earned for its lucky owner a hundred times the amount paid for it in the course of its racing career, and been then disposed of to stand as a sire at a stud farm, for a sum equal to the amount it had earned on the race courses over which it had been entered to run. There never was a time in the history of racing, during which stakes were so valuable as they are to-day. At one period, both " the Derby " and " the St. Leger," were looked upon as being at the top of the tree, but to-day the stakes to be bagged by winning either of these races are quite eclipsed. Races of the value of from four to ten thousand pounds seem as if in the future they would become of almost every day occurrence; at all events, several such have already taken place and two or three more of similar values have lately been announced.

II.

From the information supplied and the prices quoted, it is possible to form a fair idea of the total value of our stock of high mettled racers. Of the two thousand foals which annually come to swell the total number, or at all events to aid in keeping up the stock, many, it is proper to re-iterate, are of but slight value; some of those which are offered at the public sales do not fetch forty guineas, but despite that fact, a good average price is obtained. Whether there be 9000 or 10,000 race horses, steeple chasers and high class hunters in the country, we need not too minutely inquire, adopting either of these numbers, and placing the value of each of them at an average of £300, the figures represented for ten thousand would be, of course, £3,000,000, and taking it that such a sum has been expended, the interest of it would annually amount to, if calculated at the rate of five per cent, £150,000. The average indicated is not by any means too large, some of the breeding horses now at the stud being of very great value. The cost of maintaining a race horse and providing for its various engagements, paying travelling expenses and the riding fees of their jockeys, can scarcely be set down at less than £300 per annum. Calculating that only 2000 are so kept and travelled for racing purposes, the total in such case would amount to a sum of £600,000. Another portion of the stock, namely, that portion which is in preparation, may be set down as costing each about £200 per annum—say 1000 youngsters, at a total of £150,000, which brings up the annual bill paid by owners of race horses (interest on capital expended and keep) to a grand total of £900,000. Another £100,000 may well be added to that amount to represent those wonderful "miscellaneous expenses" which are always cropping up in connection with turf-work, so that if we set down a million sterling as the annual cost of keeping up the racing studs of the period, we feel that it will not be an exaggeration. The stakes raced for in any one year, have, we believe, never yet reached in value the sum of half a million sterling; in 1887, the value of the stakes raced for amounted to not more than £416,322. Putting the two totals against each other, it will be seen that the deficit is close upon £600,000 sterling, as between expenditure and income, which sum, along with the personal expenditure of owners who "travel the meetings," has to be got back in the betting ring, but many fail to find it there, and the conclusion to be arrived at is that the pastime must be, indeed, fascinating, which induces men to risk so much to gain so little. It has been asserted that no man (or woman) has ever yet been able to turn the running of race horses into a successful commercial speculation.

WHAT SPORTSMEN ACHIEVE.

From letters addressed to one of his friends we select the following, in reply to one in which he was asked his "bag" of grouse in a season and the number of deer fallen to his rifle. "I never," says Captain Ross, "tried to make a great bag of grouse in a day. I think sixty-five brace was the largest number of grouse I ever shot in one day. That is nothing. Two hundred brace have since then been shot in a day by one man, easily, 12th August. In 1828 I rented from the Duke of Athol a |large range of shooting called Feloar. I shot eighty-seven deer that season to my own rifle. I worked hard, up at 3 a.m., and seldom back to the lodge before 7 or 8 p.m., walking, running, or crawling all the time. This was the grandest training in the world! I believe I came to the post on the 1st of November, at Milden Hall, as fit to go as any winner of the Derby ever did at Epsom. In 1851 I shot one hundred and eighteen deer in Mar Forest. During that season I killed thirteen in one day with fourteen chances. In 1837 I killed seventy-five deer in Sutherlandshire. These are my three best seasons.

"In the Inverness-shire forest, I one day killed eight stags in twenty minutes. The deer were driven into a wood, and got stupefied. I had only one rifle—a muzzle-loader, and lost so much time loading, that I lost sight of the deer. If I had had a breech-loader, I could have run and loaded at the same time. I might have killed fifty."

CHARLES JAMES FOX.

THIS remarkable man, we are told, once remained in a gambling club for 22 consecutive hours *losing at the rate of £500 an hour*. In the year 1773, his debts amounted to £100,000; his father paid for him in all £140,000; yet he was ultimately compelled to sell or mortgage every source of livelihood or profit he had enjoyed. Sometimes he was reduced to the most direful necessity for the want of a guinea, yet he was never despondent, and even after he had lost every shilling, fatigued with his exertions in the House of Commons, and with the hours he had devoted to wine and faro during the night, he would quietly lay his head upon the gambling-table, and almost instantly fall into a profound sleep. Having one night lost an almost ruinous amount, a friend who was present called upon him next morning, expecting to find the unlucky gamester in a miserable frame of mind, instead of which Fox was tranquilly reading Herodotus. "What would you have me to do," he asked laughing, "when I have lost my last shilling?"

In a letter of 1871, Horace Walpole says: "As I came up St. James's-street I saw a cart and porter at Charles's door; coffers and old chests of drawers loading. In short, his success at faro has awakened his host of creditors; but unless his bank had swelled to the size of the Bank of England, it would not have yielded a sop or piece for each. Epsom, too, had been unpropitious, and one creditor has actually seized and carried off his goods, which did not seem worth removing. As I returned, whom should I see sauntering by my own door but Charles. He came up and talked to me with as much *sang froid* as if he knew nothing of what had happened."

ABOUT YOUNG ECLIPSE AND THE DERBY.

ONE of the Derby sensations of the year 1845 was about a horse purchased from Lord George Bentinck for a hundred guineas by Mr. Thomas Coleman—and which soon improved so much as to induce his Lordship to offer a thousand guineas to regain possession of the animal. What took place is interesting as showing some of the inner phases of sporting life.

Young Eclipse went amiss a few days before the Derby and went so bad that his owner had made up his mind not to let him run, but Lord George thought it would be as well to send him to Epsom with his and the Duke of Richmond's horses; so they were sent to Kingston, and then vanned on to Epsom. On the platform was Lord Stradbroke, who had come there to see the horses arrive, and I remarked to him it looked like rain, that the ground would soon be heavy, asking him how that would suit his horse.

"Oh," he said, "it's no matter how the ground is, my horse can't get the 'distance.'"

I think he was at 4 to 1 at that very time. On the morning of the race people heard in Epsom that Young Eclipse was to be scratched, and several who had backed him came bullying me, and said he was not amiss. General Charretie declared he would expose Lord George Bentinck and myself in "Bell's Life," if the horse did not start. Lord George upon being told what he said, replied.

"Study your own interests; you may get a good day out of the horse yet; but if you run him it may ruin him, in the state he is in."

As General Charretie and a lot kept on at me, I said, "The horse shall start to satisfy 'you.'"

To my surprise he laid up in front to Tattenham Corner. I did not think he could go half way; but it ruined him: he never recovered, and never won another race. I sold the half of him to one man for £600, and the other half after for £300, making £900 altogether for him. This is his true history. Lord George said it was through me he won the Northamptonshire Stakes with Discord, and other handicaps in the spring that year, by putting his horses in work so early to try mine. But the sweats and gallops knocked him over, as they will do any horse, if overdone with them.

A large bookmaker was never more bitten than he was over this race. I will tell you how it was. I chanced to be at Harcourt House with Lord George one day, when Gardener, his valet, came into the room, and said some one wanted to see him. " You are just in time for dinner, Coleman," said his Lordship. And I went down to dinner in the steward's room.

After dinner, when the housekeeper retired, I had some wine with the old butler, who said, " Now, Mr. Coleman, I know you can give me a turn ; if you can, I shall be obliged. What is this chestnut horse they call Young Eclipse that you have got ? " " Oh, we don't know anything about him yet ; but if you will promise not to attempt to back him yet, I'll let you know when we find out whether he is worth backing." He would not wait for that, but sent off to his bookmaker at once to back him for a pony, who, thinking it a good tip, helped himself as well, and I have been told he stuck to him to the time the flag fell, would not be stalled off, and, it is said, dropped a raker. If you want a horse in the market, tell people not to back him, and they are sure to do it.

BOBBY MUMFORD GETS A CHARACTER.

AT every Derby the public learn that the " welshing " at Epsom has been " even worse than usual." Almost every year the welshers have quite a benefit at the four days' meeting, keeping people's money, and abusing and ill-using them when they apply for their winnings. Great complaints were made to the stewards three or four seasons ago, and they were determined, if possible, to try and stop welshing at Ascot, at least in Tattersall's Ring. On the first day of the meeting Lord Hardwicke and Sir John Astley thought they would judge for themselves, and after the Trial Stakes had been decided they came into the enclosure, and carefully looked round to see if any " doubtful starters " were there. Much to their gratification they could not find any, but as they were walking out they heard " a voice, made hoarse by grog of course," shouting,

" I'll bet on the Ascot Stakes. Now, then, who'll back one to win or a place ? " and walking towards the layer of odds, they saw Mumford, the bookmaker, with a short pipe in his mouth.

" Holloa ! " said Sir John ; " who are you ? "

" Yes," asked Lord Hardwicke, in almost the same breath ; " what's your name ? "

" Mumford, sir,—Bobby Mumford. All the Ring knows me."

" Possibly," said Sir John ; " but I don't."

"Are you a member of Tattersall's?" inquired Lord Hardwicke.

"No, my lord," answered Bobby; "but—"

"Out you go then!" said Sir John; and as Mumford turned on his heel to leave the Ring with his clerk, Jackey Jacobs put a spoke in the wheel, and, without being applied to either by Sir John or his lordship, said,

"Oh, my lord, he's all right. He's a good man, Sir John."

"And who the devil are you?" replied Sir John, biting the end of his cigar and shaking a short-handled riding-whip.

"Me," answered the "chosen," in an awful fright. "Me, Sir John! Vy, I'm Jackey Jacobs."

"Are you, indeed?" said Sir John Astley. "And are you a member of Tattersall's?"

"No, Sir John," replied Jackey.

"Then out you go, Mr. Jacobs." And out Mr. Jackey Jacobs did go, whilst Bobby Mumford was allowed to remain and bet, and he has been betting ever since.

FORTUNE'S FAVOURS.

An almost countless number of anecdotes could be related under this heading; persons who have dealings on the turf, more especially, must be familiar with wonderful instances of men, who in a moment, so to say, have had their pockets lined with hundreds of pounds by the decision of a race. The following is one instance of a bit of good fortune gained on the turf: a struggling shopkeeper in the city of Worcester, had, in the course of business, contracted £2,000 of debt, and had not more than £500 to pay with. Writs were threatened, and the creditors were going "to play the very devil, and turn up Jack."

Telling his troubles one day to a genial friend, he said, "Why don't you try the turf and take a double event bet for the Cesarewitch and Cambridgeshire?"

"A what?" asked the tradesman in surprise.

The other explained that the odds (it was in those days) were £3,000 to £1 against guessing the winners of both races, and advised him to invest a sovereign on Cardinal York for the long race (Cesarewitch) and Adonis for the short one (the Cambridgeshire). It was done; the horses both won, and the creditors were paid in full, and the tradesman became in time a prosperous man, and can say with King Dick, "Richard's himself again."

Relating this tale one day to a Bristolian he made me laugh by declaring he knew a wine merchant there who sent ten shillings up to the late Mr. George Mather for a similar bet, who returned him the voucher—£1,500 to 10s. He promptly sent him a cheque for the winnings, but omitted the 10s. invested, whereon the greedy Bristol man wrote and acknowledged the receipt of the £1,500, but added, "You have forgotten the 10s. stake money. Please send it in postage stamps."

A Glasgow hotel-keeper won £3,000 by the same double event, and a young man in Edinburgh, a fishmonger's assistant, "lifted" £750 from a bookmaker over the Cardinal and Adonis.

Here is another little story about the favours of fortune:—

There is occasionally quoted, in connection with Doncaster Derby, an anecdote of a costermonger whose wife, on the Sunday morning previous to the Derby Day, sang in her sleep with great vigour, "The boy in yellow wins the day!" and, as the tale goes, Ned Timsin, the coster, when he saw the colours in question, during the preliminary canter of the horses, determined to back Mr. Merry's colt (Doncaster), and did so to the tune of nearly thirty shillings, all the money he possessed at the time that he could spare from his business. After the race was over Ned duly received his winnings (about £40), and no doubt lived happy ever after; at all events, with a fine pony and nice cart, bought with a portion of his winnings, he became a sort of king among the costermongers, and he called his pony Yellow Boy, in memory of the event.

The dreams and omens of the Derby with which we have been made familiar assume many shapes. Some dreamers see the race and take notice of the jockey and his colours; others see the number of the winning horse hoisted; others are told the name of the winner; and some dream that they read the name of the first three on the tissue which comes with the news to their club. I know a gentleman—a member of a sporting club—who saw in his mind's eye during his slumbers the tissue which contained Iroquois first, Peregrine second, Town Moor third. That seer was the special favourite of fortune, as on a previous occasion he dreamt that Rosebery had won the "Camberwitch," a dream which, for the moment, puzzled him not a little; but he was clever enough to solve the difficulty by backing the horse for both Cesarewitch and Cambridgeshire, and Rosebery, as is well known, won both of these races.

COCKING A ROYAL GAME.

In some of the old books which treat of cock-fighting that sport is designated a " Royal Game "—perhaps from the fact that at one period every palace possessed its pit. One of the most famous of these places was "the Royal Westminster." A curious old coloured print, by Rowlandson and Pugin, issued in 1808, depicts the interior of this building whilst a main is in progress. "Some of the figures are evidently portraits, representing well-known peers and pickpockets, grooms and gentlemen of the day. The rival cocks are being backed by two boys, called feeders, dressed in red jackets and yellow trousers--a sort of royal livery. The chief figure in the front row is an elderly gentleman, who seems to anticipate the loss of his side of the battle, as does also a fat neighbour on the left, and a grim individual, with a stupefied look of despair upon his face, on the right. On the left, again, a smiling countenance shows the other side of the game, while the clenched fists and breathless looks of two in the front row indicate all the agony of suspense. At the back are two men wildly gesticulating, and evidently offering odds which no one will take. At the back sits an officer in a cocked hat, and above him are the Royal arms, the lion and the unicorn, looking down composedly on the fray, whilst some roughs are laying whips and thick sticks over the heads and shoulders of their near neighbours. It is a companion to Hogarth's celebrated picture on the same subject."

The following anecdote of a cocking incident is not devoid of interest. It is related that in the course of a fight one of the birds fell, apparently dying. A man, watch in hand, stood counting the seconds ; if it did not rise to renew the combat before twenty had elapsed, it would be decided against him. The other bird stood by towering over him, and ready to renew the attack at the first sign of returning animation. On the eighteenth second the prostrate cock, in the agonies of death, kicked out with such force, that the spur passed clean through the head of the supposed victor, who dropped dead before the other breathed his last.

GREYHOUND STORIES.

MANY discussions used to take place regarding the comparative speed of the greyhound and the race-horse among our sporting ancestors, and in December, 1800, a celebrated match came off by way of deciding the point, at Doncaster, between a mare belonging to Mr. James Archer Riddell, and a bitch greyhound, the distance being three miles. It was a splendid race, the animals—both of the gentler sex, be it noted—keeping head to head the greater part of the way, but at the distance the greyhound had so much improved her position that 5 to 4 was laid upon her. The mare's rider then made a call upon his animal, which was responded to in fine style, and in the end the greyhound was beaten by a short head.

Matches, however, between dogs alone were more common, and a few years before the contest just noticed, a match was made, to be run on Stoke Down in Wiltshire, between two greyhounds solely as a test of speed—"points," in the current coursing meaning of the term, being ignored—the only thing being, that one of the competitors should kill the hare. One was soon turned out on a fine level part of the Down; it ran 15 miles in three-quarters of an hour, and was finally killed by the hound which was handicapped to carry 4lbs. weight of shot slung round his body.

A curious performance, again to be set down to the credit of the greyhound, was the following. A clergyman who was about to make a journey into France became wind-bound at Dover, and had to stay there until the weather should change. Happening one day to be out with his dog, a remarkably fine specimen, he was told by a sporting squire of a well-known hare in the neighbourhood which had run clean away from all their dogs, and was looked upon as quite a curiosity. Dr. Corsellis (the clergyman) expressed his wish to try his animal against the wonderful pussy, backed his opinion freely, and she was speedily beaten up for him. The dog turned out to be her master, and pressed her so close that she was forced to make for the cliff, and had just gained it when the hound snatched her by the neck, and they both bounded over together and were dashed to pieces at the bottom.

Some performances with hounds which have been narrated are curious, if not extraordinary. In October, 1792, for instance, a hare after being hunted for sixteen miles by the Seaford harriers, dashed into the sea close to Cuckmere, in Sussex, and swam more than a quarter of a mile from the shore before the dogs overtook her. Nearly fifteen years ago, a hunted stag adopted similar tactics, but got clean away from his four-footed pursuers and was taken a long distance out at sea by fishermen.

At Terling, in Essex, a similar event took place while the foxhounds were breaking cover. A hare dashed along one of the paths of Sandpit Wood, while at the same time a terrier was going full speed in the opposite direction. They met, the hare's skull was smashed into pieces, the terrier was flung to the earth senseless, but subsequently recovered. A similar thing occurred at Finchingfield, in the same county, the chief performers being greyhounds; in rushing at a hare from opposite sides they clashed their skulls together, and both fell stone dead. In March, 1798, Lord Ongley's harriers ran a hare through a part of eight parishes and three counties, the distance being covered in three hours. Merkin, a foxhound bitch belonging to Colonel Thornden, was tried at Newmarket against time, doing four miles in seven minutes and half a second. She was then matched to run any hound—dog or bitch—five miles over the heath, giving odds of 220 yards, for 10,000 guineas, but the offer was not accepted, and fell through because none dared take it up.

GOLFING—THE DUKE AND THE SHOEMAKER.

During the residence of the Duke of York, afterwards James II., in Edinburgh, in 1681 and 1682, he was frequently to be seen playing at golf with some of the nobility and gentry, on the Links of Leith. Two English noblemen one day debated the question with his Royal Highness, as to whether Scotland or England were entitled to the honour of originating the delightful pastime, and having some difficulty in agreeing on the subject, it was proposed to decide the argument by an appeal to the game itself, the Englishmen agreeing to rest the legitimacy of their national pretensions, together with a large sum of money, on the result of the match, to be played with any Scotsman the Duke chose to bring forward. The person recommended to him for this purpose was a poor man named Patersone, a shoemaker, who was regarded as the best golfer of the day. On being asked to play, Patersone modestly expressed great unwillingness to enter into a match of such consequence; but on the Duke encouraging him, he promised to do his best. The match was played, in which the Duke and his humble partner were of course victorious, and the latter was dismissed with his full share of the stake played for. With this money Patersone built a comfortable house in the Canongate, on the wall of which the Duke caused a stone to be placed, bearing the arms of the Patersone family, with the addition of a crest, a hand grasping a club, and the appropriate motto, " Far and Sure."

A HUNDRED GUINEAS TO A WALKING STICK.

JOHN JACKSON, a jockey of the day, won the St. Leger on eight different occasions, but his greatest, or at anyrate, his most sensational feat in connection with that great race, was when he won it on Theodore in 1822. That horse who had run successfully at two years old, was defeated a few weeks previously to the decision of the St. Leger, and from being high on the betting scale he was knocked down to the lowest point. In proof of how much he had sunk in public estimation, it need only be mentioned that on the morning of the race a hundred guineas to a walking stick was laid against him and taken. Jackson was sorely mortified at his chance for the race, and was very desirous of riding one of Mr. Gascoigne's horses, either the colt or the filly, and declared that he could win upon either one or the other. But his chance was unalterably fixed upon Theodore. The extraordinary success which ensued will be seen. He was extremely low-spirited during the whole of the forenoon, especially when he heard what was the state of the odds. As the hour drew near he walked to the ground in no very amiable frame of mind, and was weighed in due course. On inquiring afterwards if anyone had seen Mr. Petre, or his groom or his horse, he was answered in the negative.

Proceeding into the field he repeated his inquiries there, with the like success. At length he discovered a horse, at the far end of the field, led by a little stable-boy. He thought it must be Theodore: and trudging across the land, and approaching the boy, said, "Is that Mr. Petre's horse, my boy?" "Yes, sir," was the answer. "Bring him here," said the veteran, " and pull off his clothes directly ; " and proceeded to adjust his saddle, to strip himself of his walking coat, &c. The little boy assisted him to mount, and he recrossed the field in the direction of the course. When passing the rubbing-house, a gentleman asked,

"What horse is that?"

"Mr. Petre's Theodore!' said another.

"What will you lay against him?"

"A hundred guineas to one."

"Done! Done!"

And the bet was booked. Jackson, of course, heard this, and looked not very pleasant; in fact, he was mortified and ill-tempered, and had, even previous to that, let Theodore feel that he had his spurs on. But Theodore was alive and remarkably fresh and ready for the struggle.

Whilst parading in front of the Grand Stand, the objects of universal notice were the first favourites, Mr. Watt's Muta and Marion, Mr. Gascoigne's colt and filly, Mr. Poulett's Snap, Mr. Riddle's The Whig, &c., whilst Theodore was scarcely noticed. They approached the post in a body, and Jackson, who was noted for obtaining a good place, got in front. The word "Go" was given by Mr. Lockwood, and away they rushed, Theodore taking the lead almost immediately. The pace was very fast; Jackson was surprised at his own position, and said afterwards in allusion to this extraordinary race, "that when we got to the first cross-road, I had lost all my ill-temper and mortification. I turned my head for a moment, a crowd of horses—twenty-two—were close at my heels. The sight was terrific! The speed was tremendous! Theodore pulled hard, and I held him pretty tight. 'Now, my little fellow,' said I, to myself, 'keep up this speed to the top of the hill, and I don't care a straw for the whole lot.' I felt as strong as a giant, and the blood rushed merrily through my veins. Away we went; I was first over the hill, and never headed in any part of the race." After descending the hill he eased his horse a little, and was instantly on the look out for some of the favourites. He could see that Snap, a grey horse, was defeated, but the others challenged him in turns—first Marion, then Gascoigne's colt and filly—right and left; then Muta, then Gascoigne's again. Theodore, perhaps partly frightened by the tremendous thunder at his heels, still wanted to go faster ahead, but his rider so continued to use his powers as not to waste them.

Challenge after challenge was given, and as often defeated. Jackson never suffered his horse to go much in advance of the rest; holding him with a firm hand, but still going very fast, he only slackened the reins when he was attempted to be coupled. "I could," said the veteran jockey, "see head by head advance as far as my boots on each side, and when I encouraged Theodore forward I could see head by head glide backward out of my sight," observing to himself (said he), "Now, I think you are all done." He felt then that the race was his own, as he heard the exhilarating sounds from the Grand Stand as he approached, "Theodore! Theodore! Mr. Petre! Jackson! Theodore wins!" which he did in the most gallant and skilful manner by nearly a length, to the perfect astonishment of all the betting men, and of the immense crowd of spectators, who honoured Jackson with three loud and hearty cheers as he approached the scale to be weighed.

WAYS AND WORK OF AN OLD TIME JOCKEY.

IN looking for a sketch that would convey to modern readers a notion of the work undertaken by jockeys who lived in the last century, the Editor has selected an account of the career of John Singleton, who underwent during his day and generation much toil, and conducted himself in such a way as secured the respect of all who knew him.

I.

This eminent rider, who in his day was esteemed the first horseman on the turf, was born at Melbourne, near Pocklington, Yorkshire, in the year 1715, the register of his baptism in the parish church being there recorded "John, son of John Singleton, of Melbourne, baptised May 10th, 1715." The father must have been a clever person, for he supported a wife and nine children on the small wages of 4d. per day. On his death the family was dispersed, and the subject of this memoir was hired at the age of 10 years, along with other boys, to tend the cattle on Ross Moor, a large bleak common belonging to Melbourne and several adjoining townships, from thence he had a view of the Wold hills, about eight miles distant, where he heard racehorses were kept, and boys to ride them; this appears to have suggested the idea of racing in the minds of him and his companions, and induced them to catch the young horses on the common which they raced against each other, but being caught in the act and corrected for it, he, for once in his life, levanted, and was found early the next morning at the stable door of Wilberforce Read, Esq., who being in want of a boy engaged him on the splendid terms of board and lodging, which was sleeping in the stables and eating in the kitchen when there was anything to get.

Perhaps some notice of Mr. Read would not be amiss. He was a gentleman of a good family with a very slender portion, which was expended in stocking a farm rented under the Earl of Carlisle, at Grimthorpe, near Pocklington, a place adjoining the Yorkshire Wolds, then unenclosed; an extensive tract of fine elastic turf formed by nature for equestrian sports, on which both horse and rider equally rejoiced. The neighbourhood was, of course, a sporting one; every village had its annual feast, and every feast a race: the smallest prize brought a number of competitors to the post. No wonder this gentleman caught the epidemic of the country. He soon changed his bullocks for brood mares, and his calves for colts, which he trained himself. This passion for a race horse, added to a prejudice for his own breed, had at this time brought him nearly to his last stake, yet under every difficulty he still kept up the appearance of a gentleman, and though often hard spurred and whipped by that severe jockey necessity, he never swerved from the course of honour. His farm produced hay and oats for his horses, and barley for the bread, on which he and his frugal household subsisted. He was sanguine enough to think he should be able to pay his rent from the winnings of his race horses, and in consequence was much in arrear when Singleton came to his stable door. From this day began a connection which lasted nearly half a century, and a friendship that only ended with their lives. Both are buried in the same church. There is room to speculate what secret cause attracted these two worthies and formed an union from materials apparently so dissimilar. The one by birth and education of a rank vastly superior, moving in the first circles, and endued with a morbid sensibility, fearful of losing caste; the other a poor starved ragged orphan; there was nothing in common except a love for horses and a want of cash; which perhaps the gentleman only felt.

II.

The lad was delighted with the terms of his first engagement; he had got upon a race horse; hunger, cold, and all the hardships of the past were forgotten, he only saw the bright prospect of the future. There was plenty of riding at the feasts, where he soon distinguished himself, and partook of the good cheer stirring on these occasions as a reward for riding; there was no money. The prize contended for being only a saddle or a bridle, left little for the owner of the horse, and nothing for the rider, except the laurels of victory, fit emblem of fame, leaves without fruit. While yet a child in years, he became noted for his seat on the saddle and judgment in riding. A farmer delighted with winning a bridle (worth perhaps half a crown), at three or four mile heats, made him a present of a sheep which his master agreed to keep for him in lieu of wages. The produce of this ewe in a few years amounted to a dozen or more, when an event occurred to change the system.

From riding all sorts of horses, Singleton soon discovered the superiority of those which had a cross of the Arabs over the old English racer, and advised his master to put his mares to a stallion of this kind, but neither of them had any money, when Singleton gave up his sheep for the purpose, and Mr. Read agreed to give him £5 per annum for wages. One mare was put to a horse from Hampton Court stud (Mr. Gallant's Smiling Tom) which produced a filly called Lucy, which won the Subscription over Hambleton in 1736, beating a large field. In the early part of the following year, she, their only hope, being amiss, was beat. Winter was approaching, cash scarce, when Singleton planned to take her into the north, and set off for Morpeth, distant 120 miles from Grimthorpe, with only 10s. 6d. in his pocket for expenses, acting the part of groom, stable-boy, and jockey, in a strange distant place, where he knew no one, and when asked from whence he came, he said from Grimthorpe. Where was Grimthorpe? It was near Pocklington. And where was Pocklington? It was near York. He was laughed at for coming so far with a small slender filly as she appeared when compared with her competitors. At this moment, preparing to saddle and mount, all to be done by himself, then a youth, unwell and harassed with cares and fears, to his great joy a butcher from Pocklington turned up, who came to back the mare, for which purpose he had ridden all night, except resting himself and horse for a short time under a haystack. And being a stout sturdy fellow, he soon cleared a way, assisted him to mount, took the odds she was not distanced, then backed her to win to the extent of his purse. The plate was secured, with two others at Stockton and Sunderland; and this laid the foundation for the future success of both Read and Singleton.

Mr. Read bred several winners, and a filly which the Marquis of Rockingham purchased, engaging Singleton at the same time at a salary of £40 per annum; a great advance from £5, of which 20 years was then due, for which Mr. Read gave his bond. Success appears to have departed with Singleton, for though Mr Read continued his stud and his training, yet when Singleton came to reside on his property, he found his old master nearly in the same state in which he first knew him, his stud from want of proper crossing was blood without bone, and the farm without any other stock; he therefore invited the old gentleman to dinner, shewed him his bond, with twenty years arrear of interest, then threw it into the fire, and persuaded him to change his high-bred colts for sheep and cattle, thus enabling him to pass his last years in comfort.

III.

For several years before Singleton left Mr. Read he had a great part of the riding in the county, and was so successful that he had purchased estates in the adjoining township of Great Givendale, the scene of his early struggles and difficulties in life. About the year 1751 he went to reside at Newmarket, where the Marquis of Rockingham had a large racing establishment, which he placed under the superintendence of Singleton, and engaged him to train and ride all his horses which ran in the south; but during the winter months, the young stock were prepared and made ready for going into work at Swinton, near Wentworth House (the Marquis's seat), Yorkshire, by one Lund, and at the conclusion of the Newmarket Spring Meetings, when the horses' engagements were run out there, and they were intended to run for stakes at York and Doncaster (to both of which Meetings the Marquis was a great supporter), the horses were sent under Singleton's inspection, to a place called Thixendale, near Malton, where Singleton had purchased two farms, built stables, and other conveniences thereon for training, which he considered the best ground for the purpose of any in the kingdom; and from this place they not unfrequently departed to win many of the best stakes, and defeat most of the first-rate horses of the day in Yorkshire.

The Marquis was one of the supporters of the British turf, which he patronised both at Newmarket and in the country; and such was his regard and esteem for Singleton that he employed the first artist of that day to paint the subject of this memoir riding many of his favourite horses, and gave several of these pictures to Singleton, who appears to have been treated more as a humble friend than as a servant. After the great race between Bay Malton, Herod, Turf, and Askham, over the Beacon Course, at Newmarket First Spring Meeting, 1767, for 500gs. each, the Marquis ordered a gold cup to be made, on which the figures of Bay Malton and his rider are richly chased, with the pedigree and performances of that celebrated horse engraved thereon, also a statement that it was offered, and not accepted, to run any horse, giving him 7lb., either over the flat for speed, or over the six mile course for stoutness, and that he presented this cup to John Singleton, the rider of Bay Malton. Singleton at the same time received a Silver Salver, on which is engraved all the above horses and their riders contending in the race, from an eminent silversmith, who, though he lost his money on the race, sent it as a mark of his admiration of his riding. He continued at Newmarket until the year 1774, when he resigned his green jacket in favour of Christopher Scaife, who had married one of his nieces. During his residence at Newmarket he rode many of the great races besides those in which the Marquis was engaged, and also kept and started several horses in his own name and that of his confederate, Mr. Ottley, and was so successful that he educated and provided for many of his poor relatives, besides purchasing some valuable farms and the major part of the township of Great Givendale; on this latter he built a house and stables, and on leaving Newmarket, came to reside there, breeding a few horses which he ran in the country, but without his usual success, which he attributed to being unable from age and infirmities to give them that attention he had formerly done.

IV.

In November, 1769, he married Mrs. Jackson, widow of Peter Jackson, a rider of some note, and the nephew of Thomas Jackson, one of the best horsemen of that day. She was a person of some attainments, and the nobility and gentry who attended the Newmarket meetings called upon Singleton to see his stud, and their ladies to taste Mrs. Singleton's cakes and made wines, for which she was celebrated. In 1774, they came to reside upon his estate at Great Givendale, where he supported the character of a country gentleman, keeping a hospitable house, respected by his neighbours, and beloved by his dependents. He died in January, 1793, leaving a widow and four children, two of them sons, of one of whom a short memoir is given. His widow survived him a few years, and is buried near him. His posterity possess the estate, with several pictures, and other memorials of the turf in olden time, depicting and illustrating the stirring scenes in which he moved. They also appear to inherit a little of his spirit, breeding and starting a racer now and then in a quiet way; and one of them distinguishes himself as a gentleman jockey. Singleton appears to have been treated more as a humble friend than a servant, and that he deserved it by his faithful services, no greater proof can be given than that he had only two masters during half a century, and his attachment to both forms an honourable trait in his character. From the pictures now extant of Singleton, he appears to have been about the middle size, with a broad chest, a strong arm, and a quick eye, to which may be added a cool head and nerves which nothing could shake, for in the last years of his life he could lift his full glass of wine without the least tremor. See him mounted for the race, see him going out to course, observe a set out, the condition of his greyhounds and his hunter, the celebrated Merry Batchelor, his dress and gold-laced hat, the costume of a squire of that day, and Pat would say, "There goes a raal jintleman," and he was such by nature. He retired from a dangerous profession after fifty years spent in it, without a stain on his character. Thus is shewn what genius and perseverance can perform. In his race through this life he started the last of his village, at the end he was the first.

"Act well your part, there all the honour lies."

THE BOLD BENDIGO AND JEM BURN.

ONE of the bad signs of the times is the revival of pugilism in so far as public sentiment will admit of its revival. "Sparring" is now a recognised sign of the times, and in London, on Sunday evenings in particular, exhibitions of the "manly art" of self-defence are now given with much regularity—these shows being attended by persons of good social position. On occasion "set battles" are also brought off, and some of the sporting journals of the day devote a large amount of space to the prize ring. Books too are at present being published in record of former feats, and from these many anecdotes can be called as to the deeds and *personnel* of former heroes of the "P.R." Of these, it will be sufficient to give one or two by way of sampling the bulk. Of Bendigo the bold whose name was Thompson, we are told that almost no better man ever stripped. After his fight with, and defeat of Caunt, in a little speech made on that occasion he said, " I am backed chiefly by Nottingham weavers, by men who subscribe their pound or ten shillings a piece, and who cannot afford to lose. Now there are certain rules belonging to the P. R., and I have kept to them, not only for my own credit, but for the benefit of those friends who, though poor, always backed me to their last shilling." Thompson, *alias* Bendigo, has been accused of being a shifty fighter, but he never adopted such tactics unless when matched against heavier and stronger men than himself. When standing up to Looney, one of the hardest fights he was ever engaged in, there was no tumbling-down, and when he overcame Deaf Burke, the latter actually thought people were throwing stones at him, so rapid and effective were Bendigo's blows.

Bendigo was, in spite of being a prize fighter, a bit of a moralist, as was seen by his taking his friend Jem Burn to task. Burn's better half was either dead or was living apart from her husband, and his daughter, an attractive young girl of seventeen, served in the bar. Jem was often out; in fact, rather gay, and about this Bendigo often took him to task. As might be expected, Miss Burn had many admirers, and Bendigo told her father that he should not leave her so unprotected. He told Jem more than once that if he did not alter he would give him a thrashing. Now, when Bendigo was sober, his instincts were most manly, and it was only on one occasion that the daughter by coming into the parlour prevented a fight between him and her father on her account.

ONE WAY OF WINNING A WAGER.

The following feat certainly out-herods Herod; but my readers shall have it exactly as I myself had it, accompanied with the following remark—" Nothing, we are led to believe, is impossible with God; nothing was improbable of the late John Mytton."

He was one day engaged to dine with a friend at some distance from Halston, and came, as usual, in his tandem. After dinner, the conversation turning on the danger of that mode of harnessing horses, from the little command the driver can have over the leader, Mytton at once expressed his dissent from this doctrine; and being under the influence of the "rosy god," offered to bet a pony (£25) all round, that he would *that night* drive his tandem across the country into the turnpike road, a distance of half a mile, having in his progress to get over a sunk fence, three yards wide; a broad, deep drain; and two stiff, quick-set fences, with ditches on the further side! This bet was taken by several of the party present to the tune of £150 and upwards; and after the necessary preparations, all turned out to see the fun—although in justice it should be said, as Mytton was then under age, it was not only proposed to him that the bets made should be off, but he was strongly persuaded not to make the attempt. This, however, with him had always a contrary effect; and twelve men with lanterns on poles having been procured, to aid the light of the moon, on the appointed signal being given, away went Mytton.

"The first obstacle was the sunk fence, *into* which, as may be expected, he was landed; but the opposite side being on a gradual slope, from bottom to top, the carriage and its inmate, by dint of whipping, were drawn out without receiving any injury. Nowise disconcerted, he sent his team at the next fence —the wide drain—and such was the pace he went at, that it was cleared by a yard, or more; but the jerk pitched Mytton on the wheeler's back. Crawling over the dashing-leather, he resumed his seat and got his horses again into the proper direction, and taking the two remaining fences in gallant style, got safe into the turnpike road, and won his wager. This occurred at Mr. Walford's of Cronkhill, about four miles from Shrewsbury."

HOW BOOKMAKERS NAME HORSES.

THE majority of the bookmaking fraternity have a decidedly rough and ready way of pronouncing the names of horses, the nomenclature of which is out of the common. It has to be admitted, however, that the English bookmaker is generally equal to the occasion, and, whether in ignorance, or in fun, or in sheer contempt for all but "plain English," transforms the foreign names into something grotesque but unmistakable for betting purposes: so that Filho da Puta becomes Fill-up-the-Pewter, La Fille Ma-Gardée becomes the Female Guard, and Scherz becomes Shirts quite naturally. Owners of horses at one time gave them very ugly and unbecoming names, such names as cannot now be put in type with any sense of propriety. Then they indulged in names of a portentous length and outlandish appearance, such as the members of " the Ring," whose numbers have increased so much as to entitle them to consideration, might resent—time being money—on the ground of the minutes wasted over the multitudinous syllables and over the many " refusals " at the various obstacles of pronunciation. A bookmaker, for instance, might well be angry if he had to vociferate in his incessant fashion: "I'll lay agen Alamahatamaha," or (a real pitfall) Aphrodite, Badroulboudour, or even Bucephalus (which comes out of the turfite's mouth in the form of " Buckyfailus "), Cumberhzepha (which is scarcely fair even upon " a scholar and a gentleman "), or Coticula, Demosthenes or Dulcamara, Euphrosyne or Eurydice (which is a dreadful trap from its suggestion of " the bones," the last four letters), Guadaloupe, Hamadryad or Harapha, Inamorato or Icarus, Je-ne-sais-quoi, Kerenhappuch or Kutusoff, Laurestinus or Lycoris (which, of course, becomes Liquorice), Meleager or Montesquieu, Nepenthe or Onesander (which is divided into One-sander, and, of course, pronounced Wun-sander), or Othothea, Passamaquoddi or Przedswit, Quetlavaca, Ramschoondra or Rastopchin, Sir-Ulic-McKilligut (abbreviated almost necessarily into the plural of the last syllable), Tatharangtangtang or Tenducci (" I'll lay agen Ten Ducks "), Vergissmein-nicht (or Ferguson's Night), or Volontiers (which becomes volunteer), or Vulpecula, Wegenkorb or Wowski, Xiloaloe, Ynysymaengwyn, and Zoffani. Against such names has the bookmaker had to struggle from time immemorial, so that the money he makes is sometimes " very hard cash." It may be that the spread of horse-racing all over the globe and the more frequent and intimate intercourse between English and foreign turfites have made our home-bred bookmaker more tolerant of foreign names ; but his feelings ought to be harrowed as little as possible by his own countrymen now that the foreigners introduce so freely upon our racecourses their own horses, their own names, and their own pronunciation.

LORD PALMERSTON AND JOHN DAY.

I.

LORD PALMERSTON wisely sought recreation from the harassing cares of State in the sports of the field, thereby not only nourishing our national pastimes, but invigorating his own frame, and strengthening himself for those mighty intellectual contests in which during the session he was nightly engaged in the senate. And the hilarity of his spirits, both in the hunting field and on the racecourse, testify, far better than language can portray, his love for the turf and the covert side, and how great must have been the sacrifice of his feelings when he sank the sportsman in the politician !

As an owner of race horses, Lord Palmerston dates as far back as 1816, when we find him running at Winchester a filly called Mignonette, by Sorcerer, who was trained for him by "Grandfather Day," sire of "old John Day," and grandsire of the present John of Danebury, and who then resided at Houghton Down, which was within an easy ride of Broadlands. "Grandfather Day," whose portrait, taken in his great coat, on his pony, when he weighed over 20st, all visitors to Danebury must be familiar with, was a quaint old man, and as perfect an original as "Honest John" himself. Straightforward in his conduct to his employers, his thorough knowledge of his business and industrious habits gained him the entire good-will of the neighbourhood, and procured for him more horses than were to be found in any other stable in the south of England. With Lord Palmerston he was an especial favourite ; and often, when suffering from the gout, to which he was a fearful martyr, would the kind-hearted minister ride over, and sit by his bedside, discussing his horses, and making him acquainted with the topics of the day. On one of these occasions a remark he made to his lordship, and frequently quoted by him, we shall reproduce, as the amusing truth conveyed in it cannot be gainsaid. Happening to be at Houghton Down when the Ministry were out, his lordship informed him of the circumstance.

"Yes, my lord," replied the old man, "but they tells I as how *you* are the cleverest up there among them, for it does not signify which side goes out, *you* always manages to keep in."

Another remark of the veteran, from its shrewdness, also deserves to be rescued from oblivion. Alluding to some employer who had removed his horses from him in a fit of disappointment at not winning a particular race, and left his bill unsettled, he observed, "Huff and pay was bad enough, but huff and no pay was awful."

II.

With Mignonette, old Mr. Day could do nothing for his lordship ; but in the following year, 1817, he won his maiden race for him with Enchantress, a four-year-old mare, likewise by

Sorcerer; and in 1818 he "paid his bill" for him with a plate at the same place with her. For two seasons we do not come across Lord Palmerston's name, and then he appears again single-handed, but as winner, with a Rubens colt at Blandford; and until 1823, when he won the Queen's Plate at Salisbury with Biondetta, a plate at one of the small Hampshire meetings was the solitary result of his racing.

In 1824 matters looked brighter, for he had picked up at Tattersall's, by his own judgment, Luzborough, a Newmarket cast off, for £75, who for upwards of two years carried all before him in the western neighbouring districts, winning, among other races, the Somersetshire at Bath, the Hampshire at Winchester, the Oxfordshire at Oxford, and the Gold Cups at Salisbury and Winchester; and, in short, Luzborough and John Day at that time, in that part of the world, were as formidable as Fisherman and Wells were three years back; and he afterwards disposed of him to Mr. Dilly for 600 guineas. With Greyleg and Conquest, also, he made great havoc at the country meetings on the circuit, and nothing could stand up against them. Shortly afterwards, "Grandfather Day," who posted with the horses on their various journeys, as he was unable to ride from his weight, died; and the Houghton Down establishment was taken by his sons, John and William Day. The latter soon quitted his brother, and went to reside at Ascot; and "Honest John" getting a lease of Danebury, which was more adapted for his increasing business, took his son into partnership, and the horses of Lord Palmerston followed with the other employers of the stable. For the next few years his lordship did nothing worth speaking of, and had only one animal, called Waldron, in training; but in 1836, he had a slight turn of luck again, as Toothill, whom he bred out of his old mare Biondetta, won several things for him; and Ashfield, also out of her, paid his way. But in 1840, came the climax of his fortunes on the turf, as with Iliona, a filly whom he selected himself out of a draft of Lord George Bentinck's at Tattersall's, and which was knocked down to him for 65 guineas, he won the Cesarewitch and several other races, including the Southampton Stakes, for which she beat the celebrated Retriever, the winner of the Goodwood Stakes and the Chesterfield Cup. This rare bred mare, for she was got by Priam out of Galopade's dam, Lord Palmerston had not intended to train, and she was turned out in the paddocks at Broadlands with a view of being ultimately put to the stud; but honest John was so struck with her when he saw her, that he implored his lordship to send her up to Danebury to be trained. This he did, and the result is well known; the old man was wont to narrate, with great zest and spirit, the interview he had with his lordship when he came to settle with him and pay over the stakes.

"Nothing could exceed his lordship's great kindness," added the veteran, in that emphatic manner so peculiarly his own, and which gave such dramatic power to his language. "He saw me directly, shook me by the hand, gave me joy, handed me a chair, ran his eye over the bill, never objected to a single item; and when I offered to give him a check for the difference, which was over fifteen hundred, he got up and gave me a pen with his own hand, and concluded his interview by saying, 'John, I will do anything for you.'" And truly he did keep his word, for the old man never knew what it was to be denied, and would knock at Carlton House-terrace, or go down to the House of Commons to him, with all the confidence of a Cabinet Minister.

III.

On one occasion, during a visit to "the House," John found his way into the corridor, and was proceeding to pass the door when he was stopped by a policeman, who asked him what he wanted. To this inquiry he replied, "I want to see Lord Palmerston, and I am John Day!" The policeman, who, I suppose, knew nothing of racing, and took John, with his white neckcloth and eternal umbrella, for an elderly curate in search of a Crown living, refused him admittance, and told him Lord Palmerston could not be disturbed. This put "John" out terribly, for he had that persuasive and dignified manner about him that told very much in his favour. And he was the more annoyed because he had got a crowd of people round him. However, his patience was not long tried, as the present Lord Strafford (then Lord Enfield,) passing by, took compassion on him, and with his proverbial good nature said he would see what he could do for him, and, passing him through an inner door, to the great astonishment of the policeman, returned to him shortly, and said Lord Palmerston would come to him in a few minutes. That he accordingly did, to "John's" great delight; and, after shaking hands with him most kindly, asked him what he had come to see him for. "Why, my lord, I have got a son, I have brought him up as a doctor, and he wants an appointment to a poor law union in Hertfordshire; I have had him 'tried very high,' and he has won his trial very easy, and I am sure you will give it to him." "To be sure, John," answered the kind-hearted Premier, who then entered into a discussion on the Derby that promised to be of such duration that "John" thought it time to give him a hint, to the effect he was afraid he was detaining him, as he knew *he* (Lord Palmerston) had plenty to do. His lordship then shook him again by the hand; and, just as he parted with him, "John" turned round and amused him beyond measure by saying, "Mind, my lord, you write to the right man this time; the last time, you recollect, you wrote to the wrong one." Probably the annals of Parliament cannot furnish another instance of a Premier quitting his seat in the House of Commons to see an old and faithful servant.

THE ROYAL COCK PIT.

WITH the Restoration, the turf and the sod assumed new leases of life, and both at Newmarket and at the Royal Cockpit in St. James's Park, proof was given of the natural impulse of Englishmen. Mains were fought by day and night between the selected cocks of different countries, and although, as in racing, the records previous to the middle of the last century were not preserved, there is every reason to believe that the strains of blood in cocks were handed down in as pure a state as in the case of horses, from the cockers of the "Merry Monarch's" time to those of the Victorian era. Of the Royal Cockpit nothing now remains, the steps leading from Queen-street to St. James's Park alone telling, by their name, "the Cockpit-steps," where the site of the historic rendezvous was. It is, however, easy for the lover of antiquities, aided by the characters drawn for him by Shadwell, and the description of the Newmarket pit by Macaulay, who has left on record the fact that "on rainy days the cockpit was encircled by stars and blue ribands," to picture to himself the groups that frequented it for the purpose of watching the exertions of the best birds in Europe; I will not say in the world, in case I might strike the susceptibilities of the lovers of Indian game, to which breed may, without question, be accorded, if only on the ground of antiquity, most honourable mention. A curious old work on the subject gives the following description of the Royal Cockpit:—

"It is situated on the south side of St. James's Park, from

which it has its entrance, and was erected in the reign of Charles II., who, having been himself fond of the sport, is said to have frequently honoured it with his presence, when matches were made and fought amongst his nobles. It is the only place where long mains and great 'Subscription Matches' are fought in the metropolis, some of which are for considerable sums between opulent individuals, who procure their cocks from different parts of the country, and others (particularly of the subscription matches) by many members on each side, who breed their cocks in distant counties, but fight them only in town, of which description many matches are annually fought during all the Spring months, when it may be said cocks are in the finest feather and highest perfection. The cockpit is circular, and completely surrounded, with seats six tier deep, exclusive of a rail, with standing room all round the summit of the uppermost seat, forming in the whole a perfect amphitheatre. The centrical circle, upon which the cocks fight, is a raised mound of earth, surrounded with boarding, about 20ft. in diameter, and should, according to the technical term of the sport, be covered with a fine green turf, denominated sod, in conformity with the general acceptation of the word in the sporting world, where by 'the sod' is implied cocking. In all mains or matches fought in the country part of the kingdom, cocks invariably fight upon the sod, but as it is an article difficult to obtain in the metropolis, and would be inconvenient and inapplicable during hard frosty weather, when many matches are fought, matting upon the surface is substituted in its stead. On each side the circular mound, at its extremity, and exactly opposite to each other, are two small seats for the setters-to, who retire to those seats during long fighting, or when ordered by the bettors and spectators so to do. Directly over the centre is suspended from the dome, by a chain, a very large circular branch containing a great number of candles, affording a profusion of light—for nearly all the matches fought here are very unnaturally decided by night, the company going to pit at six o'clock in the evening. At the hour previously agreed on, the bags containing the cocks are brought into the pit by the feeders, or whoever they may appoint; they are there received by the setters-to, whose qualifications depend upon a quick eye, a light hand, and an agile heel, without the whole of which, celebrity can never be acquired in their way. The cocks, being taken from the bags, are most scrupulously compared in feather and marks with the original description entered in the match-bill on the day of weighing. This ceremony gone through, the feeders retire from the centre of the pit, and the setters-to are then the sole possessors, with the cocks in hand. In this state they are shown to each other, beak to beak, and, if they show fight, are tossed upon the mat, and the battle begins."

READY MONEY BETTING.

HAD ready-money betting been the rule of the turf some twenty years ago, the honour of several noble families would never have been in peril. When a man, especially a nobleman, bets on honour—that is, to speak plainly, on credit, it is imperative, if he loses, and wishes to maintain his good name, that he should pay what he is due on the Monday after the race. To save his honour, and in order not to be known as a defaulter, he will make any sacrifice to be prompt in settling—he will pawn his wife's diamonds, sell off his stud of horses, mortgage his lands. But were it the rule to deposit the stakes before the race, it is not in the least likely he would be led to perform any of these actions. It is the hope of "better luck next time" that lures on the credit-bettor after a loss; had he to write a cheque at the time of making each bet—which is probably months before the event on which he bets falls to be determined—he would be apt to think twice before doing so.

It is credit betting that draws men into a long series of transactions on future events. If a man loses heavily, say on the race for the two thousand guineas, and his horse does not win, he must pay or become a defaulter. If he cannot pay, then he foregoes all interest in future events, on which he may stand well, and which might come off in his favour. If a defaulter, all bets that any person may have with him are "off," and he may have heavily backed some horse for the coming Derby which might win the race, and by doing so put ten thousand pounds to his credit! Men who bet largely on credit sometimes find themselves in such a position.

When there is betting for ready money only, there will then be a chance that men will become temperate in their speculations, and bet within their means. A time when there will be no betting we do not believe in. As for the assumption that shop-boys steal occasional half-crowns for the purpose of betting, it is unworthy of much consideration. There is a famous old remedy for such petty larceny. A hungry person who takes a loaf of bread deserves our commiseration. Anyone, on the contrary, who robs his master or cheats his creditors that he may "back the favourite" for the Derby or a "good outsider" for the Oaks, deserves no mercy except such as lies in the taste of the cat.

GROUSE DRIVING SPORT.

THE following plea for grouse driving speaks for itself: "For those who can devote September as well as August to the moors, grouse-shooting on three days of the week over dogs is most enjoyable, killing at leisure and showing your twenty or thirty birds at the end of the day, not to speak of half-a-dozen hares and a couple of blackcock, and, when the shooting is well mixed, a few brace of partridges. But do give me the delight of an occasional drive—well planned and carefully executed. Let the day be a fine one, in early September; a little sun, but not much; just a capful of wind blowing in the proper direction, the late heather beautiful in its purple sheen, the decaying flowers in some places emitting a faint odour, the atmosphere clear and bracing. Anon a murmur of several distant voices is borne to our attentive ear by the gentle breeze; nearer there can occasionally be heard the ear-pleasing chuckle of a fine old cock, or the bleating of a small flock of black-faced sheep. Hark! It is a faint cry of 'Mark!' that at length reaches the listeners. In the distance there is seen a bird or two rising and falling. Straining our eyes—more and more birds rise and disappear. The ghillies are hard at work a-down the valley, and the warning 'Mark!' sounds more distinctly. 'Bang, bang!' It is the advanced guard who has drawn first blood by a right and left. Now we are at full cock; there he comes—one! again, two! Capital. More and more birds reach us, although, with a chum, I am in the rear. Anon the shooting becomes furious, and grouse positively rain upon the heather. We are eleven guns in all, and I am eighth in the line, but in less than twenty minutes I have thirteen birds, having missed four that I tried for; my companion has been more fortunate, sixteen birds has he laid low—not bad work for two in the rearmost rank. Those in front have of course had the pick of the birds, and they have fallen fast and furiously. In a little time they came in a perfect cloud, but scores of them escaped—choice was embarrassing; sometimes two men killed the same birds. It is a pity the grouse come on us so quickly—thirty or forty miles an hour; a flash, and they are either dead or a mile distant, before one has leisure to take stock of his shot. It is a grand three-quarters of an hour of keen excitement, with birds enough for triple the number of guns. Five hundred and thirty number in all the slain, and assuredly a thousand have escaped the dread display of artillery. The business, while it lasts, is somewhat bewildering! it requires a cool head and a steady hand. For one hour and three-quarters were we in the batteries, and for full twenty minutes of the time the grouse were a sight to see; at first they came as single spies, then in twos and fours, all disposed of with unerring aim, number two being ready should number one miss; then, after these advanced guards have been disposed of, there arrives the battalion, hundreds of birds! You will of course say it was a massacre; well, well, do not let us quarrel; grouse, you know, are born to be killed. What then does it matter if they are killed in twos or tens? But I shall not go further in the argument—we agree to differ."

TIPSTERS' TRICKS AND TEMPTATIONS.

A COMPLETE collection of the advertisements issued by those parasites of racing, and a plain statement of the results achieved by following the advice of touts and tipsters would form an interesting record of human credulity. From the bulk of these announcements, a few may be given by way of example, with the comments made upon them by the collector :—

I

"Many a poor man has laid the foundation of a princely fortune by a lucky chance such as now presents itself. Enormous odds. Monster double event.—Cesarewitch and Cambridgeshire. Two clippers, saved expressly, are sure to be favourably weighted, for such an artful game has been played by the cleverest men on the Turf that the handicapper has been effectually deceived. Do not miss this golden opportunity of winning a great stake at a little risk. Terms for the secret, fourteen stamps; or I can obtain £3,500 to £1, or £1,750 to 10s., or £875 to 5s. Established twenty-four years.—John Garland, Leicester-square, London.

"I shall be wonderfully successful at Doncaster. Back my extreme outsider for the St. Leger for place only. It is a certainty he will be one of the first three. As to the Great Yorkshire Handicap, I consider it as good as over. I am in the secret, and know that nothing has a chance with a certain "flyer" that is in at a ridiculously light weight. Try me in this meeting, and you will be glad you did. Fourteen stamps the week. Established twenty-four years.—John Garland, Leicester-square, London."

Mr. John Garland deserves a passing notice. He boasts that the "Admiral" has been "effectually deceived;" but seeing that this was advertised some time before the weights for the Cesarewitch and Cambridgeshire appeared, it does seem a little premature. But the terms are somewhat remarkable. You can have the "secret" for "fourteen stamps" or you may receive £875 for 5s. if you prefer it, and he has been established twenty-four years. Wonderful! And if this game of 3500 to 1 has been going on for twenty-four years, is there a bookmaker still in existence, and Garland not a millionaire! But, Garland, where is the outsider you promised?

II.

"Cesarewitch and Cambridgeshire—Mr. Gaywood begs to announce that he is in possession of first-class information direct from the stables. Backers of horses wishing to secure a good investment at long odds in these important handicaps should send their address to Mr. Fred Gaywood, Leamington, who last year advised Actæa, Cambridgeshire.

"Hermit will win the Leger.—Mr. Gaywood will attend the Doncaster races, and execute commissions at the post on Hermit to win the Leger. Gentlemen sending commissions will please let them reach Mr. Gaywood not later than Wednesday next to the Post-office Doncaster. Winnings will be remitted direct from Doncaster."

Mr. Gaywood was the gentleman who, if I mistake not, some time since had a "system" also. However, he appears to have given that up, and taken Hermit instead. All the world now knows that it was not necessary to "forward the winnings direct from Doncaster."

III.

Now comes a "mysterious" notice by a "retired bookmaker." Do they ever *retire* by the way? As it is a "forbidden book" we would rather not touch it, and trust our example will be universally followed—

"Important notice—the forbidden book—a key to the mysteries of winning on the Turf. By a retired bookmaker. Post free, thirty stamps.

Address, G. H., 172, King's-road, London, S.W. Opinions of the Sporting Press [Query—What paper?—ED.] 'A wonderful book, and would be cheap at ten times its cost.' [Copyright.]"

IV.

"Leger winner 40 to 1.—No Hermit! no Achievement!—Mr. Thomas Martin's outsider will win and surprise everybody. Advised Marksman alone (second) for the Derby. Enclose six stamps and promise per centage.—Address, 16, Victoria-terrace, Liverpool-road, Holloway, London."

Mr. Martin's is a bold dash, and evidently is just a rough chance at any outsider, and as he would have no Hermit and no Achievement, we shall probably hear no more of Mr. Martin, at least under that name.

V.

The next to which attention is drawn is that emanating from Mr. Ryley, the "well-known backer of horses," as he styles himself—yes, and rather too well known to some bookmakers, if he be, as he says, the real Riley; and one would have thought he would be more likely to succeed under some less "well known" cognomen.

"A certainty for the Leger.—Ryley, the well known leviathan backer of horses, will send the name of the horse that is certain to win, on receipt of post-office order for 5s. and stamped directed envelope (order payable to Frederick Ryley, General Post-office, Birmingham).—Address, Havannah House, Constitution Hill, Birmingham. This is the greatest certainty I ever knew, and the public are aware that I have sent some of the best things of the season."

DIFFICULTIES ATTENDING HORSE-RACE TRIALS.

WARY as the trainer himself may be, however keen-eyed his assistants, and let the surrounding points of vantage be scanned and examined as keenly as they may, it is wonderful how frequently the result of a trial is seen and spread abroad.

Some years ago a three year old was undergoing preparation on a high northern training ground. In early days he had performed very moderately. He was not fashionably bred, and had died out of the memory of the public altogether. The colt was, however, so good that, if treated with any degree of lenicncy by the adjuster of weights, one or both of the great autumn handicaps at Newmarket were nearly certain to fall to his lot. Towards the close of the summer it was determined that his merits should be severely tested; and very early one morning, before aught was astir on the moor, and with no discernible witnesses, save owner and trainer, the colt was "asked a question." He answered it in a manner so unexpectedly clever that those interested in him hugged themselves at the bright prospect of gain which opened out before them. As their exultation was at boiling pitch a ragged, dishevelled form rose above the crest of a neighbouring hollow, and approached the party. Consternation pictured on their faces, they gazed upon the unwelcome intruder.

"It's only Fond Jemmy," exclaimed one of them, with a sigh of relief, as the poor, addle-pated creature, walking up to them, displayed a large basket of mushrooms, which he had collected in the neighbouring pastures.

"Jemmy," he continued, in a seductive tone, "hast thou seen aught? We're nobbut giving t'horses a bit of a gallop!"

"Nay," said Jemmy, carefully avoiding the speaker's eye, and staring fixedly into vacancy, "Ah hevn't. Mebbe ye'll want a few misherums."

A glance was exchanged by the two principal conspirators, and Jemmy was directed to hand over his succulent burden then and there; and with a bright half-crown clasped tightly in his dusty fist, he moved hurriedly away towards the town. Luckless and mistaken liberty! Had the reward been confined to the shilling which usually repaid the mushroom gatherer's exertions, all would have been well. Half-a-crown was too much for Jemmy to carry unbroached. An early visit to the Black Lion was the natural consequence. One threepen'orth was consumed; a second; and when a third dram of unsweetened Nicholson had been despatched he grew talkative. It chanced that one very acute member of the brotherhood of touts was taking his "morning" in the same establishment, and pricking up his ears at the disjointed sentences uttered by the weak-headed tippler, he soon extracted from him the secret of the trial at early dawn. Jemmy, it appeared, had seen the spin, and notwithstanding his infirmity, retained sufficient Yorkshire cunning to deny the fact when first taxed with it on the moor. Now that his tongue was loosened he described with such accuracy to his tempter how the short-legged bay, who carried his head so low, had beaten the others to a stand-still that the shrewd listener—himself a great believer in the prowess of "Le Médecin,"—putting this and that together, was able to place the information, within a few hours, at the disposal of his London employer. The latter quietly took advantage of it. Owing to an extraordinary and unprecedented blunder, the good thing did not come off. Had it done so, the disburser of the half-crown and his allies would have discovered that the amount which they had backed their colt to win was considerably less than the great stake for which he was stood by the Metropolitan bookmaker, who had acquired his information through the tipsy babbling of "Fond Jemmy."

OF THE ODDS OBTAINED IN BETTING.

It is interesting to know that very large *odds* have frequently been obtained against a horse's chance of winning a particular event. An Edinburgh gentleman took 500 to 1 against Hawthornden winning the St. Leger, and that horse was victor in the race. On a recent occasion £100 to 5s. was betted against a horse; but it is necessary to state, by way of explanation, that by the disreputable dodge of a forged telegram the horse was reported to be *scratched* when the bet was offered and taken. Double and triple events, from the magnitude of the odds which can be obtained, always look tempting to novices in betting. Old stagers are easier to satisfy—a single event is enough for them. A gentleman residing in Glasgow negotiated in the beginning of the present year a triple event, which, had it proved successful, would have placed the handsome sum of £4,000 in his pocket! The horses he selected were Footstep, which won the Lincoln Handicap; Austerlitz, which won the Grand National Steeple Chase at Liverpool; and Saint Leger, which did *not* win the City and Suburban Handicap at Epsom. The first and second events having proved successful as stated, the bettor had an opportunity of winning money by hedging over the third horse, which figured at one time in the betting quotations at 12 to 1. The twelves in four thousand, therefore, at one time, represented the value of the bet. The odds given on a double or treble event are represented by multiplying the figures which are offered against the horses singly—say, Footstep at 20 to 1, and Austerlitz at 33 to 1, the odds for the double event, at these figures, would be 666 to 1—very handsome odds indeed, but they are rarely realised.

NOVEL FOX CHASE.

ONE Saturday afternoon, as two young gentlemen from Preston were out rabbit shooting on the banks of the Ribble, above the halfpenny bridge at Brockholes, they espied what they supposed to be a dog swimming up to the neck against the stream, its head being only just above the water, and it appeared quite exhausted. Some distance higher up, and not far from Sunderland Hall, there was a number of ducks swimming to and fro, and it soon became evident that the animal was not a dog but a fox, and that it had its eye upon them. The young fellows increased their speed, and in a short time came up with it as it still swam towards the ducks. One of them levelled his gun, but Reynard, as if he quite understood the intention, dived, and for a moment became invisible, until the report died away, when he lifted up his head again. At this juncture one of the young men fired at him from a gate, but with no better success, and the matter became quite exciting. The fox was within fifty yards of the ducks, and evidently unaffected at the balls which had twice whizzed within a few inches of him, he slackened rather than increased his speed. The youngest of the sportsmen then climbed up into an oak, thinking he could have better aim from such an elevation than from where he stood. But the distance between him and the fox rapidly increased, so that when he fired, the shot fell short by several yards, and the fox escaped once more. The men then ran after him until they got near to the Red Scar, the ducks having gone in that direction on seeing their enemy. The young fellows soon came up with him, and they fired together, but they did not reach him. They were not, however, only losing their powder and shot, but their tempers likewise; so that, as a final effort, they each loaded again, and determined either to mark him or to take to the water and swim after him. They both fired at the same time, when, as usual, the "cunning thief" bobbed his head under the water again, and when next seen he was thirty yards in advance of them. Tantalising as this additional failure was, it was rendered much more so when they observed him give a jerk in the water, he having come up with the ducks, and seizing one of them, carried it in triumph to the opposite bank. Here his good luck deserted him. A young gentleman with a dog happened to be on the other side, and, on seeing the fox carrying a duck, the dog made after him in spite of his master. He caught him near the Nab's Head, and although the fox bit him in several places, and was more than twice his size, he never lost his hold. The two young fellows got across in a boat, and along with the gentleman in question proceeded to the scene of the combat. The dog had made his teeth meet in the fox's groin, and in this way held him. As shown by the marks of blood on the ground, the fox had dragged the dog after him for forty yards, and it was with the utmost difficulty that the dog was pulled away.

"THE BLUE RIBAND OF THE TURF:" ORIGIN OF THE PHRASE.

THE world is indebted to the late Lord Beaconsfield for an account of the interview between Lord George Bentinck and himself, during which the phrase was, it may be said, coined. The following narrative embraces all the particulars incident to the disposal of Lord George's stud, which included Surplice, a race horse that won both the Derby and St. Leger of 1848.

"The world has hardly done justice to the great sacrifice which he made on this occasion to a high sense of duty. He had not only parted with the finest racing stud in England, but he parted with it at a moment when its prospects were never so brilliant, and he knew this well. He could scarcely have quitted the turf that day without a pang. He had become the lord paramount of that strange world so difficult to sway, and which requires for its government both a stern resolve and a courtly breeding. He had them both : and though the black-leg might quail before the awful scrutiny of his piercing eye, there never was a man so scrupulously polite to his inferiors as Lord George Bentinck. The turf, too, was not merely the scene of the triumphs of his stud and his betting-book. He had purified its practice and had elevated its character, and he was prouder of this achievement than of any other connected with his sporting life. Notwithstanding his mighty stakes and the keenness with which he backed his opinion, no one, perhaps, ever cared less for money. His habits were severely simple, and he was the most generous of men. He valued the acquisition of money on the turf because there it was a test of success. He counted his thousands after a great race as a victorious general counts his cannon and his prisoners.

"A few days before—it was the day after the Derby, May

25th, 1848—the writer met Lord George Bentinck in the library of the House of Commons. He was standing before the bookshelves, with a volume in his hand, and his countenance was greatly disturbed. His resolutions in favour of the colonial interest, after all his labours, had been negatived by the Committee on the 22nd, and on the 24th, his horse, Surplice, whom he had parted with among the rest of his stud, solely that he might pursue, without distraction, his labours on behalf of the great interests of the country, had won that paramount and Olympic stake, to gain which had been the object of his life. He had nothing to console him and nothing to sustain him, except his pride. Even that deserted him before a heart which he knew at least could yield him sympathy. He gave a sort of superb groan—

"'All my life I have been trying for this, and for what have I sacrificed it?' he murmured.

"It was in vain to offer solace.

"'You do not know what the Derby is,' he moaned out.

"'Yes, I do; it is the Blue Riband of the turf.'

"'It is the Blue Riband of the turf,' he slowly repeated to himself, and sitting down at the table, buried himself in a folio of statistics.

"But on Monday, 29th, when the resolution in favour of a 10s. differential duty for the colonies had, at the last moment, been carried, and carried by his casting vote, 'the Blue Ribands of the turf' were all forgotten. Not for all the honours and successes of all the meetings, spring or autumn, Newmarket, Epsom, Goodwood, Doncaster, would he have exchanged that hour of rapture. His eyes sparkled with fire, his nostrils dilated with triumph, his brow was elate like a conqueror, his sanguine spirit saw a future of continued and illimitable success.

"'We have saved the colonies,' he said, 'saved the colonies. I knew it must be so. It is the knell of free trade.'"

ONE OF LORD KENNEDY'S FEATS.

CAPTAIN HORATIO ROSS writing in a letter from the Carlton Club, 17th December, 1866, says, "I have just recollected a performance of Lord Kennedy, which I do not think has been surpassed. He backed himself for a considerable sum to shoot forty brace of grouse, and ride from his shooting quarters, Feloar, in Perthshire (the same I subsequently rented from the Duke of Athol), to his house, Dunottar, near Stonehaven, and back to Feloar in a day! He started of course very early— rain falling; he killed the forty brace by about nine a.m. He then changed his dress on the hill-side, and mounted a clever hack, which he rode the first seven or eight miles—there was no road for that distance; he then had a tolerable road to Dunottar, along which he had relays of horses. From Feloar to Dunottar is about eighty miles. He got back to Feloar about eight p.m., having shot forty brace of grouse, and ridden one hundred and sixty miles in fourteen and a half or fifteen hours, and was not in the least knocked up by it."

ARE BOOKMAKERS AS BLACK AS THEY ARE PAINTED?

The bookmaker is not quite the dreadful person he is occasionally represented as being—he does not sit waiting till the apprentice comes in with his master's till, or till the merchant's clerk, on his way to the bank, calls with a handful of the pound notes he has embezzled. No, the bookmaker knows his customers, he has his regular clients who enter his office in the most courageous manner: they do not sneak in by a back door or by some secret passage as do the clients of many of our stockbrokers. The business of the bookmaker is to accommodate all comers. For the benefit of those not well versed in betting, it may be stated that betting between personal friends or acquaintances has now almost entirely ceased, the bookmaker being able to accommodate all who desire to bet, which is a far preferable mode of speculation for those concerned. Bets made by one friend with another ought to be discouraged. No harm can happen to the layer of the odds (the bookmaker) : that is, if he gives attention to his business, and makes what is known as a fair and square book. He has, in some important races, as many as from twenty to fifty horses against which he can bet, and as each bettor has his own idea as to the animal which is likely to win the race, it will be seen that the professional layer of the odds has plenty of chances to take enough of money with which to pay those of his clients who back the winning horse and have a little left to reward him for his own trouble.

HOW THE MARQUIS OF WATERFORD FLOORED THE COCK OF THE NORTH.

A very good story is thus related of one of the Marquis of Waterford's little adventures. His Lordship while one day driving in his carriage on one of his estates in Ireland, observed a person bouncing about with a small brass cock stuck in his hat. Wondering who the man could be, the Marquis asked his coachman the question.

"It's Tim Brady, from Belfast, my Lord, who calls himself the Cock of the North, and wears that thing in his hat that every one may know him, and everybody's frightened of him," was the reply. That was enough to excite the Marquis's emulation. "Here, my man, I want you," he called out.

"You dub yourself the Cock of the North, and everybody's frightened of you," he said, when the bruiser, not in the slightest degree abashed, came up to the carriage door. "Now, look here," taking a fiver from his pocket, "here's a five-pound note. What do you say to a turn up? If you beat me the note is yours; if I beat you the cock is mine."

Brady was delighted, and as he stripped already felt the crisp bit of tissue paper between his fingers. The Marquis quickly divested himself of his clothes, and put the strictest injunctions upon his servants that they were not to interfere. The pugilist went to work with the intention of making it sharp and short, but got such a floorer for his precipitation that in the next round he thought it best to go upon a cautious tack; but very soon he discovered that his rough style was no match for that of the Marquis, who had graduated in the most scientific schools, and after half-a-dozen very short rounds Mr. Tim Brady threw up the sponge. With a knife his Lordship cut the brass effigy out of the crestfallen bruiser's hat, and put it in his pocket. "If I ever hear any more about the Cock of the North, you may expect to see me, and I'll give you a bellyful of what I have only given you a taste of to-day."

A STATESMAN AT PLAY.

The gambling records of a hundred years ago, in which the gaining or losing of thousands is reported as if it was only shillings that were changing hands are really remarkable, and cause people to wonder where all the money that was lost at play came from. Facts and figures of the most striking kind can be brought forward to prove the magnitude of the gambling transactions. Thus at White's Club in one week of 1772, three brothers lost £70,000, while the interest of the money Lord Foley's two sons required to pay their debts of honour came to £18,000, per annum. On the 4th February of the same year, Charles James Fox sat down to play hazard at Almack's, and played until five in the afternoon of the 5th. An hour before he was a winner of £12,000, but at dinnertime (five o'clock), when all play was discontinued, he had lost all that, and £11,000 as well. Resuming play after dinner, he kept on until Thursday, the 6th, when he was obliged to go and take part in the debate upon the Thirty-nine Articles, and it was then remarked he did not speak with his customary eloquence, but it seems wonderful that he could make a speech at all, but he did, and then dined. Afterwards (1 a.m., Friday 7th) he went to White's, where he remained drinking until 7 a.m., from thence to Almack's, where he won £6,000, and between three and four o'clock the same afternoon he started for Newmarket.

Two nights afterwards his brother, Stephen Fox, lost £11,000 at Almack's, and another brother of his dropped £10,000 more on the 13th. In those days people took a more practical view of gambling than we do, arguing that if a single individual lost £100,000 and became a beggar, in all probability his loss converted half-a-dozen beggars into wealthy men. Captain Gronow relates how, at one time, Lord Robert Spencer and General Fitzgerald kept a faro-bank at Brookes's, and that the former having bagged £100,000 as his share of the proceeds, followed the example set by General Scott and Colonel Panton, and cut gambling altogether. Others again played and lost and then left off for good; George Hartley Drummond, the banker, being one. He only played once in his life, when he lost £20,000 to Beau Brummell, and his partners would not allow him after that to be connected with the banking house.

PRIZE FIGHTING ON THE DERBY DAY.

IT is curious to mark how pugilism was mixed up in everything in the brave days of old. Men cared less for their skins then, and were physically braver than they now are. We allude here, of course, to the unlettered classes. A man with a grievance did not go in for the underhand certainty of a revolver, or a knife, in a difference with a fellow creature; but went rather for the comparatively even betting which characterises a bout with fists between two foes of average qualification. In the earliest accounts of the Derby more prominence is given to the boxing which came off during the meeting, than to the racing itself. The former is dismissed very curtly; and, mind you, we are speaking of times comparatively modern. *Bell's Life* was started in 1822, in which year the great race was won by a horse called Moses.

Small indeed was the space devoted by *Bell* to the history of the Epsom Summer Meeting in the year of grace 1822. There were only three days devoted to racing, it is true; but less could hardly be said about them. The fights were of more general interest than the races; and *apropos* to them, we must record our sympathy with the ladies who were unwilling spectators of the combat, being "snugly wedged in." Under the head of "Sporting Chronicle" the news runs in the following manner: On the Wednesday (May 22nd) the Downs appear to have been less numerously occupied than the spectator had hitherto observed them to be, "but the sports were very good." In order to diversify the sports on Thursday, and to gratify the plebeians and commoners, "a subscription purse of 25 gs. was collected for a fight between Dick Curtis, a man of first-rate talent, and the younger Cooper, the gipsy. It took place in the railed hollow where the plate horses saddle, and in the hurry to encircle the field of blood, hundreds of elegant females had a peep, if they chose, as they were 'snugly wedged in.' A smart battle of twenty-two minutes' duration was fought, and much science displayed. After exchanging several hits, Curtis floored his adversary by a muzzler on the throat. The gipsy placed a taking facer; but he was countered, and sprung upon with astonishing alacrity, and both fell in a struggle. The third and fourth rounds were manfully maintained; but Curtis out-fought his adversary at all points. In round seven, Cooper gave a turn to the battle by getting him down; but after this it was 'Moses' to a 'hackney.' Like the former, Curtis showed all the blood, science, and activity he was destined for; and it was no discredit to Cooper to have had enough from the hand of one of the best fighters of the day. Curtis won it carefully, but easy. A second terrible ruffianing battle was fought on the extremity of the course. It was meant at first for love, but hostilities were suspended whilst a purse of £5 was raised. It lasted 18 minutes only, but time was so busily spent, that the faces of each were as round as puddings; there was no sight between them, nor could a nose be seen! Their names were Baddely and Hodgekins, navigators; and the former won it, if it could be called a win!"

"FEE-FI-FO-FUM."

SUCH was the nickname given to a former Prince of Wales by the stable-boys of Newmarket. It was in 1784, that George Fourth commenced his short career on the turf. Not an ill-looking man was George, nor as yet over-bulky, when he went to Newmarket at the age of three-and-twenty, and ran his first horse, Hermit, against Surprise, in a match, and lost it. At the palace the doings of "Rowley" were, if possible, outdone by the prince's friends, the Lakes and other "macaronies," who spent their substance recklessly enough. Once the brothers, the Prince of Wales and the Duke of York, went on a royal progress to the North, when the doings in the way of eating and drinking, gambling, betting, and racing, were of what the French call "Homeric" character. So far as can be discovered, very few of the worshipful company were ever sober, but the progress was nevertheless a glorious one, for did not the appropriately named "Tot" win the Doncaster Cup, and make such heart as "Fee-fi-fo-fum" was endowed withal swell within his mighty and well-padded bosom. But this royal racing saturnalia was doomed to a sudden and inglorious conclusion. This came about through the "Escape affair," which brought the Prince of Wales, or rather his jockey, Chifney, into collision with the Jockey Club, who, in spite of the sycophancy of the period, held their own sternly against all the influence that could be brought to bear upon them. Escape was an unhappy beast, destined to bring trouble upon everybody connected with him. In his youth he contrived to embed his fetlock in the wood-work of his box; and the exclamation of the groom, "What an escape!" as he was rescued from his perilous position, gave a name to the ill-omened racer. He was, as sporting people have it, a "rabbit," or an "in-and-out runner." Fit one day to "run for a man's life," he was "as slow as a funeral" the day after to-morrow. Hence, when everybody expected him to win the Oatlands, his stable companion, Baronet, won instead; and he ultimately convinced the Jockey Club that he had been "pulled" by Chifney, either on his own account, or on that of his employer. What the real merits of the case may have been, it is now impossible to discover. Sporting writers insist in maintaining the unspotted honour of owner and rider, but be the truth what it may, the Jockey Club held an opposite opinion, and his royal highness had no option but to retire from the turf. So the prince shook the dust of the Heath from off his feet; and the Rowley Mile knew " Fee-fi-fo-fum " no more.

PHANTOM FORTUNES.

ONE of the most noted advertising tipsters of a few years ago was a person who took the signature of Montgomery—probably he is to-day publishing his lures under some other name. A perusal of his announcement will prove interesting: it was as follows:—

"L. C. Montgomery's system has been proved by time, and time proves all and everything. Backers of horses are advised to lose no more, when a method of betting is at hand by which they may individually clear thousands. A marvellous fortune may be made by any turfite. A minor speculation procures it. For the direct proofs of this great secret, forward an addressed envelope—L. C. Montgomery, 131, Great Conduit-street, London-road, Leicester. 'An honourable and lucrative system'—Sporting Press. (See below.)

"A prodigal and glorious success attends L. C. Montgomery's system at nearly every meeting. For good fortune, large profits and unceasing effect it stands unrivalled. Each individual who follows this remarkable system procures a rapid and immense fortune—it stands out in the clearest light, and builds the most munificent incomes. After a careful examination of the sources from which this code is derived, all backers are thoroughly convinced of the superiority of its plan, the wealth-producing powers of its action, its originality, and thorough genuineness. By its agency a few pounds are, in a short period, metamorphosed into some thousands sterling; previous losses are changed into great gains, and the system readily proves itself the best one extant, independent of a crowded impetus of foregone existences, and all their complex activities. The various ideas and plans which are so marvellously intermixed with the superior intelligences of this system are all admirable workers in their spheres, which prove it the most genuine and lucrative of the many systems of betting. In all these instances it is without comparison. £100,000 may be made by any one by the speculation of a few pounds. For particulars of this marvellous secret enclose stamped addressed envelope to L. C. Montgomery, 131 Great Conduit-street, London-road, Leicester, and you will receive full particulars per return mail.

"N.B.—Great success at the West Drayton meeting, likewise at York immense stakes cleared. Great success will occur at the meetings next week. All commissions to be forwarded without delay."

This individual had the audacity to circulate an immense mass of printed notes, in which was inserted a paragraph stated to be taken from the *Pall Mall Gazette*, recommending and approving of the system by which thousands of pounds could be gained. It is needless to say the *Pall Mall*, on its attention being called to this document, entirely repudiated all knowledge of the paragraph in question, and published for some days its indignant denial thereof; but in the meanwhile can any one tell what mischief may not have been done?

The writer of this article can give an instance of the lavish way this man had distributed these papers. A rector of a small village in an out-of-the-way part of Somersetshire, forwarded to me, just after the Derby, one of these letters of this L. C. Montgomery, and underlining the statement purporting to be taken from the *Pall Mall*, he writes, "*Can this be true?*" Now, my friend is about as unlikely a man as exists to have anything to do with horse racing, never was on a race course in his life, I should think never made a bet, and whose name could not be in any way known to this Montgomery. Yet on such apparently unfruitful soil there is a penny stamp and the paper, &c., so admirably got up, thrown away. It is dreadful to think of the immense circulation this atrocious scoundrel has given to his villany. Here is an extract from this wonderful epistle, which is taken from a statement sent to one of the Metropolitan magistrates:—

"Calling attention, with the view of putting people on their guard, to a printed circular which the writer says is being widely circulated at present, and may, he apprehends, have most mischievous consequences, a copy of it having been addressed to himself, a poor clerk with a family, among others. It is upon the subject of betting, and purports to emanate from a person who alleges that he has discovered a principle of backing horses by which 'winning to any amount is reduced to a certainty,' and that in the years 1864, 1865, and 1866 he carried it out with the most incredible success. He offers to impart his secret for £100, and on receiving a written agreement guaranteeing him in addition £900 out of the first £9000 cleared by the person to whom he shall communicate it. For less, he adds, he cannot divulge the process entirely, but for every £10 invested he guarantees a return of £60 a week; for £20 invested, £160; for £30, £330; for £50 invested, £700 a week: and 'so on,' he says, 'deducting 10 per cent. as commission.' He says, further, that statistics clearly prove that there are every week, and have been ever since the establishment of racing, several horses on which you may stake £1000 with the positive certainty of 'landing every bet,' and then he puts down certain amounts alleged to have been won by the adoption of his system, 'starting with £100 capital'—namely, in 1864, £30,000; in 1865, £28,400; and in 1866, £29,000; adding that 'all calculation is baffled when an attempt is made to arrive at the point where the profits of this infallible system really terminate.'"

THE MAKING OF A SPORTSMAN.

(By Nimrod.)

Never was constitution so murdered as Mr. Mytton's was; for, what but one of adamant could have withstood the shocks, independent of wine, to which it was almost daily exposed? His dress alone would have caused the death of nine hundred out of a thousand men who passed one part of the day and night in a state of luxury and warmth. We will take him from the sole of his shoe to the crown of his hat. He never wore any but the thinnest and finest silk stockings, with very thin boots or shoes; so that in winter he rarely had dry feet. To flannel he was a stranger since he left off his petticoats. Even his hunting breeches were without lining; he wore one small waistcoat, always open in the front from about the second of the lower buttons; and about home, he was as often without as with his hat on. His winter shooting gear was a light jacket, white linen trousers, without lining or drawers—of which he knew not the use; and in frost and snow he waded through all water that came in his way. Nor is this all. He would sometimes strip to his shirt to follow wild-fowl in hard weather, and once actually laid himself down on the snow in his shirt only to wait their arrival at dusk. But Dame Nature took offence at this, and chastised him rather severely for his daring. On one occasion, however, he out-heroded Herod, for he followed some ducks "*in puris naturalibus*"—*Anglicè*, stark-naked—on the ice, and escaped with perfect impunity. He was the only man I ever knew who, I think, at one time of his life, might have stood some chance of performing the grand Osbaldeston match over Newmarket, from the ease with which he performed immense distances on the road on his hacks. He would ride, several times in the week, to covers nearly fifty miles distant from Halston, and return thither to his dinner. Neither could any man I ever met in the field walk through the day with him *at his pace*.

I saw him, on his own moors in Merionethshire, completely knock up two keepers (who accompanied him alternately), being the whole day bare-headed under a hot sun. (One of these keepers—whom I procured for him in Cheshire—was rather a crack walker, and a noted man with his fists.) He had the stomach of an ostrich before it was debilitated by wine, and even against that, it stood nearly proof to the last; but, it appears, he once met with his match. Himself and a friend left London together with eighteen pounds of filbert-nuts in his carriage, and they devoured them all before they arrived at Halston. To use his own words, they sat up to their knees in nut-shells. But it was often alarming to witness the quantity of dry nuts he would eat, with the quantity of port wine which he would drink ; and on *my* once telling him, at his own table, that the ill-assorted mixture caused the death of a school-fellow of mine, he carried a dish of filberts into the drawing-room with him, for the purpose of " clearing decks," as he said. Among other peculiarities, he never carried a pocket-handkerchief, for he never had occasion for the use of one ; he very rarely wore gloves, for his hands were never cold ; and, although he never wore a watch, he always knew the hour.

COCK-PIT SWELLS AND ROUGHS.

MANY vivid descriptions of the work done in the Cock-pits used to be published half a century ago, some of them being embodied in substantial volumes, many of which are now scarce and consequently valuable. The following sketch may help to give modern readers some idea of this pastime of their grandfather's day. Passing through Storeys-gate to Queen Street, the visitor found himself upon the top of a flight of stone steps, called " Cock-pit Steps," which led into a maze of streets and alleys, that in time conducted him to Tufton Street. Around a building which was large when compared with its surroundings, and had a *ci-devant* ecclesiastical air about it, was congregated a string of carriages, some coronetted, and groups of fighting men, jockeys, speculators and link boys.

The portal was guarded by a keeper to whom all tickets had to be shown ; then, passing through a small entrance hall and pushing a spring door, the visitor entered the building, the interior of which gave far more convincing proofs of the original purpose for which it had been designed than the exterior. Several columns supported narrow galleries which were entirely devoted to the coops or pens of the feathered " Gladiators," who, " eager for the fray," were crowing defiance at one another, notwithstanding a curtain of sacking, that hung before each, and kept him in darkness. In the centre, could be seen the pit ; unlike the rat or dog pit, which is sunk and hedged in by wooden sides, this was raised like a stage, and covered with matting, so that the action of the combatants might be more on a level with the eye, and none of the beauties of the game lost to the devouring eyes of the enthusiastic spectators. The place was a dingy hole, and when seen empty by daylight, it seemed scarcely credible that polished, aristocratic sportsmen could endure the tainted atmosphere, the close, sickening odour of damp straw and stale sawdust, to which must be added the reeking effluvia of the " great unwashed."

The best places were occupied by the early comers, and behind them was seen a crowd of dandies. There were Sir William Wynn, Ralph Benyon, Sir Bellingham Graham, Dr. Bellyse, Colonel Mellish, Dick Thornton, Captain Barclay, and dukes and lords of turf celebrity. In the background might be seen the stolid mugs of Jem Belcher, young Cribb, Molyneux, Richmond, Tom Olliver, Gentleman Jackson, and other " pugs," whose bravery and honourable conduct earned them the patronage and friendship of the " Corinthians," and the right of entrée into every place where sport was going on. Fun, chaff, and chatter were soon at blood-heat, everybody talked at once, so there was plenty of noise and few listeners. Presently a movement and bustle without gave notice that someone extraordinary had arrived; then in came " Tommy Hughes," the gentlest of roughs and the proprietor of the drum, bowing and scraping and ushering in the " first gentleman in Europe," accompanied by his brother, the Duke of York, and supported by his beloved and attached companions, foremost among whom was Beau Brummel, then in the zenith of his power.

MACAULAY'S PICTURE OF NEWMARKET.

THE great historian writes thus of Newmarket at the date indicated—reign of William III. "William went to Newmarket —now a place of business rather than of pleasure, but in the autumn of that age the gayest and most luxurious spot in the island. It was not unusual for the whole Court and Cabinet to go down to the meetings. Jewellers and milliners, players and fiddlers, venal wits and venal beauties, followed in crowds. The streets were made impassable by coaches-and-six. In the places of public resort peers flirted with maids of honour, and officers of the Life Guards, all plumes and gold-lace, jostled professors in trencher caps and black gowns. For on such occasions the neighbouring University of Cambridge always sent her highest functionaries with loyal addresses, and selected her ablest theologians to preach before the sovereign and his splendid retinue."

NEWMARKET IN THE TIME OF QUEEN ANNE.

THE following account of this remarkable racing town was penned during the reign of her august majesty, Queen Anne— "I took the opportunity to see the horse-races, and a great concourse of the nobility and gentry, as well from London as from all parts of England; but they were all so intent, so eager upon the sharping part of the sport, their wagers, their bets, that to me they seemed just so many horse-coursers of Smithfield; descending, even the greatest, from their high dignity and quality, to picking one another's pockets and biting one another as much as possible, and that with so much eagerness, as it might be said they acted without respect to faith, honour, or good manners. There was Mr. Frampton the oldest, and, as they say, the cunningest jockey in England. One day he lost 1,000 guineas, the next he won 2,000, and so alternately. He made as light of throwing away £500 or £1,000 at a time as other men do of their pocket-money, and was as perfectly calm, cheerful, and unconcerned when he had lost £1,000 as when he won it. On the other side, there was Sir. F. Wragge, of Sussex, of whom fame says he has most in him and least to show for it, relating to jockeyship, of any man there; yet he often carried off the prize. His horses, they say, were all cheats, how honest so ever their master was, for he scarcely ever produced a horse but he looked like what he was not, and was what nobody could expect him to be. If he was as light as the wind and could fly like a meteor, he was sure to look as clumsy and as dirty and as much like a cart horse as all the cunning of his master and the grooms could make him; and just in this manner he hit some of the greatest gamesters in the field. I was so sick of the jockeying part that I left the crowd about the posts and pleased myself with observing the horses."

MESSRS. GLITTER AND FLASH OUTWITTED.

NEVER in the annals of gambling were two sharpers better outwitted than by a well known Captain of Lancers who took them on at their own game. One or two incidents of the work in which they engaged may be narrated.

"Glitter and Flash" will serve equally as well as the real names for the fellows who met their match. They tried it on with some of us at billiards, but we let them have the table to themselves. Somehow they got hold of the dashing Lancer, and invited him to dinner at the "Canute Arms." The bait took, and while the bottle was being briskly passed, the game of hazard was introduced, and when the Captain left he was a winner of thirty pounds. Prior to introduction of the dice, the sharpers had contrived to get an invitation from their guest to make him a return visit next day.

We need hardly say the engagement was duly kept, and soon after dinner the Captain was asked if he had any dice, and replied that gambling was never allowed here. There was no moving him, and the guests in consequence made no very late stay. The same worthies (?) went to Marlborough races, where they fell in with a Swindon Landlord, whom we will call Ready. Glitter and Flash had made a plant on a knot of young (and somewhat green) fellows, and asked Ready if he would join them at cards, telling him that they would take care he should be winner. "Of course," said Flash, "you understand." "Quite," said Ready; "that'll be all right." Ready walked off winner of a good round sum. The "sharpers" called next day at Ready's house, and ordering wine, to which the landlord was invited, they soon began to propose a "settling." Ready, feigning ignorance, said he had nothing to settle. "Why, we told you yesterday you were to win." "And I did as you told me," said Ready; "and, what's more, I mean to keep it." Ready was very ready with a blow, and they knew it. Chapfallen, they walked out of the house, and very quickly left the town which had so little served their purpose.

SPORTSMEN'S FISH.

NOTHING very new can be said about angling—it is an old-fashioned art still pursued in the same old fashion that was in vogue when Isaac Walton wandered rod in hand by "the purling brooks that threaded through the flowery meads of England's rural scenes." As in shooting there are *battues* where the birds of sport are frightened into flocks, or grounds on which, at least, the pheasant is preserved into the veriest tameness, so in many parts of the country there are stretches of protected water filled with fish in order that some people may obtain the chance of posing as mighty anglers; but one small fish ingeniously lured from its liquid home is worth a whole basketful taken from a preserve where the animals are merely stored for capture. In France the fishermen of Brittany sow the sea bottom with cod roe brought from Norway to attract the sardine to their nets, but sprats may be taken in millions without bait of any kind. Men, too, sit in a punt on the river Thames, delighted when they take a few gudgeon—the bottom having been previously baited in order to lure the fish to the place, but that is not angling any more than shooting in a battue is sport, nor are dace or gudgeon fishes worth the trouble of catching. The Salmon is both a creature of sport and a fish of value. To capture the venison of the waters with success implies the fisher to be a man of mettle; it requires no end of skill and finesse to play a twenty pound salmon, in a stream of very "mixed water," and it is not the first time that a fish of the kind has caught the fisher; few except those who have been at such work have a knowledge of the prowess of a big salmon so long as it can fight in its native element. The feat of capturing a hundred roach or dace cannot be placed against the grassing of a newly run (from the sea) twenty pound example of Salmo Salar. But it is the gamesome trout that is the angler's fish *par excellence*. No denizen of our lochs and streams affords better sport, and the fish is a common one and acceptable in all its varieties, whether it be the far-famed inhabitant of Loch Leven or the fierce monster of Loch Awe. Trout can be captured in many fashions, it can be made the victim of a well devised fly, or it may be taken with the humble worm, and with other baits, real or artificial. Scotland may be named as the home of the trout, that fish finding breeding and feeding places in the ten thousand lochs and streams of stern Caledonia. Pike and perch are likewise plentiful in Scottish waters, as are also eels, but against this fish the people have a long-standing prejudice, and few are found who will catch them, although they are excellent as food. This prejudice will doubtless in time wear out; already a commerce in eels is being established, large numbers of these fish being annually sent to the English markets where they command a high price.

WHO ARE THE "TOUTS?"

I THINK it will be conceded that the man who professes to instruct and advise should know more of his business than he who is to be taught. The tout, or horse watcher (to use the

WHO ARE THE "TOUTS?"

term originated, I believe, by Admiral Rous) should have some knowledge of a horse. The simple record that a horse had a gallop on a certain day would go a small way towards predicting a winner, unless the style in which the work is gone through, and his appearance after it, are taken into consideration; and in the case of a trial, it is little to find out which horse came in first, unless the weights that each horse carried are correctly known; but more especially, perhaps, the great advantage supposed to be derived from obtaining these "Reports from Training Quarters," as those papers which indulge in this luxury call them, is this—that no animal under the immediate eye of the horse watcher shall be able to be specially prepared for a great race without his observing and reporting thereon.

When a horse watcher has a thorough knowledge of horse-flesh, has discovered or been told the weights carried in a trial, and is able to give his employer information of a dark horse being secretly prepared for some great event, he has done his duty, fulfilled its requirements, and earned his weekly salary. Now, does he do this? Within my knowledge and experience he does not.

The class of men mostly employed in this diplomatic, secret, and most delicate service are chiefly decayed tradesmen, broken down gamblers, and discharged stablemen, invariably fond of liquor, not given to strict adherence to truth, *sanguine beyond measure*, because always hoping for the great good chance which is to "give them a turn" at last, and not very particular about the information they send provided something goes up and is paid for. I appeal to any one acquainted with these men if this is an exaggerated account? But let us, for the sake of argument, allow that a horse watcher is capable and zealous, *can* he do this duty such as I have sketched it?

He cannot.

Early last year, in the spring, being at Newmarket, while walking on the Heath with a trainer, I mentioned something about a report as emanating from a local reporter to one of the papers. I was immensely amused at being told:

"Why, sir, that man never comes on the Heath at all; he stands on the road, and looks through a glass, and gets a stable lad to talk to in the evening, and the boys being all up to it, he is gammoned with anything!"

So much, thought I, for the *important Newmarket intelligence*. From that time I have frequently looked at these "reports," and have had many a laugh at the extraordinary inaccuracies they contain; but it is surely enough to mention Hermit's name to show what *benefit* these reports must have conferred on the readers of them! Then, again, in the case of Plaudit! What accounts of his trials and his wonderful gallops without turning a hair, when at the time the horse was lame, and only taking walking and gentle canters as exercise! Surely the furnishers of these reports could know very little, if anything, of the real condition of these horses. And again as to finding out a " dark " horse—one who was being specially reserved—could there be a plainer instance than that of Tibthorpe? Here men were watching and writing week after week, and day after day, and not one even discovered that there was such a horse, and yet he was specially and carefully trained under their very noses! These cases happened all quite recently, and they could be multiplied by scores. I will not do more than just allude here to the annoyance it is, and must be, to owners and trainers to have a man constantly approaching as near as he dares to you, anxious to watch and report upon your horses—it is a nuisance in this way, it annoys you, as you know, and does no benefit to any one. It is as if a man were desirous to find some secret in a merchant's house, bribes a clerk, and then finds the clerk has taken the bribe but only gives half the information required; in fact, it is a practice that brings dishonour on the employer, and ruin and loss upon the employed and those who expect to benefit by it.

CROCKFORD'S CLUBS IN LONDON AND NEWMARKET

AFTER he had become pretty well known as a betting man, safe for any sum he betted to—Crockford started a house at Newmarket, which he made comfortable to those visitors to whom he extended his hospitality, and he was no niggard in dispensing the good things of life at his table. Nor were persons invited to his house simply that, when heated with good wine, he might rob them at play. He was then a betting man and made a book, laying or backing as he thought best for his own interest, but the greater number of his visitors, to use the slang of the turf, were "as fly as he was." They were not all spiders who walked into his Newmarket parlour; as many of his visitors, on occasion, left Panton House with their pockets stuffed with crisp Bank of England notes. Another feature of

Crockford's behaviour helped him to connection and wealth—he never, when he lost, required to be asked for money but paid off hand; nor did he, when reputed to be rolling in wealth, forget himself: he was invariably polite and courteous. The devil, indeed, never was so black as he has been painted, and Crockford was not the fiend of the race course that some writers have taken a delight in describing him to be. "Crockford's" in St. James's Street, London, was the most luxurious club house then known; erected quite regardless of expense, it became one of the sights shown to country cousins by town relations who possessed the right of *entrée*, or who knew a member, or the Steward of the Club. Two or three houses had been knocked down to provide a site for it, and no expense was spared to render it splendid, and make it attractive to customers, who were waited upon by footmen in gorgeous liveries, and had their palates tickled by the gastronomic delicacies of Monsieur Ude. There were over eight hundred members, and the house was placed under the management of a committee of their number, to whom Crockford conceded all that was asked. Gambling was, as a matter of course, the business or recreation of all who came to the place; figuratively speaking, the rattle of the dice was heard morning, noon, and night, tens of thousands of pounds changing hands as if they were so many halfpence.

No such style and luxury had ever before been presented in connection with club house comforts; the wages paid to the cook at Crockford's, coupled with the liberal presents from *habitués* of the house, of which he was the frequent recipient, afforded at one time a theme of great wonderment to the gossip-loving public. "Would that I were a cook," said caustic Douglas Jerrold; "I do not get half for feeding the brain which that man gets for feeding the belly!" But club cooks have always been of importance, and Ude, who had been secured by Crockford at a salary of a thousand pounds per annum, was not a man to under-rate his own services. The *chef* of the great gambling house always maintained that it was an easier feat to compose an opera than to invent a new dish. "Many things," said Ude, "can be done by rule or measurement, but you cannot in that way invent an *entrée* that will be worth tasting; no, the higher arts of my profession are due to the sympathy which brings the necessary inspiration, and that may come in a moment and be gone almost before you know it has come to you."

LORD GEORGE BENTINCK'S DUEL.

As so many incorrect accounts of Lord George's duel with Squire Osbaldeston have been published, it is better that all the facts should be known of this interesting chapter of turf history; they are as follows: Heaton Park, which has long since been abolished as a race meeting, was, at the period of which we treat, the Goodwood of the north-west, and patronised by the *élite* of the racing world, who were the guests of the noble owner of the domain. John Scott always took a large string there, and the prizes were worth running for. The riders were nearly all gentlemen jockeys, but divided into two classes, one of which stayed at the House, and the other at Manchester, which was within four miles of Lord Wilton's seat. A feeling had long prevailed among the less aristocratic division that they had not a fair chance given them in the handicaps, and that too much favour was shown to a noble lord, who, hardly second to any wearer of a silk jacket, was supposed to mesmerise the judge's eye. To strike a shivering blow at such an apparent monopoly had long been resolved upon by the members of the "lower house," and Rush proved a fitting instrument in their hands.

Rush was a rare bred horse, and the Squire gave four hundred guineas for him at Doncaster. Anxious to know what his form was, he hired a mare of old Job Marson to try him with; and agreeing upon the weights, so that there should be no mistake about his having a good horse, he got upon him himself, and put a jockey on the mare, and at six o'clock on the morning of the St. Leger they were galloped on that course. On getting to the Red House, the Squire found Rush pulling double over the mare; but discovering a lot of touts at the judge's post, he stopped him, and allowed the mare to go in by herself. The report of this trial no doubt got Rush favourably handicapped at Heaton Park; and on the first day of the races he ran in the Trial Stakes, but from some cause or another, into which we will not inquire too closely, was "nowhere." The next day he was started for the Cup, and a gentleman was "put in" to get all the "house money," and another commissioner was equally diligent at Manchester. Opening at 10 to 1 he finished at 2 to 1, and as the Squire was walking down to the post to canter up, Lord George Bentinck cried out, "200 to 100 against Rush." "I'll take 100 to 50," replied his rider, and finding him go so well with him, as he returned, he said, "My lord, you can make it 200 to 100," which the latter booked. Waiting on Lord Wilton, who rode William Scott's mare, Lady le Gros, and who was backed for pounds, shillings, and pence, until they got to the distance, he came away and won in a canter, as he had previously told Mr. Orton, the judge, he should do. Of course, this sudden improvement in Rush's form created considerable sensation, and very unparliamentary language was made use of in respect to it, which was not diminished in intensity by his winning the last day another race, although he only pulled through by a head.

Leaving immediately after the races for the purpose of cub hunting, the Squire had not time to ask Lord George for the money he had won off him, and the matter stood over until the following Craven meeting at Newmarket. Seeing Lord George standing with his back to the rails in the coffee-room yard, the Squire thinking he had had full time to digest his loss, applied to him for the sum. Drawing himself up to his full height, Lord George exclaimed, in his haughty passionate tone, "that he was surprised he should be asked for it, and that the affair was a robbery, and the Jockey Club considered it so." On this sudden onslaught being made on him, the Squire's fingers itched for his lordship's nose; but prudently recollecting that at Newmarket the person of a member of the Jockey Club, or even of their humblest menial, is regarded with as much sanctity as that of Dalia Llama in Thibet, he restrained his feelings, but added, in a firm tone, that he "*should* pay him."

"Can you count?" rejoined Lord George.

"I could at Eton," was the curt reply of the Squire; and after he had had the notes slowly dealt out to him, he remarked to his lordship the matter would not end there, and that he should hear from him again,—an announcement treated by the scion of the House of Portland with proud defiance.

The sequel was soon guessed; but Lord George gave out he would not go out with our hero.

"Tell him, then," said he, "I will pull his nose at Tattersall's and those who know me, are aware I always keep my word!"

This latter threat was more than the fiery lord could stand, and he placed himself in the hands of the late General Anson, than whom a more fitting person could not have been selected to conduct a delicate affair of this description. Wormwood Scrubbs, as favourite a spot for settling aristocratic differences as Moulsey Hurst used to be for deciding pugilistic ones, was "the fixture" for the next meeting of the pair. The hour was six: the morning a lovely one. The lark sang his matin carol, and a ploughman, "who whistled as he went for want of thought," was driving his team in the field adjoining the battle ground, as it was occupied by the combatants. Lord George, wrapped in a large cloak which well set forth his magnificent stature, while the preliminaries were being arranged, kept walking round and round in a circle, his proud spirit chafing at his position; and if he felt nervous it was very excusable. For to stand up at twelve paces against a man whom he had so openly insulted, and who had been known to kill ninety-eight pheasants out of a hundred shots when staying with Sir Richard Sutton, was no laughing matter. Moreover, to be hurled into eternity from such a world as that in which his lordship had been living for years, would try the nerves of any man.

Not having brought pistols with them, General Anson applied to the Squire for the loan of one of his, which he had borrowed for the occasion from Sir St. Vincent Cotton; and having obtained it, he and Mr. Humphrey, who "waited on" Mr. Osbaldeston, crouched under a ditch to avoid being seen by the ploughman, and loaded them. On the Squire's pistol being handed to him, he was told by his second he must not fire at his opponent, as he had been assured by General Anson that Lord George felt he could not shoot at him after insulting him, and the latter gave Mr. Humphrey to understand he would not do so. Screwing himself up, so as not to give a chance away, and with his pistol close to his side, he quietly waited the signal. But the General with the laudable desire to preserve Lord George's life from so dead a shot, desired the Squire to keep his eye on him, when he would give the word "fire," after calling one, two, three. By this means the latter's aim, even if he had directed it, which was not the case, was diverted, and when the signal was delivered Lord George's bullet went over the Squire's head, and the latter's ball fell wide of its object.

"I did not think you were so bad a shot, Squire," cried the General, laughing; to which he replied, rather ominously, "*The next time it might come off differently!*"

Happily, however, enough had been done to satisfy the honour and prove the courage of both these sporting lions, and Lord George hastily quitted the ground, without even observing the usual courtesy of saluting his opponent; and so ended the attempt to break up the monopoly of handicapping at Heaton Park.

WHAT WILL WIN?

Even the Derby is not always won by the horse which is pointed to on public form, and several instances have occurred in which a despised "outsider" has borne off the great and coveted prize. "Don't always trust *appearances*," is a motto of universal application, and many a good sporting man has discovered this to his cost. Was ever such an unpromising looking winner as Hermit ever seen? What a miserable creature he looked on that coldest of Derby days as he walked round the bush in the centre of the paddock perfectly unnoticed and overlooked by the gapers after the favourite. His coat fairly stood up straight on his back and loins, and he looked tucked up and unequal in appearance to a selling plater. It was given out that he was suffering from an affection of the kidneys; and yet his win was not only a decisive one, but it brought more grist to his owner's mill than any recorded in the history of the race. According to my calculations, he has been indirectly the means of bringing to his owner at least £60,000 in the nineteen years he has lived since he won that remarkable race, while indirectly he must have added immensely to the value of the Blankney stud.

On that memorable Derby-day, when Hobbie Noble had to yield to an Irish outsider, memorable as the wettest and muddiest on which the great race was ever run, as two sporting men were making their way across the Downs they were stopped by an Irish tramp.

"Would you like to know the winner, gentlemen?" he said, touching his hat.

They laughingly assured him they should very much like to know it.

"True, then, and I'll give you the tip—it's Dan'l O'Rourke; he's the boy that'll make the dirt fly!"

They laughed, give the fellow a coin, and went on their way without bestowing a second thought upon the bog-trotter's tip; but when that rank outsider came thundering over the soddened ground through the pelting rain, steered by Frank Butler, shooting past Hobbie Noble, when he seemed certain of winning, followed by two other outsiders, Barbarian and Chief Baron Nicholson, they wished they had availed themselves of the tramp's hint. It was a splendid compliment that Lord Glasgow paid Frank when he gave him a check for £300, and told him he might have won on any of the first four horses.

ONE OF FORTUNE'S FROLICS.

PERSONS who visited Germany when "the tables" were in full swing, say five and twenty years ago, had no end of gambling stories poured into their (usually) willing ears. These tales were of course chiefly told of persons whom fortune most favoured; good luck never lacks a chronicler; about bad luck the less said the better. I was told while dining one day at Homburg of a rather remarkable piece of play on the part of an Englishman who had just newly come to the town and had never before ventured to put a coin on the table. Whilst sitting, on the day after his arrival, listening along with some friends to the strains of a fine band, he suddenly moved from his chair and exclaiming, "I have an idea," walked away to the roulette table, his friends following him; pushing his way into the front, he paused for a moment to survey the scene, and then taking out his pocket-book he selected two notes each of the value of a thousand francs, and without the slightest hesitation, but to the consternation of the assembled company, planked them down on No. 7. It was so unusual to back a single number for more than a dollar or a couple of dollars at the very most, that even the croupiers who were working the table shared in the general surprise expressed by the looks of the company. For the time play ceased, those at work preferring to look on at the unexpected scene. Round whirled the machine, away went the ball of destiny on its course, the spectators looking on in breathless expectation. A few moments elapse, the ball becomes eccentric in its leaps and bounds, but finds at last a resting-place in the little cell—No. 7. "Wonderful, wonderful!" exclaimed everybody, and there was a general buzz of excitement at such a wonderful stroke of good luck. The player seemed the only unconcerned person among the group, and pocketed the huge sum he had won in a spirit of tranquillity. Quitting the room, he very sensibly said to his wife, "That will do, I think, for one season—let us leave the place," and by the next train they were speedily borne away from the scene of their good fortune. Why the gentleman staked his money on number seven, I never heard, but there would doubtless be some cause or reason for his doing so.

SOMETHING LIKE A WALK.

MANY a good story has been told of that most famous of all Scottish sportsmen, the late Horatio Ross of Ben Wyvis, and among others the following :—

"A large party were assembled at Black Hall, in Kincardineshire, about the end of July or beginning of August. We had all been shooting snipes and flapper ducks in a large morass on the estate called Lumphannon. We had been waddling among the bulrushes up to our middles for seven or eight hours, and had had a capital dinner. After the ladies had gone to the drawing-room I fell asleep; and about nine o'clock was awakened by the late Sir Andrew Keith Hay, who said : 'Ross, old fellow, I want you to jump up and go as my umpire, with Lord Kennedy, to Inverness. I have made a bet of twenty-five hundred pounds a side that I get there on foot before him.' Nothing came amiss to the men of that day. My answer was, 'All right I'm ready;' and off we started there and then, in evening costume, with thin shoes and silk stockings on our feet.

"We went straight across the mountains, and it was a longish walk. I called to my servant to follow with my walking shoes and worsted stockings, and Lord Kennedy did the same. They overtook us after we had gone seven or eight miles. Fancy my disgust. My idiot certainly brought me worsted stockings, but instead of walking shoes a pair of light Wellington boots! The sole of one boot vanished twenty five miles from Inverness, and I had now to finish the walk barefooted. We walked all night, next day, and the next night—raining torrents all the way. We crossed the Grampians, making a perfectly straight line, and got to Inverness at one p.m. We never saw or heard of J. Hay (he went by the coach road, *via* Huntley and Elgin, thirty six miles further than we, by a good road) who appeared at ten a.m., much cast down at finding he had been beaten." The entire distance covered by the two gentlemen was ninety eight miles; while Sir Andrew did one hundred and thirty-six. And it must be borne in mind that they started after dinner, after a hard day's shooting, and in fearful weather.

TRADING IN RACING TIPS.

VERY few persons, except those who have studied or become acquainted in some way with the surroundings of horse racing, have any idea of the active trade which is at present carried on in racing tips or prophecies—thousands of which on a busy race day are eagerly purchased. In addition to the tipsters who are constantly advertising in the newspapers, there are men and boys and even women who sell tips for all the days of the races in the street at the trifling charge of a penny. In London in particular a big trade is done in the prophetic line as will be gathered from the following remarks which appeared recently in a popular periodical.

From the end of March to the middle of November (the regular racing period in fact), the army of London street vendors is considerably augmented by members of the tipster division. In some cases they distribute their wares—buff-coloured envelopes containing what they are pleased to term " certainties " for the various races of the day—through the medium of boys or men, who regularly perambulate certain thoroughfares trying to induce passers-by to part with coin of the realm, in amount ranging from one penny to sixpence, in return for one of the precious envelopes and its contents. Others of the fraternity (and now that certain sporting journals have made it a rule not to insert any of their advertisements, their number has largely increased) rely upon their own personal powers of persuasion to effect a large sale. Any open space, such, for instance, as that in front of the Sessions House at Clerkenwell Green, which is always a favourite position for tipsters, serves their purpose.

Sometimes a tipster is satisfied to take up his position standing in the roadway, but most of them aspire to the dignity of a horse and trap, usually a four-wheeled conveyance, and having drawn up in as prominent a position as possible, they commence operations somewhat as follows :— " Now, gentlemen, here I am again—the same old spot—and, if I may say so, the same valuable information to afford you. I hope some of you profited by the tips I gave last season—made their fortunes, I daresay ! I don't see many old faces here to-day ; ah, that's it, depend upon it, gentlemen ! Now, then, I have here in my hand a list of absolute certainties ; can't be beat in fact, none of them, supposing always you understand, gentlemen, that they are trying. I get the best information to be had for love or money ; yes, gentlemen, money I pay for my information, and then I expect to get a little return for it out of you. Why don't I keep it to myself and win cheap ? That's just what I do, gentlemen. I had a capital day yesterday (or the day before, or last week, as the case may be), and so had you if you followed my advice, and will again, believe me—you can't help it. What does that gentleman say ? If I won so much what did I do with it ?

Well, I'll tell you, gentlemen. I lost it again ; not at betting, though. No, I can generally manage to win at that ; but cards, gentlemen, cards. My luck at cards is just something awful, and what I win on the course I lose on the card-table. It is a fact, gentlemen, I assure you. If I could stick to betting and leave cards alone I should be all right ; but I can't, and that's why I am before you to-day."

After a good deal of this sort of thing he commences business in real earnest.

" One penny a time ; that's my price, gentlemen. One penny only for five—six—seven certainties ; they can't lose one of them, as I said before if (always if, it will be observed) they are trying. I can't guarantee that, can I ? "

And so on to any extent.

A season or two ago, out of sheer curiosity, we invested in the " specials " of one of these prophetic individuals to the extent of exactly half-a-crown, and found, by carefully comparing his predictions with results, that he was right once out of nine times ! And yet, judging by what we have seen, these men do a roaring trade. On one occasion in particular, the morning of a big race, we saw no fewer than 103 " specials " sold to a crowd of eager purchasers in less than one hour !

The valuable information that these men obtain is nothing more or less than that to be obtained by buying a daily paper on the morning of the day, and basing calculations accordingly. One of them, indeed, went so far as to tell us (in confidence) that he did not even go so far as this, his plan being the extremely simple one of putting the names of all the probable starters into a hat, shaking them up, and taking as his "certainty" the one that he happened to encounter first when dipping his hand in ; and he gave us to understand that he found his envelopes sell as well as those of anyone else.

UPS AND DOWNS OF TURF LIFE.

Many stories and sketches are extant of the ups and downs encountered in the course of their career by those who endeavour to " make a living on the turf." Men who one week are going about almost shirtless and shoeless, will be feasting on turtle the next, a happy turn of fortune's wheel having lifted them from a state of beggary to one of affluence for the time being.

The annals of the race contain examples of many such cases; the race-course is a place on which a person can rise as far as making money is concerned. Only the other day a story went the round, of a man who visited a race-course on Tuesday morning with no more than a couple of sovereigns in his pocket and by Friday night was able to leave for home with the handsome amount of seventeen hundred and seventy pounds.

The following is a true story of a turf career which was not a little remarkable, that of Harry Hill, who began his life as boots at a small hotel; getting tired of the blacking-brush and desiring to see a little more of life than could be viewed within the narrow limits of a country inn, he bought a table, a thimble, and a few peas, and started for the race-courses. He did wonderfully well, never letting any one find the pea. After a while he discarded thimble-rig and took to the book-making line, but as he seldom paid when he lost, people called it welshing. However, when he'd made a little pile, he, like a good many others, turned honest, and paid his losses like a man. By-and-by he rose to the dignity of ownership, scratched his horses at the last moment, was very particular as to *how* his jockeys rode and all the rest of it, and made so much money at the game that he was able to add usury to his boot-blacking, thimble-rigging, welshing, book-making, horse-jobbing antecedents. His great delight was to assemble a party of loafing vagabonds about him, tell them stories, and get drunk in their company. But, with all his cunning, he could not save himself from the ups and downs of turf life. He laid heavily against a certain horse in the St. Leger of 1853, having squared the jockey; but the jockey having been bowled out of his little game, he was compelled to win, and Hill dropped £20,000; soon afterwards he lost £40,000 among the blacklegs of the Stock Exchange. And, though he had amassed large sums during his career, and was mean and miserly in his habits, denying himself every luxury except a little harem, he left no wealth behind him.

COLONEL MORDAUNT AND OTHER COCKERS.

COCKING flourished exceedingly during the reigns of the four Georges, and was at its height about the commencement of this century. When a conviction or two was gained against different persons, under Martin's Act, for practising it, then gentlemen abandoned the sport; and since then it has only led a fitful and declining existence. Among the last generation of cockers may be named the Earl of Derby, grandfather of the present peer, whose breed of black-red cocks, with white legs, is famous to this day. Lord Sefton, his contemporary, was just as keen a hand, and also bred black-reds, with willow legs, and the special peculiarity that when "cut out," or trimmed for the pit, by having their long hackle-feathers cut short, their necks would always show white. Sir Harry Goodricke, too, had a famous strain of black-breasted reds, with yellow legs; and this excellent breed was preserved after his death by Mr. Lane Fox, of Bramham, who is never behind hand where anything in the way of sport is concerned.

One of the most enthusiastic cockers ever known was Colonel Mordaunt, who lived about 1780. He had one of the best strains of game-cocks in England; and, having vanquished all his compatriots, proceeded with his birds to India to pit them against the best birds in that country—no small undertaking in those days. Colonel Mordaunt, however, suffered a defeat, partly from the great difficulty of transporting his birds, in good health, to India, and partly no doubt because he found in that country game cocks superior to the best he could produce. A somewhat similar experiment has been tried in very recent times, and it is the opinion of those who have made the trial that there are now in India strains of game-fowl superior to any which are bred in Europe. A very clever picture was painted, by Zoffany, of the great main fought at Lucknow, in 1786, between Colonel Mordaunt and the king of Oude, which contains portraits of the distinguished personages who assisted thereat. The prints of this picture by Earlom are well known to collectors of valuable engravings, but are now very scarce.

One of the greatest of English cockers was Dr. Bellyse, of Audlem, who died in 1829. For many a year he was the principal figure at the great mains which were yearly fought at Chester in the race-week. He bred largely, rearing seven or eight hundred chickens, and his favourite breed was the white piles, which in later years became so famous as the "Cheshire piles," and are valuable even to this day. Setting an example which many have since followed, Dr. Bellyse drifted back to the brown and black-breasted red birds, which have, after all, stood the test of time better than any more fancy colours.

Cheshire was always a great county for cocking. At Chester races the Irish brown-reds would put in an appearance. Lancashire would bring her black-reds from the walks of Lords

Derby, Sefton, and others; and many a good Staffordshire dun was brought to try conclusions with the famed "Cheshire piles;" while Cholmondeleys, Egertons, Warburtons, and Wilbrahams hung over the pit and backed their respective birds against the best of the strangers. Great mains were fought between Lord Mexborough and the Cotton and Meynell families; and Lichfield, Manchester, Preston, York, and Newton, each and all, were the scenes of mains, when enormous sums changed hands.

The "feeders" of those days were held in higher repute even than the more celebrated trainers of race-horses are now. Gilliver, a Staffordshire man, was at the head of them; and Potter, who for years managed Lord Derby's cocks, was equally noted. The feeder's province was to select, try, train, and deliver the cock into the pit properly "heeled" and ready for the contest. The setter then took charge of him, and there is no less difference between various "setters-to" than between jockeys. Much depends on him; for it requires great skill to handle a beaten cock to the best advantage, while a slight transgression of one of the rules of the pit would at once give the battle to the adversary. Potter and Gun were names of note in former days as setters-to; Davis and young Gilliver in more recent times, while Charles Faultless had no equal for "heeling" birds, *i.e*, fastening on the artificial spurs to the best advantage—a very difficult and nice job.

THE BITER BIT.

AMONG the many piquant anecdotes related by Mr. William Day in his interesting "Reminiscences" the following story is told about Mr. Norman Buchanan who at one time officiated as commissioner to Mr. Merry. Once whilst travelling to Doncaster races, Buchanan hit upon an ingenious scheme for adding to his revenues. Soon after leaving Kings Cross station, he carefully counted the number of the several cords or fringe forming the tassel at the end of the sash by which the carriage window was drawn up; and on arriving at the first stoppage, he left the carriage for refreshments. A gentleman who had been watching his movements, and suspected his intentions, in his absence did the same and, like him, left for the refreshment rooms. They returned together to their respective seats.

Norman soon began dandling the tassel in a careless sort of way and casually said to the gentleman opposite him,
 "How many ends are there on this tassel?"
To which his friend replied:
 "Perhaps there are sixty."
 "Well," said Norman, "I give the correct number nearer than anyone else for a pony" (£25).
 "I am a pretty good guesser generally," quoth the other; "I will lay it you, and I will tell nearer than you if you will give the number first."

The bet was made. Norman said he should think there were forty-nine, fearing to give the exact number, lest it should have been looked upon as suspicious. The other said he would make it even numbers and say fifty and of course won. At this Buchanan was furious. He appealed to his friends to know if he were called upon to pay, alleging that his opponent had been betting on a certainty, as he could not have guessed the exact number without knowing it. But it was a clear case of diamond cut diamond, or the biter bit, and they were all against him. He had to pay, got well laughed at for his pains, and sought refuge in his ulster and somnolency.

LORD GEORGE BENTINCK'S WORK ON THE TURF.

This unfortunate nobleman (he is supposed to have committed suicide) was a keen turf reformer, and was able to place the art of horse racing on a business footing. One of his reforms was to provide for the masses—a portion of the company that previously had little thought or attention bestowed on their wants. He forced stewards, trainers and jockeys to come out punctual to that time they had never hitherto professed to keep. He heralded, for the benefit of every spectator within sight, the names, by numbers, of the field preparing to start; and, to perfect this part of his design, suggested that fine treat—the saddling, walking and cantering the horses before the stands. Previous to these admirable arrangements, many a man, wearied of waiting, left the course ere the race he came to see was run; or, thanks to an indifferent card and one transient view, without a glance at the horse he had pinned his faith to. But, useful as were the improvements introduced by Lord George Bentinck for the benefit of the public, they were put into the shade by his reform of turf abuses. He cleared the race-courses of England of defaulters by his stringent code of laws; he suppressed the prevalent system of false starts, and he was constantly ready and active to put down swindling in whatever form it reared its hydra head. The memory of the great reformer of turf abuses and race-course monopoly will live as long as an Englishman has any taste for the amusement, or any sympathy and admiration for one who alone effected what a whole body allowed themselves unequal to attempt.

SOME REMARKABLE WAGERS.

AMONG the many curious wagers which have from time to time found their way into books or newspapers the following may be thought worthy of being preserved in this volume. A remarkable bet at the great odds of 1,000 to 50 guineas was decided by the fact that diplomatists no more than their weaker brethren, are averse to "that one bottle more." The gentleman laying the £1,000 had heard, on what he considered trustworthy authority, that the preliminaries of peace between France and England were signed on a certain date; his opponent, who wagered the £50, was of opinion that the signatures were not attached until the next day. The first was wrong, the second was right; for though all had been arranged at table, and the secretaries had been informed they were signed, that ceremony was subsequently postponed until the next morning should wear off some of the fumes of the ambassadorial wine.

A match at swallow-shooting deserves to be chronicled. Captain Ross has explained it in a letter. "The bet was £100, and with Mr. George Foljambe I undertook to shoot ten brace of swallows with a pistol and single ball in one day. An immense number of swallows built their nests all round the towers of Rossie Castle, and I shot the match there. 'The Squire' was staying with me at the time, and saw the match shot. I shot well, as the shots were pretty long ones, the towers being three stories high, and a half-sunk storey. I caught the birds as they were hovering, with wings extended and pretty stationary, before going into their nests. I finished the match before breakfast." This match has scarcely a parallel.

Many had thought the swallow-shooting a bet between Lord Kennedy and the Captain, and attached to the narrative was a laughable one about the swallows being placed under a dish-cover at the breakfast table, but the Captain explained that this feature, which he repudiated as connected with that affair, must have arisen out of the following : "A year or two before I shot the swallows with ball," said Captain Ross, " Lord Kennedy betted me £20 I did not shoot twenty brace in a day with a gun (he had no idea of the number at Rossie Castle). I sent them to him in a box, and they arrived while he and a party were at dinner, and were brought into the dining-room. He sent me the £20, and said in his note, ' that it was the most expensive *entrée* ever handed to him.' "

MR. SHORT ODDS AND JIMMY HIRST.

In days now long passed away there were more " characters " on the turf than there are to-day. Then there was more originality ; now all who follow the sport of Kings are very much alike, looking, so to put the case, as if made in the same mould. Among the " eccentrics " of the olden time was to be numbered a bookmaker named Richards who had been nicknamed " Mr. Short Odds," because of the miserable prices he laid in betting. He was distinguished by the queer figure he cut on the course, dressed in brown breeches, brown drill gaiters, a brown coat and an old fashioned sort of jacket, called a spencer, which was white in summer, and always with a choice flower in his button-hole. Richards began life as a stocking-weaver, and began his betting career at the cockpit. Shrewd and lucky, he soon advanced to higher things, and made a book for some of the Northern races, progressing, until, at last, he became a big man in the Ring. He was eccentric in all he did ; going to Newmarket it was his custom to drive one horse and lead another behind his gig, and after going a stage, he would change them about, putting them alternately between the shaft. His own corn always went with him in the gig, and a regular cargo of stockings as well. These he would fain on all occasions have made his cheque book, as he always wanted to pay his clients with them ; and whatever purchases he made he always tried hard to make a bargain of exchange and barter. Just fancy nowadays any butcher, well known upon the turf, when he had laid against the wrong horse, proposing that the winner should take it out in sides of beef or sucking pigs, though even that would be better than stockings, as you can dispose much more quickly of ribs of beef than you can of hosiery. "There's Richards, if he hasn't come out hunting with an umbrella!" cried some gentlemen once when that worthy put in an appearance at a meet. "Short Odds" was always ready for a bet, so, coming up to the group, he answered, "And I'll bet you five hundred you'll not hunt with or without an umbrella when you're my age." "Who's to hold the stakes?" asked one. "Oh, there'll be some one of you left, perhaps, when I'm gone; we'll leave it to him," was the reply. Richards was very particular about stale bread; he used to lock it up in the sideboard till it was a fortnight old, and put back the crust if he could not finish it. This, however, was only a fad, and there was nothing of the miser about him. Old "Short Odds" managed to make a pot of money and to live to be nearly eighty.

Among the regular visitors to Doncaster Moor in the early years of the present century was Jimmy Hirst, the miser, dressed in coat, trousers, and hat of sheepskin, and a waistcoat of drakes' feathers. In his curious carriage, made without nails and drawn by dogs, asses, or a bull, he would shower among the people notes on the Bank of Rawcliffe for twopence-halfpenny each. These notes bore his own portrait, showing him in his noble equipage, with his gun in his hand, attended by pigs, dogs, and foxes, the inscription running as follows: "Bank of Rawcliffe, No. —. I promise to pay John Bull, or bearer on demand, the sum of FIVE halfpence. 18—. For the Governor and Company of the Bank of Rawcliffe, JAMES HIRST."

This eccentric character lived to the great age of ninety-one, and was present at the St. Leger, in his usual state, a few days before he died. His will was in keeping with his life. It was his desire that he should be carried to the grave by eight old maids, each of whom was to be paid half-a-guinea. As eight old maids, however, sufficiently strong for the office, could not be found, the corpse was borne by eight widows—what a moral against celibacy!—to the solemn music of a bagpipe and a fiddle, the former being played by a Scotch shepherd, the latter by an inhabitant of the village where the old man died.

FALLING AMONG THIEVES.

THOSE who used to attend the numerous prize fights which were wont to be held in the palmy days of the ring had to take pot luck of a rough and ready kind so far as accommodation was concerned, and submit quietly to be robbed as well, resistance being out of the question except at the risk of death. When the fight between Caunt and Bendigo took place, the roughs of London, Birmingham, and Nottingham formed themselves into three separate bands to levy black mail. A party of gentlemen, who remembered the days of Tom Spring, chartered a drag and drove down to the place in the style they were accustomed to of yore. "I put on," to tell the story in the words of one of the narrators, "a new white hat, a white Chesterfield wrapper, a bird's-eye scarf, with a magnificent pin, and had a box seat. We reached the gate. 'Pay here,' said one of a knot of fellows, armed with sticks. 'How much?' 'Ten bob a nob.' The money was paid, and in return we received a yellow ticket. We reached a second gate, where a second lot of ragamuffins made a similar demand. 'We've paid at the other gate,' I said.

"'Then pay again,' was the answer. There was no help for it, so we paid again, and got a blue ticket, which we found only passed us to the third gate, where we paid a third time, and, after receiving a pink card, found ourselves in the field with the ropes and stakes.

"While I was looking at the preparation a smart smack on the top of my hat called my attention to a gentleman whose force of character was visible in his countenance, and who demanded a sovereign for a front seat and some straw. I gave him the sovereign, and in exchange he gave me the straw, and another thump on the hat, telling me to sit down. Being stout, I could not very well sit down upon the ground all at once, and knelt upon my straw. In another moment I experienced a most painful sensation—a man was kneeling on the calves of my legs. 'Are you aware,' I remarked mildly, 'that you are kneeling on my legs and causing me great pain?' 'Am I?' he answered stolidly, but without moving. 'Get up,' I cried, 'get up.' 'Oh, ah, I shouldn't wonder,' he said, in the same tone, and, putting his arms under mine, he placed the end of a stick under my chin, and positively trussed me. I could neither speak nor stir. They rifled my pockets, took my watch and pin, forced my hat over my face, rolled me over, and then told me to sit still and watch the fight!"

"Ah," remarked a friend to whom he told the story, "I

was there ; but I walked with the mob fourteen miles in the oldest clothes, had nothing with me but a cotton pocket-handkerchief and a captain's biscuit, but, by——! they took both. But I don't mind such trifling inconveniences to see a good set-to ; and I met another of my own way of thinking. There was a young fellow, a thoroughbred one, returning home ; his coat and hat were gone, and his torn shirt gave indications of a struggle. 'I think,' said an oily, white-chokered, Chadband-sort of fellow, ' that the treatment you have experienced will sicken you of such disgusting exhibitions.' 'Not a bit of it,' was the reply ; ' I don't care as long as they leave me my trousers.'"

CHARLES JAMES FOX AND OTHER GAMBLERS.

ENORMOUS sums of money at one time changed hands at gambling tables about the end of the last and in the first quarter of the present century, and many stories have been published regarding the luck experienced by particular players. As all well read people know, the famous Charles James Fox was one of the seekers of fortune at the faro table, at which and at other games he lost almost incredible amounts. Night after night he was to be found at the table of one or other of the clubs, where he lost enormous sums, ran himself hopelessly into debt, and had often to borrow a guinea of one of the waiters to pay an importunate chairman, and in consequence was always in the hands of the Jews. One night he won £8,000, the greater part of which he had to pay away as he stood at the table, he would then stake the rest, and leave the room as penniless as he entered it. His father left him £154,000, but this did not cover his liabilities, and a few years afterwards he was compelled to sell everything he possessed in the world for the benefit of his creditors. Writing to a friend he said, "I have not a guinea, nor have I had for some time, and I am all the happier for it." Considering the way in which he squandered his guineas when he had them, this last remark was probably true.

Crockford is alluded to on another page, but there were gambling clubs before Crockford's day, of which the Cocoa Tree, in St. James's-street, was an example: it was a resort of fashionable gamblers. There, after the play was over, or the Houses of Parliament had risen, peers, politicians, and men about town might be seen supping at little tables, covered with a napkin, in the middle of the coffee-room, upon a bit of cold meat or a sandwich, and drinking a glass of punch to refresh themselves before adjourning to the gambling room, where they would remain till morning. An amusing anecdote in connection with "The Cocoa-tree Club" (1780) used to be related by Horace Walpole. "Within this week," he says, "there has been a cast at hazard at the Cocoa-tree Club, the difference of which amounted to a hundred and four-score thousand pounds. Mr. O'Brien, an Irish gamester, had won £100,000 off a young Harvey, of Chigwell, just started from a midshipman into an estate by his elder brother's death.

"O'Brien said, 'You can never pay me.'

"'I can,' said the youth; 'my estate will sell for the debt.'

"'No,' said O'Brien; 'I will win ten thousand, and you shall throw for the odd ninety thousand.' They did, and Harvey won. It is to be hoped he left the gaming-house a wiser man."

Some ladies of the period were even, it has been written, greater gamblers than the men. The Duchess of Cumberland set up a gambling-table in her own saloon, and she and her sister, Lady Elizabeth Luttrel, presided at it with great profit to themselves. Lady Elizabeth was so *clever* at cards that she almost invariably won. When the London drawing-room became rather too warm for her she migrated to Germany, but being detected there cheating, she was condemned to draw a barrow, to which she was chained, through the streets; and, being a second time discovered at the same game, was thrown into prison. More than once we hear of women attempting to commit suicide on account of their losses! and no wonder, when one has been known to lose as much as £3,000 at a sitting.

LORD GLASGOW ON THE TURF.

THE late Earl of Glasgow was in his day one of the best known men on the turf; he bred and owned race-horses on a large scale, and when he died on the 11th March, 1869, he was greatly missed in racing circles. He was a heavy bettor either way, never being afraid of asserting his opinion, no matter the cost. There is a story told of how Lord George Bentinck looked in at Crockford's on the eve of the Derby of 1843, and expressed his readiness to take 3 to 1 about his horse Gaper.

"I'll lay it you," said Lord Glasgow.

"Yes," said Lord George, in his rather mincing way, "but then I want to do it to money."

"I'll lay you 90,000 to 30,000," immediately responded the other.

The Earl's generosity was almost boundless. It is said that he once fed half Paisley in a time of distress, and not a man dared to give him a word of thanks without being assaulted. When the hat went round for some Turfite who had fallen upon evil days, he never put in less than a ten or a twenty pound-note. Forty years after their connection had ceased he has been known to send a jockey a fifty pound-note for "auld lang syne," if he had won a great event.

His lordship's fondness for the turf led him to leave the Navy where it was expected he would make a big mark, but he preferred to live a free life and not to be fettered by the calls of discipline. He settled down at his seat, Hawkhead, near Paisley, in Scotland, giving himself up entirely to hunting, racing, and shooting. Hither came such congenial boon companions as Old "Q," Sir John Heron Maxwell, and Sir James Boswell. What nights these choice spirits must have had together! What wine they must have drank—enough to float a man-of-war! What wild pranks they must have carried out!

Of course, everything was decided by a bet, to win which there was nothing too rash, too dare-devil, or extravagant to perpetrate. One night, after the bottle had been passed pretty frequently, a dispute arose between Lord Kelburne and Lord Kennedy—one of the wildest and most reckless, whether of life, limb, or purse, of the set—as to which was the better coachman. A match for five hundred was at once proposed and accepted. It was to be decided then and there; such hot-blooded and impatient spirits could not wait an hour, an instant.

Up sprang my lord, rang the bell, and, although it was midnight, ordered two coaches and two teams to be immediately ordered and got ready at an hotel close by. The landlord, probably used to such extraordinary freaks upon the part of his noble patron, lost no time in complying with the request. The vehicles and horses were brought out, and made ready as quickly as hands could accomplish the task. Up mounted the rival coachmen, seized the ribbons, and off they started on their trial of skill. The night was dark as Erebus, but they dashed on as if it had been broad daylight; the road was so narrow that two waggons could scarcely pass abreast; the coaches swayed, threatening to topple over every minute, and, more than once coming into collision, narrowly escaped being upset. Lord Kelburne was winning easily, when he arrived at the top of a hill where two roads met, one leading to the sea, the other to Ardrossan, where the match was to terminate. Never a lucky man, his usual ill-fortune attended him on the present occasion—he took the wrong road. On he went through the blinding darkness, and, not hearing any sound in the rear, chuckled to think he had left his rival so far behind. The noise of his wheels prevented him hearing the dash of the waves towards which he was so rapidly approaching, but presently his seasoned nostrils detected a scent of the briny in the atmosphere; he grew doubtful, pulled up—just in time ! He was on the very verge of the sea; a few more paces and horse, coach, and rider would have been among the breakers. As it was, he lost his bet, and very nearly his life.

SPORTSMEN'S APPETITES.

"HALTING one day at Moon's Hotel, the landlord, Mr. and Mrs. (the 'Squire's' mother) Osbaldeston, told us that the Marquis of Huntly, afterwards Duke of Gordon, and the Marquis of Anglesea, had just left, having taken lunch after a grand *battue* at Up Park, and had started for London, for dinner. Moon said he had taken them in, on separate silver plates, no less than twenty-five mutton-chops! Allowing that they would be Welsh mutton, it was a pretty little meal, washed down with five bottles of claret." Of what would their *dinner* consist ?

After the mutton-chop story was told, others were of course related. "When Regent's Park had not a house upon it except the farm-house, my friend H— told me he was invited by 'old Willan' to take 'pot luck' with him. Each had a leg of mutton placed before him, and thus each could help himself as he pleased."

We have all heard of the pic-nic where each of the gentlemen, six in number, had brought a leg of mutton; the ladies preferred some daintier food, and thus each gentleman was left to eat his own leg.

A gentleman having a very small family to cater for, was constantly bewildered in his attempts to provide variety in his purveyorship of butcher's meat. In making his purchases he found it convenient (and probably studying his own taste) to frequently send home a small shoulder of mutton; none can deny that it has greater variety in it, and more moisture, than any other ovine joint, but his wife's taste, in this matter at all events, did not coincide with that of her lord and master (?), and, after repeated hints that, even when smothered with onions, her aversion was as strong as the vegetable, and the "cold shoulder" an utter abomination, she said if another were sent home, "you may cook it, for," said she, "I will not"—strong words from a weak stomach.

A fortnight after, orders were issued for marketing, and the lady being asked what would be most approved, the husband was told that neither beef nor veal would suit, as it had been served several days; lamb was not in season, and there seemed no alternative but mutton. The usual question of what joint was met by the stereotyped "Any part; no matter what." "Shoulder won't do, we know, how about a leg?" "Too large," was the reply. "A loin?" "Too fat; we said we didn't like it." "A neck, then?" "No; we don't want anything for boiling, and a neck is not calculated for roasting." "Then what d'ye say to a breast?" That was instantly negatived as "nasty, bony, thin stuff, we never have!" "Then which must we have, the head or the entrails, as there's little else left?" The ultimatum was, that it must be a shoulder after all.

HOW LORD GEORGE BENTINCK SOLD HIS STUD.

LORD GEORGE BENTINCK's abandonment of the sport of Kings and the sudden method in which he disposed of his stud was much commented on at the time of its occurrence. Lord George in his day was a tower of strength on the turf and did much to place racing on a proper business footing, but notwithstanding his vast expenditure and his desire to have animals of supreme merit, he was never able to win the Derby, a race on the winning of which he had set his heart. At one period he thought he possessed an animal capable of winning the coveted prize in Gaper, and thinking so he backed it to win him a very large sum of money, over a hundred thousand pounds, it was said at the time; but his horse was unsuccessful, the blue riband falling to a horse called Cotherstone, which Lord George fortunately had backed to win him a pretty considerable amount, probably over £25,000. It was at the race meeting of Goodwood, three years afterwards [1846], that he negotiated the sale of his stud of thoroughbreds, jockey and all, offering them first of all to Mr. George Payne.

"The lot, Payne," said he to George Payne, at Goodwood, "from Bay Middleton to Little Kitchener" (his "feather weight" jockey), "for £10,000. Yes or no?"

"I will give £300 to have till breakfast-time to-morrow to consider the matter, Bentinck," replied George Payne. "Give me till then, and I will say yes or no."

"With pleasure, my dear fellow," said his lordship, with nonchalant acquiescence, apparently not giving the matter a second thought, till reminded of the circumstance by Payne handing him a cheque for £300 over his muffin, refusing the offer with as much nonchalance as it was made, and returning to his morning paper without further comment.

Then Mr. Mostyn, seeing the negotiation concluded, said very quietly, from the lower end of the table, lifting his eyes for an instant from his letters—

"*I'll* take the lot, Bentinck, at 10,000; and will give you a cheque before you go to the course."

"If you please," replied Lord George, and the bargain was concluded.

SQUIRE DIMSDALE'S DEATH RIDE.

The following brief narrative although it may read like a romance is in reality a true enough story. It relates to the closing adventure in the life of a Yorkshire county gentleman, and provides us with one more illustration of the old saw, the ruling passion strong in death. The old man, Squire Dimsdale, of Ilkley, lay on his death-bed. In his day there had not been a finer type of his class in all broad Yorkshire. A gambler, a racing and hunting man—most of his tastes, and his affections, were equine. In his young days, when George the Third was King, he had led a wild life, as most men did at that era; had shot a man whose wife he had run off with, and committed many other violences and excesses that rendered him a terror to the country round. But having played his part on the stage of life, there came at length the cue for his exit, the curtain being about to be rung down. It was an awful night; a tempest was raging without, tearing among the branches of the trees and dashing the rain against the windows as though it would beat them in. In the great hall the assembled grooms and huntsmen, huddled over a fire of blazing logs, sat dozing, for the doctor had said the master could not live the night through, and they were every moment expecting to hear that the old man's soul had passed away upon the wings of the storm. Suddenly they were awakened by a trampling of feet without and a woman's voice in entreaty; and they had hardly sprung from their seats when the door burst open, and in stalked the Squire, arrayed in his scarlet coat, hunting cap and boots, but with a face so deathlike that the men shrank back in terror, almost thinking it was his spirit; the nurse was clinging to his arm, and imploring him to go back to bed. But he was not to be persuaded or turned from his purpose, he shook off the woman and ordered one of the grooms, to "Put a saddle on Lightning Bess; get out the dogs. I'll have one more run before they put me under the turf. Give me a glass of brandy. I never was in better fettle."

No one had ever dared to disobey him or cross his lightest whim, and the old habits asserted themselves instinctively. The entreaties of the nurse, the only one who dared to uplift a voice, were unheeded; the mare was saddled, the hounds brought out, and with the strength of fever, augmented by the bumper of neat brandy which he had swallowed, the old Squire walked out of the hall, and with just the assistance of a hand put his foot in the stirrup, threw himself across the mare, and started for his last ride. The tempest had by this time abated, and the flying clouds gave passing gleams of moonlight. Wild with delirium, the dying man struck the horse with his spurs, and, with a yell that sounded inhuman, dashed on, followed by his trembling and horror-stricken servants. The fabled ride of the Wild Huntsman could not have been more ghastly. With reckless frenzy he breasted fence after fence, leaped hedges and ditches and every obstacle in his path. The mare he was riding seeming infected by the demoniac spirit of her master, while the hounds barked in harmony. None of his followers could keep pace with him, and it was only now and again by the fitful moonlight that they caught sight of his flying figure far ahead. All at once they heard a wild shriek, and then Lightning Bess was dashing on riderless, the pack still following in full cry. When they came to the spot where they had seen him fall, they picked up Squire Dimsdale dead. He had sworn he would never die in his bed, and his word was kept.

CHARLES DICKENS ON BATTUE SHOOTING.

A FEW years since a nobleman being about to shoot in an outlying wood in which there was little or no game, ordered his keeper to put some pheasants in over night. The poachers did not on this occasion get at the secret, as they sometimes do. In the morning came my lord and his party—pretty good shots all of them—and famous sport they had : so good, in fact, that after lunch they wanted to go back to the big wood ; but the keeper hesitated, and when pressed, explained that " it was of no use, my lord, going there again ; they had killed a hundred and eighty and odd pheasants already, and he had only turned down a couple of hundred."

This is the ridiculous side of the question ; but there is a lower deep. Pheasants well fed may be kept at home, and it may be presumed that, in many instances, or on great estates, they are not fed on the farmer's produce, or, if so fed, that the tenant gains in rent what he loses in game—though this would be rather strong presumption in a case last season, where, on the property of a noted game-preserving peer in Suffolk, towards the close of an autumn afternoon *three hundred* pheasants were counted round a tenant's barleystack. But then, when the battue is over ; when, to paraphrase Dryden,

> They are all shot down and vanished hence,
> Three days of slaughter at a vast expense,

where do they go ? To market generally, to compete with the expensively dairy-fed pork and poultry of the farmer class, who feed their landlord's more sacred animals for nothing. After one of these double-barrelled festivals in Essex last year, pheasants and hares were sold at a *shilling a head*, and rabbits were cheaper than meat or poultry. We know a parish within an easy rail-ride of London, where farmers with lands overrun with game, are obliged, when they want a brace of pheasants or a hare, to send to Leadenhall market and buy them. And their landlord, who does not shoot himself, hires his shooting out to a stranger.

We have referred to the popularity of the Master of the Foxhounds : we mean, of course, the master who takes pains to make himself liked by all classes ; who does not forget the farmers in the game season, or the farmers' wives in personal politeness or payment for poultry. But who is hated like a battue game preserver, especially a pheasant-preserving parson ? Ask the farmers in Nottinghamshire, say in Sherwood Forest; ask them in Norfolk or in Suffolk; or, if a great landlord doubts, let him try the toast ingeniously proposed by the Secretary of the Farmers' Club, and give at a lively agricultural dinner after the tally-hos have died away, "the truly British sport of Battue Shooting," and let him, in a neat speech, thank the farmers for having enabled him to kill hundreds upon hundreds of hares and pheasants in a day, "and trust they will still continue to enable him to show sport to his fashionable guests."

For a battue, it is essential to concentrate an enormous head of game in a confined space. Thus, after birds have been bred on the plan of a well-managed poultry-yard, hatched under hens, and fed regularly on chosen spots, they are driven, if partridges, into selected turnip fields, and if pheasants, into coverts, where certain rides or paths have been stopped up with netting, so that the tame birds may not *run* out of danger.

LUCK IN GAMBLING.

GAMBLERS are great believers in luck, and are always on the outlook for omens or tips of some kind to guide them. This has always been so, and is the case to-day in various cities where lotteries are still permitted, and where men and women adopt extraordinary modes of finding out what they hope may prove a successful figure. Curiously enough, some people of more than average common sense believe in luck at cards, and of the foibles of such persons, many curious tales have been told, but none is more curious than the following of the late Lord Lytton. He used to play whist very frequently at the Portland Club, but could never be induced to play when a member of the name of Townend, a very harmless and inoffensive man, for whom he had conceived a violent antipathy, was present. He firmly believed that this man brought him ill-luck. One afternoon, after he had been playing with an uninterrupted run of luck, it suddenly turned, upon which he exclaimed, "I'm sure that Mr. Townend has come into the club." Some three minutes afterwards in walked this unlucky personage. Lord Lytton finished the rubber and retired.

Of the gambling last century, Walpole tells that in 1775 at Almack's they played only for rouleaux of £50 each, there being frequently as much as £10,000 in gold upon the table at the same time. Their mode of playing was very extraordinary. Upon entering the room they either turned their embroidered velvet coats inside out for luck, or changed them for others of frieze. They put on pieces of leather, such as used to be worn by footmen when cleaning knives, to save their lace ruffles; to guard their eyes from the light, and to prevent their long powdered hair or wigs from being tumbled, they put on high crowned straw hats adorned with ribbons; and that they might appear to take their gains and losses with the same equability, they sometimes concealed their features beneath masks. Each gamester had a small bowl edged with ormolu to hold his stakes or his winnings.

Men who lost heavily had to fly to the Jews, who advanced them money at exorbitant interest. It was a common occurrence for young men of fashion to lose fifteen or twenty thousand in a single night. There is a story told of a young nobleman who, after losing £11,000 at a sitting, won it back in a single hand at hazard, upon which he exclaimed with a great oath, "Now if I had been playing *deep* I might have won millions!" Many will no doubt wonder what his idea of playing deep would have amounted to.

Lord Holland, it is related, had to pay £20,000 to settle the gambling debts of his two sons. The following paragraph speaks for itself, it is extracted from *The London Chronicle* for August 13th, 1775:—"On Wednesday morning two ladies of distinction, having a dispute at a card party, repaired in their carriages to a field near Pancras, and fought a duel with pistols, when one of them being shot in the left arm, the affair terminated."

At a later period than that just referred to, an extraordinary move was made in the gambling way. Four members of the aristocracy, three of them noblemen, set up a faro bank at Brookes's. So determined were they to keep all the plunder to themselves that they were their own croupiers, and took three guineas an hour each from the joint concern as payment for their trouble. And there, night after night, might they be seen dealing the cards. It was a good paying spec; each of the four realised between three and four hundred thousand. A Mr. Paul, who had made a large fortune in India, dropped into the place on the night of his return to England; before quitting the hell he lost ninety thousand pounds.

OLD COACHING DAYS.

THE inns all along the Great North Road, where twenty (read fifty) years ago the postillions had to sleep spur on heel, when a great division on the twelfth of August was at hand, and the ostler muttered "horses on" in his dreams, are nearly all merged into farm-houses; but racing recollections will hover about them, albeit the bar snuggery has become a cheese room, and Herring's St. Leger winners which once adorned their walls are dispersed into all lands. These were the texts on which the jolly landlord discoursed without any bidding, to favoured groups by the hour, till the mail bugle was heard in the distance, and the guard and the coachman bustled in to deliver themselves of the news and receive something hot in return. "What's won?" was invariably the first question from April to November; and Boniface as invariably remarked to the company, "I told you so." For racing news, and, in fact, for any other kind of information, guards were at that date as good as a telegraph. One day in 1843, a quiet clerical friend remarked to us that he could get no rest all night in one of the Lancashire mail coaches because the guard would roar out "the cure," in reply to some speaker, at nearly every house they passed—it was the name of the horse that had won the Champagne Stakes—the Cure.

ABSURD STORIES ABOUT MR. MERRY.

ONE of the many absurd and often contradicted stories which have for the last twelve or fifteen years been in circulation about Mr. James Merry, has again cropped up in a column of a sporting newspaper. "A capital story, which I will give as it is chronicled by a well-known authority," says the writer in the sporting journal, "is told of the late Mr. Merry, whose happy knack of getting out of difficulties was proverbial. A terrible rumour had gone abroad among the Falkirk people that their member had allowed one of his racehorses to run in a race on the Sabbath on the Continent, and it was solemnly determined that he should be called upon for an explanation of such godless conduct. The day arrived. The largest hall was crowded, the 'meenister' himself put the question. Mr. Merry rose to answer. 'It is quite true,' he said, 'that having sent a horse of mine to the Continent, I did so far forget myself as to conform to the customs of the country in which I was staying, and allow him to start for an important prize on the Sabbath-day.' ('Oh, oh!' and loud groans all over the place.) 'But, gentlemen, I must add that before I thought about the day on which the race was to be run, I had backed my horse very heavily with the French, *and I won their money and brought it back to spend in auld Scotland.*' And straightway all true Scots in that room felt their hearts touched, and waving their bonnets exultantly over their heads, the assembly joined in three cheers for the canny member, and then dispersed, singing 'Auld Lang Syne.'" Like several other tales told about the great Scottish sportsman, this is a "pack of nonsense."

Another of the anecdotes of which Mr. Merry has been a fertile source, runs as follows. On one occasion he was "heckled" on the hustings as to his opinions on the vexed questions of Church Rates, the Law of Hypothec and sundry other abominations in Scottish eyes. He had been previously coached by his secretary as to the answers he ought to give, and was just opening his mouth to reply when a voice exclaimed, "An' hoo aboot the Decalogue, mon?" Mr. Merry looked perplexed, the word was unfamiliar to him, but supposing it must be one of the questions as to which he had not been duly instructed what to say, he boldly avowed in his broad Lowland Scotch dialect, "I'm for abolishin' it."

WAGERS ABOUT WORDS.

THE following note written by Admiral Rous many years ago has been published by Mr. John Corlett of the *Sporting Times.*

If, according to Chesterfield, it was in his time absolutely necessary for a gentleman to study orthography, lest one false spelling should fix ridicule on him for life, it is now equally incumbent on a fast gentleman to study Johnson, that he may be able to defend himself, and to avoid being picked up by a dear friend, who may have a design on his purse.

For the last thirty years, Raindeer, Refirrible, Dier, Bay window, *infortunate, have been baits to pick up country flats both amongst the sharpers in London and the lowest of the betting fraternity at Newmarket. A celebrated trainer left a written document to his son, S.R., who was in the first class of jockeys, to beware of Raindeer, Refirrible, and Dier!

In 1832, a trap was laid for a young gentleman, who arrived in Paris with more money than brains. A, an ex-M.P., said to B, "I was very *in*fortunate at the club last night." "*Un*fortunate, you mean," remarked B. "No, *in*fortunate," replied A. "Why, you have been so long abroad you have forgotten your English. I will bet you 1,000 francs that the word *in*fortunate is not to be found in Johnson;" and B turning to C, asked, "Will you go halves if I increase the bet?" C consenting, A and B chaffed one another, and added bet to bet till the stake amounted to 50,000 francs! The money was paid. A and B divided the spoils, and it was subsequently discovered that the confederates had for years made an income out of the "*in*fortunates."

Pretended disputes and subsequent bets upon the spelling of refirrible had a special run through the night houses of the Haymarket in the winter of '57-'58, when "plants" were being continually made by sharpers upon likely subjects, always to be decided by Johnson. My correspondent adds: "In my own experience I have never hesitated in concluding that anyone whom I have heard trying to raise a bet upon the spelling of refirrible or dier was a 'sharp;' and on more than one occasion, where I have had an excuse, I have denounced the 'plant,' but I have never known of the attempt being made in a private circle and by an honourable man."

Another correspondent says: "From my own personal knowledge, the spelling of the word Raindeer is the oldest catch bet, but it cannot be done without a previous arrangement with a confederate to introduce the subject. It is exactly the same as getting a friend to say, 'He has caught cold by sleeping in a *dank* bed,' when flats will bet that he is wrong, thinking he intends to say *damp*, which is synonymous. Also, the word 'compete,' which is not to be found in Johnson, or even in Vine's Dictionary Appendix. *Displosion* is another catch bet, and *referrible* has won more money than any word in the English language."

IN A LONDON GAMBLING CLUB.

A WRITER in the *British Weekly* thus describes what he saw: "I was introduced to the proprietor—a Jew, of course, and a highly objectionable one. In aspect he is near of kin to some melodramatic stage villains usually considered impossible. Bulky, with a big oily face and heavy, fleshy nose, his black eyes, large as they are, have hard work to see over his cheeks, and it is extremely improbable that he has seen his toes for the last ten years. He was 'got up' regardless of expense—and taste; gold *pince-nez* put a kind of note of interrogation into his expression; spotless linen, a marvellous tie, heavy gold watch-chain, trousers of horse-cloth pattern and irreproachable spats— magnificent attire! but it simply intensified his blackguardly appearance. He joked with me for a few minutes in thick, sugary tones, accompanying his jokes with hoarse chuckles, and occasionally poked me in the ribs in a painful manner. In spite of his condescending jocularity, it was evident he was taking my measure. He concluded I must be as big an idiot as my introducer, I suppose, for he complacently hung up my membership notice on the wall, and gracefully pointed to the baccarat table. A very nice gentleman had all this time been consuming a Welsh rabbit at a small table, and I wondered whether he had made some mistake in the number of the street door. He looked the essence of respectability, and his benevolent gravity was more reconcilable with a prayer-meeting than a gambling house. I half expected he would pray; but no—he rose just as I turned to go to the table, stretched himself comfortably, and took a seat at the game. His presence gave an aspect of sobriety to his end of the table, but it was almost too ludicrous. He played in the same sedate, benign manner in which he ambled through his supper—and won.

"The players were a very mixed lot; a good number of them bore an openly unscrupulous look, though I saw no overt robbery whilst there. Clerks of inferior outward smartness and not very well dressed, five or six retail traders and a few cattle-dealers, a money-lender or two, shopmen on good wages and the usual nondescripts—these, so far as I could judge and pick up from conversation, formed the bulk of the forty-five or fifty men round the table. There were several skilled mechanics and a sprinkling of very ordinary labourers. During the night a few young fools such as my introducer came in, but left shortly for scenes of greater liveliness. Truly the room was depressing; no attempt at comfort was made. Bare wooden benches round a deal table, covered with faded green baize; no carpet of any kind; walls dirty and greasy, bearing traces of beer and tobacco-juice and ornamented solely with a great number of printed rules and orders of the committee—this, lit up from half-a-dozen glaring burners, was not an attractive picture.

"Play went on with great regularity and with little in the way of disorder. There was more talking and swearing than at more respectable clubs, and at times the din grew to pitch enough to incite the flashy Shylock to interference. Then he shone forth in all his glory as he demanded order. He did it with the fatty sternness of tone so much in vogue with his kind, as who should say, '*Now*, gentlemen, *I* want you to enjoy yourselves, but *really*—well *come* you *must* be quiet, you know.' After delivering his charge he smiled expansively over the room, replaced his cigar between his ponderous lips, and resumed his stroll, rattling watch-chain and money. Two or three mechanics originally with but little in their pockets, hung anxiously over the table, watching the luck of the sixpence or shilling which, if not the last which remained, was very near it. Soon they had lost all. They waited about for some time, for a drink or anything else that might turn up. One, with a haggard face—perhaps he had lost the whole of his wages (it was Saturday) —managed to borrow five shillings and sat down again. The bank raked it remorselessly in, and in a few minutes the man rose and rushed down the stairs, followed by the mocking laugh of Shylock, who had keenly enjoyed the poor fellow's agonised face. Another, also a mechanic, had just as wretched luck. He staked sixpence at a time, and played ahead until he had but a shilling or two left. Then he commenced to be cautious, and laid his money down at intervals. It was no use; he was doomed. The last sixpence went; he quietly lifted his chair back, and as quietly walked to the door. There was no small pathos in his departure, but the repulsive proprietor leered with sneering pity, and seemed to be saying to himself, 'He'll come back.' Perhaps he was right. The man had certainly lost several pounds, and just as he passed down the stair, Shylock moved after him and whispered something in his ear. The fellow smiled in a ghastly manner, and went off shaking his head. Shylock came back and encouraged me to take the vacant chair—kind man. I thought I had better play a little, and so sat down.

"To-night the bank had all the luck, and I don't think any but the bankers rose winning. A red-faced, healthy cattle-dealer, well-dressed, and of great self-reliance, if looks go for anything, lost sovereign after sovereign. He calmly changed five-pound notes with great good humour. But he was evidently an *habitué* of the place and an old gambler. Doubtless he ran the bank when he could get the chance; and I expect he goes to the club several nights each week, playing ahead when he can't get the bank, and knowing that all his losings will be made up.

"The continued luck of the bank seemed to have the effect of making the great majority of the players fiercely reckless. A man seated on my right maintained a rigid face each draw of the cards till he saw his florin swept away, and then he ground out in an undertone a hideous volley of oaths. Down went another florin, or maybe two, and a fresh combination of imprecations followed the stake into the bank. How much he lost it is not easy to say; but he played regularly for over two hours, and did not win once in ten times. His originality in swearing was the most remarkable thing about him. Not only did he invent new oaths, but he displayed the most extraordinary ingenuity in new arrangements of old ones. The recent novelist who invented the tasteful expression, 'slap me crimson,' did not beat this shopman."

ABOUT "HEDGING."

"WELL then, what is hedging? You promised to explain it to me," said a novice in turf matters, to a master of the finesse of racing.

"So I shall, my boy—no bet is a good bet till it is well hedged, has become a maxim on the turf."

"I have heard the maxim often enough, but to me it is as a door that is locked because I have not the key to it."

"Well, here is the key: listen."

"All right, I will."

"You back a horse that is to run in a certain race to win you a hundred pounds at the odds of say 50 to 1; if the horse loses, you will lose your two pounds of stake money. To save yourself you can 'hedge' as it is called, that is, you can, providing the animal you have backed comes to a shorter price, 'lay off' a portion of the cash you expect to win at the current rate of odds: let us imagine that the horse finds favour in the betting and comes in time to be quoted at 25 to 1, you can then lay 50 to 2, which leaves you in the position of having nothing to pay if your horse loses the race, and of winning fifty pounds should it prove successful; that in brief is an explanation of 'hedging;' do you understand the principle?"

"Oh yes, I think I do, but who do you hedge with, and what if the price does not lessen?"

"Well that is a risk you must run; the horse may, of course, recede instead of 'come' in the betting, or it may not even run, on the other hand it may come to a still shorter price than I have indicated, so that you lay off to still more advantage. The bookmaker you deal with will, as a rule, take your hedging money."

NO. 2,224: MISS MITFORD'S CHOICE!

DOCTOR MITFORD, father of Miss Mitford, the popular authoress of "Our Village," was seldom free from pecuniary cares, indeed he was constantly in monetary hot water, and on one occasion during the girlhood of his daughter, he was saved from great distress by drawing a big prize in a lottery of the period. The circumstances under which this ticket in the lottery was purchased are worth relating, more especially as the story was more than once told by the lady herself.

"The Doctor took his little girl with him to the lottery office to choose the number, when a quantity of tickets was laid down on the counter for her to select from. She at once fixed upon the number 2,224. There were difficulties in the way of the Doctor's possessing himself of that ticket. It was one that had been divided into shares, all of which had not been taken by the same office; and he wished to procure a whole ticket. The child (Miss Mitford) could not be induced by any persuasion to relinquish her first choice. What was to be done? The little girl, as all who knew her at that early age will agree, was a 'spoilt child,' and her father—superstitious as every gambler appears more or less to be—allowed her to have her own way. The sixteenth she had fixed her heart upon, she carried home with her; the remaining shares of the number were bought up from the other offices at a considerable advance in price; and the Doctor on the drawing of the lottery, received £20,000, the largest prize that was then given as the fruit of—we cannot say his wisdom and discretion."

GOOD ADVICE TO ANGLERS ABOUT KILLING TROUT IN AUGUST.

It was on a beautiful autumn evening that my brother and I went down the river side for a few hours' trout fishing. I carried the rod, he the basket along with the landing net, which we used for heavy trout at particular parts of the stream. The sun was just setting behind the Grampians as I put up my rod, and its rays fell with a peculiar splendour on the golden corn fields which lay on all sides, and glanced with slanting ray on the stream at which I purposed to begin my labours. Before I was ready it had disappeared, leaving behind it only a few crimson clouds, the welcome token of continued good weather. In a few minutes more I was nearly ready. My rod was up, my line through the rings, and my cast line was dangling at the end of it, with three flies attached to it. Some will, doubtless, think that this being the case I was quite ready to begin, but they are mistaken, the most important part had yet to be done. I now bring forth a small tin box from my pocket and open it; it is filled with meal, but not altogether with meal, the meal swarms with maggots. Not the maggots that one generally sees, small, decrepid-looking animals, but great, fat, substantial maggots, enough to tempt the most epicurean trout that ever swam, and furnish him with a supper fit for an alderman.

Some anglers, I know, have an aversion to fish with maggots: they don't like to handle them, and hate the very sight of them. The sooner they overcome this prejudice the better, for it is merely a prejudice. After the interesting little creatures have been for a day or two in meal, and got their complexions improved, nothing can, in my opinion, be more beautiful or cleanly. But let that be as it may, I would have all such sensitive anglers bear in mind that with whatever dislike they may view them, the trouts don't share in their foolish prejudice. Many a fine trout will come out of his haunt, and make a dash at a fly with a maggot on the end of it, when it would have treated the fly wanting the maggot with the utmost contempt. Well, then, it was with profound satisfaction that I pounced upon a great fat maggot, and put it on my trail fly, and in like manner fastened others on the two bobs. All was ready now, and I knew that I had a good chance of basketing a few trout, although it was the month of August. I fished down the river with some success, but I knew that the time was not come yet, so I reserved the best places for the dusky hour that was approaching. The minutes flew quickly past, and at last the time came, and with the time came the place and man. It was a large deep dam, quite smooth or nearly so—a place, in fact, where during the day an angler would not have got a single "offer," unless in a good breeze of wind. It was just getting dark when I commenced to thrash the water at this spot, and in good sooth I did not thrash in vain. At every throw a fine yellow trout, sometimes two or three, made a dash at my hooks, and I generally managed to land one of the competitors for my favours. The bank was high, and I had to stand on the top and throw, while my brother sat at the bottom, and took out the fish as I successfully brought them to the side.

The way I worked my flies, or rather maggots, was this. I threw out a considerable line, and allowed them to sink a little, and then gently drew them in a semi-circle towards the edge. I found it was better to sink them slightly than to draw them along the top of the water. Perhaps some will think that I could have got as many fish if I had put my maggots on common bait hooks instead of flies. To some extent they are right. Supposing the maggots stuck on the hooks, all would be well, but the worst of maggot fishing is that the maggots are constantly falling off, or being bitten off by the trout; and when this happens with bait hooks, then the fish have no lure to attract them at all; whereas, although a maggot falls off a fly hook, there is still the fly to tempt the dwellers in the stream, and though they don't bite at it so voraciously as at the maggot, yet you have always the chance of getting something. I still remember that night at the dam; it is a white night in my fishing calendar. I got trout after trout, till my brother began to complain of the weight of the basket, and of the constant efforts he had to make in landing the fish. At length, from want of maggots, I had to stop, and with a glorious basket, full almost to the brim with splendid trout, averaging ½lb each, I retraced my steps homewards, thoroughly convinced that for the month of August there was nothing like maggots and the evening for effective work. I would advise all anglers at that time of the year to try the plan, and I am greatly mistaken if they do not succeed.

MYTTONIANA.

For about twenty years (he died at the age of thirty-eight), John Mytton of Halston was a tower of strength in the world of sport, and was known in all its departments. It may indeed be said " he died of the pastimes of the period." In his life which was written by his friend " Nimrod," many of his doings are recorded, and it is to the pages of that work we are indebted for the following anecdotes :—

No phase in Mytton's character is so interesting as that which is illustrated by his exploits in riding and driving. During the period of Sir Bellingham Graham's hunting Shropshire, he performed several gallant feats in the field. Whilst suffering severely from the effects of a fall, and with his right arm in a sling, he rode his favourite horse, Baronet, over Lord Berwick's park-paling at Atsham, near Shrewsbury, to the astonishment of the whole field; Sir Bellingham himself exclaiming—

"Well done, Neck-or-nothing! you are not a bad one to breed from!"

With the same hounds he signalised himself greatly in a run from Bomer Wood to Haughmond Hill, when the river Severn brought the field to check. Three or four of them managed to get their horses into a boat, but Mytton scorned such assistance. " Let all who call themselves sportsmen," he exclaimed, "follow me!" and, dashing into the stream, gained the opposite bank, and was one of the very few who saw the fox killed.

I have spoken of Mytton as a shot, and I believe no *sportsman* need be superior to what he was at one time of his life. For myself, I only knew him as a game shot, as the term is, never having seen him with either pistol or rifle in his hand. It has, however, been represented to me that he was a most superior marksman with a rifle, so superior indeed as to be able to hit the edge of a razor at the distance of thirty yards, and occasionally to split his ball! " *Credat Judæus* "—I do not add " *non ego ;* " yet I never chanced to hear of such a wonderful performance. He was the dread of the owners of the minor gambling-tables who frequent country races, for he was given to break their banks in more ways than one. I have said, he was often a great winner; but he would demolish the entire apparatus if he suspected any unfair advantage to be taken of himself, or of any other person in the room. At Warwick races, in 1824, he and his companions not only broke a *rouge-et-noir* table to atoms, but gave the proprietor of it and his gang a sound drubbing into the bargain. He was once, together with some others, surprised by the Mayor of Chester, in the act of playing hazard, in a room hired for that purpose, on the *Sunday* evening previous to the races; but on seeing his worship enter he put his winnings into his hat, the hat on to his head, and then walked away unnoticed, being taken only for a spectator. He was losing heavily one night at Chester, when he turned very faint. "Take him away," said somebody; "he's too drunk to play."

"No, no," answered a friend at his side; "wash his mouth out and give him another chance." They did so, when he not only won all his money back, but a good stake to boot.

GAMES OF CHANCE AND GAMBLING.

THE following opinion given by one of our best written journals—*The Spectator*—is worthy of consideration.

In games of chance you do learn to realise practically what it means in life to have the odds against you, as men so often must have them against them in much more serious matters, and matters where it is far less possible to calculate the amount of the odds against them. You might learn, too, and often do learn, how much piquancy is given to otherwise very stupid occupations by the uncertainty of the issue. And you certainly get a very good opportunity of practising equanimity in small reverses and magnanimity in small successes.

If a game be made more cheerful by a little of the excitement of pure chance as to who will be the gainers and who the losers,—as games have been made and will be made more cheerful as long as human nature and youth remain what they are,—we can see no more harm in losing small sums for such a purpose than in losing them for the purposes of a cooling drink in summer or a hot drink in winter. But the difference between gambling and almost every other amusement is that it combines no advantage of a higher order with the advantage of excitement. It does not involve exercise; it does not teach anything, unless it be a little coolness and self-control; it does not cultivate the sense of beauty, like gazing at beautiful scenes; it does not sustain the body; and, unless very moderately indulged in, instead of refreshing and restoring, it rather heats and exhausts the mind.

Another writer pithily says, "Gambling is not gambling when you gamble within your means."

BILLIARDS IN PARIS.

THE following remarks which are certainly worthy of perusal were written by a well-known authority, Captain Crawley—more than twenty years ago.

Every town has a character of its own, and so has every billiard room. In Paris, the fashion is to have several tables in one long apartment. This is a bad plan; the tables are too close together, and the players incommode each other. The number of lights, and the prevailing want of ventilation to such rooms, make them hot and "stuffy." After an hour's play at one very celebrated place, not a thousand miles from the Palais Royal, I had as severe a headache as ever I got in the old reading room of the British Museum; and that, most of my readers of literary tendencies may remember, was a splitter!

Then, again, the public rooms of Paris are a little too public. People come and go, and smoke and yawn, and chatter and walk about, as they do in the *cafés*. Frenchmen do not appear to understand the grace and comfort of doing nothing in a quiet, unobtrusive way. They shift about in their seats, they make remarks about Jules's hazards and Henri's cannons with a loud voice; they assert their liberty by incessant calls upon *garçon*, and frequent small orders for *café-noir* or *eau sucrée;* they seem to regard a public billiard room as a lounge, and the players as performers in some pretty little entertainment got up for their especial benefit.

As for the players in the public rooms of Paris, I think, upon the whole, that they are rather worse than the generality of those I have seen in similar places at home. They play with less finish and aplomb than Englishmen. One reason for this, is the extreme size of the balls; and another, the breadth and flatness of the tips of the cues. French players of the ordinary sort seem to care less about the choice of their cues than we do. Moreover, they play with much heavier cues than are commonly found in English billiard rooms. What we at home call a French tip, or top, for a cue does not appear to be much valued in Paris. Then, again, they play too hard and too recklessly. Of course, I am referring to the play of public rooms. In the clubs, and in private houses, in France, you will find some of the best players in Europe—careful, cautious, scientific, and full of *finesse*. Occasionally, too, in the public rooms you will see—as with us—wonderful players of the Berger and Roberts school, expert in hazards and unfailing in cannons; men who glance from ball to ball with the eyes of eagles, and shoot the object ball into the very centre of the pocket with unerring exactness; men who judge distances with more than a rifleman's expertness, and make all their strokes with a suddenness and decision that is really admirable.

But these are the exceptions. Your ordinary Frenchman plays billiards as he dances and fights, with vivacity and smartness, but without exactness or anxiety. It was my pleasure and my pain to see some very excellent and some very execrable play in Paris. Any man who really likes the game would be delighted to watch M. Berger make his fifty or sixty at a break. Such smoothness and grace—not in the player alone, but in the strokes; such excellent judgment as to strength and distance; such admirable calculation as to the effect of each individual hazard and cannon, and the situation of the balls after the stroke: nothing finer in the way of billiards can be witnessed in England—if we except Roberts, Hughes, and, perhaps, some three or four other professional players.

But as for Jules, Christophe, and Edouard, it is, as the Yankees say, a caution to see them knock the balls about. Arms, and legs, and cue at all angles; and then what self-approving looks after every successful hazard! And the noise, the continual patter, chatter, and laughter, why it would be a terrible infliction to a looker-on, if it were not so excessively droll and un-English.

This is, however, but an insular way of looking at French billiards. There is another aspect of the game. Every little *café* and *estaminet* in Paris, almost every poor little *cabaret* in the provincial towns, has its billiard table, at which the people play for two or three sous a game. Why cannot we have billiard tables in our coffee-houses and beer-shops? Why must a simple game of fifty up never cost less than sixpence or eightpence? To the working man, billiards is practically a forbidden game. He cannot afford eightpence for an hour's amusement. Surely, now that the dining question is before the public, the recreation question might attract some attention.

What reason is there for making billiards an expensive game? A good table, cues, balls, marking board, &c., can be bought for fifty guineas; and one would suppose that ten or fifteen shillings a week would be ample return for an outlay of that amount. Ten shillings a week would give £26 a year for rent of room and table—fifty per cent. on the capital invested. At threepence a game, only forty games per week—seven a day—would be necessary to make up the amount required. But then, ah! I forgot that!—there is the license. Magistrates, on whom the power of licensing rests, look upon billiards as a gambling game, and are, therefore, very chary in granting the privilege. Why, what nonsense this is. There is really—and I speak from a long experience—less money expended in wagers and drink in a billiard room frequented by respectable middle-class people than there is in an ordinary skittle-alley. Moreover, tavern-keepers require no special license for billiards. It is included in their general permission to vend excisable liquors, or is obtainable for the mere asking. I contend that billiards is an excellent in-door game, equally adapted to the lord and the labourer. Our system, and our way of looking at the amusements of the people does, however, deter capitalists from investing money in billiard tables.

STOCK EXCHANGE GAMBLING.

THE following "definitions" were recently given in the pages of the *Gentleman's Magazine*:—

A "punter" means a person who speculates for small amounts. At baccarat or on the turf he operates generally for shillings, half-crowns, or crowns, or the smallest amount the banker or bookmaker will accept. In this way he is distinguished from the "plunger," who operates for large amounts.

A "bucket-shop" is a stockbroker's office which is frequented by and kept for the convenience of "punters." Such institutions are almost invariably owned by what are called "outside brokers," an industrious and enterprising class of practitioners, who have, however, no more connection with the Stock Exchange than they have with the Vatican.

As regards the operations which are technically known as

"bulling" and "bearing," accounts, it may be stated, are adjusted on the Stock Exchange about once a fortnight. In other words, unless there be a special arrangement that the transaction is to take place at once, if you buy a stock your broker pays the owner for it, or if you sell he delivers it to the buyer, at the next account. Now, suppose that a week will elapse before the next account comes on, and suppose also that for some reason or other you are led to think that a certain stock will get dearer, or "go up," as it is termed, in the meantime. It is evident under these circumstances that if you were to buy a certain amount of the stock to-day, and then, if the stock gets dearer in the intervening time, to sell it again, you would have two transactions to carry out on the account day, and that you would benefit by them. In the one case you would have to pay the price at which you agreed to buy the stock; in the other you would have to receive the higher price at which you agreed to sell it. So that by buying the stock at one price and selling at a higher price you would make a profit. This is what is called "bulling," "bearing" being the converse operation. The "bear" thinks, for one reason or other, that a stock is going to get cheaper, or to "fall" in price. Consequently, while the stock is dear he sells it to be delivered or handed over to the purchaser at a future date; and then, if, as he expects, it does get cheaper, he buys it again at the cheaper price, and makes his profit by delivering it to the purchaser, who has to pay him the higher price. Of course, if the stock should get dearer, he (the "bear") has to buy it at the dearer price, if he be not already possessed of it, so as to complete his contract with the purchaser, in which case he would make a loss by having to give more for the stock than he gets for it. In the same way, if a "bull" buys a stock that falls in price, he must, if he does not want to invest his money in it, sell the stock at the lower price, in which case he loses the difference between the two prices. This is, generally speaking, the theory of a Stock Exchange account, and of "bulling" and "bearing."

In practice, however, "bulling" and "bearing" are usually, as Mr. Labouchere once said, merely betting transactions. As a rule, the "bull" does not pay for all the stock he has bought, nor does the "bear" deliver all the stock he has sold. What they do, in most cases, is merely to give or take a cheque for the amount which is represented by the difference between the price of the stock when the contract was made, and the price it is at when the contract is concluded. Still, it is important to notice that either party can legally call upon the other to perform the whole contract. The "bear," by tendering the stock sold, can demand the whole of the purchase-money. The "bull," by tendering payment, can demand delivery of the whole of stock he has bought.

"HIS ROYAL HIGHNESS" ON THE TURF.

His Royal Highness deigns, and that is, not infrequently, to put in an appearance at Newmarket, Epsom, Doncaster, Goodwood and Ascot. Royalty rarely misses any one of these meetings, but his favourite racing town is Newmarket, and he likes it because the natives do not mob him whenever he stirs abroad. I met him, says an American Journalist, in Highstreet there a week or so ago strolling along quite unattended and unnoticed. He was got up in correct sporting fashion, and wore, among other striking things, a pair of long yellow ridingboots, which well set off the handsome legs and ankles of which His Royal Highness is inordinately proud. At Newmarket, the Prince enjoys his freedom, and likes it, and walks along whistling and whacking his big boots with a whip as though life was worth living there, at any rate.

His Royal Highness does not often make a bet, but then he rarely misses a good thing. His racing counsellors are reported to be Sir Frederick Johnstone, Lord Alington, Sir George Chetwynd, and Mr. Mackenzie, the latter a rich Scotch laird who claims to be descended in the direct line from the ancient kings of Scotland. These four sportsmen know pretty well all that is worth knowing about form, trials, and jockeys and trainers' gossip. His Royal Highness does not bet for himself, his commissions being executed chiefly by the gentlemen named. He wins much oftener than he loses, because his advisers take care to give him what they believe to be the very straightest of straight tips.

The royal sportsman has made several efforts to become the owner of good flat racers, but his speculations have been unfortunate. He has had better luck with steeplechasers, in which department his right-hand man is Lord Marcus Beresford, brother of the Marquis of Waterford, and chief sporting member of a famous Irish sporting family. Lord Marcus, years ago, tried to enjoy himself like a Marquis upon the slender portion of a younger son, got into difficulties, and was set upon his legs again by being appointed official starter to the Jockey Club, at a salary of £1000 a-year. Lord Marcus and John Jones, the Epsom trainer, persuaded the Prince to purchase the horse Magic, which has turned out almost a first-rate steeplechaser at three miles. The animal has won several races in the royal colours—purple and scarlet with gold braid—and won them on his merits.

TRUE STORY OF A LOTTERY TICKET.

I.

This is a true story and does not require much telling.

In the days when money lotteries and big prizes were a great fact, old Jacob Mathers, a retired exciseman living on his pension in the town of Dundee, bought a half of ticket number. 1824, for a lottery shortly to be drawn; it cost him fifty shillings. He did not mention the fact of his purchase to any of his family, and in the course of a few days the transaction had altogether quite faded from his memory.

II.

Within three weeks after the purchase of the ticket, stricken down with great suddenness by a stroke of apoplexy, Jacob Mathers died, and was gathered to his fathers, and, sad to say, in the space of a fortnight's time his widow followed him to the grave. Two daughters and one son were left to mourn their parents; the daughters, however, were tolerably well provided for, having each fallen heir in right of their mother to a sum of sixteen hundred pounds. The son was manager of a rope work in the town, at a salary of two pounds a-week, in those days a good wage, but very little came to him from his father's estate.

III.

Old Jacob's library of books and philosophical instruments were sold by auction. Among the books was a copy of "Sturm's Reflections," which his step-niece, who also acted as a servant, was fond of reading, and that book she had determined on buying at the sale, which was not a matter of much difficulty as it changed hands for the sum of one shilling and five pence. After the death of the old man the house was broken up, the

Misses Mathers having determined to start housekeeping in Edinburgh, where several of their friends resided.

IV.

They wanted Bella to go with them, and it came out in consequence that Bella was the wife of young Jacob, as he used to be called. They had been privately married at Perth five months previously, and at once began the cares of housekeeping in humble fashion in a small house near the "Ropery," of which Mathers was manager, and among the household gods of the young wife was her carefully treasured book, the before mentioned "Sturm," which, however, had been laid aside for some time during the bustle of furnishing their modest home.

V.

One evening after tea, Mathers was busy reading to his wife paragraphs from a newspaper, for which, along with two neighbours, he was a subscriber. "Listen to this, Bella," he said. "With regard to the lottery which was drawn in London five weeks ago, it is considered somewhat curious that the second half of the capital prize of £16,000 which fell to ticket no. 1824 has not yet been claimed, the first half having been promptly demanded immediately after the drawing; now that we make known these facts a claimant for the second portion of the prize will, in all probability, speedily turn up, 'it is not every day that a sum of £8,000 goes begging for an owner.'"

VI.

Jacob Mathers always left his house early to go to the rope work, where he breakfasted and did not again come home till one o'clock, the dinner hour. Great was his astonishment one forenoon, two or three days after he had read about the lottery ticket, to see his wife coming along the rope walk to the shed in which he had his desk. She looked somewhat excited as she reached him. "What is wrong, Bella?" he said. "Nothing, Jacob," she replied, "only look at that," and she handed him a slip of paper partly written and partly printed.

VII.

It was the missing half of the lottery ticket number 1824! What she said about it can be told in very few words. "When you read about it the other night I was quite sure I had seen it somewhere, but could not think of the place. I sought over all my drawers, and in my boxes, but it was not to be seen, and

I was giving up the search as a bad job, when all at once I thought this morning of my book, so I took it off the drawer head and sat down to look it over ; at first I missed finding it, but as a last resource tried for it again, and there it was sure enough stuck to the back of the engraving of the rising sun at page 197. Oh, Jacob, I was so glad when I found it, for at one time I began to think I must have seen it only in my sleep, but it was in 'Sturm,' where your father must have placed it and forgotten it, after he had bought and paid for it. Oh, Jacob, it's an awful fortune, isn't it?"

No after record is extant, but doubtless the pair flourished and lived happy during the rest of their lives.

HOW THE PUGILIST OF THE PERIOD IS TRAINED.

SULLIVAN, " the great American pugilist," as he has been called, has dictated to a reporter, the following narrative of how he trains.

I get up about six o'clock and start out on a five-mile walk. When I return from that exercise I am rubbed down with a coarse towel, and rest for about half-an-hour, then I am ready for breakfast. That meal consists of chops or beefsteak and a cup of weak tea. I am not allowed to drink coffee, because coffee has a tendency to make a man bilious. Tea if not too strong, and you don't drink too much of it, is good for the nerves. Nearly all people who have grown to an old age have been very fond of their cup of tea. That fact proves that tea is a good thing for the human system. After breakfast I sit awhile, read the newspapers, or chat with my trainer, and then for half-an-hour I exercise with two-pound dumb-bells, or swing a small pair of Indian clubs. I also skip a rope. That may seem a very womanish exercise, and the statement may make some people smile. But the fact is that skipping the rope is an excellent exercise for limbering up the joints; almost every joint in your body receives benefit. Another exercise I indulge in is punching the football, which is suspended by a rope from the ceiling, all these exertions occupying the time until the dinner hour. They are continued pretty constantly one after the other, slowly and easily, and not to the degree of fatigue.

For dinner I eat roast mutton, roast beef, or roast chicken. I eat only the lean of the meat at this or any meal; the fat is cut off and thrown aside. I consider chicken, boiled or roasted, good food; the meat is dry and somewhat strengthening. There is no choice between roast beef and mutton—one is as good as the other.

After resting a while after dinner, I get out on my long walk and run—for a distance of twenty miles I walk and run, alternately. This is the most severe exercise of the day, and has for its object the strengthening of the legs and the wind. When I come in from the long run I am rubbed down with a coarse towel, after which I jump into a bath tub with salt in the water, or, if I am in a neighbourhood where there is sea-bathing I take the benefit of that. I also let the water run over me in a shower. Then I am rubbed dry with a coarse hand towel, after which my trainer rubs me down with his hands—always rubbing in a downward direction, not both ways. The object of this rubbing is to harden the flesh; if you rubbed both ways instead of one it would have a tendency to make the flesh sore, because under this high training the flesh becomes very sensitive until, under proper treatment, it begins to harden. By this time it is six o'clock. After dressing myself in ordinary costume I pass away the time for an hour in reading or chatting, and then I have a good appetite for supper. That is not such a heavy meal as breakfast or dinner. I generally eat a little cold chicken, some dry bread (I always eat the bread dry) and drink a bowl of weak tea. As a rule I eat no dessert, though I am sometimes allowed a little rice pudding. I don't smoke or drink any kind of liquor, though for dinner I sometimes take a bottle of Bass's ale. The drink, taken in a very moderate quantity at the noon meal, I consider beneficial; it is, to a certain extent, strengthening. I go to bed at nine o'clock, and it is almost needless to say, I enjoy a good night's rest. The reason I don't eat fat is because fat makes fat. The object of training is to get rid of surplus fat, to develop your muscles, and to harden your flesh, and to get what fighters call your "wind" all right. Again, as to eating, I do not eat a large quantity of food, but I eat three good meals during the day, and I eat food that is adapted to make strength. I don't indulge in what cooks call "palate ticklers." I suppose many business men eat more than I do, but I don't think their appetite can be a healthy one. Then, again, they eat a light breakfast, a moderate lunch, and consume a large meal at the close of the day.

CHARLES DICKENS AND HIS BETTING CASHIER.

THE following interesting little story was recently sent by a correspondent to the *Athenæum*.

"The circumstances of which I told you some time since relating to the misconduct of a confidential servant of Charles Dickens through a betting transaction, and which were told to me by Mr. Walker, late District Superintendent of the Metropolitan Police, are shortly as follows. I cannot give the date of the occurrence, but it would probably be some years before the death of the great novelist. One afternoon this confidential servant had, as usual, to take into the bank the sum of £70, or thereabouts, the amount of that day's takings, I believe. Leaving this sum of money in a bag on a table in their usual business room, he left the room for a few moments to change his coat: on returning, the bag of money was gone. This was his statement to Mr. Dickens. Of course his master was extremely surprised at the occurrence, but as he never had had any reason to doubt his truth or honesty he hesitated to disbelieve his story. It seemed, however, so mysterious that he thought it better to send for a detective officer. So Mr. Walker came, heard the story privately from Mr. Dickens, and then expressed a wish to see the man alone. Mr. Dickens called him, and, without mentioning the profession of Mr. Walker, left them together. Perhaps the man suspected who Mr. Walker was, for as he told the story over again to the latter, Mr. Walker noticed an uneasy look upon his face, and that his lips trembled. His story over, the man was dismissed, and Mr. Walker then saw Mr. Dickens again, and told him that the man knew more about the matter than he chose to tell him. Mr. Dickens was both surprised and troubled, for, as stated above, he had reposed the most implicit confidence in him for many years. However, he was sent for again, and told in presence of Mr. Walker that the latter was a detective officer, and that if he had anything else to disclose in connection with the loss of this money he had better tell it then. The man then fell on his knees before Mr. Dickens, begging his pardon, and confessing that he had himself taken the money, having just lost heavily (very nearly the amount of the sum stolen) by the Derby. Mr. Dickens reproached him for his conduct, and said that if he had come to him and told him of his loss he would have paid it himself, but that now, having abused his confidence, he could never trust him again. He then discharged him from his service, but said that in consideration for his previous good conduct, and to save him from starvation or an ill mode of gaining a livelihood, he would settle upon him for life an annuity of £60. I believe the above account is a substantially accurate version of what Mr. Walker told me some five or six years ago."

VALUE OF RACEHORSES: "DONCASTER."

Mr. Corlett, who is one of our most informed commentators on all matters relating to the racehorse and horse racing, writes in one of his letters to a Scottish newspaper with which he is in constant communication. It was said that it was because the Duke of Westminster was a Plutus that Doncaster sold for £14,000, which was far beyond his value. And yet it must be borne in mind that Robert Peck, who was in a much more humble position, was quite content to give Mr. Merry £10,000 for the horse, and the worst day's work he ever did was when he took £4000 profit for him. Though Doncaster won the Derby, and was beaten by only a head for the St. Leger, I have never looked on him as having been in the highest class. He was, however, an honest Derby winner like St. Gatien, and not, like so many others, merely "the horse of a day." He improved as he went on. As the Yankee humourist said, "I never argy agin a success." Consequently I have no stones to throw at a horse that won the Derby, and that at five years of age won the Ascot Gold Cup and Alexandra Plate, and who was also a winner of the Goodwood Cup. These victories, gained under heavy weights and over long distances, stamp Doncaster as being a horse of the most desirable class, as we have here guarantees of speed, weight-carrying powers, stamina, and soundness.

I now come to a consideration of how the Duke of Westminster has fared with his £14,000 bargain. Since 1879 he has won in stakes alone considerably over £100,000, nearly all of which has been gained by Doncaster and his son Bend Or. In addition to this we must add £7000, for which Doncaster was resold, and £17,000, the price of Ormonde. During the last ten years the earnings at the stud of Doncaster and Bend Or have been at the lowest estimate £4000 a year, and finally, what is the present value of Bend Or? If he is worth a penny he is worth £10,000. From this it will be seen that the original £14,000 has brought in about £160,000. There is, of course, the forfeits to be deducted and the training expenses, but against them I have not, with the exception of Ormonde and Bend Or, taken into calculation the value of the various sons and daughters of Doncaster and Bend Or now in training, that have been sold or that are at Eaton. Ormonde comes of the Stockwell line. What a change has come over the turf since 1860, the year when the stud of the late Lord Londesborough was sold at Grimston. In that stud were three St. Leger winners—viz., Stockwell, West Australian, and Warlock. Stockwell was then in his prime, and so was West Australian, who was the best horse that John Scott ever trained.

"When again," writes that famous historian the "Druid," "shall we see 20,689 guineas made in an afternoon—twenty-three brood mares averaging 409½ guineas, one brood mare and her two brood mare daughters making 2990 guineas, and three St. Leger winners—chestnut, brown, and roan—standing up to the hammer in the self-same ring?" How little could the "Druid" see into the future. This sale was up to that time perhaps the most famous that had been known, and there were buyers from all parts of the earth. The Duc de Morney, it was well known, had set his heart on one of the stallions, and it was amidst the groans of Yorkshire that his bid of 3000 guineas for their great favourite, West Australian, was made, and the hammer fell. The winner of the Two Thousand Guineas, Derby, and St. Leger, and Gold Cup at Ascot, little more than ten years old, and himself the sire of a filly that had just won the Oaks, for 3000 guineas! What would be the price of such a horse now-a-days? Mr. Naylor had at that time just made his appearance on the turf, and his purchase of Stockwell for 4500 guineas was as much talked about as that of his son, Doncaster, for £14,000 twice seven years afterwards.

Again quoting the "Druid"—"The thousand for which Stockwell was put in soon became four thousand five hundred. *We never heard such a price bid in a ring before.* Never again shall we see three St. Leger winners, and such St. Leger winners, and twenty-three of the very choicest mares possible to be gathered together sold for 20,689 guineas," said the "Druid." Never again, indeed, but not as the "Druid" prophesied. What would he have thought of the possibility of £37,000 for two horses, one of them a roarer and the other without winning honours in England? That Stuart is anything like as good as West Australian was may be doubted, and yet he may be a very good horse all the same. One of the most famous of the American political writers has said that "one million dollars touched American soil when the Derby winner Diomed came charging down the gangway from the ship that had brought him from England." The appreciation for the English thoroughbred that led him to write these lines is not dead in the American breast, but survives with additional force. Extravagant as appears to be the price that has been paid for Ormonde, who shall say that as a commercial speculation it will not prove as remunerative as was the Duke of Westminster's £14,000 purchase of Doncaster? and will not the wonderful breed of horses in America of which Diomed is the common father be enriched by the admixture of the blood of the horse that many believe to be the very best that ever was foaled?

HOW TO BRING UP YOUR BOYS.

A LAIRD in Strathaven, who owned a quarry, and was reported to be worth "a gey twa-three bawbees beside," was curling one day, and his foreman, whose name was Lawrence, was playing with him on the same side. The laird was very anxious that he should take a certain shot, and he cried out in this fashion, "Noo, Jock Lawrence, d'ye see whaur my broom is? Lay yer stane doon there, and, as sure as death, I'll gie ye my dochter Jean, if ye do it." Birr went the stane oot o' Jock's hand, and went trintling along to the very spot where the laird wished it. "Capital! Jock, capital! Ye couldna hae dune better, and ye can get Jean the morn if ye want her." "Ye maun gie me something else than Jean, laird, I hae got her already. We were married at Gretna Green sax weeks since, and we've been thinking of asking your blessing ever since, but something aye cam' in the way." The laird was dumfounded when he heard the news, but he compromised matters by saying, "Aweel, aweel, Jock, I'll let bygauns be bygauns. A man that could lay doon a pat-lid like that is worthy o' the best and bonniest lass in Lanarkshire; keep her and welcome, and ye'll maybe get the matter o' sax hunner pounds wi' her. Keep her, Jock, and if ye hae ony laddie weans atween ye, bring them up in the fear o' the Lord and the knowledge o' curlin'."

OUR SPORTS AND PASTIMES—THE PROFESSIONAL ELEMENT.

THE following pertinent observations on this much discussed subject have been abridged from a daily Scottish newspaper:
We presume that the £300—besides the honours—gained this year, 1889, by Serjeant Reid at Wimbledon, is a good deal more than his wages as a servant in the Post Office. In a similar way some football players think they see their way to making more by their *feet* than they can ever hope to do by their *hands* or their *heads*, or both combined. We hear that overtures to some of our very best exponents of football have just been received from England, asking them to enter the ranks of professional players. Some of our clubs are indeed in quite a ferment over the affair. It would appear as if England were determined to beat Scotland at this game by means of her own sons. Now in this there is grave cause for anxiety to all lovers of true sport. There is, besides, ground for regret for the sake of the young men who are giving themselves over to a professional career in the football field and at the shooting range. It is beside the point to argue that if we are to have professional cricketers and golfers we may as well have professional marksmen and football players. There is a manifest difference. Cricket and golf professionals are usually teachers of their games, and can secure employment, even to old age, as such, besides being employed as club makers, caddies, and green keepers. On the other hand a young man, with 30s. a week in an "honest" employment, may foolishly resign this to accept £200 or £300 a year as a football player, forgetting that his ability to play the game in first-class style can only last for a very few years. This is so even if not maimed for life in the rough play now so common—and often fatal. What has a footballer to look to after those few years? The same remarks apply to marksmen, who cannot long hope to have the steady eye and firm nerve requisite to take a first-class position before the target. In both cases there is then no field for a situation as a teacher of the art either of shooting or following the "leather." Besides these personal objections to young men giving up useful and honourable employment for following a "game" as a profession, there is the objection founded upon the degrading of sport by professionalism. Our principal football clubs in the West are against professionals, and mean to decline matches with English

clubs which have bribed away some of our best Scotch players. We might have alluded to another distinction between, say golf and football. The one game is played in the quiet of a country or coast links; the other is too often played in presence of a howling and excited mob, with all the coarse instincts and passions of a Spanish bull-fighting ring. Our young men should think "once, twice, and even thrice" before accepting a short, brilliant career in such circumstances, in lieu of the honour for the amateur game and fair wages in some productive industry.

MULTIPLICATION OF GAMBLING CLUBS IN LONDON.

WE are indebted for the following remarks to a paper on "Tempted London" in the "British Weekly."

If any argument were needed to prove that gambling-clubs in London are widely known, it is easily found by a visit. The very fact that every one of the vast number of clubs scattered throughout the metropolis manages to thrive splendidly, is quite sufficient indication of the influence which they can exert. Year by year they increase in number. In one district, where three years ago no such club existed, there are now four, each with a large membership. Particularly is this growth remarkable in the case of genuine "working-men's" clubs. Clerkenwell has always been noted for places of this kind, but of late years the district has become fairly alive with them. Soho of course takes the palm for low establishments of all descriptions, but even there the growth has been very noticeable; at the present time there is scarcely a street in Soho in which there is not at least one house devoted to gaming, and in each of two of the streets there are six. These twelve houses include coffee-shops, restaurants, "national" clubs, and even a laundry—in all of which there are regular illegal gatherings. Go into the northern parts of London and you find them growing up in one shape or another, from the quietly-conducted hell, recently established in one of the finest streets in Hampstead, to the dirty clubs where working-men and lower-class shopmen lose their shillings and sixpences in Highgate or Mildmay. Or cross the water and inquire into the state of affairs in Camberwell. Is it for a moment imagined that the club near the "Elephant and Castle"—upon which a raid was made a few months ago is the only one in that part? There are a score and a half or more in the southern districts; and—what is very much to the point—in these same districts there were not one-third of the number a few years since.

The average Briton shuts his eyes to these things. He doesn't approve of them himself, nor does he make any use of them; and there is something to be said for his blindness. But when the evil spreads day by day, and its influence becomes ever more strong, it is surely time to see. At any rate, strong expression might be expected of that social disapproval the very weakness of which is mainly responsible for the extent of the evil as it stands just now. Of course you may walk about the streets of London for years and never know what is going on around you. But is that good ground for denying that there is anything wrong? Walk past the clubs, it is ten to one you wouldn't recognise them; you notice a chocolate-painted window bearing, in gilt or white letters, "Working Men's Club," or some such thing, but it doesn't seem to you that gambling is the *raison d'être* of the club. The very fact that you are not inclined personally for playing chance-games, that you are not given to frequenting public-houses, and don't care for questionable company, is the most excellent reason in the world why you remain ignorant of gambling-clubs, or if you do know that there are such places, why, you imagine that they are few and far between. It is quite possible for a man to move freely in the world and yet never have the faintest idea of the ramifications of gambling. He doesn't happen to be thrown into contact with the set of people and circumstances which could enlighten him, or if he has rubbed shoulders with them, he had not the curiosity to make inquiries, or to listen even to what is said. All the more personal respect is due to him in many ways, for there is a large and loud-mouthed section of the public whose morbid curiosity is more repulsive and disgusting than even the vice against which it is directed; but let him not undertake to say that because he doesn't see the evil it therefore does not exist.

FONDNESS OF THE CLERGY FOR COCKING.

COCKING seems to have been well patronised by the country clergy. In 1609 Robert Wild, a *Nonconforming* minister, wrote a poem in which he described with great unction all the phases of a well-fought main. But the passion among the black coats and white chokers came down to a much later period, as is proved by a story told by Grantley Berkley. In describing a visit he had made to a cockpit, in company with a friend, he said, " Never shall I forget the amusement of my friend when I pointed out to him a rather tall, dingy figure, in black coat and waistcoat, kerseymere breeches, and brown top-boots looking as if they had seen much wear and tear or had never been brushed or blacked. The elderly gentleman was very busy taking his gamecocks out of their bags, which he sent to fight on our side. My friend was intently watching him, and asked, as the first bird was taken out, ' What the devil is that parcel tied to one of the bird's legs ? ' ' His battle money,' I answered ; ' my reverend friend always stands his own battle money in preference to standing any share in our main, and by so doing generally loses, as his birds are not as good as ours.' ' But why do you call him your reverend friend ? ' inquired the other. ' Because he is a regularly beneficed clergyman of the Church of England,' was my reply." It was remarkable that the two great cockers of the present century, Dr. Bellyse and the Earl of Derby, died within a few years of the passing of the Act which interdicted their favourite pastime.

NO FRIENDSHIP IN HORSE DEALING.

AMONG the many nice readable anecdotes which appear from time to time in *Baily* a good selection might be made as the following example will show—Amongst the men hunting with the new forest hounds was one Wise, Dicky Wise, quite a character in his own way, who always rode with a spare stirrup leather round his neck for the benefit of any of his neighbours who might break one. Wise once had a deal with a sporting butcher of Southampton, also a " bit of a character." Jack Hewitt he was called, who came from Bath and horsed one or two coaches. Wise's horse was a rank roarer, while the butcher's nag had an awful spavin, but after a little talk they agreed to exchange horses right away without any examination. Next day Hewitt, while out hunting, discovered the roaring but kept quiet about it. The following day Wise rode his horse with the hounds and while returning by way of the High Street he passed Hewitt, who was standing at a shop door. The horse was going on three legs and Wise halooed out to him, "No friendship in horse dealing, Mr. Hewitt, no friendship in horse dealing." "Quite so, old man, tit for tat," was the prompt reply.

THE DERBY IN THE HOUSE OF COMMONS.

OF late years it has not been necessary to move the adjournment of the House over the Derby Day, as the great race has fallen to be run at a time when the House has risen at any rate. But there have been several debates on the subject of the Derby Holiday, and it may prove interesting to state that the "Blue riband" of the turf made its first appearance in Parliament on May 18, 1847, when Lord George Bentinck brought forward a motion, of which he had given notice, "that the House at its rising do adjourn till Thursday." In his speech on the occasion Lord George stated that for more than half a century the Derby day had been a recognised holiday. Mr. Joseph Hume, then a power in Parliament, objected to the noble Lord's motion, not being able to see why the Derby should have preference in the House over everything else, Lord George's motion being number 18 on the paper. The Speaker, however, overruled the objection, and it was agreed to. The motion was repeated in 1848 by the same member and was again opposed by Mr. Hume on account of there being an important Scotch bill on the paper for that day. Mr. Bright also opposed the motion, although on principle the hon. member was not averse that the House should at times have its relaxation; he thought it, however, not in consonance with the dignity of Parliament for the House to adjourn on account of a horse race. Lord John Russell replied, giving his consent, and, among other arguments, said " the clerks would have to sit for some time at the table waiting to make a House; and," said his Lordship, " as it seems the practice to look upon to-morrow as a national *fête*, I have acquiesced in the motion." Next year (1849) a division was taken on the question whether the House should adjourn; which was carried by 138 to 119, giving a majority of 19 to the holiday seekers. In the course of the debate Mr. Aglionby hoped a motion would be submitted that on every Derby Day in every future year the House should then be adjourned. In 1850 the holiday was agreed to, Mr. W. Sharman Crawford and Mr.

Hume protesting. In the years which have followed, the holiday (when Parliament was sitting at the time) has always been carried, as Lord Palmerston said in 1860, "to adjourn over the Derby Day is part of the unwritten law of Parliament."

It need scarcely be explained that the adjournment is moved on behalf of the servants of the House, who could not otherwise witness the race, if any of them should be desirous of going to Epsom on the occasion of the Derby being run. The distance from London to the racecourse being only about 16 miles, and the race being usually run for at three o'clock, those members of either house of Parliament who felt inclined to witness its celebration could do so if they pleased; there would be a sufficient number of members left to make a House.

KING OF THE GAMBLERS.

A DETAILED "Life" of this "King of the Gamblers" would be of extraordinary interest, especially if it contained sketches of the players at his club, which at one time was the resort of kings, princes, and nobles of high degree. Had it been thought when "Crocky" was a boy that he would become one of the notorieties of his time, and die worth half a million of money, a veritable and correct chronicle of his sayings and doings would doubtless have been forthcoming; but there is no such biography in existence, and so his career is surrounded with a haze of exaggeration, all that he did in the way of evil having from time to time been magnified, whilst some of his many good deeds have persistently been looked at through the wrong end of the telescope. Bred a fishmonger, in the days of his youth he became well versed in the ways of London's great piscatorial bourse, where for years he was known as a successful trader, and was able in time to save what he was wont to speak of as "a little bit of money." The following is a creditable feature of his character. "One of the salesmen with whom Crockford often had a deal in the way of his business, fell into misfortune. Becoming security for the sum of a thousand pounds on behalf of a near relative of his wife, he found himself one morning called on to pay it, but having unfortunately made several bad debts of magnitude, he had no alternative but to cry *peccavi*; to crown his distress, as one of his children lay on her deathbed, his furniture was seized, and but for Crockford, would have been sold; he it was who came to the rescue and brought comfort to the parents in their day of distress. He purchased not only the furniture, but the lease of the house as well, paid the funeral expenses of the child, lent the salesman a couple of hundreds to be going on with, and was never the man to say he had done it."

SINGULAR GAMBLING CIRCUMSTANCE.

ONE of the magazines published in the year 1827, contained the following narrative :—

A few years since two fellows were observed by a patrol in the New-road, busily engaged beside a lamp-post; closely watching them, he discovered that one was tying up the other, who offered no resistance, by the neck. The patrol interfered to prevent what he considered to be murder, when he was assailed by both and pretty severely beaten. His shouts, however, brought the watch to his assistance, and the parties were secured. On being examined before a magistrate the next morning it came out that the men had been gambling, that one had lost all his money to the other, and had at last proposed to stake his clothes. The latter demurred, on the plea that he could not strip his adversary naked should he lose. "Oh! don't give yourself any uneasiness about that," was the reply; "if I lose I shall be unable to live, and you shall hang me, and take my clothes after I'm dead, as I shall then, you know, have no occasion for them." This arrangement was assented to, and the fellow having lost, was quietly submitting to the terms of the treaty when he was interrupted by the patrol, whose interference he so angrily resented.

A CLEVER BACKER OF RACE HORSES.

AN Edinburgh gentleman, well known as "The Chief," who occasionally frequented some of the English racecourses, and whom I met in two different seasons at Ascot, landed some bets under rather curious circumstances. One day "The Chief" observed a horse taking its preliminary canter in a condition that led him to infer that it was *not intended* to win, but in a twinkling, nature relieved the animal of its load to such an extraordinary extent, that within a minute or two it became quite like a different horse. "I'll back it now," resolved "The Chief," and taking stock of the colours it carried he speedily found that a good price could be got, which was always "a consideration" with him. "It just won anyway it liked; a lot of people looked surprised, but from the curious way in which the bookmaker took stock of my tartan trousers, I thought he was going to welsh me. I got my money all right," said "The Chief."

Another time when I was present at Ascot, "The Chief" made a nice little hit by backing a horse called Blenheim, ridden by Fordham, which beat Prince Charlie. "I don't know how it is, but I feel a rather strong presentiment," said Mr. M'Nab ("The Chief"), "that the Prince will be beaten this time." "Yes," I said; "but which of the other two will do the trick, Blenheim or Somerset?" "Look here," he said, "it's the chief consideration; the bookmakers are wanting 6 to 1 *on* the Prince. Now we can back both of the others and even then win a little money. We can get 7 to 1 about Blenheim, and 8 to 1 against Somerset, but I think Fordham is on the one that will win. I feel sure the Prince will lose the race. I hear, too, that one of the big swells has laid £6,000 to £1000. My conscience! that *would* be a haul for the ring, if the Prince were to be beaten; what do you say, shall we venture and divide our winnings?" In the end we backed the Prince's two opponents, putting a fiver on each, so that we won £35 and lost £5, leaving us a bonus of £15 each as the outcome of "The Chief's presentiment."

NIMROD'S LITERARY WORK.

THE above name, that of "the mighty hunter," was selected as the *nom de plume* of a writer who some fifty or sixty years ago made his mark, not only in the sporting literature of the day, but also in the *Quarterly Review* when that great periodical was conducted by John Gibson Lockhart, and was a tower of strength in the literary world. The literary work of Mr. Apperley (that was the family name of the writer) became in demand, and his pen was requisitioned by several editors well able to pay for his contributions. This modern Nimrod began life in the army, and in his earlier days took part in all the sport that was going. It was the sinking of his bank account that impelled him to try his fortune with the publishers, to one of whom in London, Mr. Henry Colburn, he proposed to write a book of hunting episodes, and the proposal was favourably received, but as he himself tells us, "No sooner was I in Regent Street, on the road to my hotel, than my course was at once changed. I chanced to meet a very old friend and brother sportsman, to whom I communicated my intentions, together with the result of my interview with Mr. Colburn, when the following parley took place:—

My Friend. "You are wrong in thinking of writing a book. Go to the *Sporting Magazine:* it will answer your purpose much better."

Myself. "The *Sporting Magazine!* That will never do; it is a mere Cockney concern, and no *gentleman* writes for it."

My Friend. "Never mind that. Take my advice, and go to the proprietor of it. If *you* write for it, other gentlemen and sportsmen will soon do so also."

Mr. Apperley made a hit with his letters to the periodical named, "they were so fresh, so genial, so full of anecdote, and so happily combining the tastes of the sportsman, the scholar, and the gentleman. From an unknown work the *Sporting Magazine* became the talk of town and country, and Nimrod's name was in everybody's mouth. The price of the monthly number was raised from two shillings to half-a-crown, with occasional five-shilling parts, and the circulation doubled in less than two years' time from his engagement."

The proprietor of the Magazine was not unthankful, but remunerated his successful contributor in a style that was then, as indeed it would be now, wonderfully liberal; he paid him twelve hundred a year, and kept up for him, besides, a stud of hunters. It is not unjust to say that the articles contributed by Nimrod to the periodicals that willingly accepted, and paid for them, would not easily find a place in the Reviews or Magazines of to-day. Now sporting literature presents different features, but "Nimrod" was a giant among the men with whom he collaborated

HOW FRED SWINDELL BEGAN BUSINESS.

It has been said that what started him on the turf was a bet of a hundred pounds to one against Charles XII. for the Liverpool Cup. He had "faced the music" long before then. His own account is that fifty-two years ago he was a working-man in Manchester, and there formed the acquaintance of a saddler, who used to bet for the trainer of Mr. Watt's horses. Mr. Watt had in the St. Leger of that year two horses called Belshazzar and Rockingham, the former of which was a favourite.

"One night," said Mr. Swindell, "I called in to see this saddler, when he said, 'Hast tha' any money about tha'?'

"I told him I had just drawn my week's wages, and I daresay I might be able to borrow a pound or two.

"'Then,' said he, 'get tha' out, and put it all on Rockingham for the St. Leger.' I did as he told me, and that was my first start on the turf."

So shrewd a man as Mr. Swindell was not long in discovering that it was by laying against horses rather than backing them that fortunes were made, and he shortly joined the ranks of fielders. Fortune was not altogether in his favour at first. He had got hold of a horse for the Northumberland Plate as being a "safe 'un," and he betted every shilling against it he possibly could. Feeling rather nervous, he went on some steps to see the race, and to his horror the "safe 'un" won in a canter. "There wor I," he said, "dead broke, and there was a fellow just above me who had backed the horse—we will call him Greyleg—screaming like mad, '*Greyleg* wins! *Greyleg* wins!' and, as the winner went past the post, in his excitement he yelled, '*Greyleg's* won!' and brought his fist down on the top of my hat with such force as to knock it over my eyes—and I broke all the while. I didna like it."

LORD PETERSHAM'S STRANGE VISITOR.

His lordship having arranged to attend a prize fight asked one of his friends of the "fancy" to call for him at the residence of his mother, Lady Harrington, with whom at the time he was residing. Knowing the mill was to take place at an early hour he had requested that breakfast should be served sooner than usual, telling his mother that he had an engagement out of town. Every attention was of course given to his request, breakfast being on the table at the time agreed upon, and while her ladyship was waiting for his lordship to come down, a footman announced that a gentleman wished to see him. Thinking it was some one her son had invited to breakfast, Lady Harrington ordered him to be shown up. A very flashly-dressed individual entered the room, and without waiting for him to give his name she advanced to receive him. Taking everything for granted, she began apologising for her son not being down, and asked the visitor to join her at table.

"Thanks, my lady; I *should* like a pick as we've a long drive before us," he at once said. During the meal, observing that his manners were somewhat strange, she tried to ascertain the gentleman's calling, and caught the idea that he was in the army.

"You have been abroad, I presume?" she inquired.

"Never, my lady," replied the visitor very quickly; "it was one of my name, but no relation, that went across the water at his majesty's expense."

"I thought perhaps you might have served in Holland."

"Oh, I see, your ladyship," he said, brightening up; "you mistake me for Dutch—" At that moment the entrance of the footman with the newspaper interrupted his speech.

"What is the exact time?" inquired her ladyship

The reply was, "Nine o'clock, my lady." At those words up jumped the stranger so quickly that he dropped his cup and saucer; the genteel veneer vanished in an instant, and in a voice and tone familiar to the "Dials" he exclaimed:

"Then I'm blest if we shan't be too late for the 'mill;' it comes off at half-past ten, and we've to call in Wind-mill Street for the bird's-eye fogles, and to pick up Heavy and Handy, the fighting Life Guardsman, at the barracks." While the countess was speechless with astonishment at this extraordinary lingo, in came Lord Petersham, to discover to his great astonishment that Mr. William Gibbons, of pugilistic notoriety, had been breakfasting with his mother.

TAKING A TIP FOR THE CESAREWITCH.

A CLEVER Edinburgh backer of horses obtained an excellent tip for the Cesarewitch of 1867 in the following manner: Taking a walk after dinner on the road leading to the Doncaster Town

Moor he observed a man sitting on a form reading, apparently with great attention, a newspaper. Casting his eye on the paper as he passed he saw the reader was holding it upside down. That seemed rather a curious way of reading a paper; but the gentleman quickly discovered that the holder of the news-sheet was not reading, but listening with an attentive ear to the conversation of two persons in an adjoining garden. By-and-by they left, and the pretended reader rose and walked off on his way to the town. He was at once joined by the gentleman from Edinburgh, who, as he told the writer, "smelt a rat." However, to make an end of the story, the Edinburgh gentleman discovered that the pretended reader had been listening to the arguments of two well-known votaries of racing, and had found that the result of their conversation was to the effect that the third horse in that day's St. Leger could not be beaten for the forthcoming Cesarewitch, and their conclusion proved to be correct. The animal which formed the subject of their conversation was Julius, which won the race in question.

THE LORD OF THE VALLEY.

MAJOR WHYTE MELVILLE met his death in the hunting field while in pursuit of his favourite pastime. The horse of the unfortunate gentleman while galloping over a ploughed field fell and Mr. Whyte Melville fell with it, breaking his neck. The deceased soldier and author was much esteemed in his lifetime, and had almost no compeer as a teller of hunting stories and as a writer and reciter of hunting poems and songs, some of the latter being often sung; the following verses are from his hunting song, "The Lord of the Valley." They have the true ring of the thoroughgoing sportsman about them:—

> Hard on his track o'er the open, and facing
>   The cream of the country, the pick of the chase,
> Mute as a dream, his pursuers are racing.
>   Silence, you know's the criterion of pace.
> Swarming and driving, while man and horse striving,
>   By hugging and cramming scarce live with them still,
> The fastest are failing, the truest are tailing,
>   The Lord of the Valley is over the hill!
>
> Yonder a steed is rolled up with the master,
>   Here, in a double, another lies cast;
> Faster and faster comes grief and disaster,
>   All but the good ones are weeded at last.

Hunters so limber at water and timber,
    Now on the causeway are fain to be led,
Beat, but still going, a countryman sowing,
    Has sighted the Lord of the Valley ahead !
There in the bottom, see, sluggish and idle,
    Steals the dark stream where the willow-tree grows,
Harden your heart and catch hold of your bridle,
    Steady him ! rouse him ! and over he goes.
Look, in a minute, a dozen are in it,
    But forward ! hark forward ! for draggled and blown,
A check though desiring, with courage untiring,
    The Lord of the Valley is holding his own.
Onward we struggle in sorrow and labour,
    Lurching and lobbing, and "bellows to mend ; "
Each, while he smiles at the plight of his neighbour,
    Only is anxious to get to the end.
Horses are flagging, hounds drooping and lagging,
    But gathering down yonder, where press as they may,
Mobbed, driven, and hunted, but game and undaunted,
    The Lord of the Valley stands proudly at bay.

Now, here's to the Baron, and all his supporters,
    The thrusters, the skirters, the whole of the tail ;
And here's to the fairest of all hunting quarters,
    The widest of pastures, three cheers for the Vale !
For the fair lady rider, the rogue who beside her
    Finds breath in a gallop his suit to advance ;
The hounds for our pleasure, that tune us the measure,
    The Lord of the Valley that leads us the dance.

HOW DICKY RAYNER WAS "DONE."

MR. RICHARD RAYNER, a well known English horse dealer residing in Edinburgh, told the following little story of how he was one time "done" in buying "an 'unter" by a pawky old Scotchman. "Look here, Mr. Rayner," said the seller of the horse, "you can buy or no, just as you like, my price is eight and forty notes." "Yes, yes," said Rayner, "I don't object to the price but I want—" "Oh, he's a real honest beast, I do assure you, and you must just take him as he is." And so he changed hands. Taking him to a meet one day, the horse, much to the chagrin of his new owner, came down on his knees. Rayner told his late owner of the fact, and threatened to return him on his hands, but the canny Scotchman quietly replied, "Oh, man, ye needna' fash, I tell't ye that ye wad hae to take him as yo saw him, as he was a real honest beast, in fact he often threatened to come doon when I had him, and noo he has keepit his word."

DELIGHTS OF TROUT FISHING.

Some anglers delight in pike-catching, others try for perch; but give me the trout, of which there is a large variety, and all worth catching. In Loch Awe, for instance, there is the great lake trout, which, combined with the beauty of the scenery, has sufficed to draw to that neighbourhood some of our best anglers. The trout of Loch Awe, as is well known, are very ferocious, hence their scientific name of *Salmo ferox*. This trout attains to great dimensions; individuals weighing twenty pounds have been often captured; but its flavour is indifferent and the flesh is coarse, and not of a prepossessing colour. This kind of trout is found in nearly all the large and deep lochs of Scotland. It was discovered scientifically about the end of last century by a Glasgow merchant, who was fond of sending samples of it to his friends as a proof of his prowess as an angler. The usual way of taking the great lake trout is to engage a boat to fish from, which must be rowed gently through the water. The best bait is a small trout, with at least half-a-dozen strong hooks projecting from it, and the tackle requires to be prodigiously strong, as the fish is a most powerful one, although not quite so active as some others of the trout kind, but it roves about in these deep waters enacting the parts of the bully and the cannibal to all lesser creatures, and driving before it even the hungry pike. Persons residing near the great lochs capture these large trout by setting night lines for them. As has been already mentioned, they are exceedingly voracious, and have been known to be dragged for long distances, and even after losing hold of the bait to seize it again with great eagerness, and so have been finally captured. These great lake trout are also to be found in other countries.

GAMBLING CHAT.

The following are notes of a conversation among some who were at the gambling tables at Monaco.

"And how have you disposed of your wife?"

"She is in another compartment, she would not allow me to travel hereabouts without looking after me."

"And have you been playing?"

"Yes, and been pretty successful. I have often lost, but on

the whole I have made about 9,000 francs; and I just want to-day to make it up to 10,000, and then I will leave off."

"You have been very, very lucky."

"I have been lucky all through this year. Nearly all my horses won—I won eleven races out of fourteen, that was not bad; and then my yacht won the race at Boulogne."

"I gained sixteen napoleons," said the young lady, "the last time I was at Monte Carlo."

"The last time I was there," said the former speaker, "I got out at Monaco, had a fine chop and a small bottle of champagne at the Hotel de Nice. I felt so comfortable, I felt as if I could break the bank in no time. I drove to Monte Carlo and commenced. I could not get a chair at first, and that does not suite my lameness well, for I require to lean on my stick. I did not get on well at first, but I soon got a place in the second row, and then it was not long till the man in front of me turned round and said, 'I am *broke*, you can have my chair.' I sat down, pulled in my chair, and set to work, and in less than half-an-hour, I had made 960 francs. I staked the odd sixty and lost them, and then stopped playing for that day."

"It is not every one who is so lucky," said his friend.

"No," he replied, "there are two or three fellows in my hotel who are evidently played out, they look very dejected, and are just going to leave."

"Do you know anything about Captain Bentley?" said his friend, after a pause.

"The last time I heard of him, he was boots in some hotel in Australia."

"He was a great swell."

"Yes," was the reply; "he presumed upon his position, and it was a splendid position if he had only taken care of himself. He was the showiest man I ever knew; he was almost as bad as Colonel Rowan, who would never sit down unless he had a chair in front, to stretch out his feet upon, lest he should bag his trousers. He was a brassey fellow, though. The last time I saw him was when he sent me a note, asking if I would call on him. He said he wanted to settle with me, he owed me a 'tenner.' Well, I did call, and the first thing he said was, 'I want you to lend me £150.' I said I was not a money-lender, besides did you not say in your note that you wanted to settle with me, and you know you owe me a trifle? 'O yes,' said he, 'that is all right, but I thought that was the best way to bring you. Come, now, will you oblige? if not, it can't be helped.' Well, ultimately, I gave him £60; it was all I had at the time, and I have never seen or heard of him since. However, I got £30 of my £60 from some of his friends, who owed him some money."

"The last I saw of him," said the younger gentleman, "was when he was staying at 'the Grosvenor,' and that was just before he left. Splendid apartments he had there, and I suppose the bill is not paid to this day. Did you hear about his leaving?" he continued.

"No," was the reply; "what was it?"

"Two gentlemanly-looking men called, and found him in his dressing-gown and slippers, sitting at breakfast. 'Captain Bentley, I presume I have the honour of addressing,' said one of them.

"'You never made a greater mistake in your life. Captain Bentley has just left me this moment; there he is getting into that hansom at the door.' Whilst the two officers hurried down to the hansom, the Captain disappeared, and has not been seen in this country since."

HOW THE JOCKEYS ROSE TO POWER.

FOR more than fifty years the jockey has been the chief factor in all turf operations. Before that time he only held a subordinate position, namely, that of a smart and trustworthy groom, and leading patrons of the turf only sought his society for business purposes. If he made from £300 to £500 a year he was in the forefront of his profession, and as a rule his wagering was of little account. His masters never dreamt of overwhelming him with wealth, much less of placing themselves under his personal guidance in turf or financial matters. He rode round the country from meeting to meeting, and worked very hard for every penny he received. The jockey's ambition then was to become a trainer, so that he might escape from the drudgery and risks of his profession and place himself in a position to make provision for his old age. The occasional departures from this rule altered little the normal state of matters until the plunging era of twenty-five years ago set in. Then there ensued a wild competition amongst reckless gamblers for the services of the first-rate men and boys of the profession, and as a result of this high-bidding a system of extravagant payments, and still more extravagant presents to the riders of winners, was inaugurated. The practice of heavy betting by jockeys followed naturally upon this state of things, with the inevitable result that certain riders found themselves so influential in turf affairs as almost to believe themselves masters of the situation.

L. S. D. OF A GREAT PUGILISTIC EVENT.

THE financial aspects of the battle between Sullivan and Kilrain fought in America, in the month of July 1889, have been set forth as follows :—

The stakes fought for were the largest ever known in pugilism, Sullivan's fists earning for him 10,000 dols., the sum each side had deposited in the hands of the stakeholder.

Besides this principal sum, Kilrain and Sullivan wagered 1,000 each at the ring side, just prior to the beginning of the fisticuffs, and almost every man in America had wagered something on the result of the fight.

Ten thousand dollars were won and lost among the sports at the ring side, though Sullivan had been the favourite from the very start, and odds had been placed on him every day.

Besides the money won and lost in wagers, there was the immense expense of the show itself. Thousands of sporting men flocked to New Orleans ; the Southern railways reaped a rich harvest of car fares.

There were 2,122 tickets sold to the fight.

Of this number 722 brought 15 dols. each, and 1,400 were sold for 10 dols. a piece.

The total receipts consequently were 24,830 dols.

The railroad company was paid 1.25 dols. per ticket for transportation, amounting to 2,652,050 dols.

Bud Renaud and Pat Duffy were given jointly 25 per cent. net receipts for managing the affair, and this mounted to about 5,544 dols., leaving about 16,000 dols. to be divided between the backers of the fighters after all expenses have been paid.

Of course, there are heavy training expenses to be borne, Muldoon alone receiving 300 dols. a week, it is said, for getting John L. in condition.

Sullivan will be about 20,000 dols. richer when the stakes are paid and the business settled, while Kilrain, though a loser in the main stake, will be only a slight loser by his defeat.

Referee John Fitzpatrick has 500 dols. for Kilrain, which was collected by subscription on the train while returning from the fight. Marsh Redon subscribed 25 dols. of this sum.

BEAU BRUMMEL'S LUCK AT CARDS.

THE celebrated Beau Brummel of "I once ate a pea" notoriety was a keen hand at cards and often played with a considerable degree of success. He was in possession of a talisman to which he attributed his good fortune, it was a lucky sixpence he had picked up in the street. Once, in a gambling house, he found Tom Sheridan, Brinsley's son, who was a luckless, impecunious dog, with ten pounds' worth of counters before him, tempting Fortune. "Let me be your partner, Tom," said the Beau, "and we'll go shares in the winnings." This being acceded to, he put two hundred to the ten, and in less than a quarter of an hour had made it fifteen hundred. Handing over seven hundred and fifty to his partner, the good-natured spendthrift said to Sheridan, "Now go home, Tom; give your wife and brats a good supper, and never play again." In course of time the Beau lost his lucky coin, and from that hour always protested that fickle Fortune had turned her back upon him.

BILLIARDS.

IT cannot be said with any degree of accuracy whether this fine pastime originated in France or Italy, but it was the French who sent the game to this country, and it is supposed to have been known in England so early as the sixteenth century. Shakspeare mentions it. Originally the game was played with two balls only.

The game of billiards did not become popular or fashionable in France until the reign of Louis XIV. The "Grand Monarque" was a great sufferer from indigestion, and his physicians advised him to play billiards for exercise. A billiard-table of the style of the day was erected in a room near the "Œil-de-Bœuf" at

Versailles. Here the courtiers congregated and applauded the king, who, of course, always came out victorious. Madame de Maintenon was forced to attend the games in the capacity of marker, and recouped herself by quizzing his majesty when he missed. At that time the billiard-table was a clumsy affair; the cushions had no elasticity, the pockets were very wide, and the cues were devoid of tips. This rendered the making of many of the favourite modern shots impossible. Tips were invented by Mangin about sixty years ago. Until the year 1830 billiard-tables were square and very clumsy objects.

ART OF PLACING HORSES IN RACES.

OWNERS and trainers of race horses have often a fortune in their grasp without knowing it, in other words they may possess a horse capable of winning the Derby and yet be ignorant of the fact. Horses upon which at first very little store have been set frequently turn out to be of great value, able to win valuable stakes and then bring a great sum of money for use at the stud. To be able to inform his employers how best to " place " his horses constitutes one of the chief merits of a trainer. It is no use to enter a slow plodding horse in a short distance race where speed is the one quality required, nor, on the other hand, is it of any use entering a horse suitable for a five furlong course, in the City and Suburban or Cesarewitch handicaps.

Some owners and trainers have a happy knack of so placing their horses as to win nearly every race for which they are entered. The *Swan* was a horse of that kind, it won no end of races for its owner, and there are several others which might be mentioned as being equally useful during their career on the turf. A gentleman possessing a stud of only half-a-dozen race horses will often enough have a larger winning account at the end of the season than an owner of three times the number, just because he knows what to do with them or how to place them so that they may, by winning a few races, earn their keep and pay for the entries made on their behalf. To be able so to place one's horses as that each will win a couple of races in the course of the season implies a good knowledge of the business of racing. Men with big studs usually strive to win the larger stakes, but as these stakes are fewer in number, and there are numerous competitors, so their chances of success are proportionately lessened; but when a Cesarewitch, Cambridgeshire or Liverpool Autumn Cup is won, the money that can be earned is worth adding to one's bank account. On the two former races it is quite possible to lift from the ring a round sum of sixty or seventy thousand pounds, and even more money than that sum represents has before now been won.

Some followers of racing, but not many, it must be confessed, set their hearts on winning the Derby or some other classic race, and think that is better than gaining a big sum of money over a handicap. As a rule, money is the main object of all turf strivings, and trainers who can so advise as to the selection of races to be battled for as to bring grist to the mill are sure to get plenty of horses to train and "place."

ONE OF MYTTON'S PRACTICAL JOKES.

HE had a parson and a doctor dining with him one evening at Halston, and at a certain hour of the night they mounted their horses to return to their homes. Having a carter's frock, and a brace of pistols, loaded with blank cartridges, at hand, Mytton mounted a hack, and by a circuitous route headed and met them on the road, when, letting fly both barrels at them, and calling to them to "stand and deliver," he declared they never rode half so fast in their lives as they did from that place to Oswestry, with himself at their heels. He once stopped and robbed, on this same road, his own butler, who was returning from the town with a sum of money he had just received from the agent. The man had boasted that no one should ever rob him; but on Mytton suddenly putting a pistol to his head by the green gates, he meekly gave up both the money and his watch.

Mytton was fond of, as well as very good at disguising himself, in which way he played off another trick on the butler. Strolling one summer's evening about his grounds, he came across a beggar who was taking his road up to the house. The Squire at once proposed that they should exchange clothes, or, at least, their outer garments, and the other being naturally nothing loth, the metamorphosis was quickly completed.

Bidding the man stay where he was, and with a tattered hat over his eyes, and otherwise capitally got-up, he returned to the Hall, where but a few minutes previously he had been sitting at the dinner-table. Here, he begged in vain of his own servants; they only jeered at him; but, at length, on his asking for something to drink, they offered him the dregs of a barrel, which he indignantly refused. "You fare too well," said he, "and get saucy in your places, or you, who can have so much good wholesome beer whenever you choose, would never give a fellow-creature such stuff as this." Some of the household now began to fight a little shy, but the butler, hearing the noise, came out at once and ordered the sturdy mendicant off the place, threatening to, if he did not actually, send for the constables.

But, in the interim, imprudently venturing to put his hand on the beggar's shoulder, Mytton sent him reeling, as he did one or two more of the men who came to their superior's assistance. They then let the dogs loose, when he at once rushed off to the bear, who more readily recognised her master, and, released from her chains, raised herself on her haunches in his defence. This let out the secret, as none but Mytton would have dared to have done so much with Nell, as she was called; and often afterwards, greatly to the butler's and the other servants' annoyance, would the small-beer story be told against them.

Then, again, during harvest-time Mytton went in the garb of a countryman to Jones, at the Queen's Head, at Oswestry, and asked for work. The terms being agreed to, at so much a week for the job, the master stood a pot of strong beer to bind the bargain, and then the new hand quickly called for another, which he seasoned with brandy. It, of course, ended in his getting very riotous, and when just about to thrash the landlord, who was going to turn him out, a customer recognised the Squire, and the joke happily resulted in no serious consequences to those upon whom it was tried.

RACING CONSPIRACIES.

MANY of the professional betting-men are highly superstitious, and are believers in dreams and omens. A voluminous series of instances might be collected, both of anecdotes which have appeared in print and of others which have not yet found a resting-place, but are floating about the ring, and are occasionally narrated in the hotels, public-houses, and billiard-rooms frequented by bookmakers and betting-men. One of these stories relates to the doings of John Gully, at one period well known to the turf as an owner of horses, a manipulator of races and a gigantic and bold bookmaker—a man who dealt in tens of thousands and thought nothing of winning or losing twenty or thirty thousand pounds. In the days of his youth Gully had gained his bread as a professional prize-fighter—a pugilist in fact—and to that circumstance may be attributed, it has been said, his losing many thousand pounds over an animal called Prizefighter, which ran in the race for the St. Leger in the year 1843, but was fated only to get third, being beaten by Nutwith and Cotherstone, the animal which ought to have proved the victor. As a matter of fact the latter horse was "pulled," in order that Prizefighter might win, and if he had proved successful, would have earned for Gully a sum of fifty thousand pounds. Such "arrangements" are not unknown on the turf even at the present time, and the conspirators of 1843 were properly punished by the race being won by Nutwith, because Cotherstone, pulled in favour of Prizefighter, could have won that year's St. Leger as easily as he won that year's Derby, beating a field of twenty-two opponents.

A WAIF'S TIPS.

I BECAME conversant with a very curious series of Derby tips some thirty-five years ago in Edinburgh. A waif of the horsey kind, who was a constant frequenter of Laing's Bazaar, in the Lothian Road, and who was thought to be a little weak in his intellect, gave the winner of the Derby for seven successive years. This person's name was Jamie Skinners, who will doubtless be remembered by many, as he was well known to the frequenters of the Horse Bazaar in question, and no person could ever understand how poor Jamie came to be so versed in Derby lore as to name the winner so often as he did. Personally I was only cognisant of one of his tips. It was of Flying Dutchman, which won the Derby of 1849 for the Earl of Eglinton. But I know on good authority that he also gave Orlando and Surplice in the years in which they won. In those days there were no penny papers devoted to sport, nor was sporting news so common as it has now become. Few persons, comparatively, talked about such matters, and the knowledge displayed by poor Jamie was long one of the mysteries of Laing's Bazaar. Jamie in his day was patronised by Ramsay of Barnton and Sharp of Hoddam.

DAN DAWSON'S CRIME.

MANY narratives have been already given of the trial and execution of Dawson for the crime of horse poisoning, but the following brief narrative contains all the particulars: Great was the astonishment when one fine morning one of the best known loungers about the stables in that town, one Daniel Dawson, a horse watcher, a jolly boon companion that every one liked, and who up to this time, had been regarded as an honest man and a faithful servant, was arrested, together with a nondescript named Cecil Bishop, for these atrocities. Dawson was known to be employed by several betting men as a tout; and although there was no evidence to prove that any of them had actually instigated these men to the crime, it seemed difficult to discover any other motive for its commission than bribery to put a favourite out of the race. The trial of these scoundrels took place in May, 1811, at the Cambridge Assizes, and Bishop, who had turned King's evidence, was put in the witness-box. The horse, for the killing of which they were actually indicted, was the Eagle Colt, the property of Sir Frederick Standish, at Newmarket; but Bishop, when in the witness-box, made a clean breast, and told the whole story of the various poisonings committed by him and his confederate, and the different devices they had resorted to. Sometimes the deadly drug was given in a hollowed-out bean, sometimes it was introduced into the trough, at others given in a bolus. In the case of Eagle every precaution seemed to have been taken in locking up the drinking troughs in his stable, but by means of a fine crooked syringe Bishop had contrived to infuse a dose into the water, and, watching at a distance, as soon as he saw the horse drink, rushed off with the news to Dawson. On some technical point, however, Dawson was acquitted on this charge, but only to be arrested before he could leave the court on another of having poisoned two brood mares and a hack in the years 1809-10, and at the next assizes he was convicted and sentence of death passed upon him. The curious part of the case is that he never peached upon his employers. Several very influential Turfites endeavoured to procure a remission of the extreme penalty of the law, but without effect, yet to the last he was buoyed up with the hope of reprieve, and had behaved throughout the trial with the greatest levity. As the saying is he died "game," for when he was being taken in an open cart, as was then the fashion, to the place of execution, recognising some old pals, he shouted out, pointing to his manacled hands, "Good-bye, my Newmarket lads; sorry I can't shake hands with you!"

The following is another story of horse poisoning: The day before Sim Templeman was to ride Marcus for his second St. Leger, that and some other horses were standing at the Doncaster Arms. During the afternoon an ill-looking fellow that nobody knew entered the kitchen, and taking out his pipe, seated himself beside a huge boiler, from which the lads were every now and then drawing water for their charges. There was no one remaining in the kitchen except a maid-servant, whom the stranger sent out to get him a pot of beer. The lads continued to draw their water, and presently a girl came in with her kettle, and was placing it under the tap, when the fellow said: "I wouldn't take my tea-water from there, if I was you; it looks so yellow and greasy." "All right," said the girl; "I'll get it outside." The next morning two horses were found dead in the stable, and upon being opened, arsenic poisoning was at once discovered to be the cause of death; while Marcus, who had won the stakes two years previously, and whom everybody fancied, came in last, and died during the day. It may be remarked that the owner of Chorister won £7,000 at very low odds. Then the incident of the loafer and the water was remembered. There was no doubt that he had put a quantity of arsenic into the copper, at the risk, not only of poisoning the horses, but any number of human beings as well.

MODEL YACHT SAILING ON THE SERPENTINE FORTY YEARS AGO.

WHAT are all those mimic skiffs I see, coasting from shore to shore—cutters, sloops, and schooners, now on their beam-ends, now sliding in between the swans, which scarcely deign to turn aside their feathery breasts, bent back like Roman galley beaks? These, at least, are playthings. Not at all. One of the boatmen, with a straw in his mouth and his hands in his pockets, informs me that they form the squadron of the London Model Yacht Club, and that they are testing their powers for the next sailing-match. I am not quite sure that those grave-looking men with long poles, watching the performances of the different craft, are not the members of the Club. That big man there may be, for anything I know, the Commodore—for they have a Commodore, and rules, and a club-room, and they sail matches for silver cups! Look into "Bell's Life in London," a week or two since, and there you will find full particulars of the next match of the Yacht Club, "established in 1845," which is to come off in June next for a handsome twelve-guinea cup, and which informs us that the measurements must be as follows: "The length multiplied by the beam not to exceed five hundred inches over all; the keel for cutters or yawls, not more than two feet, six inches; and for two-masted vessels, two feet, ten inches, on the level of the rabbit, with not less than four inches counter." It is a very serious sporting matter. The Vice-Commodore of the sister Club at Birkenhead having proposed, by advertisement, to change the flags of the Club, "the white ensign to be without the cross," &c., the editor of our sporting contemporary gravely objects, "that the alteration of our national ensign cannot be legally made without the written sanction of the Admiralty." Fast young boats, these!

For the cup last autumn, fifteen yachts started, and the different heats lasted the whole day; the America, modelled on the lines of the famous Yankee boat, coming off victorious. It is a pretty sight to see these little cutters driving along under full sail; and many an old gentleman, standing amid his boys, I have noticed enjoying it to his heart's content. After watching them for some little time, one's ideas of proportion get confused; they look veritable ships sailing upon a veritable great lake; the trees, the men, the sheep on the shore, swell into immense proportions, and it seems as if one were contemplating the fleet of Lilliput from the shores of Brobdignag.

MR. CHEERFUL'S BETTING-SHOP.

The following admirable sketch is evidently from the pen of Mr. Charles Dickens. It is extracted from an article which appeared in one of the early volumes of "Household Words," at a time when "Betting-shops" were so numerous as to have become a clamant nuisance which Dickens did his best to satirize and show up.

Passing, the other day, through a dirty thoroughfare, much frequented, near Drury Lane Theatre, we found that a new betting-shop had suddenly been added to the number under the auspices of Mr. Cheerful.

Mr. Cheerful's small establishment was so very like that of the apothecary in Romeo and Juliet, unfurnished, and hastily adapted to the requirements of secure and profitable investment, that it attracted our particular notice. It burst into bloom, too, so very shortly before the Ascot Meeting, that we had our suspicions concerning the possibility of Mr. Cheerful having devised the ingenious speculation of getting what money he could, up to the day of the race, and then—if we may be allowed the harsh expression—bolting. We had no doubt that investments would be made with Mr. Cheerful, notwithstanding the very unpromising appearance of his establishment; for, even as we were considering its exterior from the opposite side of the way (it may have been opened that very morning), we saw two newsboys, an incipient baker, a clerk, and a young butcher, go in, and transact business with Mr. Cheerful, in a most confiding manner.

We resolved to lay a bet with Mr. Cheerful, and see what came of it. So, we stepped across the road into Mr. Cheerful's betting-shop, and, having glanced at the lists hanging up therein, while another noble sportsman (a boy with a blue bag) laid another bet with Mr. Cheerful, we expressed our desire to back Tophana for the Western Handicap, to the spirited amount of half-a-crown. In making this advance to Mr. Cheerful, we looked as knowing on the subject, both of Tophana and the Western Handicap, as it was in us to do; though, to confess the humiliating truth, we neither had, nor have, the least idea in connexion with those proper names, otherwise than as we suppose Tophana to be a horse, and the Western Handicap an aggregate of stakes. It being Mr. Cheerful's business to be grave and ask no questions, he accepted our wager, booked it, and handed us over his railed desk the dirty scrap of pasteboard, in right of which we were to claim—the day after the race; we were to be very particular about that—seven-and-sixpence sterling, if Tophana won. Some demon whispering us that here was an opportunity of discovering whether Mr. Cheerful had a good bank of silver in the cash-box, we handed in a sovereign. Mr. Cheerful's head immediately slipped down behind the partition, investigating imaginary drawers; and Mr. Cheerful's voice was presently heard to remark, in a stifled manner, that all the silver had been changed for gold that morning. After which, Mr. Cheerful reappeared in the twinkling of an eye, called in from a parlour the sharpest small boy ever beheld by human vision, and dispatched him for change. We remarked to Mr. Cheerful that if he would obligingly produce half-a-sovereign (having so much gold by him) we would increase our bet, and save him trouble. But

Mr. Cheerful, sliding down behind the partition again, answered that the boy was gone, now—trust him for that; he had vanished the instant he was spoken to—and it was no trouble at all. Therefore, we remained until the boy came back, in the society of Mr. Cheerful, and of an inscrutable woman who stared out resolutely into the street, and was probably Mrs. Cheerful. When the boy returned, we thought we once saw him faintly twitch his nose while we received our change, as if he exulted over a victim; but he was so miraculously sharp, that it was impossible to be certain.

The day after the race arriving, we returned with our document to Mr. Cheerful's establishment, and found it in great confusion. It was filled by a crowd of boys, mostly greasy, dirty, and dissipated; and all clamouring for Mr. Cheerful. Occupying Mr. Cheerful's place, was the miraculous boy; all alone, and unsupported, but not at all disconcerted. Mr. Cheerful, he said, had gone out on "tickler bizniz" at ten o'clock in the morning, and wouldn't be back till late at night. Mrs. Cheerful was gone out of town for her health, till the winter. Would Mr. Cheerful be back to-morrow? cried the crowd. "He won't be *here*, to-morrow," said the miraculous boy. "Coz it's Sunday, and he always goes to church, a' Sunday." At this, even the losers laughed. "Will he be here a' Monday, then?" asked a desperate young green-grocer. "A' Monday?" said the miracle, reflecting. "No, I don't think he'll be here, a' Monday, coz he's going to a sale a' Monday." At this, some of the boys taunted the unmoved miracle with meaning "a sell instead of a sale," and others swarmed over the whole place, and some laughed, and some swore, and one errand-boy, discovering the book—the only thing Mr. Cheerful had left behind him—declared it to be "a stunning good 'un." We took the liberty of looking over it, and found it so. Mr. Cheerful had received about seventeen pounds, and, even if he had paid his losses, would have made a profit of between eleven and twelve pounds. It is scarcely necessary to add that Mr. Cheerful has been so long detained at the sale, that he has never come back. The last time we loitered past his late establishment (over which is inscribed Boot and Shoe Manufactory), the dusk of evening was closing in, and a young gentleman from New Inn was making some rather particular enquiries after him of a dim and dusty man who held the door a very little way open, and knew nothing about anybody, and less than nothing (if possible) about Mr. Cheerful. The handle of the lower door-bell was most significantly pulled out to its utmost extent, and left so, like an organ stop in full action. It is to be hoped that the poor gull who had so frantically rung for Mr. Cheerful, derived some gratification from that expenditure of emphasis. He will never get any other, for his money.

MR. SNEWING'S DREAM.

No winner of the Derby was ever more spoken about than Caractacus which won the great race for Mr. Snewing, who it is said had dreamt that he would secure the Blue Riband with a horse of that name. Mr. Snewing was a man who had a considerable idea of his own powers, and always believed he would be somebody on the turf. In the Great Exhibition of 1851, he was much struck with a piece of sculpture representing Caractacus being led in chains to Rome. He was so struck with the mien of the hero and his resounding name that he at once determined to look out for a racehorse, and, when he had secured one good enough, to name him Caractacus, and win the Derby with him. So great was his faith that he laid down a butt of sherry and vowed not to touch it until his dream was realised.

Not much of Caractacus was heard until he was a three-year-old, when, after his running in the Great Metropolitan, there was a perfect *furore* to get on him for the Derby. He seemed to be fairly running away with the Metropolitan, but Jimmy Grimshaw riding him to a standstill, Elcho caught him in the last stride and beat him by a head, with the famous Asteriod a head in turn behind him. Elcho was a first-class horse, and when he won the Goodwood Stakes, Lord Coventry committed the only wild and extravagant act of which he was ever known to be guilty. When Elcho passed the post he said nothing, but, with a perfectly rigid face, took off his hat and solemnly sat on it. After the Metropolitan, two or three defeats of Caractacus cooled the public ardour for him, and when he went to run for the Somersetshire Stakes he was a despised animal. He won in a canter, notwithstanding that Grimshaw broke a stirrup-leather, which he caught and held between his teeth as he finished, otherwise having "weighed close," he might have been short of weight. Caractacus did not arrive on the course until immediately before the race, and he left directly afterwards. As a rustic said, "He came here to win, and he win'd."

The number of people who vowed to eat Caractacus, bit and bridle as well, if he won the Derby was extraordinary, and yet with a stable-boy in the saddle he beat the largest field that ever went to the post for that race. Not long after this Mr. Snewing retired from the turf, and at his farm, near Watford, we had the satisfaction of tasting the famous Caractacus sherry. Mr. Snewing gave a dinner to a small party of us, and everything we tasted, except the wine, was "home made." The fish came out of the brook that ran by his house; the poultry was from the farmyard; the mutton was fed on his own land, and the partridges were shot there. Even the bread was baked in the house, and made from flour ground on his own premises. Mr. Snewing was full of racing stories, and he told us that passing every now and again the paddock in which Surplice gambolled as a foal, he was so much struck with his splendid appearance that he at once backed him for the Derby.

DREAMS ABOUT CARACTACUS.

CARACTACUS was the hero of several dreams and omens. About the date of the Derby Day a farmer took a prize at a local competition for a plough-horse of that name. The prize-taker was elated by his success, and being a "bit of a turfite," accepted his good fortune as an omen, and backed Caractacus for that year's blue ribbon of the turf, much to his satisfaction, and to the scorn of some of his friends, who laughed at his chance.

The following is a *bona fide* story relating to the Derby of 1862.

"I hope you are enjoying yourselves, you and your friends, at the Great Exhibition. As I know you will be going to see the Derby, I may tell you that in a dream last night I was there too, and saw the race; it was won by a horse which was ridden by a pale-faced lady in a blue silk bonnet and white silk dress. There! That will be a striking novelty, I think, in connection with the Derby."

Mr. Snewing's colours were the same as given by the writer, and the boy as he came past the post on Caractacus was exceedingly pale. The above letter was written by a Scottish lady to her husband, who at the time had occasion to be in London; he read the part of his wife's letter to his friends at breakfast, but took no more thought of the matter till he saw Mr. Snewing's colt winning in the identical colours pointed out by his wife, and then, of course, felt annoyed at not having backed the horse; his companions, too, had laughed heartily over the lady's communication.

The horse was ridden by a lad named Parsons, of no fame as a jockey, and who, when he weighed in after the race, could not pull the scale down : and, awful moment of suspense ! the bridle had to be sent for. Another objection would have been taken, namely, that the horse had not gone the proper course, but the objector was five minutes late in making it.

HOW TO PERPETRATE A LOTTERY FRAUD.

With reference to the drawing of a big prize in a foreign lottery scheme, in the summer of 1889, there is reason to believe that a fraud was committed, the police at any rate think so. In order to make clear the *modus operandi*, adopted in carrying out the supposed swindle, it is necessary to give a description of the method of drawing the numbers. These, from one to ninety, are firmly fitted into as many small hollow balls, which are placed in an urn with glass sides. The urn is turned round, and at each turn one ball containing a number is drawn out by a boy, who is usually an orphan, and is given a couple of florins for his pains. Only five of the balls are drawn. The numbers inside them are taken out by the officials, in the presence of a sort of commission and of the public. The numbers and balls are carefully examined, and the eighty-five remaining in the urn are counted. The five drawn numbers are immediately made known, and whoever has backed these numbers is declared the winner.

At the Temesvar drawing, which was so lucky for —, a peculiar incident occurred. When the boy who was to act as drawer appeared, the manager of the Loto informed him that his services were not needed, and sent him home, giving him, however, the two florins. A second boy appeared, and was treated in precisely the same manner, when a strange lady suddenly came upon the scene, bringing with her a young lad. The woman requested the manager, as a great favour, to allow her companion to draw the numbers, as she herself had staked money upon them, and felt sure that the boy would bring her luck. The request was granted and another Loto official put on the boy the official blouse always worn by the drawer, and the numbers were extracted. The inquiry which took place, established the following facts :— —— was seen in frequent conference, some days before the drawing and on the morning of the day itself, with the woman and the boy, and with the two Loto officials already mentioned. At the right time —— came to Vienna to back at three different Loto offices five

x

numbers to be drawn at Temesvar, as it is allowed to back numbers in Vienna for the drawing at that place. The woman gave a false name during her stay and disappeared with the boy immediately after the successful *coup*. Her name is not known. ⸻ as well as the two Loto officials, have undergone long examinations at the hands of the Police Commissioners. All three protested their innocence. ⸻ said that he had invented a system, which made winning inevitable, and stated in proof of his assertion, that he had won no less than four large sums since March last—namely, 14,000, 18,000, 36,000, and now 480,000fls. It is rather curious that three of these amounts, including the largest, were won at Temesvar. It is also remarkable that ⸻ gave up his profession, and established at Werschetz, in Hungary, a Loto office—may be in order to learn his system. But he soon abandoned the business, and settled in a handsome house at Pesth. How he succeeded in getting at the five numbers is not yet known. Possibly, it was some clever sleight of hand on the part of the boy, who is suspected to be ⸻'s son. A similar case occurred at Genoa some years ago.

THE FATE OF MR. MERRY'S HORSE, DUNDEE.

THE following is a good Dundee story : " I was up to the neck in Dundee for the Derby after this. I had seen his dead heat and defeat of Maggiore at York, and could not believe in his defeat. I should have worn his colours, only yellow and black was a little too 'pronounced' for a tie. So I kept up the steam without. But my 'fate' was near. 'I would not be too sanguine about Dundee winning, if I were you,' said my wife. 'Why not ?' 'Because I dreamt he did not win. I cannot tell you why. All I know is he appeared to be winning, and then he seemed to get into a maze, which lost him ground, and then he got into another, and was beaten.' This was strictly prophetic. Dundee, about a fortnight before the Derby, showed symptoms of giving way on one of his fore legs ; but Matthew Dawson's exquisite skill kept him at work. He ran his race well to 'the Bell,' when the doubtful leg gave way, but still he struggled on with three legs, showing all his old gameness ; and just when he appeared to have his race again won 'he got into another maze,' for the other leg gave way, and he finished second to Kettledrum, with Diophantus third, in the fastest Derby ever run. My wife never dreamt about horse-racing again, and I shall always think that it was the anxiety of a good wife for the welfare of her husband, in the early days of her wifehood, that caused her to dream about the incidents I have related."

The following is another story about Dundee—*Apropos* to that year's Derby, which, as turfites know, was won by Kettledrum, it is told that all sporting Paisley was "mad about Mr. Merry's horse" (Dundee)—all but one man, who kept constantly sending away money to Messrs. Holt and Crook, the betting agents at Leeds, telling none of his companions, however, for what horse he was sending the cash. Every Saturday for a few weeks before the race he sent his half or whole sovereign to the firm named. When news of the result of the race arrived at Paisley on the Derby afternoon, and it became known that Dundee had only obtained the second place, "all Paisley" was stricken with grief—all, that is, but the man who had sent his remittances to the Leeds firm of Holt and Crook. Much to the astonishment of his "pals," he was laughing in a fine spirit of contentment, and was immediately assailed by his friends for such a display of levity in the hour of disappointment. "Let those laugh who win," was his reply; "I never put a penny on Dundee; I backed the winner." "What! you backed Kettledrum!" was the wondering response from the assemblage. "Yes, I did," was the reply. "And how did you come to do that?" was next asked. "Because I dreamt two months ago that it had won."

PUGILISTS AFTER THE FIGHT.

People, says Sullivan, the American pugilist, sometimes express surprise that prize-fighters recover so quickly from the punishment they receive in a fight. After the fight is over the fighter is given a hot bath that takes the soreness out of him and keeps the blood in circulation. If he has bruises the blood hasn't time to congeal. For very bad swellings the tincture of iodine is used. If your eyes are all bunged up you simply apply hot water, just as hot as you can bear, and that will soon reduce them to their natural state. I suppose the great secret of the fighter's quick recovery is the fact that he is in such a high state of health nature does most of the work. They say if you cut an Indian with a hatchet—I mean a strong, healthy Indian that hasn't been soaked in bad whisky—the wound will heal of itself in a few days. Give a white man the same kind of blow and it will kill him. A fighter don't feel so bad while battling; he is in a state of activity, and the excitement helps to keep him up. After the fight he feels stiff and sore. Between the rounds his mouth is sponged out to prevent the saliva from gathering and sticking in his throat; he is freshened up by the ice-water applied to his head just behind the ears with a sponge; this is a very sensitive part of the head, and there the application is especially beneficial. Stimulants are sometimes given, but it depends on the condition of the man. If he is weak they will give him a swallow of brandy and Vichy water. Brandy is used because it is quicker in its action than whisky.

I am sometimes asked to give a scientific description of the fistic art. I don't know that any man can do that any more than one man can tell another how to succeed in life. There are a good many things to be taken into consideration, and you have to consider them and decide upon them quickly at the time, and one man's judgment may lead him to act one way, and another man's judgment may lead him to act in an entirely different manner. In boxing, it may be said, however, that there are only seven scientific blows and seven parries. These blows are, first, on the right side of the face with the left hand; second, on the left side of the face with the right hand; third, on the left pit of the stomach with the left hand; fourth, on the left side of your opponent's ribs, with the right hand; fifth, on the right side of his ribs with your left hand; sixth, directly at the centre of the face, covering, if the fist is sufficiently large, the chin, throat, nose, and both eyes. This is considered what the boys call a "daisy" blow when well given. Seventh, the upper cut with the right. This blow strikes under the chin, and if the other man carries his tongue between his teeth it is bad for the tongue. There is another blow called the "chopper"—raising the right hand up and bringing it down with crushing force on the bridge of your antagonist's "smeller."

PLEASURES OF MOORLAND SHOOTING.

The following notes are from the pen of a sportsman who has been long at work and knows what he is writing about.

The heaviest bags are made at the beginning of the season. Each succeeding day renders the birds stronger and wilder. Of course the extent of a bag depends on a variety of circumstances; as for instance, the inherent merits of a moor; the goodness or badness of the breeding season (if the breeding has been unusually early, the grouse are often very wild even on the twelfth;) the perfection of the available material, in the shape of dogs, keepers, &c.; and last, but not least, the ability of the shooter to shoot.

As many as two hundred brace have been bagged by one man in one day, it being noted that the man was a specially good shot, shooting over a specially good and well preserved moor. Moreover, in his case three or four sets of dogs were ranging at one time over adjacent ground, each set attended by a couple of gillies provided with guns. In such well-stocked ground, at least one set of dogs might always be found "pointing" at any given instant; to this point the shooter rode on a pony provided for the purpose, and, taking a gun from the hand of the attendant gillie, walked up to the dogs and knocked over his birds, resorting, if necessary, to the second gun carried by the second gillie. After finishing off that "point," he remounted his pony and rode off to a neighbouring set of dogs, which by this time had in turn found game; and so on throughout the day. In short, the effect was practically that of four men shooting on different hills.

The above enormous bag is probably without a parallel. However, upwards of one hundred brace have often been shot by one gun in one day. The reader may naturally exclaim, "What useless slaughter!" and to this exclamation many good sportsmen may say, Amen. But it must be remembered that the rents paid for shooting are high; so also are the attendant expenses of travelling to and fro; so of dogs, keepers, gillies, &c.; indeed, on a moderate computation, each brace of grouse costs the average of sportsmen at least one guinea—some much less, many much more—while the season available for the sport is little longer than a fortnight. Taking into consideration these circumstances, it is not surprising that the tenant of a moor endeavours to make hay while he may. Moreover, it is now a recognised custom that, in order to recoup himself of a portion of his outlay, the tenant makes arrangements with a salesman either in London or his neighbourhood, who buys all birds sent to him at so much a head, so that the sportsman has to shoot for his pocket. The quantity of grouse sent south from the Highlands during the fortnight following the 12th constitutes a traffic of itself, for which the various railway companies compete by means of printed direction cards forwarded to the various shooting lodges, for the purpose of being affixed to the game boxes.

On the other hand, to prevent the occupant of a moor from becoming a wholesale slaughterer, or rather poulterer, as has sometimes happened, many landlords let their hill on the condition that the number of birds shot off it during the season shall not exceed a fixed limit. This limit is generally a liberal one, and is seldom attained; more frequently, indeed, it is so high above the possible yield of a moor as to suggest the suspicion of a trap for the unwary, much like the notice in old recruiting placards, which specified that recruits for H. M.'s—th Lancers would not be allowed to hunt their horses above three times a week.

MISCELLANEOUS MOORLAND SPORT.

ONE of the great charms of moorland shooting, compared with others, is the uncertainty of what game may next rise before the gun. Your dogs may now be pointing at a grouse, a blackcock, a snipe, a duck, or (alas, on too many moors) a hill hare—we say alas, because these hares are very numerous and scarcely worth shooting, while their weight is troublesome to the gillie who carries the game bag. Moreover, when disturbed, instead of speeding away like his prototype of the plains, a hill hare sits up on his hunkers, and raising his fore paws in the air, looks calmly in a dog's face; a most tantalising temptation for young pointers, and one scarcely to be resisted by crack trained setters of any age.

These hares (whose fur becomes white in winter) have of late years increased enormously, owing to the extirpation of the stoats, weasels, hawks, &c., resulting from the modern system of gamekeeping.

Towards the top of high hills, where the heather slopes are replaced by stony ground, and scantily sprinkled over with grass and moss, the sportsman occasionally comes across a flock of ptarmigan. This bird, which resembles a hybrid between a grouse and a pigeon, is exceedingly wary and difficult to find. His plumage, white in winter and speckled in summer, so nearly resembles the colour of the ground which he frequents, that by crouching close to that ground he is often passed unobserved by his enemies. Of course, in seeking so shy a bird the dogs of the sportsman must be kept well "in the heel."

On the 20th of August the black game come into season. The birds usually effect ground clothed with wood, and, above all, with birchwood. Although it is certainly satisfactory to hear the "thud" with which a fine old blackcock comes down when shot, yet he is not much encouraged by rigid grouse preservers on account of his ill-treatment of the latter named bird.

By the 25th of August the grouse have become very strong, and, having now been under fire for a fortnight, are getting very shy. The first storm of wind and rain which afterwards occurs renders them as wild as hawks. From having restricted their society solely to their own family circle, the coveys now unite, and form packs which at a distance might be taken for flight of crows.

Henceforth, throughout the waning year, it is a hard day's work to shoot ten brace even on the best hill; and these ten brace must be picked up by long range snap shots with a wire cartridge.

TATTERSALL'S.

"TATTERSALL'S" is a name that is constantly turning up in the newspapers to the puzzlement of many of those persons who are not "horsey" and do not bet. "Tattersall's" is a combination of livery stables and sale yard for the disposal of horses. It also contains a suite of rooms devoted to persons who take an interest in horse racing. "Tattersall's" has existed for more than a hundred years. A slight sketch of the history of the firm was given upon the occasion of a banquet held in celebration of its centenary in the year 1865.

The following extract from what was said is most interesting. It is now one hundred years ago—"bar one"— since my great-grandfather, who was best known to his contemporaries by the name of "Old Tatt," leased from the then Earl Grosvenor the piece of ground on which he established our business, long and familiarly known as "The Corner;" and by his honesty, uprightness, and integrity, he secured the respect and confidence of all who knew him. The then Prince of Wales, afterwards George the Fourth, was a constant attendant at the establishment in the time of my grandfather, and it was by his own desire that the bust of his Majesty, which stood in the old yard, was placed there, where it remained until we were "turned out;" and it is now "up" in our new yard at Albert Gate. I remember hearing many strange stories concerning the Prince and his companions at the old Corner. Among them, one of a postchaise and four galloping into Newmarket at night, his Royal Highness riding the leaders, and Charles James Fox the wheelers. My great-grandfather was succeeded about the end of the last century by his son, my grandfather, who had likewise the reputation of being a man of strict integrity and honour, and who was also a good deal connected with the Prince of Wales, as he was for many years associated with the Prince as joint proprietor of the *Morning Post* newspaper. In 1810, my father and uncle succeeded to the business, which they carried on, I might say, with credit and success, for nearly half a century. No men, perhaps, were ever more popular with all classes, and no men, I believe, ever made more sincere friends; and among others I may mention the name of an English nobleman, who was a model in every relation of life— the late Duke of Richmond. Time—and the Marquis of Westminster—have, however, driven us out from our time-honoured locality, and we have secured a spot as near to " The Corner " as we could get; but although we have changed our habitation, we have not changed our principles, and we hope to be still honoured with the confidence and patronage which we have for so many years enjoyed. A hundred years ago horse racing and betting were confined to noblemen and gentlemen, and bookmakers were as little dreamt of as railways or electric telegraphs. But bookmakers have since arisen, and horse racing has become far more popular, even amongst persons in humble ranks, who some few years since would as soon have thought of keeping a tame elephant as a race horse, or of " making a book." In 1815 my grandfather opened a small room for the accommodation of bookmakers, who had hitherto been accustomed to walk about the yard, picking up a stray " pony " whenever they could. That room has become an institution of the turf; and in our new premises neither time nor money have been spared to make the room fitted for the object for which it has been erected. I attribute the great success of my family as being due to their untiring industry and integrity, and the uprightness of their dealings. My grandfather used to say that he told more lies than any man in England, but that, like those of a counsellor, they were all " briefed " to him.

GAMEKEEPERS' TIPS.

We are glad to see that several of our nobility have spoken out their minds on the malpractice that has been so common— viz., for their servants to expect a liberal discount from the tradesmen when they go round to pay the bills. But there are several evils amongst us connected with the system of tipping, that might as easily be put a stop to as this. And we beg to draw the attention of our readers to that pernicious custom, that obtains amongst sportsmen, of feeing gamekeepers, believing that if we can open the eyes of game preservers to the evil, we shall be rendering a great boon to the public at large.

Indeed, the practice in these days of battue shooting has obtained such proportions, that a visitor to a friend's house for a few days' covert shooting will find, that unless he is prepared to give the head keeper a good tip, it is precious little sport he will get on his next visit.

Why should this be so? It is easily obviated. Let all masters give strict orders that none of their keepers shall receive any present on pain of dismissal, and let them also particularly request their guests to adhere to this rule, and we venture to say that the evil will rapidly vanish, and gamekeepers will be as civil, and will put Mr. A., or Mr. B., in just as good positions as His Grace the Duke, or "his lordship" of—.

In illustration of this, we adduce a case which has recently come within our notice, and of the authenticity of which we are able to vouch.

A gentleman owning a large estate was in the habit of asking down a select party of friends for his battue. Among these was one old schoolfellow and college chum, but unfortunately not over-burdened with wealth. Only once did he accept the invitation, though regularly invited year after year. At last, one day happening to meet him in London, the gentleman asked him how it was he never came to see him now? Pressed to tell him he therefore replied, "You know I'm a poor man, and can't afford it."

His friend laughed at the shallow excuse. "But I mean it. Now look here, old fellow, all your friends tip the keeper from two guineas up to a tenner for those few days' shooting. The first and only time I have shot at —— I gave the man what I could afford—I think it was ten shillings—and I never shall forget the supercilious way in which he pocketed it, without even deigning to say, 'Thank you, sir.' So, as I can't stand a gamekeeper's insolence, and can't afford a fiver, I've fought shy of your invitations altogether."

"Oh! that's it, is it?" replied the other musing, as he walked away.

Next day, on arriving home, the head gamekeeper was had up and informed that for the future dismissal would be the consequence of his receiving a present from any of his visitors. It may be imagined how he opened his eyes! However, his wages were raised ten pounds a year as a set off, and when the guests came down they were begged not to give the keeper anything, as dismissal would be the result. To guard, however, against any infringement of this law, a box was put up in the smoking room with the following notice :—" It is particularly requested that no presents be made to any of my servants, keepers, &c. ; those of my visitors who think right (though it is contrary to my wish) to give them anything are requested to put it in this box." At the end of the season the box was opened and was found to contain fifty pounds, there being several fivers amongst them. A natural inference of course is, that this sum must have been far exceeded in former years.

A gentleman who tried this plan found it, as he said, a "bad job," as the footman soon found a key that opened the box, and began at once to share the proceeds as they accumulated !

We should be glad if all game preservers would adopt some such plan as this; for the reckless and lavish system of tipping that prevails is constantly on the increase, and is thereby the means of preventing many a poor though ardent sportsman from accepting an invitation into the country during the shooting season.

GAMBLER AND DUELLIST.

It is related that Count Montroud, an inveterate gambler, who flourished about the end of the last century, was a card sharper and cheat of the worst description. He was a man of good parts, well descended, and had admittance to the best society. His good luck at play on all occasions led to suspicion, and one night he was charged by a certain Monsieur de Champagne, of the Guards, with cheating. " Possibly," Montroud answered coolly, " but I don't choose to be told so," at the same time flinging the cards in Champagne's face. A duel followed, and Montroud was run through the body, which compelled him to keep his bed for two months. His health restored, Montroud challenged Champagne again, and succeeded in killing his adversary. In this way the Count established his reputation as a man whom it was dangerous to meddle with, however strange might appear his constant run of good fortune at games of chance. Montroud was thrown into prison during the Reign of Terror, and expected every day to pass from thence to the guillotine. Noticing, however, it was mostly those who made themselves conspicuous by talking through the bars to the sentry on guard who went first, he kept as much in the background as possible, and at the death of Robespierre was set free. Released from prison, he became intimate with Tallyrand and other leading men. On one occasion Tallyrand, then Minister for Foreign Affairs under Napoleon, furnished Montroud with secret intelligence, which enabled him to gain a sum of £20,000 by operation on the Bourse. After this *coup* Tallyrand said to him, "My dear Montroud, now you have secured this large sum of money you must see about investing it. Where will you place it?" "Place it?" he answered, "why in my bureau of course."

AN ODD CATCH.

It was towards the end of the month of August that, along with two friends, I went to the river Earn to have a day's salmon fishing. There had been a heavy flood, and the water was still very high and dirty. "No use trying fly to-day," was our unanimous conclusion, as soon as we saw the water, "bait is our only chance." Fortunately, we had plenty of worms with us, so we soon put up our rods, ran out our line through the rings, and fastened on stout gut-cast lines. We had to "lead" very heavily, owing to the size of the water, and consequently we were very often fast on the bottom, or, as it is termed by the anglers in that part of the country, "fast on a *he* one."

We fished for some time without success, till we came to a stream famous for the quantity of salmon and sea trout killed in it annually. It was a stream formed by the rush of waters over a dam dyke, and is called the Lynn of Dornoch. I had not been many minutes there, till I felt a draw at my line. This sent the blood to my heart, and made me wait anxiously for a repetition of the sensation. I had not long to wait, for my line soon began to run out in that peculiar manner by which an angler can always detect the presence of a fish. Having given the fish plenty of time to swallow the bait, I struck, and sure enough my line remained taut, and I called my friends to my aid, telling them that I had hooked a fish. After waiting patiently for a few minutes for the fish to move, which it did not seem inclined to do, I began to jerk it slightly with the intention of irritating it, and thereby causing it to move. But my efforts proved ineffectual, and let me jerk as I liked, I could not make the beast stir. My companions now began to laugh, and told me that I had hooked a "he one." I was certain, however, that I had hooked a fish, and that it was still on the line, for I felt it "rugg" every now and again. Still, appearances went against me, and my line remained firmly fixed at the bottom, from which my utmost efforts could not disengage it.

My friends at last got tired of looking at so uninteresting a spectacle, and went off to their own rods, making jokes at my simplicity. Being convinced, however, that there was a fish on my line, though I plainly saw that it was caught on some stick or stone at the bottom, I still continued to use every plan my ingenuity could invent to disengage it. But I was entirely foiled, and was at last forced very reluctantly to break. I lost my cast-line, and about a yard of my line to the bargain. This put me in a very bad humour, and I was in no mood to stand the raillery of my friends, who still held out that there had been no fish at all at the line, but that it had been fastened by the lead on some stone, and that the water playing upon it had given rise to the draws which I had thought were caused by a fish. Soon after this, tired and disgusted with an unsuccessful day's fishing, we went home, resolving, however, to try it again on the morrow.

The morrow came, and after fishing for some time, one of my friends hooked and landed a fine sea trout of about 4lb. This raised our spirits a bit, and shortly afterwards we went down to our favourite spot, the Lynn of Dornoch. I was fishing, as on the day before, with bait, and after making a few casts, I struck again exactly at the place where I had lost the cast-line the day before. My friends, on seeing my dilemma, began asking me "if I had hooked another fish like the one I had on yesterday." Their sarcastic remarks, however, were soon destined to be turned into looks and exclamations of wonder, for my cast-line began to show itself more and more above the water. I soon perceived that my line was coming towards me, and at the same time I became sensible of feeling sundry "ruggs" at the line, which I could impute to nothing else than a fish's efforts to escape. Accordingly I wound up my line, and to the amazement of both myself and friends, after a short struggle, I landed a fine sea trout of about 3lb. Our astonishment was considerably augmented when we saw that the trout was not on the hook I had been fishing with, but on an entirely different one. Wonder of wonders! When it was landed on the bank, I recognised the cast-line as the one I had lost on the previous day. It would appear that in casting, my new cast-line had got entangled with the old one at the bottom of the stream, and in some mysterious way had disengaged it from the place to which it had been attached, keeping the trout a captive till my return. I had been right then, after all, and my friends had to acknowledge the fact. The poor sea trout had the worst of it. It had been kept close chained to the stone which held the cast-line all night, only to be taken out next morning from prison to die.

This was the strangest way in which I ever killed a trout. I have several times, especially in burns, lost a hook in a trout, and some time afterwards caught a trout with the identical hook in its jaws, but never before, never since, and I believe never hereafter shall I go down one day, lose a cast-line with a fish on it, and go down again next day, and hook, not the fish, but the cast-line, and draw both safely to land.

GENERAL HUTCHINSON ON THE EDUCATION OF SPORTING DOGS.

The education of the dog, the General holds, can hardly begin too soon. From his infancy he should be exercised in habits of obedience, and the simple compliance with orders which will in later years form the best groundwork for training for all purposes. The particular object in view is of course, in the case before us, service in the field; and with this object the General recommends special education to commence when the animal is six or seven months old. The first portion of training, still condemned as useless by many breakers, consists entirely of such initiatory lessons as may be taught in a room or on the road, and is, of course, a mere prelude to the "breaking to game" which is to follow. Despite their simple character, however, and the contempt in which they are held by the idle, the ignorant, these early lessons, on which the General so strongly insists, are in his opinion (and we may add in ours) the key to the whole system. That it can ever be *too early* to commence the education of any living thing which can understand the difference between right and wrong, obedience and disobedience, kindness and severity, is surely a delusion. Were no further object in view than the establishment of a mutual intelligence and kindly feeling between the instructor and the instructed, no early lessons to man or beast would be thrown away. But when, as is the case with the sporting dog, his education must be commenced by the intelligence of certain arbitrary signs and words which may be as easily acquired in a room as in the field, at seven as at twelve months old, the wisdom of letting him run riot until he is shown game, is not apparent. That he should intuitively understand the magic word "Toho" roared at him when enraptured by the first sniff of the *Perdix Cinerea*, that he should have any spontaneous intelligence of the mysteries of "down charge" or "war fence," is not to be supposed. Until he is patiently and perseveringly taught that those to him at first unmeaning and alarming cries, accompanied very often by gesture equally unmeaning, and even more terrible, have a meaning, and what that meaning is, nothing but ignorance or brutality could punish him for their neglect.

By a series of simple and easy lessons, based on a system in which rewards, not punishments, and the temper and patience of the teacher, are the only secrets employed, the young pointer or setter, or any other dog, will in a few weeks be brought to a perfect comprehension of the ordinary signs employed in the field. He will obey the "toho," the "down charge," and the "find," with more or less steadiness, and be prepared to commence the far more difficult study of "ranging" and "quartering." "A good method of ranging," insists the General, "can only be implanted when the dog is young;" and few practical sportsmen will, we imagine, find fault with the dictum. It is here, also, that the temper and patience of the breaker is most severely tried, and that undue harshness is attended with its most fatal results. The instincts of the animal will infallibly lead him to hunt, and by a gradual and cautious direction of his natural habits, the proper method of ranging may be certainly, if slowly, inculcated. But it is impossible to be too careful in checking the first free efforts of a young dog to hunt. Let the object of his search be what it may, the first effort of the trainer should be to encourage him to range freely at his own sweet will, and to take pleasure in the unrestrained act of *hunting*. Any untimely check or rating to a young and timid dog may cool the ardour which it should be our first aim to excite, and he will be perpetually running to "heel" in fancied obedience to our wishes, which certainly lie in an opposite direction. Encourage him, therefore, to hunt, when necessary, even by the example of an old dog, and let the direction of his hunting be the gradual extension and guidance of his own efforts.

As to the time at which the first lessons in ranging should be given, there is considerable difference of opinion, even among the best judges. Many good sportsmen, among whom General Hutchinson is one, would defer it until birds can actually be killed to the young dog; others incline, not unnaturally, to the belief that this is a waste of time, and that the pupil should be as perfectly broken in *all* respects as possible, before giving him a chance of spoiling a day's sport in the field. Whatever difference of opinion, however, exist on the question of time, there can be none as to the superiority of the lucid and admirable method by which General Hutchinson initiates his pupil into what he calls a "truly killing range." With the minute directions, all conspicuous by brevity and simplicity, laid down for the guidance of the trainer, we are not immediately concerned. Suffice it to say they are adopted with a view to prove *intelligible to the animal*, on which broad principle, indeed, the whole system properly stands. Thoroughly conversant with the canine character, General Hutchinson gives every dog of average capacity and docility credit for a desire to do his master's bidding, when he knows what that is. Uncompromising firmness in correcting a fault is absolutely essential in the teacher; but it is entirely thrown away unless the animal understands that he has committed a fault, and in what that fault consists. The ignorant harshness of the professional breaker, now happily far less common than of old, could not or would not condescend to explain to its victim the nature of his misdeeds; and the result was too often the timid and miserable "blinking," which was the dog's only idea of avoiding a thrashing. General Hutchinson takes a high and correct estimate of the unequalled sagacity of his four-footed friends, and nowhere is it so apparent as in his method of making a ranger; the achievement, as he justly says, "more difficult than any dozen things in the whole art of dog-breaking." In recompense, however, there is nothing so advantageous when it is at length acquired. It will abundantly repay months of persevering exertion. It constitutes the grand criterion of true excellence.

TURF SLANG.

THE "Slang Dictionary" contains a good many turf phrases, but still the students of the sporting journals will, from time to time, meet with many expressions which are neither in Johnson nor in Hotten. I have jotted down several tit-bits of slang with which every turfite is well acquainted. No doubt the list could be largely extended, but here they are as they occurred to me:—

Stayer.—A horse whose *forte* is endurance rather than speed.

Pot.—The sum of money for which a favourite is backed, and sometimes the favourite himself. When the favourite wins, his backers are said to "land the pot," or "to pull it off."

Hot, and sometimes *Warm.*—Backed for a great deal of money. A horse is said "to come hot" in the betting when he is suddenly backed for a large amount.

All out.—With nothing left *in* him. "He won, but he was *all out* to win" (*i. e.* fully extended) we say of a horse who has just pulled through.

There or *thereabouts.*—The winner, or almost the winner.

Turned loose.—Handicapped at a very light, ridiculous, or unfair weight.

Sidebinder.—Nearly equivalent to a "rib roaster"—a heavy cut with the whip to get a horse to make another effort.

Office, to give the, or sometimes to *tip* the office, is not necessarily a dishonest proceeding, but is simply to give private and exclusive information; and we often hear men assure their friends they "have it straight" from owner, trainer, or jockey.

Gruelling.—"To give a person his gruel is to kill him; expression derived from the report of a trial for poisoning." But ordinarily, the word is used with a milder signification. A greyhound has a "severe gruelling" when he has a long severe course, or a single-handed one, which thoroughly exhausts him, and makes him a subject for gruel, in fact; and this is the usual meaning of the term, which equally applies to a punishing race.

Coming with a wet sail.—Making a sudden spurt.

Hands down.—A horse wins "hands down" when the jockey is not called upon to urge him with rein or whip.

A little in hand.—To win with "a little in hand" is to win by a less distance than the race might have been won by, to keep handicappers and others in the dark as to a horse's true form.

So much for turf slang.

COST OF SCOTTISH OUT-OF-DOOR SPORTS.

It is an undoubted fact that every stag which is shot in the Scottish deer forests costs in rent, taxes, and wages a sum of £50 ; each brace of grouse that is slain on the heather may be put down as costing one guinea ! Pheasants are bred for the gun at the price of about three shillings each. All over Scotland there is sport of some kind available, trout or salmon fishing ; it has been computed, by the way, that each salmon caught by an angler who rents a stretch of water or fishes by the day will stand him in two guineas of expenses. There are about four thousand sporting estates in Scotland, big and little, some of which fetch large rents, and the total game rental of the country is not less every year than half a million sterling ! There are deer or grouse in every Scottish county, as also trout or salmon. The following are a few brief details of the rents charged.

In the county of Forfar the estates of the Earl Dalhousie fetch large sums. Invermark Deer Forest fetches £3,500 from Lord Hindlip's coffers, while Sir John Thursby, Bart., pays a like amount for Panmure House. Bechin Castle, belonging to the same estate, is let to Mr. H. C. Maxwell for £1,000 ; and Hunthill, for £850, is let to Captain W. Thomson. Mr. Rushton, of Bolton, pays £800 for Milden. Lord Airlie, in the same county, gets £1,400 for one shooting, and £600 and £500 for two others respectively.

The chief deer forests of "dear old Scotland" are situated in the counties of Ross and Inverness, and several of them bring to their owners large sums by way of rent. The great American sportsman Mr. W. L. Winans pays £8000 for Affaric and other Deer Forests, while Balmachan costs Mr. Bradley Martin £2,700. Ceanvacroc is put down at £2,650 to Sir H. B. Meux, Bart.; and Dunacton costs Mr. J. Austin, M.P., £1000. Gaick Forest brings Sir G. Macpherson Grant £2,000, Glenfeshie brings him £2,500, and Invereshie the same amount. Mr. A. Dennistown pays £1,670 for Invermoriston Forest, while Lord Burton pays £3,022 for Glenquoich Forest, and £1,200 for Glenkingie. Rothiemurchus Forest fetches £2,000 from Mr. A. H. Brown, and Meamore Forest £2,500.

In Ross-shire Mr. Cooper pays £4,500 for Achnashellan Forest, while Mr. Walter Schoolbred pays £1,000 for Castle Leod. Clenie, Grimersta, and Kildermorie Forest fetch like amounts from their respective lessees. Mr. C. E. Young pays £1,650 for

Y

Novar, Mr. J. H. Platt £1,600 to Lady Matheson for Deer Park Forest, and Mr. Cunninghame and Mr. Merry divide the £2,500 rental of Strathconan Forest between them.

The County of Perth is *the* Sporting County of Scotland *par excellence*: it contains over three hundred shooting estates and yields all kinds of sport. Among the estates of Perthshire rented at £1,000 and upward are Auchleeks to Mr. W. Pilkington for £1,000; the Barracks, to Mr. Henry Robertson, for £1,000; and Faskally for £1,200. The average price seems about £500 to £900, and almost all are rented between these figures.

The Duke of Sutherland is pretty nearly supreme in the county of Sutherland but not quite. In all the Duke lets no less than 56 shootings in this county for close upon £30,000 per annum.

In Morayshire Mr. W. L. Agnew pays £1,450 for Altyre, and Mr. G. Williamson pays the Duke of Fife £800 for Innes. Mr. Arthur Sassoon pays £900 to the Countess of Seafield for the shooting of Tulchan, and Sir A. L. Smith pays Mr. T. W. H. Grant £700 for Wester Elchies.

In the County of Caithness (from which comes the best grouse of Scotland as also the best geese) Sir Tollemache Sinclair lets Brawl Castle, at one time a famous rendezvous for early salmon fishers, to Mr. G. H. Hodgson for £675, and Dalnawilan to Mr. A. Hickman for £1,070, and Glutt and Torrens to Mr. Sydney Peel for £800. The Duke of Portland receives £600 from Major Ramsay for Watten. In Banffshire the Duke of Richmond lets Glenavon to Mr. H. Barclay for £1,460, and Strathavon to Col. Blackett for £550. Arndilly goes at £700 to Sir Ford North. A much longer list might easily be made up, but for persons desiring more particulars there is Mr. Watson Lyall's "Guide."

GAME PRESERVING, PRO AND CON.

"A PLACE for everything, and everything in its place," so somebody once said, or if he didn't he ought to have said it. Such was the moral I drew the other day after a long discussion in a railway carriage with a foxhunter. He had been inveighing against the selfish and unsportsmanlike proceedings of sundry game preservers in the favourite county of ——, who he expected would soon warn the hunt off their land altogether, and thus put an end to the noble and manly sport of foxhunting, and all for the sake of a few pheasants.

"Let us examine the pros and cons of the case," said I, "and see how the matter lies."

The line of argument I followed was, "that foxhunting and game preserving go excellently hand in hand up to a certain point, and when that is reached they separate. That it is unfair to expect that men living in the 'game counties,' and who go to great expense and trouble in rearing game, should also have lots of foxes in their coverts; and that it is a gross injustice that they should be blackguarded and written at if they object to having their woods drawn before they have pulled trigger at a long tail."

"But," said my friend, "you have no right to breed game in such quantities."

"Why not?"

"Oh! because it is putting a premium on poaching, and throwing temptation in the way of many an honest lad; and as for your *battues*, they are butchery; one might as well go and shoot barn door fowls in a farm yard!"

The first part of the above objections was easily disposed of, and my friend was forced to allow that every man has a perfect right to do what he likes with his own, so long as he does not injure his neighbour.

"I have you there on your own grounds," he exclaimed triumphantly, after I had shown him that the "premium on poaching" was no real argument against game preserving. "Rabbits! rabbits!! look at the harm they do to your neighbours' fields."

"Well, I suppose rabbits and hares do some harm," I allowed; "but is not the tenant often compensated in some way for the damage inflicted on his crops, and is the harm they commit much greater than that which foxhunters commit in breaking down fences, riding over the young corn late in the season, &c.?"

"Well, but farmers, generally speaking, are hunting men, and if they assist in breaking down their own hedges, &c., they have a right to do so, I suppose."

"I suppose they have," I replied, "but I was only speaking of the harm inflicted by hunters; and whether that harm is committed with or without their consent, I cannot see that it makes much difference. Moreover, every farmer, when he rents his farm, knows that if his landlord preserves very highly, his rent is not so much as it would otherwise be. And further, if the rabbits, &c., are allowed to increase too much, he can always leave, if his landlord refuses him any compensation. But you said just now you could see no sport in *battue* shooting. Surely that is no reason why other people should not. And if, as you allowed just now, that a man had perfect liberty to preserve game, you must confess that a *battue* is the only way of getting the pheasants. You cannot go into coverts well stocked with game day after day for an hour or two without frightening away all the birds."

"Well, I suppose I must allow that," he answered; "but what I do say is, that no man ought to breed so much game as to render it requisite to keep out the hounds from the woods."

"Well, at all events that is a concession. You began, you know, by taking rather high ground—viz., that game preserving was wrong, because it encouraged poaching. But I really think the true reason why you condemn it, is because you consider it and foxhunting as enemies. In other words, then, you hold that every other sport ought to give way to foxhunting, and that a man, though living in a game country, has no right to rear game. Might I not rather say that foxhunters have no right to expect to have everything their own way in the very heart of a game county. Some few places are by nature adapted for game, and in these, I say, that foxhunting men ought to consider the feelings and tastes of shooting men. On the other hand, a man who tries to preserve game highly, in a hunting county like Melton, &c., has no right to complain if the foxes commit depredations in his coverts. I can only say this, that if I preserve game in a game district, I would follow the example of one or two masters of foxhounds who take very good care not to have a superfluity of foxes themselves, and I would never allow a hound to set foot in a covert of mine till I had had my party down to shoot the pheasants. Now, look here, I have just been staying with a friend of mine who has been to great expense and trouble in getting up a good head of game, and who at the same time throws no other impediment in the foxhunter's way than a request that his coverts may be held sacred till after he has had his *battue*. The consequence is, that some few of his neighbours who don't care for shooting blackguard him and abuse him in every conceivable way. I don't believe a fox has ever been destroyed in his coverts by any of his keepers; but this last season, I can tell you, they have taken 100 pheasants off their nests. Reckoning five to each hatch, he has thus lost 600 pheasants, or nearly £80, reckoning a brace of pheasants at 5s. This state of things, of course, cannot be expected to last. And I am certainly of opinion that he would be quite justified in keeping foxes down within proper limits. I really think you must allow his to be a hard case—namely, to get soundly abused, and at the same time to be such a considerable loser. And so I say 'success to foxhunting and to shooting,' but let the advocates of each be reasonable, and not expect too much from each other. Do not let hunting men expect to have it all their own way in a game county, neither let shooting men think that they can or ought to turn a hunting county into another Norfolk or Suffolk."

I ceased here, for on turning round, to my great disgust, I found my companion fast asleep, so for fear lest my readers should also be getting drowsy I had better end this letter. But I think I had the best of it.

DIFFERENCES IN JOCKEYS.

Of Robinson and Chifney the following opinions were given by an observant sportsman of the olden time : " As to Robinson, his talent is unquestionable, he will ride through a church door, however awkward and refractory the animal may be on which he is mounted, but as to Sam Chifney, only let him get tight hold of his horse's head, and he'll go slap through the keyhole."

WINNING BY THE SKIN OF HIS TEETH.

A Gentleman undertook some seventy seven years ago, for a wager of one hundred guineas, to ride nine miles within half an hour, and to run five miles in another half hour. He started from Two-mile Brook, near Colnbrook, Bucks, and performed the nine miles in four minutes less than the given time. He now started on his pedestrian match, and went four miles in a few seconds less than twenty-four minutes, labouring under great distress, but he recovered his wind, and won the match, though by the skin of his teeth, having only six seconds to spare.

A LEGEND OF THE "SHIRES."

A Guardsman bold got up one morn,
He'd been restlessly tossing about since dawn ;
As he eats his breakfast he knows no bounds
To his joy, at the thoughts of a day with T.'s hounds.
His form he surveys in the glass with haste,
And he thinks his " get up " 's in perfect taste ;
And he shouts to his servant, who's waiting down stairs,

"*Make haste, and come here, Sir, and buckle my spurs!*"
That being over,
He mounts a mover
Of no small pretensions, to ride to covert;
His breeches are white, and his boots are brown,
And he looks just the fellow to cut them all down,
As he trots through the purlieus of Harboro' town;
And, thinks he "More or less,
" There's *one* thing I possess,
" That's good taste in my notion of hunting dress!
" George is neat, but although he may try the swell,
" In matter of 'get up,' he can't do it so well!"
So he reaches the meet.
As his friends give him greet-
Ing, he sees that they are all looking down at his feet.
They banter and chaff,
One gives a hoarse laugh,—
In short, they are getting too funny by half.
" Old fellow!—we really—can't—help it—don't frown,
" *But your spurs have been buckled on upside down!*"
The Guardsman frets, the Guardsman fumes,
He curses his servant, he damns his grooms;
With a terrible oath, as he rides away,
He vows that his valet shall leave him that day.
He canters back
To a quiet track
In the covert, and leaps from his horse's back;
For a brilliant idea to his mind occurs—
He'll conceal in his pocket those hateful spurs.
Now, pray do not think this a spurious story—
Spurs are won, and are worn in the field of victory;
But I ne'er before heard of their being consigned
To the pocket of one who is always inclined
To "go hard;" and although gravest doubts may arise, one
Is not sure th' arrangement's a wonderfully wise one.
But there's no time to stay—
A fox is away!
He remounts, and is soon at the head of the fray.
The fences are large, and the brooks are wide,
But nothing can turn the Guardsman aside,
And he takes them just as they come in his stride!
But his horse is blown,
And an overgrown
Dark and dangerous bullfinch brings him down.
The Guardsman gets up, and prepares, with a grace-
Ful bound in the saddle, to leap to his place.
He vaults—ha! ha! with a terrible scream,
Like that of one woke from a fearsome dream,
He reels back from his saddle, and falls to the ground,
And the blood wells out from a dreadful wound.
It was not a thunderbolt's electric shock, it
Appears he'd *forgotten the spurs in his pocket!*

HOW ANGLERS SHOULD CAST THEIR FLIES.

"BADAUD," said Major O'Gaffer on our way to the river, "I will reward your good behaviour by teaching you, rod in hand, my original method of managing a cast of artificial flies. But before putting precept in practice, I will repeat, as your memory is none of the best, the directions I gave you some years ago for refining gut and attaching droppers to a casting line. The tool sold by the tackle-makers for diminishing the thickness of gut is very difficult to manage, and does not produce the desired effect nearly so well as the method I employ. Perhaps you will remember that the gut is to be steeped in vinegar and water—one part of the former to five or six of the latter—for about half an hour. It is then to be placed in a saucer of pure water. The thicker end of one of the finest lengths must be fixed in a table-vice, the thinner end in a pair of pliers, and the gut rubbed between the finger and thumb, moistened in water, until the cotton rises equally round it. This cotton must then be removed with old linen, chamois leather, and india-rubber. The cotton or fur must again be raised and removed, and the operation repeated until the requisite degree of fineness is obtained. In order to equalise the thickness of the gut, it is necessary to work with the thicker end nearest to the operator; and to preserve its roundness, to keep it constantly turning between the finger and thumb. If the trout in your river do not much exceed a pound in weight, the gut may be safely reduced to half the thickness of stallion's hair, and if regularly done, possess more than double its strength. If the gut be stained, the vinegar and rubbing will take out great part of the colour, improving the gut very materially. The whole of the fly cast, with the exception of the droppers, is to be composed of gut thus reduced. *It never answers to tie droppers to gut of any kind*, more particularly refined gut. The dropper-fly ought to be dressed on horse-hair,—single if your fish do not much exceed a pound, double or treble according to circumstances. The last, in good hands, ought to be equal to a salmon. The reason I disapprove of gut for a drop-fly is that, in consequence of its pliancy, the hook never hangs clear of the line. Hog's bristles I have tried, but do not like them as well as hair. But it must be *good*, and good stallion's hair is not easily got. I consider it well worth a shilling a dozen strands. It is no difficult matter to knot the different lengths of gut together. The lower may be single sliding knots, but it is as prudent to make the upper ones double. The difficulty is to fix the drop-flies.

There are an infinity of methods, one worse than the other. I fancy I practise the best, so does every other fisherman you meet. One thing is certain, and that is, the old-fashioned way of looping over a knot is the worst of all. Perhaps the next is placing the dropper between the sliding knots, and securing it by means of a knot at the end. These methods have in view the facility of change. In my opinion, changing a dropper, or indeed a tail, is sheer loss of time. Indeed, if a man can dress a fly at all, he can do it in little more time than is required to change one. In case it requires removal, from the point of the hook being damaged, the shortest way is just to construct another. But a dropper does not require removing from that cause nearly so often as the tail-fly, and that I invariably make a fixture. With regard to the distance between my drop-flies, I generally allow no more than two lengths of gut between them. This enables me to use four, and even five droppers. I would fain describe my mode of fixing a dropper in such language as, were you to repeat it, would prove intelligible."

SHAKESPEARE AS A FOX-HUNTER.

A VERY clever and amusing writer in the *New Sporting Magazine* under the assumed name of "Paddy Blake," has endeavoured to prove our immortal bard to have been a fox-hunter. The adventure in Sir Thomas Lucy's park, which compelled him to leave Stratford, he properly considers as one of the wild pranks of youth, and into which an innate love of mischief and danger, but no idea of plunder or gain, had led him; but he maintains that, previous to this, he was, and must have been a fox-hunter.

His proof is merely presumptive; but I confess that it is strong, and, in my mind, conclusive. He refers to one of Shakespeare's minor poems, "Venus and Adonis," and he quotes a description of the wiles of the hare, which I fear you may not insert, from want of space, and because it does not quite come within the scope of your work; and yet I will answer, that no reader will find fault.

> But if thou needs will hunt, be ruled by me,
> Uncouple at the timorous flying hare;
>   Or at the fox which lives by subtlety;
>   Or at the roe, which no encounter dare.
> Pursue these fearful creatures o'er the downs,
> And on thy *well-breathed* horse keep with thy hounds.

And when thou hast on foot the purblind hare,
Mark the poor wretch; to overshoot his troubles,
  How he outruns the wind, and with what care
He cranks and crosses with a thousand doubles.
  The many musits through the which he goes
  Are like a labyrinth t'amaze his foes.

Sometimes he runs among the flock of sheep
To make the cunning hounds mistake their smell;
  And sometimes where earth-delving conies keep,
To stop the loud pursuers in their yell;
  And sometimes sorteth with a herd of deer;
  Danger deviseth shifts, wit waits on fear.

For there his smell with others being mingled,
The hot scent-snuffing hounds are driven to doubt,
  Ceasing their clamorous cry, till they have singled,
With much ado, the cold fault clearly out:
  Then do they spend their mouths; echo replies,
  As if another chase were in the skies.

By this poor Wat, far off upon a hill,
Stands on his hinder legs with listening ear,
  To hearken if his foes pursue him still;
Anon their loud alarums he doth hear;
  And now his grief may be comparèd well
  To one sore sick that hears the passing bell.

Then shalt thou see the dew-bedabbled wretch
Turn and return, indenting with the way;
  Each envious briar his weary legs doth scratch,
Each shadow makes him stop, each murmur stay;
  For misery is trodden on by many,
  And, being low, never relieved by any.

I can hardly conceive that any man could write thus who had not witnessed and admired all this again and again.

Now, however, comes the chief evidence. While Adonis is withstanding the solicitations of the goddess, his horse espies a filly at a little distance——

Imperiously he leaps, he neighs, he bounds,
And now his woven girths he breaks asunder;
  The solid earth with his hard hoof he wounds,
Whose hollow womb resounds like heaven's thunder.
The iron bit he crushes 'tween his teeth,
  Controlling what he was controllèd with.

His ears up-pricked, his braided hanging mane
Upon his compassed crest now stands on end;
  His nostrils drink the air, and forth again,
As from a furnace, vapours doth he send:
  His eye, which glistens scornfully like fire,
  Shows his hot courage and his high desire.

Sometimes he trots, as if he told the steps,
With gentle modesty, and modest pride :
Anon he rears upright, curvets and leaps,
As who should say, lo ! thus my strength is tried :
And thus do I to captivate the eye
Of the fair breeder that is standing by.

What recketh he his rider's angry stir,
His flattering *holloa*, or his *stand I say ?*
What cares he now for curb, or pricking spur ?
For rich caparisons or trappings gay ?
He seeks his love, and nothing else he sees,
For nothing else with his proud sight agrees.

Look ! when a painter would surpass the life
In limning out a well-proportioned steed,
His art, with Nature's workmanship at strife,
As if the dead the living should exceed :
So did this horse excel a common one
In shape, in courage, colour, pace, and bone.

Round-hoofed, short-jointed, fetlocks shag and long,
Broad breast, full eyes, small head, and nostril wide,
High crest, short ears, straight legs and passing strong,
Thin mane, thick tail, broad buttock, tender hide,
Look what a horse should have, he did not lack,
Save a proud rider on so proud a back.

Sometimes he scuds far off, and there he stares ;
Anon he starts at stirring of a feather ;
To bid the wind abase, he now prepares,
And if he run or fly, they know not whether.
For through his mane and tail the high wind sings,
Fanning the hairs, which heave like feathered wings.

"Paddy Blake" says, and I perfectly agree with him, that he " questions whether so much poetry and truth are to be found in any modern book of poems as are contained in these few lines; and, besides, there is a reality, an enthusiasm, a *vrai-semblance* about them which no man, but a real hunting horseman, could have imparted."

As for me, I shall love the bard of Avon the more on account of this new light in which he appears, and devote to him a few more of my two-minute snatches from professional business, or his and my choicest pleasures ; and I hope that you will unstarch a little ('twould do you no harm if you oftener do it), and admit this scrawl. Let 'Mr. Paddy,' however, have all the credit of the thing—he has my thanks ; and you know what I think of and feel towards you.

A Hunting Vet.

GOLDEN RULE IN BETTING.

"In all bets there must be a possibility to win when the bet is made—You cannot win when you cannot lose."

WAITING FOR A BADGER.

Hunting the badger is a somewhat novel and yet exciting sport. As the animal seldom leaves his den until towards midnight, the "meet" acquires a tinge of the supernatural, and seems "hardly canny." Observe the programme.

Scene: A tangled copse on the hill side, bordering on a large dark wood. The night is fine and clear, with just sufficient light to discern objects floating in thin air, without exactly determining their character. A deep silence reigns around, broken at intervals by the hooting of an owl, or the dismal croak of the raven, until at length the good dogs are fairly on the "slot" of the badger, when the air rings with the music of the pack. Still the huntsman can scarcely distinguish his hounds as he cheers them on, but follows the "trail" as much by sound as sight in the pale gleams of a waning moon. Time, four o'clock, a.m.

I once saw a fine badger which was caught alive by a single woodman, without the aid of either dog or gun. How did he catch it? In this way:—having observed during the day a couple of badger-holes in a certain wood, he did—what? "Dig the animal out," you will say. Nothing of the kind; for he might have thrown up a score tons of earth, circumnavigated more than one hard tree-root, and not got at the beast after all. David Grimes knew better than to waste so much labour. He waited until long after midnight, and then took a lantern, a sack, and some ropes into the wood. David inferred, and, as it turned out, rightly, that the badgers would be abroad, eating their evening meal. Arriving at the spot, he prepared his tackle; the sack, having a string round the opening, like the string of a purse, was thrust into the burrow, the mouth of the bag being propped open by a hoop; then, taking the two long strings into his hands, David ascended the nearest tree, and waited until Mr. Badger thought proper to return home. If I remember rightly, he watched and waited up in that tree for nearly three hours; so long, indeed, that he began to think the badger must either have taken fresh lodgings, or remained fast asleep in his bed. It required some patience, he observed, to sit perched up all that time, solitary and yet not alone, for squirrels climbed the neighbouring boughs, and a hawk, careering in search of food, flapped its wings within a few yards of the place. At length the woodman could dimly trace some larger animal proceeding at an easy trot. It stopped, then sniffed the ground, walking round and round up to the very tree where David was. An enemy had been there, might be still concealed in the neighbourhood, and the badger's suspicions being clearly aroused the question arose whether it were best to stay or fly. After some further reconnoitring the careful brute bolted into his hole as he thought, but the jerk proved that it was only into a sack; the woodman pulled the strings tightly, thus inclosing his victim, and then descended to secure it. No doubt the big beast would struggle violently, and try to bite through the sack. But it was all in vain; the woodman shouldered his prize, and bore it home in triumph, where afterwards it was "baited" with the best dogs in the neighbourhood.

HOW JOCKEYS USED TO DRESS IN THE DAYS OF OLD.

THE following was at one time the costume worn by some of the jockeys, who rode in the earlier races for the Derby :—

A black velvet cap with a long French peak, and a bow of black satin riband behind; long hair falling to his shoulders; a white cambric neckcloth, of ample folds, tied at the back; a long body-coat with flaps, wide skirt, three buttons at the side, where it opened, as well as in front, and behind; knee-breeches, strapped just below the knee; white cotton stockings, and black leather Oxford shoes, with long tongues and silver buckles.

CAPTAIN BARCLAY'S RIVAL.

IT was to be expected that the great feats of the Captain would excite in others the desire to outdo him, and many great feats are recorded of his so-called rivals, among others, that of one Abraham Wood of Mildam, in Lancashire, who once ran four miles on the York Course in twenty minutes and twenty-one seconds. On another occasion he did twenty miles

on the Brighton course in two hours and five minutes. A few
days afterwards he ran a quarter of a mile in fifty-nine seconds.
In 1807 he ran forty miles over Newmarket Heath in four
hours and fifty-six minutes, doing the first eight miles in forty-
eight minutes. He ran without shoes or stockings, and wore
only a pair of flannel drawers and a jacket. He did not appear
to suffer much from his exertions, and few riders were able to
keep their horses up with him. This was looked upon at the
time as being a great performance and excited considerable attention.

EPSOM AND THE DERBY.

The "blue riband of the Turf" was instituted in the year
1780, "the Oaks" having been first run in the preceding year, both
races being, of course, run on the Downs at Epsom, on which
horse racing was established by James I., when he lived at
Nonsuch. Reference is made to the custom in the time of his
successor, and in that of Charles II., who made Epsom a
second Newmarket, as being more convenient to the Court.
But the history of the world-famous races undoubtedly commences with the day (May 4, 1780) when Sir Charles Bunbury's
Diomed had the honour—an honour, the greatness of which no
one dreamed of then—of winning the first Derby, the value of
which was £1,125. Eight horses out of thirty-six which had
been entered ran. Sir Charles had the extraordinary good
fortune to win the Derby three times; the second was won by
Diomed's grand-daughter, Eleanor, who, in the same year, won
the Oaks; the third winner was Smolensko.

WHEN PROFESSIONAL RIDING BEGAN.

We have no positive data to enable us to ascertain with certainty the period when the "business" of riding races
originated, but presume it to have been very early in last
century, although the practice was continued by county
gentlemen of putting up their own grooms, long after "professional" horsemen had begun work. The first mention we find
of the regular "jockey" is in connection with the "Merlin Match"
arranged by Old Frampton, in the year 1720. The names of
the two riders, we are told, were "Jerome Hare of Cold-Kirby

near Hambleton, and one Hesseltine of Newmarket." These early riders in races were most of all noted for the inhumane mode they had of punishing the animals they rode, a system of riding which would not now be tolerated: horses being seldom flogged and very often ridden even without spurs.

CHIFNEY IN THE HUNTING FIELD.

OLD Chifney—one of the great riding artists of his day on the turf—cut but a poor figure when following the hounds, being excessively timid, a fact well known to his Royal Highness the Prince of Wales, who always ordered him to take the lead over difficult or unknown fences, a post of honour which the jockey dared not, of course, decline. One day, having had a rather severe fall over a fence which the Prince had sent him to explore, the unlucky Chifney shouted to the Prince, "A ditch, by jingo, your Royal Highness, and I have just about broken my neck over it, don't *you* try, or your neck will soon be done for!"

WHAT A JOCKEY SHOULD BE.

HE should be of a shrewd and calculating disposition, and neglect no opportunity of improving his judgment, by observation and practice in his profession. Above all, he must be a perfect master of his temper, accustomed to keep a constant check upon his tongue, possess much personal intrepidity, be honest to his employers, and of temperate habits.

MEN WITH MORE MONEY THAN BRAINS.

THE following is taken from an American newspaper, and requires no comment:—

"What became of all the things you used at the ring side when you beat Kilrain?" asked a reporter of Sullivan, the world's champion.

"Why, people grabbed them and sold them as souvenirs. We didn't get a penny for them," replied Sullivan's "trainer." "Each of us bought a soft felt hat to wear out to the ring. Mr. Sullivan threw both of them into the ring before the fight.

They only cost 4s. 6d. apiece, yet a man got £10 for Mr. Sullivan's hat and £5 apiece for Cleary's and mine. The buckets which held the ice-water which we dipped the towels in, sold for £5 each. The post which held his colours was torn up and splinters of it sold for £1 each. They even dug the ground up where the post was driven and doing it up in little parcels sold them to people anxious for mementoes. The ring rope was cut into bits and sold. I had a half dozen towels and two sponges which I bathed Mr. Sullivan with and they disappeared as if by magic. Major Hughes got the can which I had made expressly for Mr. Sullivan to drink out of at the ring and he refused £200 for it."

A MORNING WITH THE "WIZARD OF THE NORTH."

No trainer's home and its surroundings was ever more worthy of visiting than that of John Scott of Malton, or as he was often designated, the "Wizard of the North," from the success he had achieved in the art of training the high mettled racer. The following short sketch will give the reader some idea of the comforts of a trainer's home :—

Next morning I awoke to see the ground crisp with frost and the red December sun already above the horizon. In the distance was the quaint old red bricked town. I passed again by the old painted clock on the staircase, and, after the usual morning salutations, sat down to the bountiful morning meal. I will not speak of the many tempting things before me, nor how I relished them, except to say that never were muffins and pikelets finer or whiter, toast more deliciously browned, or sheep's head (a favourite morning dish there,) rump steak, and kidneys better done or more bountifully provided. On the adjoining sideboard were the gold and silver cups and plates that were the trophies emblematical of the success of many a "high mettled racer." There was, too, a peculiar knife, but I forgot what it was intended to commemorate. The beautiful painting by Herring of two of the host's favourite hunters over the fireplace has been added since. We rose from the table to look at the illustrious trainer's pupils pass before the house to the exercise ground. There they were, the *elite* and aristocracy of their species—some destined to become of world-wide fame, and distinguished sires of high-born progeny, amongst which would be many a noble steed that would bring the "blue riband of the Turf," or the cross of the Legion of Honour of the sporting world—the St. Leger—to lucky owners. With boyish pride, too, I had pointed out to me and noticed two fine and proudly-pacing animals; one a beautiful chestnut, in whom I should have recognised—but did not, so strangely were they altered—two brave horses which, but a few months before, had been prancing and comparatively-unbroken colts in the old paddock at home. The riders were of various sizes, from the full-grown jockey of the astounding height of four or five feet, to the little urchin or mannikin whose head, when off the horse, scarcely reached the stirrups.

The sturdy trainer, standing in front of the window, with one arm akimbo, and handkerchief in hand, explained to us the several names, performances, or lineage of the passing string, which comprised some fifty or sixty of the finest horses in the world. There were the veterans of and victors in many a well-fought field, whose names sounded ever to my boyish ears as "familiar as household words," and there were the untried and youthful aspirants for racing honours. There were riders, too, there. then boys, and unknown to fame, but whose names and deeds have since been on the lips of thousands—some of whom are now resting on well-won laurels, whilst others are sleeping under many a green-turf mound in village churchyards. One, whose name was familiar some thirty years ago, had arrived for a trial—George Nelson, the quondam "Admiral" of Tickhill, where he had gallantly commanded his well-known "fleet," (and which "fleet," by-the-bye, were often wont to violate the rules of temperance, although this was not permitted to take place in the admiral's scrupulously clean apartments.) There were, too, that prince of jocks, the host's brother, (Bill Scott) and quondam owner of "Sir Tatton Skyes," and many a riding celebrity whose names and memory are all that remain to the present generation. I was questioned as to my opinion of the racers as they passed, and as my phrenological development enabled me to be a pretty shrewd judge of size, shape, symmetry, and form, a spectator of, and sojourner in, this globe of ours, a pretty considerable amount of observation and experience respecting these noble animals, I flattered myself the answers I gave produced satisfaction; indeed, the gratified and pleased look of the paternal face truly indicated as much.

THE END.

NEW BOOKS AND NEW EDITIONS.

NOCTES AMBROSIANÆ. By PROFESSOR JOHN WILSON ("Christopher North"). Popular Edition. Post 8vo. Price 4s. 6d.

In issuing a POPULAR edition of this remarkable work, the editor has omitted those portions which were of interest ONLY at the time of original publication, such as matters of merely passing interest, questions of politics and science, and other affairs that have now passed out from that stage from which they were viewed fifty years ago. But there are other matters, the interest surrounding which is as great as ever—these the editor has been careful to retain. Especial care has also been taken with regard to the amusing element, with which these pages will be found laden.

THE EARLY PROSE AND POETICAL WORKS OF JOHN TAYLOR, The Water Poet, 1580-1653. Post 8vo. Price 5s.

A most remarkable man. His writings are highly descriptive of the manners and customs of the period. In 1618 he travelled on foot from London to the Wilds of Braemar, and published an account of the journey, entitled " The Penniless Pilgrimage." In the Scottish Highlands he became the guest of the Earl of Mar at a hunting encampment among the hills, all of which he saw and describes.

THE LAIRD OF LOGAN: Being Anecdotes and Tales illustrative of the wit and humour of Scotland. Post 8vo. Price 3s. 6d.

A complete, very handsome, and the only large type edition of the famous " Laird of Logan." This work was compiled by three very distinguished literary Scotchmen, namely, John Donald Carrick, William Motherwell, and Andrew Henderson, all of them authors of works relating to Scotland. This is the only unadulterated edition, and is here given to the public as it came direct from the hands of the editors.

THE WILD SPORTS AND NATURAL HISTORY OF THE SCOTTISH HIGHLANDS. By CHARLES ST. JOHN. Post 8vo. Popular Edition. Price 4s. 6d.

One of the most interesting works published on Scottish field sports. Its pages are devoted to the author's experience in deer-stalking, otter-hunting, salmon-fishing, grouse-shooting, as well as with all the representatives of animal life to be found in the Highlands, such as the eagle, wild cat, black game, owl, hawk, wild duck, wild geese, wild swan, seal, fox, etc., etc.

THE HISTORICAL TALES AND LEGENDS OF AYRSHIRE. By WILLIAM ROBERTSON. Post 8vo. Price 5s.

The County of Ayr is especially rich in story and tradition. In the centuries when feudal strife was rampant, the great county families maintained ceaseless activity in their warrings with one another. And the result of their plots, raids, enmities, machinations, and contests are to be seen in the existing social life in Ayrshire. The volume presents a series of historical tales and legends illustrative of the feudal and early social history of the shire. In every instance the author deals with facts of an intensely interesting nature.

EARLY SCOTTISH METRICAL TALES. Edited by DAVID LAING, LL.D. Post 8vo. Price 6s.

Extremely interesting early metrical tales in the original spelling, with valuable notes by the distinguished antiquary who collected the tales and issued the first edition of the book. The tales are thirteen in number, and comprise such as "The History of Sir Gray Steill," "The Tales of the Priests of Peblis," "The History of a Lord and his Three Sons," etc., etc.

BRITISH TRADE; or, CERTAIN CONDITIONS OF OUR NATIONAL PROSPERITY. By PROFESSOR JOHN KIRK. Crown 8vo. Price 4s. 6d

A companion volume to "Social Politics," by the same author, and now out of print. Regarding the latter volume, Ruskin says: "I had no notion myself, till the other day, what the facts were in this matter. Get if you can, Professor Kirk's 'Social Politics;' and read for a beginning his 21st Chapter on Land and Liquor, and then as you have leisure all the book carefully."—FORS CLAVIGERA, March, 1873.

SPORTING ANECDOTES. Being Anecdotal Annals, Descriptions, and Incidents relating to Sport and Gambling. Edited by "ELLANGOWAN." Post 8vo. Price 5s.

An entirely new and most interesting collection of anecdotes, relating to all sections of sporting life and character, such as horse-racing, boxing, golfing, jockeys, cover-shooting, gambling, betting, cock-fighting, pedestrianism, flat-racing, coursing, fox-hunting, angling, card-playing, billiards, etc., etc.

THE LIFE OF JOHN KNOX. By THOMAS M'CRIE, D.D. Demy 8vo. Stiff Paper Boards. Price 1s. 6d.

A cheap edition of this important work. The life of Knox comprises a history of Scotland at one of the most critical periods, namely that of the Reformation.

HUMOROUS READINGS FOR HOME AND HALL. Edited by CHARLES B. NEVILLE. FIRST SERIES. Price 1s.

Humorous and amusing Readings for large or small audiences, and for the fireside. This series (the first) contains thirteen pieces, such as "Old Dick Fogrum Getting Settled in Life," "The Bachelor Feeling his Way," "Mr. Gingerly's Delicate Attentions," etc., etc.

HUMOROUS READINGS FOR HOME AND HALL. Edited by CHARLES B. NEVILLE. SECOND SERIES. Price 1s.

A sequel to the above. The second series contains fourteen readings, such as "Dick Doleful's Disinterested Motives," "Ferney Fidget, Esq., in London Lodgings," "A Philosopher Getting Married," etc., etc.

HUMOROUS READINGS FOR HOME AND HALL. Edited by CHARLES B. NEVILLE. THIRD SERIES. Price 1s.

The concluding series of Mr. Neville's readings. This issue contains fourteen pieces, all of a highly humorous nature, such as "Dandy Nat's Hopes and Fears," "How Billy Muggins was brought to Terms," "Cousin Jones's Valuable Legacy," etc., etc.

HUMOROUS READINGS FOR HOME AND HALL. Edited by CHARLES B. NEVILLE. Post 8vo. Price 3s. 6d.

The three aforementioned series bound in one thick handsome volume, cloth gilt.

THE SCOTTISH BOOK OF FAMILY AND PRIVATE DEVOTION. By TWENTY SCOTTISH CLERGYMEN. Crown 8vo. Price 5s.

Morning and evening prayers for family and private use for quarter-a-year. Week day and sunday. Also prayers for the sick, forms of invocation of the Divine blessing at table, etc.

ANGLING REMINISCENCES OF THE RIVERS AND LOCHS OF SCOTLAND. By THOMAS TOD STODDART. Post 8vo. Price 3s. 6d.

If not the most useful, this is at least the most interesting of all Stoddart's angling works, of which there are three in number. The above is not to be confounded with "The Scottish Angler" on the one hand, or "The Angler's Companion" on the other, though from the same pen. The present work is colloquial throughout, and teeming with the richest humour from beginning to end.

HUMOROUS AND AMUSING SCOTCH READINGS. For the Platform, the Social Circle, and the Fireside. By ALEXANDER G. MURDOCH. First Series. Paper Covers. Price 1s.

Humorous and amusing Scotch readings, fifteen in number, and illustrative of the social life and character of the Scottish people, than which the author believes no more interesting subject can be found. Among other readings may be mentioned, " Mrs. Macfarlane's Rabbit Dinner," " The Washin'-Hoose Key," " Jock Broon's Patent Umbrella," " Willie Weedrap's Domestic Astronomy," etc., etc.

HUMOROUS AND AMUSING SCOTCH READINGS. For the Platform, the Social Circle, and the Fireside. By ALEXANDER G. MURDOCH. SECOND SERIES. Paper Cover. Price 1s.

A sequel to the foregoing, contains fourteen readings, comprising " Johnny Gowdy's Funny Ploy," " Jock Turnip's Mither in-Law," " Lodgings in Arran," " Robin Rigg and the Minister," etc., etc.

HUMOROUS AND AMUSING SCOTCH READINGS. For the Platform, the Social Circle, and the Fireside. By ALEXANDER G. MURDOCH. THIRD SERIES. Paper Covers. Price 1s

The third and concluding series of Mr. Murdoch's, popular and highly amusing Scotch readings. This issue contains " Jean Tamson's Love Hopes and Fears," " The Amateur Phrenologist," " Peter Paterson the Poet," " Coming Home Fou'," etc., etc.

HUMOROUS AND AMUSING SCOTCH READINGS. For the Platform, the Social Circle, and the Fireside. By ALEXANDER G. MURDOCH. Thick Post 8vo. Cloth. Price 3s. 6d.

The three aforementioned series, bound in one thick handsome volume, cloth gilt.

THE COURT OF SESSION GARLAND. Edited by JAMES MAIDMENT, Advocate. *New edition, including all the Supplements.* Demy 8vo. Price 7s. 6d.

A collection of most interesting anecdotes and faceliae connected with the Court of Session. Even to those not initiated in the mysteries of legal procedure, much of the volume will be found highly attractive, for no genuine votary of Momus can be insensible to the fun of the Justiciary Opera, as illustrated by the drollery of the " Diamond Beetle Case," and many others of an amusing nature, such as " The Poor Client's Complaint," " The Parody on Hellvellyn," " The King's Speech," " Lord Bannatyne's Lion," " The Beauties of Overgroggy," etc., etc.

ST. KILDA AND THE ST. KILDIANS. By ROBERT CONNELL. Crown 8vo. Price 2s. 6d.

"*A capital book. It contains everything worth knowing about the famous islet and its people.*"—THE BAILIE.

"*Interesting and amusing. It includes a lively description of the daily life of the inhabitants, the native industries of fishing, bird catching, and the rearing of sickly sheep and cattle, and gives a vivid picture of the Sabbatarian despotism of the Free Church minister who rules the small population.*"—SATURDAY REVIEW.

THE PRAISE OF FOLLY. By ERASMUS. *With Numerous Illustrations by Holbein.* Post 8vo. Price 4s. 6d.

An English translation of the "Encomium Moriae" which has always held a foremost place among the more popular of the writings of the great scholar. This work is probably the most satirical production of any age. It is intensely humorous throughout, and is entirely unique in character. This edition also contains Holbein's illustrations, attaching to which there is very considerable interest.

ANECDOTES OF FISH AND FISHING. By THOMAS BOOSEY. Post 8vo. Price 3s. 6d.

An interesting collection of anecdotes and incidents connected with fish and fishing, arranged and classified into sections. It deals with all varieties of British fish, their habits, different modes of catching them, interesting incidents in connection with their capture, and an infinite amount of angling gossip relating to each. Considerable space is also devoted to the subject of fishing as practised in different parts of the world.

TALES OF A SCOTTISH PARISH. By JACOB RUDDIMAN, M.A. Post 8vo. Paper Covers. Price 1s.

The deceased author was a person of singular beauty and originality of mind, and may well be ranked alongside of Wilson, Hogg, Bethune, Pollok, and other such standard writers of Scottish tales. The tales are nineteen in all, and comprise such as "The Sexton," "The Unfortunate Farmer," "The Lonely Widow," "The Foreboding," etc., etc.

SCOTTISH LEGENDS. By ANDREW GLASS. Post 8vo. Paper Covers. Price 1s.

Four legends, relating chiefly to the west and south of Scotland, entitled, "A Legend of Rothesay Castle," "The Laird of Auchinleck's Gift," "The Cruives of Cree," "The Grey Stones of Garlaffin."

A BANQUET OF JESTS AND MERRY TALES.
By ARCHIE ARMSTRONG, Court Jester to King
James I. and King Charles I., 1611-1637.

An extremely amusing work, reprinted in the original quaint spelling of the period. In addition to the immense fund of amusement to be found in its pages, the work is highly valuable as throwing much light on the social customs and ideas of the period. The author experienced life in connection with all ranks and sections of society, from his own peasant home in the north, to that of the Court of his Sovereign.

AMUSING IRISH TALES. By WILLIAM CARLETON.
Post 8vo. Price 2s. 6d.

A collection of amusing and humorous tales descriptive of Irish life and character. The distinguished author has been designated the Sir Walter Scott of Ireland. The tales are fifteen in number, such as "The Country Dancing Master," "The Irish Match-Maker," "The Irish Smuggler," "The Irish Senachie," "The Country Fiddler," etc., etc. All of them are overflowing with the richest wit and humour.

THE WHOLE FAMILIAR COLLOQUIES OF ERASMUS. Translated by NATHAN BAILEY.
Demy 8vo. Price 4s. 6d.

A complete and inexpensive edition of the great book of amusement of the sixteenth century. Probably no other work so truly and intensely depicts the life and notions of our forefathers 350 years ago, as does this inimical production of the great Erasmus.

There are 62 dialogues in all, and an immense variety of subjects are dealt with, such as "Benefice-Hunting," "The Soldier and the Carthusian," "The Franciscans," "The Apparition," "The Beggar's Dialogue," "The Religious Pilgrimage," "The Sermon," "The Parliament of Women," etc., etc. The whole work is richly characteristic, and is full of the richest humour and satire.

AMUSING PROSE CHAP BOOKS, CHIEFLY OF LAST CENTURY. Edited by ROBERT HAYS CUNNINGHAM. Post 8vo. Price 4s. 6d.

A collection of interesting prose chap books of former times, forming a good representative of the people's earliest popular literature, such as "The Comical History of the King and the Cobbler," "The Merry Tales of the Wise Men of Gotham," "The Merry Conceits of Tom Long, the Carrier," "The Pleasant History of Poor Robin, the Merry Saddler of Walden," etc., etc.

THE DANCE OF DEATH: *Illustrated in Forty-Eight Plates.* By JOHN HOLBEIN. Demy 8vo. Price 5s.

A handsome and inexpensive edition of the great Holbein's most popular production. It contains the whole forty-eight plates, with letterpress description of each plate, the plate and the description in each case being on separate pages, facing each other. The first edition was issued in 1530, and since then innumerable impressions have been issued, but mostly in an expensive form, and unattainable by the general public.

THE LITERARY HISTORY OF GLASGOW. By W. J. DUNCAN. Quarto. Price 12s. 6d. net. *Printed for Subscribers and Private Circulation.*

This volume forms one of the volumes issued by the Maitland Club, and was originally published in 1831. This edition is a verbatim et literatim reprint, and is limited to 350 copies, with an appendix additional containing extra matter of considerable importance, not in the original work.

The book is chiefly devoted to giving an account of the greatest of Scottish printers, namely, the Foulises, and furnishes a list of the books they printed, as likewise of the sculptures and paintings which they so largely produced.

GOLFIANA MISCELLANEA. *Being a Collection of Interesting Monographs on the Royal and Ancient Game of Golf.* Edited by JAMES LINDSAY STEWART. Post 8vo. Price 4s. 6d.

A collection of interesting productions, prose and verse, on or relating to, the game of golf, by various authors both old and recent. Nothing has been allowed into the collection except works of merit and real interest. Many of the works are now extremely scarce and, in a separate form, command very high prices. It contains twenty-three separate productions of a great variety of character—historical, descriptive, practical, poetical, humorous, biographical, etc.

THE BARDS OF THE BIBLE. By GEORGE GILFILLAN. Seventh Edition. Post 8vo. Price 5s.

The most popular of the writings of the late Rev. Dr. Gilfillan. The author, in his preface, states that the object of the book was chiefly a prose poem or hymn in honour of the poetry and the poets of the Bible. It deals with the poetical side of the inspired word, and takes up the separate portions in chronological order.

ONE HUNDRED ROMANCES OF REAL LIFE. By
LEIGH HUNT. Post 8vo. Price 3s. 6d.

A handsome edition of Leigh Hunt's famous collection of romances of real life, now scarce in a complete form. The present issue is complete, containing as it does the entire hundred as issued by the author. All being incidents from real life, the interest attaching to the volume is not of an ordinary character. The romances relate to all grades of society, and are entirely various in circumstance, each one being separate and distinct in itself.

UNIQUE TRADITIONS CHIEFLY OF THE WEST AND SOUTH OF SCOTLAND. By JOHN GORDON BARBOUR. Post 8vo. Price 4s. 6d.

A collection of interesting local and popular traditions gathered orally by the author in his wanderings over the West and South of Scotland. The author narrates in this volume, thirty-five separate incidental traditions in narrative form, connected with places or individuals, all of a nature to interest the general Scottish reader, such as "The Red Comyn's Castle," "The Coves of Barholm," "The Rafters of Kirk Alloway," "Cumstone Castle," "The Origin of Loch Catrine," etc., etc.

MODERN ANECDOTES: A Treasury of Wise and Witty Sayings of the last Hundred Years. Edited, with Notes, by W. DAVENPORT ADAMS. Crown 8vo. Price 3s. 6d.

The Anecdotes are all authenticated and are classed into Sections—I. *Men of Society.* II. *Lawyers and the Law.* III. *Men of Letters.* IV. *Plays and Players.* V. *Statesmen and Politicians.* VI. *The Church and Clergy.* VII. *People in General.*

In compiling a work like this, Mr. Adams has steadily kept in view the necessity of ministering to the requirements of those who will not read anecdotes unless they have reason to know that they are really good. On this principle the entire editorial work has been executed. The book is also a particularly handsome one as regards printing, paper, and binding.

THE LITURGY OF JOHN KNOX: As received by the Church of Scotland in 1564. Crown 8vo. Price 5s.

A beautifully printed edition of the Book of Common Order, more popularly known as the Liturgy of John Knox. This is the only modern edition in which the original quaint spelling is retained. In this and other respects the old style is strictly reproduced, so that the work remains exactly as used by our forefathers three hundred years ago.

THE GABERLUNZIE'S WALLET. By JAMES BALLANTINE. Third edition. Cr. 8vo. Price 2s. 6d.

A most interesting historical tale of the period of the Pretenders, and containing a very large number of favourite songs and ballads, illustrative of the tastes and life of the people at that time. Also containing numerous facetious illustrations by Alexander A. Ritchie.

THE WOLFE OF BADENOCH. A Historical Romance of the Fourteenth Century. By SIR THOMAS DICK LAUDER. Complete unabridged edition. Thick Crown 8vo. Price 6s.

This most interesting romance has been frequently described as equal in interest to any of Sir Walter Scott's historical tales. This is a complete unabridged edition, and is uniform with "Highland Legends" and "Tales of the Highlands," by the same author. As several abridged editions of the work have been published, especial attention is drawn to the fact that the above edition is complete.

THE LIVES OF THE PLAYERS. By JOHN GALT, Esq. Post 8vo. Price 5s.

Interesting accounts of the lives of distinguished actors, such as Betterton, Cibber, Farquhar, Garrick, Foote, Macklin, Murphy, Kemble, Siddons, &c., &c. After the style of Johnson's "Lives of the Poets."

KAY'S EDINBURGH PORTRAITS. A Series of Anecdotal Biographies, chiefly of Scotchmen. Mostly written by JAMES PATERSON. And edited by JAMES MAIDMENT, Esq. Popular Edition. 2 Vols., Post 8vo. Price 12s.

A popular edition of this famous work, which, from its exceedingly high price, has hitherto been out of the reach of the general public. This edition contains all the reading matter that is of general interest; it also contains eighty illustrations.

THE RELIGIOUS ANECDOTES OF SCOTLAND. Edited by WILLIAM ADAMSON, D.D. Thick Post 8vo. Price 5s.

A voluminous collection of purely religious anecdotes relating to Scotland and Scotchmen, and illustrative of the more serious side of the life of the people. The anecdotes are chiefly in connection with distinguished Scottish clergymen and laymen, such as Rutherford, Macleod, Guthrie, Shirra, Leighton, the Erskines, Knox, Beattie, M'Crie, Eadie, Brown, Irving, Chalmers, Lawson, Milne, M'Cheyne, &c., &c. The anecdotes are serious and religious purely, and not at all of the ordinary witty description.

DAYS OF DEER STALKING in the Scottish High lands, including an account of the Nature and Habits of the Red Deer, a description of the Scottish Forests, and Historical Notes on the earlier Field Sports of Scotland. With Highland Legends, Superstitions, Folk-Lore, and Tales of Poachers and Freebooters. By WILLIAM SCROPE. Illustrated by Sir Edwin and Charles Landseer. Demy 8vo. Price 12s. 6d.

" *The best book of sporting adventures with which we are acquainted.*"—ATHENÆUM.

" *Of this noble diversion we owe the first satisfactory description to the pen of an English gentleman of high birth and extensive fortune, whose many amiable and elegant personal qualities have been commemorated in the diary of Sir Walter Scott.*"—LONDON QUARTERLY REVIEW.

DAYS AND NIGHTS OF SALMON FISHING in the River Tweed. By WILLIAM SCROPE. Illustrated by Sir David Wilkie, Sir Edwin Landseer, Charles Landseer, William Simson, and Edward Cooke. Demy 8vo. Price 12s. 6d.

" *Mr. Scrope's book has done for salmon fishing what its predecessor performed for deer stalking.*"—LONDON QUARTERLY REVIEW.

" *Mr. Scrope conveys to us in an agreeable and lively manner the results of his more than twenty years' experience in our great Border river. . . . The work is enlivened by the narration of numerous angling adventures, which bring out with force and spirit the essential character of the sport in question. . . . Mr. Scrope is a skilful author as well as an experienced angler. It does not fall to the lot of all men to handle with equal dexterity, the brush, the pen, and the rod, to say nothing of the rifle, still less of the leister under cloud of night.*"—BLACKWOOD'S MAGAZINE.

THE FIELD SPORTS OF THE NORTH OF EUROPE. A Narrative of Angling, Hunting, and Shooting in Sweden and Norway. By CAPTAIN L. LLOYD. New edition. Enlarged and revised. Demy 8vo. Price 9s.

" *The chase seems for years to have been his ruling passion, and to have made him a perfect model of perpetual motion. We admire Mr. Lloyd. He is a sportsman far above the common run.*"—BLACKWOOD'S MAGAZINE.

" *This is a very entertaining work and written, moreover, in an agreeable and modest spirit. We strongly recommend it as containing much instruction and more amusement.*—ATHENÆUM.

*PUBLIC AND PRIVATE LIBRARIES OF GLAS-
GOW.* A Bibliographical Study. By THOMAS MASON.
Demy 8vo. Price 12s. 6d. net.

A strictly Bibliographical work dealing with the subject of rare and interesting works, and in that respect describing three of the public and thirteen of the private libraries of Glasgow. All of especial interest.

THE LIFE OF SIR WILLIAM WALLACE. By
JOHN D. CARRICK. Fourth and cheaper edition.
Royal 8vo. Price 2s. 6d.

The best life of the great Scottish hero. Contains much valuable and interesting matter regarding the history of that historically important period.

THE HISTORY OF THE PROVINCE OF MORAY.
By LACHLAN SHAW. New and Enlarged Edition,
3 Vols., Demy 8vo. Price 30s.

The Standard History of the old geographical division termed the Province of Moray, comprising the Counties of Elgin and Nairn, the greater part of the County of Inverness, and a portion of the County of Banff. Cosmo Innes pronounced this to be the best local history of any part of Scotland.

HIGHLAND LEGENDS. By SIR THOMAS DICK
LAUDER. Crown 8vo. Price 6s.

Historical Legends descriptive of Clan and Highland Life and Incident in former times.

TALES OF THE HIGHLANDS. By SIR THOMAS
DICK LAUDER. Crown 8vo. Price 6s.

Uniform with and similar in character to the preceding, though entirely different tales. The two are companion volumes.

---

*AN ACCOUNT OF THE GREAT MORAY FLOODS
IN 1829.* By SIR THOMAS DICK LAUDER. Demy
8vo., with 64 Plates and Portrait. Fourth Edition.
Price 8s. 6d.

A most interesting work, containing numerous etchings by the Author. In addition to the main feature of the book, it contains much historical and legendary matter relating to the districts through which the River Spey runs.

OLD SCOTTISH CUSTOMS: Local and General. By E. J. GUTHRIE. Crown 8vo. Price 3s. 6d.

Gives *an interesting account of old local and general Scottish customs, now rapidly being lost sight of.*

A HISTORICAL ACCOUNT OF THE BELIEF IN WITCHCRAFT IN SCOTLAND. By CHARLES KIRKPATRICK SHARPE. Crown 8vo. Price 4s. 6d.

Gives a *chronological account of Witchcraft incidents in Scotland from the earliest period, in a racy, attractive style. And likewise contains an interesting Bibliography of Scottish books on Witchcraft.*

"*Sharpe was well qualified to gossip about these topics.*"—SATURDAY REVIEW.

"*Mr. Sharpe has arranged all the striking and important phenomena associated with the belief in Apparitions and Witchcraft. An extensive appendix, with a list of books on Witchcraft in Scotland, and a useful index, render this edition of Mr. Sharpe's work all the more valuable.*"—GLASGOW HERALD.

TALES OF THE SCOTTISH PEASANTRY. By ALEXANDER and JOHN BETHUNE. With Biography of the Authors by JOHN INGRAM, F.S.A.Scot. Post 8vo. Price 3s. 6d.

"*It is the perfect propriety of taste, no less than the thorough intimacy with the subjects he treats of, that gives Mr. Bethune's book a great charm in our eyes.*"—ATHENÆUM.

"*The pictures of rural life and character appear to us remarkably true, as well as pleasing.*"—CHAMBERS'S JOURNAL.

The *Tales are quite out of the ordinary routine of such literature, and are universally held in peculiarly high esteem. The following may be given as a specimen of the Contents:*—"*The Deformed,*" "*The Fate of the Fairest,*" "*The Stranger,*" "*The Drunkard,*" "*The Illegitimate,*" "*The Cousins,*" &c., &c.

A JOURNEY TO THE WESTERN ISLANDS OF SCOTLAND IN 1773. By SAMUEL JOHNSON, LL.D. Crown 8vo. Price 3s.

Written by *Johnson himself, and not to be confounded with Boswell's account of the same tour. Johnson said that some of his best writing is in this work.*

THE HISTORY OF BURKE AND HARE AND OF THE RESURRECTIONIST TIMES. A Fragment from the Criminal Annals of Scotland. By GEORGE MAC GREGOR, F.S.A.Scot. With Seven Illustrations, Demy 8vo. Price 7s. 6d.

" *Mr. MacGregor has produced a book which is eminently readable.*"—JOURNAL OF JURISPRUDENCE.

" *The book contains a great deal of curious information.*"— SCOTSMAN.

" *He who takes up this book of an evening must be prepared to sup full of horrors, yet the banquet is served with much of literary grace, and garnished with a deftness and taste which render it palatable to a degree.*"—GLASGOW HERALD.

THE HISTORY OF GLASGOW: From the Earliest Period to the Present Time. By GEORGE MAC GREGOR, F.S.A.Scot. Containing 36 Illustrations. Demy 8vo. Price 12s. 6d.

An entirely new as well as the fullest and most complete history of this prosperous city. In addition it is the first written in chronological order. Comprising a large handsome volume in Sixty Chapters, and extensive Appendix and Index, and illustrated throughout with many interesting engravings and drawings.

THE COLLECTED WRITINGS OF DOUGAL GRAHAM, "Skellat," Bellman of Glasgow. Edited with Notes, together with a Biographical and Bibliographical Introduction, and a Sketch of the Chap Literature of Scotland, by GEORGE MAC GREGOR, F.S.A.Scot. Impression limited to 250 copies. 2 Vols., Demy 8vo. Price 21s.

With very trifling exceptions Graham was the only writer of purely Scottish chap-books of a secular description, almost all the others circulated being reprints of English productions. His writings are exceedingly facetious and highly illustrative of the social life of the period.

SCOTTISH PROVERBS. By ANDREW HENDERSON. Crown 8vo. Cheaper edition. Price 2s. 6d.

A cheap edition of a book that has long held a high place in Scottish Literature.

THE BOOK OF SCOTTISH ANECDOTE: Humorous, Social, Legendary, and Historical. Edited by ALEXANDER HISLOP. Crown 8vo., pp. 768. Cheaper edition. Price 5s.

The most comprehensive collection of Scottish Anecdotes, containing about 3,000 in number.

THE BOOK OF SCOTTISH STORY: Historical, Traditional, Legendary, Imaginative, and Humorous. Crown 8vo., pp. 768. Cheaper edition. Price 5s.

A most interesting and varied collection by Leading Scottish Authors.

THE BOOK OF SCOTTISH POEMS: Ancient and Modern. Edited by J. Ross. Crown 8vo., pp. 768. Cheaper edition. Price 5s.

Comprising a History of Scottish Poetry and Poets from the earliest times. With lives of the Poets and Selections from their Writings.

⁎⁎⁎ These three works are uniform.

A DESCRIPTION OF THE WESTERN ISLES OF SCOTLAND, CALLED HYBRIDES. With the Genealogies of the Chief Clans of the Isles. By SIR DONALD MONRO, High Dean of the Isles, who travelled through most of them in the year 1549. Impression limited to 250 copies. Demy 8vo. Price 5s.

This is the earliest written description of the Western Islands, and is exceedingly quaint and interesting. In this edition all the old curious spellings are strictly retained.

A DESCRIPTION OF THE WESTERN ISLANDS OF SCOTLAND CIRCA 1695. By MARTIN MARTIN. Impression limited to 250 copies. Demy 8vo. Price 12s. 6d.

With the exception of Dean Monro's smaller work 150 years previous, it is the earliest description of the Western Islands we have, and is the only lengthy work on the subject before the era of modern innovations. Martin very interestingly describes the people and their ways as he found them about 200 years ago.

THE SCOTTISH POETS, RECENT AND LIVING.
By ALEXANDER G. MURDOCH. With Portraits, Post 8vo. Price 6s.

A most interesting resumé of Scottish Poetry in recent times. Contains a biographical sketch, choice pieces, and portraits of the recent and living Scottish Poets.

THE HUMOROUS CHAP-BOOKS OF SCOTLAND.
By JOHN FRASER. 2 Vols., Thin Crown 8vo (all published). Price 5s.

An interesting and racy description of the chap-book literature of Scotland, and biographical sketches of the writers.

THE HISTORY OF STIRLINGSHIRE. By WILLIAM NIMMO. 2 Vols., Demy 8vo. 3rd Edition. Price 25s.

A new edition of this standard county history, handsomely printed, and with detailed map giving the parish boundaries and other matters of interest.

This county has been termed the battlefield of Scotland, and in addition to the many and important military engagements that have taken place in this district, of all which a full account is given,—this part of Scotland is of especial moment in many other notable respects,—among which particular reference may be made to the Roman Wall, the greater part of this most interesting object being situated within the boundaries of the county.

A POPULAR SKETCH OF THE HISTORY OF GLASGOW: From the Earliest Period to the Present Time. By ANDREW WALLACE. Crown 8vo. Price 3s. 6d.

The only attempt to write a History of Glasgow suitable for popular use.

THE HISTORY OF THE WESTERN HIGHLANDS AND ISLES OF SCOTLAND, from A.D. 1493 to A.D. 1625. With a brief introductory sketch from A.D. 80 to A.D. 1493. By DONALD GREGORY. Demy 8vo. Price 12s. 6d.

Incomparably the best history of the Scottish Highlands, and written purely from original investigation. Also contains particularly full and lengthened Contents and Index, respectively at beginning and end of the volume.

NEW BOOKS AND NEW EDITIONS.

THE HISTORY OF AYRSHIRE. By JAMES PATERSON. 5 Vols., Crown 8vo. Price 28s. net.

The most recent and the fullest history of this exceedingly interesting county. The work is particularly rich in the department of Family History.

MARTYRLAND: a Historical Tale of the Covenanters. By the Rev. ROBERT SIMPSON, D.D. Crown 8vo. Cheaper Edition. Price 2s. 6d.

A tale illustrative of the history of the Covenanters in the South of Scotland.

TALES OF THE COVENANTERS. By E. J. GUTHRIE. Crown 8vo. Cheaper Edition. Price 2s. 6d.

A number of tales illustrative of leading incidents and characters connected with the Covenanters.

PERSONAL AND FAMILY NAMES. A Popular Monograph on the Origin and History of the Nomenclature of the Present and Former Times. By HARRY ALFRED LONG. Demy 8vo. Price 5s.

Interesting investigations as to the origin, history, and meaning of about 9,000 personal and family names.

THE SCOTTISH GALLOVIDIAN ENCYCLOPÆDIA of the Original, Antiquated, and Natural Curiosities of the South of Scotland. By JOHN MACTAGGART. Demy 8vo. Price raised to 25s. Impression limited to 250 copies.

Contains a large amount of extremely interesting and curious matter relating to the South of Scotland.

THE COMPLETE TALES OF THE ETTRICK SHEPHERD (JAMES HOGG). 2 vols., Demy 8vo.

An entirely new and complete edition of the tales of this popular Scottish writer.

**GLASGOW: THOMAS D. MORISON.
LONDON: HAMILTON, ADAMS & CO.**

www.ingramcontent.com/pod-product-compliance
Lightning Source LLC
Chambersburg PA
CBHW020224240426
43672CB00006B/409